Songwriting

2nd Edition

by Jim Peterik, Dave Austin, Cathy Lynn
FOREWORD BY Kara DioGuardi

for
dummies®
A Wiley Brand

Songwriting For Dummies®, 2nd Edition

Published by: **John Wiley & Sons, Inc.**, 111 River Street, Hoboken, NJ 07030-5774, www.wiley.com

Copyright © 2020 by John Wiley & Sons, Inc., Hoboken, New Jersey

Published simultaneously in Canada

For general information on our other products and services, please contact our Customer Care Department within the U.S. at 877-762-2974, outside the U.S. at 317-572-3993, or fax 317-572-4002. For technical support, please visit https://hub.wiley.com/community/support/dummies.

Wiley publishes in a variety of print and electronic formats and by print-on-demand. Some material included with standard print versions of this book may not be included in e-books or in print-on-demand. If this book refers to media such as a CD or DVD that is not included in the version you purchased, you may download this material at http://booksupport.wiley.com. For more information about Wiley products, visit www.wiley.com.

Library of Congress Control Number: 2019921154

ISBN 978-1-119-67565-5 (pbk); ISBN 978-1-119-67567-9 (ebk); ISBN 978-1-119-67566-2 (ebk)

Manufactured in the United States of America

SKY10033228_020822

Contents at a Glance

Table of Contents

Foreword

People ask me all the time, "How did you become a successful writer?" If I were to answer that in the most simple way possible, I'd have to say that it comes down to three things — WORK, honesty and feeling.

I put the word WORK in capital letters to show you just how important this part of the equation is. Every successful songwriter knows that sometimes you write hundreds of songs before you stumble upon anything great, and because of that, WORK in some cases is more important than talent. I wrote for seven years before I made a dollar. And I learned that every bad song you write gets you closer to a good one. As my famous songwriter friend Marti Fredrickson says, "It took me 47 years to write that song." (By the way, he's 47; and he co-wrote "Jaded" for Aerosmith, "Sorry" for Buck Cherry, and "Love Remains the Same" for Gavin Rossdale.)

WORK can mean many different things — from the actual creation of the song, to finding the right person to produce or sing it, to networking so that someone in a position to promote it can actually hear it. You may have the best song in your pocket, but if you don't hit the ground running, it will always just be that — a song in your pocket.

If you want to be a professional songwriter, you should write every day and spend every waking moment finding others who inspire you and are dedicated to a life of music. Every good songwriter I know lives, eats, and breathes music. When they are not engaged in the important task of experiencing life to have something to draw upon, they are honing their craft. A great song is where inspiration meets craft, and craft can be developed only through hard WORK.

If you like a lot vacations, professional songwriting is not for you. If you're feelings are hurt easily, co-writing is not for you. And if you can't stand rejection, don't even think of songwriting as a career. If you think this foreword is harsh, the music business is harsher. It's my intention to steer you away from this profession now and save you the heartache. I'd rather see you admit to yourself that songwriting is more of a hobby than what you want to do for work.

Now for honesty. Your parents had good reasons for telling you to always be honest. If I had been honest with myself 20 years ago, I probably would not have gone to Duke University to be a lawyer. I got a late start writing songs, and that was only because no one believed in me enough to allow me to record their songs to showcase my voice. At 22, in the middle of the Bronx, in a crappy apartment, against the sound of two barking pit bulls, I penned my first song with Dave Citron called "Show Me."

It was horrid.

My verses described what I thought some guy was feeling. (I was into him, but he was not into me, by the way.) It was easier to fabricate someone else's truth than to deal with my own.

I did not have a handle on my own emotions and, therefore, could not write anything true. It took me years to develop an internal dialogue with myself that I could trust. Hit songwriting is about putting your real personal experiences into melodies and words that are universal and easily digested. You can embellish on your experiences, but there should always be truth at the core. How else would you be able to convey feelings or emotions in a way that the listener could relate? Put your passion for songwriting into exploring your emotions and thoughts. It will be the best therapy you never paid for.

Here comes the part you can't teach — *feeling*. When a particular subject or piece of music moves you, makes you cry, and brings you to your knees, open your heart — or the *channel*, as I call it — and listen. That's your soul talking to you. And when that happens in combination with your craft, you are on your way to a BIG song. The more feeling you put into a song, the more the listener gets out of it.

My hope for each and every one of you reading this book is that you, too, will experience the joy and healing that songwriting has given to me. And remember, it's not the money or the hits that should be motivating you — it's the music!!!!!

GOD SAVE THE MUSIC!!! ROCK ON!

Kara DioGuardi

Grammy-nominated hit songwriter.
Executive VP of Talent/Office of the Chairman, Warner Brothers Records.
Her songs have appeared on over 150 million records.
Over 40 charting radio/retail singles.
Fifteen BMI Pop Awards; Pop Writer Of The Year in 2007.
Three hundred songs released on major labels; 171 of them on platinum albums.

Introduction

Welcome to *Songwriting For Dummies*, 2nd Edition. If you're merely flipping through the pages of this book right now at the local bookstore (looking for the fast track to writing a sure-fire hit), do yourself a favor and buy it. You can thank us later! There's simply too much information packed into this baby to get a hold of in one sitting. If you've already purchased this book and are sitting down ready to discover the ins and outs of songwriting, congratulations! It's going to be a great adventure. We're riding the wave of a great songwriting revolution. What better time to be a part of this business? The record labels are still looking for memorable, meaningful, and long-lasting songs for their artists — songs that make a difference — not disposable ditties (at least this is our reverent prayer), and now there is a whole new world to explore since the digital revolution has firmly planted its feet on the ground. What you'll find in this book is a practical and lighthearted look at that impractical and unnecessarily serious subject of writing a song. We hope you get some encouragement and inspiration from our labor of love. We know that with a little work and dedication you can unleash the creativity inside you. Feel free to share it with a friend — who knows, he may be your own Bernie Taupin!

About This Book

This book was written to give you a hands-on, behind-the-scenes look at the noble pursuit of songwriting. It offers basic songwriting concepts, as well as shortcuts and slightly unconventional methods not necessarily found in other books. It's coming from authors who have "been there" and "done that" in all areas of the music business. This isn't for people who dream about writing a song, this is for those who are ready to dig in and try it. The book is also meant to be useful to the already up-and-running or successful writer who'd like to refocus his creativity or gain a little validation on what he's been doing right all along. The text of the book covers all aspects of the business and the pleasure of songwriting from the collection of ideas to the creation of a song, from creating a demo of your song to assembling a team for its marketing. It includes not only the nuts and bolts of constructing a song, but the spiritual or mystical side that gives it wings. It includes a Practice Makes Perfect section at the ends of Chapters 2 through 11 geared toward honing your songwriting skills with methods of practicing your newfound skills. It includes the latest resources to go beyond the bindings of this book and explore the outer reaches of cyberspace and the inner reaches of your limitless imagination. Above all, it debunks the idea that you have to be a virtuoso on a particular instrument or that you need years of music theory and schoolin' to write a song. All you really need are ears, a good imagination, a lot of determination, and a (reasonably) organized procedure in order to make your bid at enhancing the world through music.

Foolish Assumptions

We're assuming that you are in some way curious about how a song gets written. Maybe you're wondering if you have what it takes to write a song yourself. Perhaps you're looking for the next step in getting your song from your hard drive to the shelves of the record stores. In any case, we don't assume that you're a musical genius or that you have astounding technique, or any technique for that matter, on a particular instrument. Our whole premise is that anyone can write a song with the right inspiration, methods, and collaborators. The genius in writing a song is your ability to bring all your skills into a common focus to create a verse and chorus that, in addition to yourself, the whole world wants to hear.

How This Book Is Organized

This book is organized into six parts, which cover everything from writing lyrics to selling your songs.

Part 1: So You Want to Be a Songwriter

The first section of this book asks you to identify and assess your ambitions, prior experience, expectations, and preconceptions regarding songwriting. You'll take an inventory of the talents and skills you can bring to your own songwriting experience. We will explore the vast smorgasbord of styles to choose from when writing and arranging your songs, and assess which genres suit your style of writing. This part also shows you how to capture song ideas so they can't escape, and gives you an introduction to song structure with a discussion on song forms.

Part 2: Unleashing the Lyricist in You

This part is dedicated to channeling the "word power" and expressiveness within you into the lyrics of your next song. We give you some concrete tips for writing lyrics, including the definition of a hook and where to put it and how to use rhyme in your lyrics. We also show you the successful lyrics of many popular songs, telling you exactly what the lyricist did to achieve greatness.

Part 3: Creating Memorable Music

This part addresses how rhythm, chords, and melody come together to make a great song. All these ingredients are critical to a song's success — and we make sure you don't neglect any of them. We also explore the "cheating" side of town through the use of shortcuts and cool technological advancements.

Part 4: Cooperation, Collaboration, and Community

Our "Three C's" of songwriting might just be the ticket that "lights your fire" and starts you on your way towards a long and successful career as a songwriter. You can collaborate to write the next pop hit or try your hand at country or R&B. You can also write for many different types of arenas, such as the stage, screen, and television. The possibilities are virtually endless as you build your community spirit — just think how awesome your demos will be once you master the art of cooperation.

Part 5: Getting Down to Business

In this part, we examine how the words *music* and *business* can shake hands and be friends. From finding out just who the business players are to filling out paper-work, and from creating goals to meeting deadlines, it's the part you must force yourself to read to assure that your song is on track and being properly looked after once it's created.

Part 6: The Part of Tens

In this section we review some of the great songs throughout history. We also throw in some highly prudent and useful contracts for good measure.

Icons Used in This Book

For Dummies books are nothing if not user-friendly and fun. To this end, we have included various graphic icons in the left margins of the pages. These clever little cartoons give you an immediate "heads up" to nuggets of truth you need right away, plus snacks you can choose to save for later.

TIP

This is a lesson we've learned in our decades of experience. It can be as crass as a shortcut to success, or as heady as a gateway to your soul.

REMEMBER

This icon is the mother of all icons. This is the reminder of what you should already know through reading this book. Fight the temptation to slam down the book and cry, "Give me some credit for brains, ma!"

WARNING

This needlessly ominous icon is reserved mainly for blatant no-no's in either the creation of a song or with the business and legalities of songwriting.

TECHNICAL STUFF

This is the icon that tells you there is more to know if you really feel the need. However, you have our permission to skip over this stuff if you'd rather stay immersed in the creative flow of an artistic mindset. For those of you who love gadgets and want more techie info, these are the areas to note.

WORDS OF WISDOM

This icon indicates a "pearl of wisdom" or a quotation from one of the top experts in the various areas of the music business that we have corralled just for you.

OFF THE RECORD

This icon indicates the under-our-breath, down-and-dirty truth that you now have the dubious privilege of knowing. With whom you share these boardroom secrets is entirely up to you, but please, act responsibly!

Where to Go from Here

Please note that it's okay to skip around in this book. Although we had some crazy notion about a logical unfolding of information, truth be told, it works even if you throw all the chapters into a blender and hit "frappé."

Beyond the Book

In addition to what you're reading right now, this book comes with a free access-anywhere Cheat Sheet. To get this Cheat Sheet, go to www.dummies.com and search for "Songwriting For Dummies, 2nd Edition" by using the Search box.

1

So You Want to Be a Songwriter

We all have songs inside us just waiting to come out. The real key to songwriting is not only figuring out the combination to what unlocks that music within you, but also developing methods to capture these little gems of inspiration before they fly away. And like most gifts, there is some assembly required, so it's vital to discover the what-goes-where of a song. Also important is knowing where your taste in music might lie? Are you heavy metal, easy listening, or one of the hundreds of shades in between? It's easy to argue that a great song is a great song; still, every song seems to live and breathe best in a particular style, or *genre.* In this part, we not only look at many of the different directions your song can take, we give you everything you need to get started in your songwriting journey.

Chapter **1**

Capturing That Solid-Gold Nugget

This book is for everyone who shares the dream of harnessing the songwriting power we all have within. You've come to the right place if your heart keeps telling you to write a song, but your mind is uncertain as to the process of the craft or what's required to create a really good song. You bought the right book if you're wondering how to collect and organize your ideas. You have found the right resource if you have pieces of songs lying in notebooks and on countless cassettes but can't seem to put the pieces together. This book is for you if you have racks of finished song demos but don't know what to do next to get them heard. When you know the elements that make up a great song and how the pros go about writing one, you can get on the right path to creating one of your own.

Unless you're lucky enough to have fully finished songs come to you in your deepest dreams, or to somehow take dictation from the ghosts of Tin Pan Alley (the publishing area located in New York City in the 1930s and 1940s), most of us need to summon the forces, sources, reasons, and seasons that give us the necessary motivation to draw a song from our heart of hearts. Given that initial spark, you then need the best means of gathering those ideas, organizing them, putting them into form, and documenting them as they roll in — before it's too late and they roll right out again!

Have you ever noticed how you can remember a powerful dream just after you've awakened only for it to vanish into thin air in the light of day? Song ideas can be just as illusive. Songwriting is all about capturing the moment of musical inspiration at its source. This is perhaps the single most important element of songwriting because, like the moment that rain turns to snow, at the instant of inspiration, your mind grows wings and a song takes flight.

In this chapter, we explore the various places to mine for golden nuggets of inspiration for your songs, ways to gather that information, and methods of documenting your ideas. We also demonstrate the importance of brainstorming ideas with others to let inspiration flow, and provide simple exercises to show you the way.

Ground Zero — Before You Write a Single Note

So, you want to write songs. But writing a song can be an intimidating process. After all, where do you really begin?

Is formal music training a must?

Music training is not a prerequisite for songwriting. However, if you don't at least have some ability on the piano or guitar to help put the ideas from your head into some tangible form, you *may* be at a disadvantage. (Notice we said "may." Funnyman Mel Brooks composed the musical score to his hit Broadway show *The Producers* by humming the melodies into a tape recorder and having someone translate that into musical notes on a page.) Even if you're solely a lyricist (the one who puts the words to the music), it may be helpful to you and your collaborator (the person writing the music to go with your words) if you have a working knowledge of a musical instrument. Musical ability could also help you with the rhythm of your words and the structure of your songs. That being said, even though musical expertise is advantageous, it is not required by any means.

Although songwriting is more than just an assembly line of components to be bolted together, it doesn't hurt to know what's available in the "parts bin." A song is made up of chords (a combination of two or more tones sounded together in harmony), a melody (the arrangement of single tones in sequence — the part you sing), a rhythm (the beat or pulse of the song), and words (often called *lyrics* in the context of a song). Many successful songwriters excel in one area or another. Rare individuals can do it all. Even the ones who are a songwriting one-man band often choose to collaborate with others to come up with that magical song that comes from a blend of styles and personalities. It's your task at hand, if you are challenged in a given area, to find writers to complete your vision and contribute the expertise you lack.

Most of what I know about songwriting, I learned by being a fan of music. Truly the best teacher is listening. I emulated the styles of songs that inspired me, and gradually, over the course of many years, integrated these influences into a style of my own. The Beatle's songwriting, to cite a notable example, was heavily influenced by the American rock 'n' roll of Chuck Berry, Carl Perkins, The Everly Brothers, and Little Richard. The Beatles created songs by absorbing those influences and adding their own unique personalities. The fact that they could barely read music hardly mattered at all. They had ears!

— JIM PETERIK, PERFORMER, SONGWRITER, AND MULTI-INSTRUMENTALIST FOR THE BANDS IDES OF MARCH AND SURVIVOR, PLUS WRITER OF HITS FOR .38 SPECIAL, SAMMY HAGAR, AND OTHERS

Studying music theory, history, and arrangement can only enhance your abilities as a writer, but it would be a mistake to infer that formal training is a necessity to write a great song. Music appreciation classes can open your eyes and ears to what you should be listening for in songs, but you really don't need anyone to tell your foot when to start tapping or your lips to break out into a big smile when the chorus hits — that's just the power of great music. Start with your love for the songs you hear and then tap into all you have to express in your soul.

If you're still not convinced that you don't need training, consider the fact that some of the greatest songs ever written were composed by people with virtually no formal music training. Folk music, chants, delta blues, country, and rock 'n' roll all got their start with people who had the raw talent to create songs. On the other hand, many legendary composers have extensive musical training in all forms of music, including classical composition. It's all good. Just don't let the so-called "rules" hold you back or keep you frozen.

In college, my harmony teacher told me at the end of the semester, "You know all that stuff I taught you about avoiding parallel fifths? Forget about it! If it sounds good, just do it!" By the way, that was the only formal music training I ever got, other than two years of piano and a few years of saxophone lessons. I earned a C+ in that class. It is my belief that life is the best teacher, and listening to and enjoying a good song are perhaps the best ways to learn to do it yourself.

— JIM PETERIK, WRITER OF 18 BILLBOARD TOP 10 HITS INCLUDING THE PERENNIAL FAVORITE "EYE OF THE TIGER: FEATURED IN ROCKY III

TIP

Although some songwriters do well with the trial-and-error method, the more you know about music, the better chance you have to write a great song. The more adept you can become at an instrument, the easier it will be to create and demonstrate the ideas in your head. You do not need to enroll in a college course to study music, because there are other ways to get instruction in music theory, composition, instrumental performance, and voice at a per-session rate. Qualified, reasonably priced private teachers can be located through your local music shop or record store or in the back pages of the local "freebie" entertainment newspaper and through a simple Internet search. Finding someone who inspires you will make songwriting a lot easier.

Being prepared when inspiration strikes

Ideas will come into your brain while you're in the strangest of places, at any time of the day or night. You've probably heard stories about how some of the greatest hits were born. Paul McCartney has said some of his best songs came to him in his dreams. Billy Joel also got the song "River of Dreams" from — you guessed it — a dream. And Sting, former lead singer of the group The Police, awakened in the middle of the night, wrote a song in ten minutes flat, then went back to sleep. The song? "Every Breath You Take." (Makes you want to get plenty of shut-eye, now doesn't it?)

TIP

When a melody or a lyrical idea pops into your head, make sure you have a way of freezing it in time. Try to carry with you, at all times, a notebook to jot down ideas and a digital recorder to capture your musical phrases. Never fool yourself into thinking you'll remember the ideas when you get home. And don't think that "If it's really so great of an idea, I won't forget it." Some great songs will never be heard because the songwriter couldn't reconstruct some once-in-a-lifetime moment of inspiration. Those cool ideas that you know you'll never forget will be "dust in the wind" if you don't have the discipline to write them down or hum them into the recorder when they hit.

REMEMBER

A flash of inspiration may hit you when you least expect it. Be ready to catch it — then be prepared to work hard at turning the initial idea into a finished song.

Finding you own inner voice and expression

So you aren't being awakened in the middle of the night by divine inspiration? Not to worry. You can find a way to tap into that inspiration even if it hasn't quite found its way to your bedside just yet. We go into this process in greater detail later in this book, but just know there are methods that enhance the likelihood that you'll soon be listening to your inner voice of inspiration.

In the meantime, take a look at the unique ways you look at and feel about the world around you, the moods you project in life, and all the emotions will undoubtedly be projected in your songs. These emotions are a great place to tap into when you are looking for ideas and inspirations to begin your songs. In other words, write about what you know and feel, and you're sure to come up with something unique (because even though you thought your mother was lame when she said it, there really is only one you).

WORDS OF WISDOM

We are always chasing that perfect song in life, that magical moment where the stars align. But nothing is ever perfect. Those imperfections echo our humanity. These songs are true expressions of what our lives are like, imperfect but worn; comfortable. But the chase is fun, and we keep on chasing. Meanwhile, we take pictures along the way and document our feelings through words, through phrases, through titles of songs and through performance as well.

— GEOFF BYRD, SINGER–SONGWRITER, PRODUCER, AND CREATOR OF THESONGWRITINGACADEMY.COM

Some writers are able to project a powerful optimism through their melodies, chord progressions, and lyrics, while others are able to project wonder, a bittersweet sadness, or pure intense anger. But very few songwriters can project all these emotions within a single song or even on one complete CD — so don't pressure yourself to cram in every possible emotion all at once. Let it out in single doses to begin with.

REMEMBER

Whatever the mood or genre, all great songs have the ability to move people, to make them *feel* something.

Psychologists say that songs can put us in touch with our feelings. We all know what it feels like to be happy, sad, afraid, or in love. Often, a song is what puts us in touch with those emotions — instantaneously.

Expressing your authentic feelings in a song can be therapeutic to you as a person; those feelings can also be the clay from which a lasting song can be sculpted. If your audience can see a little bit of themselves within your song, if they can identify directly with what you are saying, your song just may stay in their hearts and minds (and their iPods) long after it has dropped off the Billboard charts. When there is an issue you feel passionate about, when you are swept away by some new fad or idea, when you are moved to tears by a movie or the passing of a loved one, or when you've recently fallen in or out of love — these are the subjects and feelings that will resonate in your song.

CAPTURING THAT LOVING FEELING

In a survey based on performances, sheet music, and record sales, *Variety,* the entertainment trade paper, once named the 100 most popular songs of all time. An analysis of the themes of those 100 titles showed that about 85 percent of them were love songs. And many of those blockbuster golden oldies are still generating new recordings after 50 years.

OFF THE RECORD

Of all the songs I've written or co-written, the ones based on personal experience, like "Eye of the Tiger" (co-written with Frankie Sullivan; hasn't everyone felt at one time or another like the underdog trying to beat the odds), "Hold on Loosely" (co-written with Don Barnes and Jeff Carlisi; I based the lyric behind Don's title on some advice my future wife once gave me), and "The Search Is Over" (co-written with Frankie Sullivan; the idea of taking for granted what's most precious to you) became some very long-lasting hits — proving the point that our own experiences are perhaps more universal than we think.

— JIM PETERIK, WRITER OF 18 BILLBOARD TOP 10 HITS

WORDS OF WISDOM

Whatever moves me to write a song is usually a pretty good reason. I can really only write about what I feel in my heart. On September 11, 2001, I received a call from a good friend of mine who works on the rooftops in Manhattan. He was just witness to one of the great tragedies of our or any time, as he heard a huge explosion and watched helplessly as the first of two jet aircrafts crashed into the World Trade Center. He called me and said that when he looked around, all of his co-workers had tears streaming down their faces. I said to him, "This has got to be the day America cried." As I watched the images of destruction all that day, I started to sing a melody that seemed to mirror my emotions at the time. The next day I called up my good buddy Jim Peterik and told him that there was a song to be written here that could possibly do some good. I sang him a piece of the melody I had in my head. The first words out of Jim's mouth were, "In the shadow of the Statue of Liberty" to which I added, "In the torchlight of the land of the free." From there, with the help of Ma Bell, digital recording, and the grace of God, a song was born. We are proud to say that the fruits from our labor of love became the title song to The Day America Cried album, helped raised some money, and hopefully expressed a few emotions locked in so many hearts. That's the power of a song.

— JOHNNY VAN ZANT, LEAD SINGER OF LYNYRD SKYNYRD AND VAN ZANT

Creating the mood

As the chapters of this book unfold, you'll see the elements that come together to make a great song. But it all starts with you — who you are and what feeling or mood you're able to project. The number of people who will be able to connect with and relate to the mood you're creating will determine just how successful your song will be.

In some great songs, the mood of the music matches perfectly to the lyrics. Minor chords often become the basis for sadder, deeper, and more introspective songs. Listen to "New York State of Mind" (written and sung by Billy Joel), "New York Minute" (written by Don Henley, Daniel Kortchmar, and Jai Winding; sung by Don Henley), or "Paint It Black" (written by Mick Jagger and Keith Richards; performed by The Rolling Stones). Major chords generally result in happier and more optimistic songs like "You Are the Sunshine of My Life" (written and sung by Stevie Wonder) or Survivor's "High on You" (written by Jim Peterik and Frankie Sullivan). In other songs, the mood of the lyrics is in direct contrast to the vibe of the music, such as in Elton John's deceptively happy ditty "I Think I'm Going to Kill Myself" (written by Elton John and Bernie Taupin) and in "I'll Never Fall In Love Again" (written by Burt Bacharach and Hal David; sung by Dionne Warwick). That bittersweet contrast between the words and the music is often what gives a song its potency.

The greatest intimacy we share with our audience as songwriters (and our greatest responsibility) is the transference of the mood we have created within a song. Taking that idea a bit farther, we're also sharing with our audience the mood we happened to be in as we were creating the song. It's a thought-provoking notion that when we respond emotionally to one of the great classics, we're actually feeling a little bit of what the composer was feeling at the moment of creation, even if it was many years ago. Such is the transcendent, timeless nature of songwriting.

Drip, Drip, Drop: The Six-Step Process

Well now you have your notebook at your side, a gross of freshly sharpened pencils, and your digital recorder in your bag, and you're just waiting for the next drip of inspiration to hit you on the head. First off, don't expect miracles right off the bat. Your first ideas might not be ready for prime time. But there is really no such thing as a bad idea, only ones that may need to be refined, clarified, or made more unique and clever — and real. Remember, you've got to start somewhere. Try to set aside some time each day to be inspired and to write your thoughts down. Before long, those moments you set aside will become an oasis in the often dry climate of a typical day. The more you practice your craft, the better your odds of coming up with that one special song that the world really wants (or needs) to hear.

WORDS OF WISDOM

When writing a song, if you're afraid to suck, you'll never write a note.

— JEFF BOYLE, SINGER-SONGWRITER OF "CUBS WIN" AND A MULTITUDE OF TV COMMERCIALS INCLUDING COORS LIGHT AND MCDONALD'S

Songwriting can take an enormous amount of patience and hard work. Fortunately, there's a lot of fun to be had along the way. In that spirit, we have compiled — for you — the six steps to writing your first song:

1. **Find a message you feel passionate about.** Choose a cause that resonates with you (a sure bet is anything about love — or lack of it!). Write about the girl you've been too insecure to ask out or that guy that you wish would take notice of you. Write about what interests you. Write about what you know. Keep it simple. If a subject is vital to you, it just might be vital to others as well. Similarly, if you don't care about a subject, don't expect others to either.

2. **Find a simple melody.** So many new songwriters get in over their heads trying to be complex to win friends and influence publishers. Songwriters are not paid by the note — we're rewarded by the connections we make in the synapses of our audiences' brains. Often the easiest melodies are the longest lasting.

3. **Find a simple set of chord changes.** Search your piano keyboard or your guitar for this needed element of your song, use a program like GarageBand, or search the Internet and local clubs for the musicians that can furnish your words and melodies with a comfortable music bed.

4. **Find a place to write.** Find a quiet, peaceful setting to clear your mind, light some incense, and let the melodies and emotions flow. If this is not possible, any chaotic subway station will do. Other key places to write: supermarkets, flea markets, soccer matches, PTA meetings, in the car, and anywhere else where the distractions merge to zero.

5. **Find a nine-foot Bosendorfer concert grand piano in an ancient cathedral and let your fingers land sensuously on the keys as you compose your masterpiece.** If this is not possible, pick up any old instrument that's lying around the house and see if you can coax some sound out of it. It's really all about what you're hearing *in your head*. If you can imagine what the finished song will sound like, you can write it on your late Uncle Louie's banjo for all we care.

6. **Find the confidence within yourself to put your heart and soul on the line and share your song with others.** It's through this loop of constant feedback that you learn how to improve your songs. Resist the urge to discount everything but positive reaction. Likewise, you should resist the urge to devalue the positive reactions. Breathe in the accolades, and weigh the brickbats. Take it all in, but before making any changes, always consult your heart for the truth.

Pay Attention: Stop, Look, and Listen

Living and breathing are good places to start when writing a song: being observant to all that is swirling around you, making note of your own reactions to situations, taking notice of other people's reactions in similar situations, and trying to put yourself in the other guy's shoes to better empathize with what he might be feeling. Like they say in all those contests, "You must be present to win!" By keeping your feelings close to the surface and refusing to disown even one sentiment, you are opening a panorama of emotions that can be channeled into a song. The melodies that enter our consciousness when our guard is down and our inner antennas are up are perhaps the most authentic of all.

WORDS OF WISDOM

I always tell people, and it's the truth, "I Believe" was written at about three in the morning . . . I was hearing the melody and I thought, "This is pretty." I just had to get up and play it.

— ELIOT SLOAN, SINGER AND SONGWRITER WITH BLESSID UNION OF SOULS

REMEMBER

As a writer, don't get discouraged if you hear echoes of a song you've been slaving over in a new song that just came on the radio. Theses melodies and ideas are out there somewhere in the cosmos; it's just a matter of being in tune and being receptive to what's coming in. Perhaps someone else just happened to access that idea before you did. At least it shows that you're paying attention to inspiration and are most likely on the right track. So keep the faith, and remember that it happens the other way around too — next time it could be you who gets there first for that melody or lyrical concept!

Finding the inspiration zone

What inspired you to write that song? This is an age-old question that fuels many a conversation. You are probably familiar with the quote, "in the beginning was the word," but from a songwriter's perspective you could rephrase that statement as "in the beginning was the thought." A thought, idea, or inspiration is where all songs begin. It is the genesis of all musical masterpieces. I can hear you say "sounds simple, but how do I actually get the party started?" There are many techniques and methods to go about this, but the bottom line is that you need to tap into your inner voice to listen to those brilliant thoughts that are just waiting to come out and be revealed — you need to find a way to "get in the zone" and let inspiration come bubbling to the surface.

This is a common phenomenon in the sports world where athletes are able to slow down time and get into "the zone" of competition — a place where there are no distractions and everything seems to be effortless. For the songwriter, it's just as important to get in the zone. So how do you do it? You simply quiet your mind and pay attention to your inner self. This may be difficult for the average person to fathom, but with practice it is attainable to all who seek the ability to tap into a place of higher authenticity.

OFF THE RECORD

Coming from a professional athlete's point of view, Dave Austin uses this method on a daily basis with his coaching clients. The core of the work he does is "the process" of getting athletes into the zone quicker and having them stay there longer — the results his players get speak for themselves.

Every successful songwriter has experienced this phenomenon more often than not when composing music and writing lyrics. You've probably heard a story or two about how an artist says their ideas come to them seemingly from nowhere. There is a perfect example of this when Michael Jackson, the King of Pop, said, "I wake up from dreams and go, wow, put this down on paper . . . that's why I find it hard to take credit for songs I've written. I feel that somewhere, someplace, it's been done and I'm just a courier bringing it into the world." From Stevie Wonder to Paul McCartney, and probably Mozart to Bach, songwriters have been listening to that inner voice of inspiration and wisdom and have passed those thoughts along to the masses.

Some basic tips for getting in the zone:

>> **Clear the clutter:** Quiet your mind in a peaceful setting or surroundings.

>> **Set an intention:** Determine what you want to accomplish, or set your sights on a particular subject or topic of interest.

>> **Let your mind wander:** Accept whatever thoughts want to appear.

>> **Allow inspiration to flow:** Don't judge or censor what shows up.

>> **Listen and record:** Let your pen go as you jot down your thoughts onto a notepad or speak them into a recorder.

>> **Visualize and fantasize:** Expand on any thoughts that are in line with your intention or subject matter.

>> **Review later:** Don't immediately critique your work, but take a break and then review after you've allowed for time to reflect and a change of scenery. More than likely you will be blown away at what showed up during your "in the zone" session.

If you are adept at playing an instrument or are able to sing what comes to mind, make it a practice to record your sessions for future playback. Sometimes the best ideas come out of the blue and are hard to capture when you "come back to earth" and are trying to remember them.

Whence and how they come, I know not; nor can I force them.

— WOLFGANG AMADEUS MOZART, SPEAKING OF WHERE HIS IDEAS ORIGINATED

TIP

There are many great workshops that help songwriters find inspiration. One such program that has led to a participant getting a record deal out of those inspired sessions is Creative Expressions, which can be found by visiting www. creativeexpressions.com.

Coming up with concepts for songs

Before you set your pen to paper to write the words (also known as lyrics) to your song, it's good to have a concept (a sort of idea roadmap) that points the way to your final destination — a finished song. If you can write out one sentence that explains what your song is about (this sentence is called a *thesis*), you're on the right track to the kind of clarity and focus needed in a good song. Refer back to your thesis often to make sure the words you're coming up with still support your initial concept. If your lyrics start taking you in a different direction, it could be a sign you need to change your thesis. Who knows — perhaps you need to write two separate songs.

WARNING

Make sure each song that you write has one cohesive idea that flows from start to finish and that all the lines support that idea. If there is more than one concept fighting for life, neither will win.

TIP

One of the first things you should ask your co-writing partner is, "What matters most in your life? What do you feel passionate about?" Hopefully there is some common ground between you and your partner. Sit and talk for as long as it takes to find a concept that resonates and feels real to both of you. At least then you'll stand a fighting chance of writing a decent song.

Here are just a few of the subjects that have provided concepts for songwriters since the beginning of time — the headings are general, but the emotions you harness and the situations you create around these subjects are what will set your song apart from the others:

>> **Love:** The most universal of all feelings is surely the gold standard when it comes to subject matter for your song. Refer to "I'm Yours" (written and sung by Jason Mraz), "Lovesong" (written by Simon Gallup, Roger O'Donnell, Robert Smith, Porl Thompson, Lol Tolhurst, and Boris Williams; performed by The Cure, 311, and countless others), "Forever" (written by Chris Brown, J. Jones, B. Kennedy, A. Merritt, and Rob Allen; sung by Chris Brown), and "I Just Can't Stop Loving You" (written by Graham Gouldman and Eric Stewart; sung by Michael Jackson and Siedah Garrett). Take a week off from work and make a

list of the couple of thousand more you can think of on your own! Or better yet, just Google "love" and spend a gazillion years compiling a complete list.

>> **Friendship:** As a sub-genre of love, the bonds of friendship can bring out some of the strongest, sweetest emotions known to man. Refer to "I'll Be There for You," best known as the theme song for the TV series *Friends* (written and performed by The Rembrandts [Phil Solem and Danny Wilde]), "Umbrella" (written by Terius Nash, The Dream, Christopher Stewart, Kuk Harrell, and Jay-Z; sung by Rihanna), "Put Your Records On" (written by Corinne Bailey Rae, John Beck, and Steve Chrisanthou; sung by Corinne Bailey Rae), and "You've Got a Friend" (written and sung by Carole King; James Taylor's only #1 pop single).

>> **Family:** The family unit and its members have been the springboard for countless great songs. It's easy to see why. Your family most likely supplied you with some of your first memories — whether they are good or bad! The nature of those memories will probably determine whether your song is filled with sorrow, joy, regret, love, hurt, admiration, disdain, the desire to distance yourself from them, or your commitment to get closer. Refer to "Ready, Set, Don't Go" (written by Billy Ray Cyrus and Casey Beathard; sung by Billy Ray Cyrus), "In My Daughter's Eyes" (written by James Slater; sung by Martina McBride), "Cleanin' Out My Closet" (written by Eminem and Jeff Bass; sung by Eminem), and "The Riddle" (written by John Ondrasik; performed by Five for Fighting).

>> **Conflict:** Songs of war, strife, struggle, and broken hearts have helped countless generations deal with and heal the wounds of conflict. Verbalizing the feelings common to the heart of mankind is one of the songwriter's most sacred privileges and responsibilities. Refer to "Ordinary People" (written by John Legend and will.i.am; sung by John Legend), "Broken" (written by Jason Wade; performed by Lifehouse), "Lips of an Angel" (written by Hinder, Brian Howes, and Rey Casiano; performed by Hinder, and later by country music artist Jack Ingram), "Paralyzer" (written and performed by Finger Eleven), and "Breathe You In" (written by Steve Augustine, Joel Bruyere, Trevor McNevan, and Arnold Lanni; performed by Thousand Foot Krutch).

>> **Loss:** When the pain and devastation of a loss and the deep disappointment of losing can be put into a great song, you have a very effective delivery system for an all-natural cure. Your song will become popular with people who can relate to and draw healing from the sentiments you've expressed. Refer to "Forever & Always" (written and performed by Taylor Alison Swift), "One Sweet Day" (written by Mariah Carey, Walter Afanasieff, Wanya Morris, Shawn Stockman, Nathan Morris, and Michael McCary; performed by Mariah Carey and Boys II Men), "Wake Me Up When September Ends" (written by Billie Joe Armstrong/Green Day; performed by Green Day), "Here Without You" (written by Brad Arnold/3 Doors Down; performed by 3 Doors Down), and

"You're Beautiful" (written by James Blunt, Sacha Skarbek, and Amanda Ghost; sung by James Blunt).

» **Music and song:** Because of every songwriter's inherent love for what he does, writing about the object of his affection has been very popular since time immemorial. Refer to "I Write the Songs" (written by Bruce Johnston; sung by Barry Manilow) and "Remember the Name," which describes the life of making it big in the music industry but has a life of its own within the sports arena as a popular "pump up" song (written by Takbir Bashir, Ryan Maginn, and Mike Shinoda; performed by Fort Minor).

» **Towns, travel, and touring:** Famous places and natural wonders are always good stepping off points for a songwriter. Hiking, biking, driving, and exploring the world can supply you with endless reasons to write. Refer to "Route 66" (written by Bobby Troup; most recently sung by John Mayer, but also 40 or more other artists including Nat King Cole Trio and The Rolling Stones), "Dani California" (written by Anthony Kiedis, John Frusciante, Flea, and Chad Smith; performed by Red Hot Chili Peppers), "Fly Away" (written and sung by Lenny Kravitz), and "Somewhere Over the Rainbow" (written by Harold Arlen and E. Y. Harburg; recently covered by Hawaiian singer, Israel "IZ" Kamakawiwole).

» **Faith, hope, belief, God, and spirituality:** Although all very different subjects, we have put them together because they tend to intersect in some key areas. Looking for meaning outside of ourselves, believing in something greater than us all, searching for feelings beyond that which our five senses can validate, and looking for strength when you seem to have none have been the impetuses for some of the world's greatest songs. Refer to "I Believe" (written and performed by Blessid Union of Souls), "Meant to Live" (written by Jon Foreman and Tim Foreman; performed by Switchfoot), "Jesus Walks" (written by Kanye West and Che Smith; sung by Kanye West), and "I Still Haven't Found What I'm Looking For" (written by U2 and Bono; performed by U2).

» **Motivation, inspiration, and sports:** Going against all odds, overcoming obstacles, or simply getting pumped up for the big event is a powerful way to breathe life into a song filled with emotion and determination. Whether you're rooting for the underdog or the top dog, who couldn't use a cheering section in their corner? Refer to "Welcome to the Jungle" (written by Axl Rose and Slash; performed by Guns N' Roses). Although not originally written for this purpose, *Rolling Stone* magazine rates it "the greatest sports anthem." Also refer to "Eye of the Tiger" (written by Jim Peterik and Frankie Sullivan; performed by Survivor), "My Hero" (written by Dave Groule, Nate Mendel, and Pat Smear; performed by Foo Fighters), and "We Are the Champions" (written by Freddie Mercury; performed by Queen).

>> **Death, dying, heaven, and hell:** These subjects have been the source of speculation, inspiration, and intrigue since time began. The concepts of the afterlife, lost souls, and past lives fill the pages of songbooks, and now, more than ever, there is a tendency for many of us to check out our lineage through the centuries. Refer to "We May Never Pass This Way Again" (written and performed by James Seals and Dash Crofts), "Live and Let Die" (written by Linda McCartney and Paul McCartney; performed by Wings), "I Can't Hear the Music" on the album *All the Lost Souls* (written and sung by James Blunt), "I Knew I Loved You Before I Met You" (written by Darren Hayes and Daniel Jones; performed by Savage Garden), "Soul Meets Body" (written by Ben Gibbard; performed by Death Cab for Cutie), and "Like You'll Never See Me Again" (written by Alicia Keys and Kerry Brothers, Jr.; performed by Alicia Keys).

>> **Politics, protest, and going against the grain:** To register their feelings of disagreement or disillusionment, some people picket; some cause destruction; and some participate in marches, demonstrations, and strikes. Songwriters usually grab a pen, run to a piano, and attempt to express their frustrations through music. Love them or hate them, these songs are sure to invoke powerful emotions — note that lyrics in this category tend to fall prey to "explicit" warning labels more often than not. Refer to "Testify" (written by Rage Against the Machine and Zach De la Rocha; performed by Rage Against the Machine), "American Idiot" (written by Billie Joe Armstrong and Green Day; performed by Green Day), "When I'm Gone" (written by 3 Doors Down; performed by 3 Doors Down), and "What's Going On" (written by Marvin Gaye, Al Cleveland, and Renaldo Benson; sung by Marvin Gaye).

>> **The future, the past, and the present:** Some songs look back upon a bygone day, or even just yesterday; some look hopefully, pessimistically, or presciently into the future; and some are rooted in the good old here and now. Whatever your vantage point, a lot of material can be stitched together from the fabric of time. Refer to "Time in a Bottle" (written and sung by Jim Croce), "If This Was Your Last Day" (written by Chad Kroeger; performed by Nickelback), "Yesterday" (written by John Lennon and Paul McCartney; performed by The Beatles), "Right Now" (written and performed by Van Halen), and "Dust in the Wind" (written by Kerry Livgren and Steve Walsh; performed by Kansas).

>> **Fads, crazes, and passing fancies:** Who could forget all these timeless songs that either drive you nuts or get you off your butt to dance? The fact is they have made an indelible impression in our memory banks. Start with writing the ones you have a true affinity for, and then move to the ones that you're commissioned to write for big bucks by a major motion picture company. Refer to "The Twist" (written by Henry Ballard; sung by Chubby Checker), "Y.M.C.A." (written by Henri Belolo, Jacques Morali, and Victor Willis; performed by The Village People), "Macarena" (written by Monge, Antonio Romero, and Rafael Ruiz; performed by Los Del Rio), and "Cha Cha Slide" (written and performed by DJ Casper).

>> **States of mind:** This ever-popular subject, which ranges from sanity to insanity, elation to depression, and all stops in between, has always provided some good therapy for writer and audience alike. Refer to "When I Fall From Grace" (written and sung by Geoff Byrd), "Soak Up the Sun" (written by Sheryl Crow and Jeff Trott; sung by Sheryl Crow), and "Pocketful of Sunshine" (written by Natasha Bedingfield, Danielle Brisebois, and John Shanks; sung by Natasha Bedingfield).

We have, of course, only touched the surface of the subjects that may inspire you to create a song. Anything in life is fair game to write about. It's up to you to find unique and compelling ways of presenting these ideas and concepts through your words and music. Finding the subjects you're most passionate about, the ones that "strike a chord" in you, will make it easier to write a song that you're satisfied with and that will connect with others.

TIP

The better the source of inspiration, the better the song will be. If you come across a very compelling cause that moves you, use that as your motivation to write a compelling song. Let's say you meet a girl that knocks you out — use that inspiration to make sure the song you write about her will knock *her* out. From author Jim's experience, when writing music for a soundtrack, the better the movie script was from which he was basing a song, the better the song tended to be. Always look for the highest form of inspiration that you can find when setting out to write a song.

WORDS OF
WISDOM

Some notes, chords, and basically the same words have been used since the days of Beethoven and Bach. . . . What makes a song a timeless thing? I basically write about love and life because they are always current.

— SMOKEY ROBINSON, LEGENDARY R&B AND SOUL SINGER/
SONGWRITER, AND THE KING OF MOTOWN

Setting your antennae to listen for lyrics

There are song titles, song concepts, catchy phrases, rhymes, rhythms, and reasons all around us — you just need to keep your eyes and ears open, and consider practically everything as a potential candidate for a song. If you think of a phrase that sounds interesting, scribble that down in your notebook under "potential titles" or "intriguing phrases" to be used in the context of a future song.

Take a look at some of the places a songwriter might find lyrical stepping off points, story ideas and concepts, and catch phrases:

>> **Evesdropping:** The next time you're at a restaurant, tune in to the conversation at the table next to you. (Usually, the diners are talking so loudly you won't have to strain.) You may catch a glimpse of a conversation that could spark a song.

OFF THE RECORD

One day while Jim was on a writing trip in Nashville, he was at a local eatery with a fellow writer. They couldn't help overhearing two young ladies discussing their love lives in the booth behind them. As the blond girl was listening to the brunette recount the wonders of her current beau, the other one sighed and said, "Now that's true love." Jim and his friend looked at each other, quickly paid the bill and went to his piano room to write "Now That's True Love" in about an hour and a half.

>> **Situations you or your friends may be involved in:** There is nothing more real to write about than actual situations. The dynamics of people's lives can provide thousands of stories. Obviously it's okay to enhance or modify a real-life story (after all we're usually writing fiction here), but many writers at least base their song on the interactions of real people.

>> **Items in the news:** You'll find an endless supply of song ideas just by reading the daily newspaper and watching CNN. Of course it's important to watch actively — not only taking in and comprehending the events, but also taking the implications of the events to the next stage and searching for the motivation behind them. As you're doing all this, you are considering different situations for the emotional impact they could have in the context of a song and just how deeply the event impacts you.

TIP

Thinking "outside the box" is a songwriting goal. It's vital to look at every implication of a situation to find the perfect theme for your song.

>> **Items in magazines or blogs:** Magazines and blogs can be a great stepping off point for a song. Well-written articles can inspire an idea, and colorful ads can transfer a feeling of what's considered current in the world of pop consciousness. Magazines and blogs are basically just another way for a writer to keep his "ear to the street."

>> **Television, movies, and videos:** This is a big and vibrant category when it comes to shaking loose some great ideas from that head of yours. Just the feeling that a certain movie evokes can be enough to write a song. The message contained in so many series and shows can sometimes be harnessed into a song. In good drama or comedy, the interactions between people can serve as a template for relationships in your song. Often, there is a particular character that you're drawn to or can identify with. Write about him

or her or from *his or her* perspective. And who can resist the temptation of looking at the latest YouTube offerings — the stuff that shows up there can be an endless supply of ideas.

OFF THE
RECORD

The song title "The Search is Over" (written by Jim Peterik and Frankie Sullivan; performed by Survivor) was a phrase that Jim Peterik jotted down in his notebook after he heard it said on the evening news program.

Making up music "dummy" style

Everyone has a melody inside of them. The simplest three notes put together just right can be a melody that lasts for ages. That song you whistle while doing the laundry, walking the dog, mowing the lawn, driving, or taking a shower could be a tune you've already heard, such as the latest Black Eyed Peas smash or an Elton John classic — or it could be something you've just pulled out of thin air.

WARNING

To avoid a potential copyright infringement suit, it's critical to know the difference between a song you've heard somewhere before and one you've come up with on your own. If you think you've heard it before, screen the charts, your memory banks, and your record collection to make sure it's original. It's well documented that soon after Paul McCartney began writing "Yesterday" he went around singing it for friends to make sure he had not stolen its melody from an old song. He was finally convinced that he'd just written a new and original classic.

A working ability on guitar or keyboard can also help you experiment with and eventually find a melody for your song. When you finally put the music together, you can create a suitable bed against which you can road test your lyrics and eventually perform your finished song. Although certain people can write entire songs "in their head," most of us need an instrument at our disposal to help coax the ideas from our cranium.

OFF THE
RECORD

Although Jim says he is far from a virtuoso on the keyboard, he uses a process he coined "creative noodling" to help create ideas. He simply dials up an interesting sound on his keyboard synthesizer (generally a reassuring combination of piano and strings, although for edgier ideas perhaps a distorted electric piano setting or clavinet), and lets his fingers find their way across the keys. (Let's call it "The Columbus Method" — just find a "key" and land on it!) Often the sound itself will dictate the type of musical idea he comes up with. Try to keep a digital recorder close by to catch anything close-to-good. One truism that we've learned is this: "If I don't have my recorder handy, I most certainly *will* come up with a good idea that I *won't* quite remember later!"

One fast-track method of getting in the groove to writing your songs is to learn from the masters and not try to reinvent the wheel. A quick and effective way to begin is to grab one of your favorite tunes and use it as a "dummy song" to build your own without having to start from scratch — kind of like cut and paste in your computer's word processing program. The key here is to remember that this is just a method of getting you in the flow of creating a song, and not a means to rip off copyrighted material from the best of the best! Begin by dissecting, or picking apart, the greats by using the reverse engineering route to isolate the structure, lyrics, and melody to see what works in a great song. Not only will you learn by doing, but you can focus on just one aspect at a time. As a bonus, you will also be practicing your craft without the tendency of repeating old habits or familiar ways of doing things, thereby allowing yourself to learn something new.

The more you use a "dummy" song as your teacher and collaborator, the stronger your songwriting muscles become — and as a bonus you'll get some of the best training in the business for no money down!

WORDS OF WISDOM

The better you can become on your instrument of choice, the easier it is for you to consistently come up with good song ideas. It is also helpful when you can demonstrate to others how your song goes. Facility is not a prerequisite for writing a song, but it sure can help the process along.

— JEFF JACOBS, SONGWRITER, ARRANGER, AND KEYBOARDIST WITH FOREIGNER

On-the-Go Tools of the Trade for Recording and Organizing

Practically anyone can write or co-write a song after getting the hang of being an open vessel for inspiration. Ideas for concepts and melodies can come from anywhere, but documentation and organization of those special moments of illumination are crucial — although often a tedious but necessary evil part of the process. As with any other craft, songwriting requires a few tools of the trade — a simple notebook, recording device, rhyming dictionary, and Thesaurus, to name a few. But don't forget the computer and a slew of musical instruments and software programs as well — the latter is covered in greater detail in other chapters.

REMEMBER

Have you ever had an original melody in your head all day long, only to lose it by evening? This is why the notebook and the recorder were invented! Having learned the hard way to disregard the statement, "If it's really a great idea, don't worry. . . I'll remember it," many good melodies and ideas have fluttered away because there wasn't a net to catch them. And unfortunately, some of these rare butterflies only come around once in a lifetime — guaranteed!

Have a notebook or a digital means by which to capture those fleeting thoughts with you at all times! Time and time again you'll be glad you did because no matter how easy and simple that thought seems when inspiration strikes, trust us, it will be gone quicker than you can say "brilliant idea!" If you get caught with your pants down and have nothing handy with which to record your great thought, call your voicemail and leave a message to retrieve later. No matter how embarrassing it may be to have someone else beat you to the phone and hear your "crooning in the moment" message first, you'll be glad you did it!

Using a digital recording device

Any songwriter — whether aspiring or accomplished — should at all times carry an inexpensive, hand-held digital recorder. Better yet, always carry your cell phone or a Flip video device that can document the visual setting of your inspiration. Quality of sound is not nearly as important as merely documenting the idea. Extra batteries are always a must.

When you're driving down the road or waking up from a profound dream, and you think of a great line or words for a song, grab your recording device, press the Record button, and do the following:

1. **Start saying or singing the words or melodies that come to mind. If you're recording lyrical ideas, say them slowly and intelligibly.** With musical ideas, make sure that if you don't have an instrument handy, you give your melody a count off (as in 1, 2, 3, 4, start) so you can tell later where your musical phrase starts. It's also essential to hum the "root note" (the tonic or base note of any chord) of the key you are in, if you possibly can, so that your melody has a musical reference point when you review it later.

2. **State the date, time, your location, and anything else to help you identify the moment of creation.**

3. **Identify the working title of the song you're creating — or, if it's something new, give it a working title.**

Recording your ideas is one thing, but without a system for organizing and naming all the files you record, your ideas can be lost or extremely hard to find again. A month from now, you probably won't remember that the song you just thought of is buried deep within your hard drive . . . or on an entirely different computer. With all the time you'll spend searching for the song in question, it's probably easier to start a new song.

The world of digital recording has leaped forward at hyperspeed. For example, Todd Rundgren was able to record an entire album on his computer's inexpensive Reason program (a music software program that creates a virtual studio and instruments), and many commercial albums have now been produced on Garage-Band (a computer software program designed for the music hobbyist). But when it comes to merely documenting song ideas, you can simply use the recording function on the latest and greatest cell phone. There is even a multitrack format available to iPhone users where you cannot only memorialize the idea, but can also lay down a keyboard track, do a vocal, and add a harmony to boot! The whole song can be represented so that all the band needs to do is learn it and add their individual expressions to the final recording.

There are a zillion digital recording options out there now, and nearly every audio company now offers some type of simple digital device (featuring stereo condenser mics and usually a tiny monitor speaker). Some even have outboard effects such as *reverb* (echo) and *compression* (squashing the signal) for a more distinctive sound. Musicians can now e-mail demos to their writing and/or production partners whenever inspiration strikes! Because new technology is spitting out faster than new books are printed, rather than suggest one or two models, we suggest that you simply do an online search using the keywords "audio company digital recorders," or some variation of that, to find the latest and greatest new devices out there. But if you prefer "old school," stick with a notepad or cassette recorder (that still does the trick!) — just make sure you stock up on blank cassette tapes before they become obsolete!

On a biking tour in Europe, Jim labeled the idea-catching cassette he carried in his shoulder bag "July 6, '01 — Vienna to Prague." At least he'd be ready to write a few polkas and maybe even a waltz! Entry #1 was marked "Melodic hard rock thing in Austria." As he was winding through the streets of some quaint Austria town, he heard the sound of American rock-and-roll emanating from a boom box in someone's living room. The music was like hearing from an old friend. He stopped his bike and, into his recorder, he sang a new idea that was inspired by the mood of that moment. Jim always tries to classify an idea by genre and include any details that may help bring to mind the genesis of the idea. He also uses a star rating system (one through four), indicating his level of excitement about the idea. In this situation, the next entry was "work on possible Skynyrd seed" — perhaps a stepping off point for my upcoming writing session with them. After that he entered "Boy-band type rock." When Jim got home, he filed this tape with hundreds of other cassettes arranged by month and year. If Jim is having a creative dry spell, he spends a lot of time going through those tapes. Take a look at Figure 1-1 for an example of Jim's Vienna to Prague J-card.

> (Back Home) 6. Forgive Me work on.
> 4. Dream Song moody. ***. Wild h America!!
> 3. Good Alternative piece in plane from Prague.
> Side II

> July 6, 2001 Vienna to Prague
> Jim Peterik

> July 6, 2001 Vienna to Prague Bike Ride Tape
>
> Side A
> ** 1. Melodic Hard Rock thing in Austria. 2. Work on
> poss. Skynyrd seed   "American English" in Trebón.
>
> Side B
> *** 1. Boy Band type Rock (Layla style modulation).
> In Cerviche   "You Took the Music With Me"
> new chor.

FIGURE 1-1:
A sample J-card.

TIP

A J-card is the paper card inserted in the plastic storage case of <u>audio cassettes</u>. The card gets its name from being folded into the shape of the letter J (when viewed from the side) to fit inside the cassette's case.

Jotting down ideas in a notebook

As a songwriter, at any stage of success or experience, it's always a good idea to carry along (in addition to your portable recording device) a traditional notebook as well as a pen or pencil. Making notes is fast, easy, and you never need to wait for it to boot up or load an app. If you happen to be versed in notating music, it may be preferable to get a notebook that contains staff paper — pages that are pre-lined with the five lines of the musical staff. This would be for jotting down melodies and their accompanying chords in note form. As for your standard note-book, we recommend one of the spiral ones divided into three or more sections, with pockets lining each divider panel. This notebook configuration can help you organize your creative output in the following ways. If you purchase a five-section book, here's how your notebook could be organized:

>> **Section one:** The first section could be for the miscellaneous ideas, phrases, titles, concepts, observations, rhymes, and pieces of lyrics that you're likely to collect as you go about your day.

>> **Section two:** This section could be "songs in progress" — the ones that may have a verse but no chorus, a chorus but no verse, a rhyme with no reason, or a reason with no rhyme. It's wise to notate on these pages the current date and a cross-reference to the exact cassette or file folder where the corresponding musical tidbit can be found. This section might include songs with a few permanent or "keeper" lines (you know, the ones you're really satisfied with), and the rest of the song composed of dummy lyrics.

REMEMBER

The *dummy lyrics* are lines that serve to fill up the correct amount of space that the line should occupy, but it's usually made up of temporary words off the top of your head or substandard stuff that you fully intend on replacing at a later date. That being said, about half of the words that end up in Jim's finished songs start life as a dummy lyric. That may be because when you take the pressure off yourself to be brilliant, it often opens up creativity you didn't even know you had.

>> **Section three:** This section is reserved for finished lyrics. We suggest you leave a few pages between songs to allow for the inevitable rewrites.

>> **Section four:** You could make section four a list section — songs to be finished, songs already finished, projects in progress, and ideas on whom to pitch your tunes to. (Refer to Chapter 17 on marketing your song.)

>> **Section five:** In this section, you can just doodle your brains out until inspiration strikes, or make lists of songs already written and ideas of which artists might be appropriate for each song. If you have an upcoming writing appointment, you may want to write down some *seed ideas* (starter ideas that could spark creativity in you and your collaborator). If you're writing with a specific artist in mind or will be collaborating with a specific band or artist, you may want to put together lists of prospective titles and concepts that seem in keeping with your target artist.

TIP

In the pockets of your notebooks, keep the scraps of paper that you originally used to scribble down ideas. It's great to have these crude representations when your song hits #1 — which, of course, is entirely possible. Also keep in these pockets anything connected to a song's creation, such as the paragraph in the magazine that triggered a song, the photo of the girl who broke your heart and triggered a song, and so on.

WORDS OF WISDOM

I generally write my lyrics in progress on the right-hand page of my notebook. I keep the left side reserved for what I call "spare parts" — phrases that occur to me that relate to the song I'm working on, alternative lines, alternative titles, trial phrases, and ideas I'd rather not forget. These "left page words," as I like to call them, can be worth their weight in gold, especially a few days later when you need some fresh inspiration.

— DON BARNES, SINGER, GUITARIST, AND SONGWRITER WITH .38 SPECIAL

REMEMBER

Always put your name, address, and contact number somewhere near the front of the notebook (perhaps on the first page or on the cover) with the words, "If found, please return to. . . ." Also, make note of the date the book was started and the date of your last entry.

Practice Makes Perfect

As you go about your daily routine today (or any day, for that matter), try to notice everything that enters your consciousness. In that receptive state, be sure to have a digital recorder or a notebook close by, ready to catch your inspirations. Write down all observations, feelings, and realizations that you have that day, even if they seem trivial at the time. If you think of a catchy phrase, see an intriguing headline in the newspaper, notice a slogan on a bus as it's going by, or incorrectly hear something your child says to you, jot those things down, too. When you get home, try to find a little quiet time and look over your crop of ideas from the day. Audition them all as potential candidates for future songs. If the mood hits you, set your notebook on your piano, and if you happen to play, open your notebook to today's bounty and, informed by your own inspired words, see where your fingers take you. Try the various phrases and ideas against the music of your mind. Who knows. Before you know it, you may have a good start on an awesome new song.

Take the phrase that strikes you the most and start building a song around it. Have some fun with it. Now start your file of song ideas. Your writing sessions will become much more productive if you have a decent way of putting your thoughts and concepts on paper or on tapes. You might have a thought one day that you believe can be really good material, but you're not sure where it may take you. Now, if you've been disciplined enough to store away these thoughts for future use, when the moment comes that you can now take it further, you'll be able to recapture that original thought and let it inspire a whole new song when the time is right.

SAYING HELLO TO A GOOD IDEA

In Dave's opinion, it's always fun to be around Jim because you never know when something said or seen is going to become the new title for a song or part of its lyrics. Just being around such a prolific songwriter has also proved to help Dave raise his own antenna without much additional effort on his part. Case in point: One day Jim and Dave were in a meeting together, and Jim (who had just written the title track for the debut CD of our new artist) needed to get to another meeting across town. Everyone excused themselves and left the room, but before we knew it, Jim and Dave got to talking about something else and time slipped away from them. (If you know either of these two, you'd agree that this is not very unusual!) A while later, the CEO of the record company came back into the room and told Jim, "Boy, you're bad at goodbyes."

Jim immediately took out his pocket notebook and wrote down the words "bad at goodbyes," saying what a great song idea that was. Dave agreed — so much so that he couldn't get that phrase out of his head. That night he awoke in the middle of the night, his mind filled with the words to that song. Good for him that he had a pad of paper and pen available by his bedside so he could quickly write down the words floating around in his mind.

REMEMBER

If you let your mind go and let your imagination take flight, writing songs can be easy. But being able to do this takes practice and discipline. Be ready for that moment of inspiration, and always be prepared to catch those thoughts before they float on by. Even though they seem so simple at the time and so easy to remember, they'll haunt you forever if you decide you're too busy or lazy to write them down!

Chapter **2**

Looking at the Genres: From Country to Rock and Everything in Between

As a songwriter, you're presented with a broad menu of styles, or genres, from which to choose. Many songwriters settle on at least two or three musical directions in which they want to specialize, usually mirroring their personal taste in music and drawing from their background and influences — although you might want to keep it to one or two to get your feet wet. Some songwriters can write outside their field of expertise and stretch themselves — often with the help of a collaborator versed in that genre. Other times, a writer's song that's intended for one marketplace can find a home outside its original genre by a clever recasting of the arrangement.

In this chapter, we look at the different genres of popular music, and see how you can vary your songs — in both writing style and arrangement. We also explain how to tailor your lyrics, melodies, and chord progressions to fit each genre.

The various musical genres we take a look at include the following:

>> **Singer-songwriter:** When you write strictly for yourself and seek what defines you personally, the rulebook goes out the window.

>> **Rock:** This broad spectrum of styles ranges from hard to soft, with a zillion styles in between, and has been around since the mid-1950s.

>> **Pop:** Ranging from Billy Joel to Michael Jackson (the King of Pop), and from Christina Aguilera to Lady Gaga, this genre is perhaps the most widely known and commercially accepted.

>> **R&B, urban, and hip-hop:** This ever-expanding segment of the music charts started life in the 1940s, took off with Smokey Robinson, the King of Motown, and hasn't stopped to catch its breath.

>> **Country:** Spanning from traditional to *pop* or *alternative country,* both twenty-first-century fads, this genre continues to be a force to be reckoned with for the serious songwriter.

>> **Gospel and Christian:** Defined today mainly by its lyrical content and subject matter, this genre now encompasses most of the musical styles.

>> **Blues and folk:** The granddaddy of several other styles, the imprint of blues, both lyrically and musically, is undeniable.

>> **Jazz:** This chapter would be incomplete without a mention of this style, which basically created a bridge between classical forms and contemporary songwriting.

Creating Your Own Style: The Singer-Songwriter

A singer–songwriter is a musician who writes, composes, and sings their own material. It's considered a genre of its own because it defines itself by often breaking traditional songwriting rules and depends on the unique vision of the artist. Success in this category depends on how well the artist's vision relates to public taste and whether the audience cares enough about the artist as a person to listen to what they have to say. The singer–songwriter genre tends to be very personal and sometimes confessional. It's a form that isn't so much learned as it's lived.

A lyric that was once deep and thought-provoking might be considered whiney or self-indulgent, depending on how "in vogue" the singer-songwriter genre is in any given year.

If you're a performing songwriter, your goal should be to create a unique voice and persona through your songs. Although issues like good song form, effective use of poetic devices, and solid musical hooks and ideas are a given, the overriding objective is to separate yourself from everyone else and isolate whatever it is about you that makes you unique. It may be a point of view, a complete diversity of musical styles, or the unique way you look at life. Whatever it is, *you* define this genre — not the other way around.

The list of singer-songwriters goes on and on; they invented for themselves a style all their own. Bob Dylan, James Taylor, Carole King, Joni Mitchell, Paul Simon, Cat Stevens, Kenny Loggins, Bruce Springsteen, Sheryl Crow, Alanis Morissette, Jewel, and Melissa Etheridge are a few of the singer-songwriters. One characteristic that's shared by all these artists is this: There's no mistake about who you're listening to as soon as you hear them.

Back in 1984 when I was on the road with Survivor, we were staying in Beverly Hills when I wandered into the hotel bar to have a drink. As I drank a cold one, I noticed the young girl performing at the piano. As I started to focus on what she was playing and the words she was singing, I soon realized this was not your typical lounge singer recycling standards and top 40 hits. She was singing future classics. I went over and sat at the piano bar (one of those pianos with seats positioned all around it where the piano itself becomes your table), and I sat mesmerized by the stories of her life. When she finally took a break, I introduced myself to the young Tori Amos. Her sense of unshakeable confidence and knowing who she was totally bowled me over. Without any false modesty or boastfulness, she just knew that she would make it and that she had everything it took to make it in this business.

— JIM PETERIK, PERFORMER, SONGWRITER, AND MULTI-INSTRUMENTALIST FOR THE BANDS IDES OF MARCH AND SURVIVOR, PLUS WRITER OF HITS FOR .38 SPECIAL, SAMMY HAGAR, AND OTHERS

If your primary ambition as a songwriter is to perform your own material, study the lyrics of the artists previously listed (along with any of your personal favorites) to compare your vision with theirs; then ask yourself:

>> Just who am I, and how can I best put my personal vision into a song?

>> How do I reach deeper inside than ever to examine what's important to my soul?

>> How can I develop a style of songwriting, arranging, and singing that, when it comes on the radio (or is heard from the lobby of the theater), will immediately be recognizable as mine?

The singer-songwriting category is one where being unique is not an option — it's a necessity!

Looking for Mainstream Success: Commercial Appeal

If your intent is to find a large audience and sell your songs to the masses, you may want to concentrate on one of the following four mainstream genres because record labels and publishers look primarily for songs and artists that can be marketed commercially on radio and satellite stations. One thing to keep in mind when selecting your genre is to pay attention to how each one can vary widely in lyric and melodic style, chord progressions, and rhythm, and even how the production qualities feel — the characteristics that tend to contribute to their audience appeal.

Many labels and publishers are looking to market songs in the modern day to TV, video games, and as ringtones. These placements account for a significant percentage of total revenue, as the industry is no longer run by radio placements. At music conferences, I have heard this buzz phrase, "TV is the new radio." This has and will affect what types of music labels and publishers are looking for. A great example of an artist who has broken into pop culture from a media placement is the band The Shins from the work they did with the music for the movie Garden State!

— STEVE "SKILLET" KILLEN, GUITARIST, SESSION PLAYER, AND FOUNDER OF HERON BLUE RECORDING WORKSHOPS

When you look in terms of professional baseball, there are the minor leagues and the spotlight of the majors. Songwriting genres can be thought of in a similar way — niche markets and commercially appealing platinum domination. One is not necessarily better or more creative than the other, but in terms of commercial success and revenues generated by the masses, the major-league songwriting home runs are "hit out of the park" in the following groups of musical genres.

Rock

Rock music was born in the mid-1950s from its ancestors: rhythm and blues. As a songwriter, this is one genre that can satisfy many cravings. The genre of good old rock music is the foundation of a multitude of subgenres.

If this is your style of interest, take a look at the following subcategories of rock, and see where you might fit on the continuum and how you can tailor your own writing to correspond.

REMEMBER

As Chapter 4 mentions, the musical riff (often played on guitar) is a component in the rock genre. As a songwriter, if you're a bit weak musically, try to find a guitarist who can create an original signature sound for you in the same way that the Edge does for U2, Keith Richard does for The Rolling Stones, Eddie Van Halen does for Van Halen, Jimmy Page did for Led Zeppelin, or Slash did for Guns 'N Roses.

Old-fashioned rock 'n' roll

This genre started in the wild mid-50s when people were looking for the perfect escape with acts like Bill Haley and His Comets ("Shake, Rattle, and Roll"), Chuck Berry ("Johnny B. Goode"), Jerry Lee Lewis ("Great Balls of Fire), and of course, the King of Rock and Roll himself, Elvis Presley. The rockabilly performing songwriters like Buddy Holly ("Peggy Sue") would be a major influence on the "British Invasion" acts and the songwriting of the Beatles — then later the more blues-influenced Rolling Stones and the blues-rock groups like Traffic, Cream, and The Moody Blues.

Today, this genre finds expression as a hybrid of blues-rock in a variety of acts such as George Thorogood and The Destroyers, Brian Setzer, Black Crowes, The White Stripes, and John Mayer. However, opportunities for the songwriter are a bit limited in this genre because it's full of bands and artists who usually write their own songs. If you love it, however, then write it and pray that a new band is forming (or form one yourself!) that's ready to kick butt with some good old-fashioned rock 'n' roll!

TIP

Songs in the old-fashioned rock 'n' roll genre generally base their chord progression on the basic blues progressions ("Hound Dog" and "Johnny B. Goode" both use the 1, 4, 1, 5, 1 progression — or E, A, E, B, E progression) and they just bump up the tempo. Messages are pretty straightforward, although Chuck Berry notably stretched its boundaries with the pretty darn literate lyrics (considered rock 'n' roll poetry) of "Sweet Little Sixteen."

Hard rock

As you turn up the decibels and distortion, mic up the drums from a distance (to capture the raw room ambiance), and perhaps focus your lyrics on more extreme, explicit, angry, and controversial topics, a genre known as *hard rock* comes into the focus. Filling this genre are artists and groups such as AC/DC, Black Sabbath, Aerosmith, Joan Jett, and Van Halen, as well as those bands considered more "classic rock" in terms of style, such as Pink Floyd, Led Zeppelin, Jimi Hendrix, The Who, and the Grateful Dead (classic rock has a tendency to write politically charged material and to sway toward psychedelic sound scapes, rather than extreme, explicit, or angry).

Because hard rock is such a live-performance-oriented genre, it's difficult to write it in the confines of a writer's cubicle at a publisher's office — the bands themselves generate many of the songs written in the hard rock genre. It's also not a form that encourages the *outside song* (the song written by someone outside the band and pitched by that writer or his publisher). Songs are often fallen upon in open-ended jam sessions, where the musicians turn up the volume and interact musically until they fall into some sort of set pattern over which song structure and lyrics are placed.

If your songwriting is verging into the hard rock side of music, it's time to look at the menu of choices to see just how loud, extreme, and radical you want to go. This genre includes many subgenres such as:

>> **Heavy metal:** For example, Megadeth, Metallica, Static X, and Ozzy Osbourne. This subgenre is defined by overdriven and distorted electric guitars generally playing a minor key and an often classically inspired riff underneath manic, shouted vocals.

>> **Speed metal** (subgenre of heavy metal): For example, Anthrax, Slayer, and, perhaps "the fastest guitar alive," Sweden's Yngwie (pronounced Ing-vay) Malmsteen. This is where heavy metal is played as fast as humanly possible, and then sped up from there.

**OFF THE
RECORD**

The Swedish sensation Yngwie Malmsteen used to play for Stormer and then Keel — he's had and still has an amazing solo career and sells tons of CDs worldwide. *The Guinness Book of World Records* checked this guy out for his speed — that's how fast he was at his peak — but Nigel Rojas (lead guitarist for The Orange Sky, a reggae-rock band from Trinidad that was Yngwie's 2005 tour opening act), pushed the envelope and set new velocity records with the speed of his fingers!

Punk rock

Featuring bands such as The Clash, X, Sex Pistols, The Ramones, Good Charlotte, and Green Day, this subgenre is all about alienation from society, making a fashion statement, and speaking to a depressed economic and sociopolitical condition through music with all its rough edges left in. Punk songs usually contain anywhere from one to three chords and are arranged in a stripped-down fashion. Tempos tend to be exceptionally fast. Vocals are generally sung at the edge of hoarseness.

Alternative rock

Initially, this genre emerged with cult acts that were on independent labels and received their exposure through word of mouth, but some bands achieved commercial success and mainstream critical recognition, such as The Cure, REM, Nirvana, Soundgarden, Pearl Jam, Nine Inch Nails, Stone Temple Pilots, and Smashing Pumpkins. Sometimes referred to by the media as *Grunge* (referring both to the grungy distortion present in the guitars and to the often negative themes of songs), this genre has been around for over 20 years and shows no signs of losing steam. In fact, in the mid-2000s, after almost a decade of domination by rap-rock and nu-metal bands, this genre has hit its stride and emerged anew with the commercial success of bands such as Vertical Horizon, The Killers, and Kings of Leon — and a diverse group of acts that cross over to this category including Lifehouse, Nickelback, Incubus, Jimmy Eat World, and Shinedown.

OFF THE
RECORD

Modern rock is a term commonly used to describe a radio format that primarily plays alternative rock music — from acts such as U2, Coldplay, System of a Down, Staind, Nickelback, Puddle of Mudd, and Linkin Park. This category is a modern blend of decades and genres combining the slick production values (big guitars) and song craft (big choruses) of the '80s, with the attitude of the new millennium. Modern rock also samples from other genres such as rap, metal, and hip-hop.

Progressive rock

Musical acts such as King Crimson, early Genesis, Hawkwind, Yes, Rush, Pink Floyd, Emerson, Lake, and Palmer (ELP), and System of a Down pushed the technical and compositional boundaries by going beyond the standard rock song structures. This is music with a grand vision, musically, lyrically, and visually. This genre incorporates expansive musical arrangements, sometimes written for full symphony orchestras, into what are essentially rock melodies. Progressive rock draws themes from classical sources both literary and musical and has served as inspiration to genres such as post-rock, avant-garde metal, and neoclassical metal. The style has actually experienced a bit of a rebirth in the early years of the new millennium, with many of the signature songs by progressive rock acts being sampled and scratched into new music by groups in the electronic subgenre of rock.

When I was a member of Survivor, we would usually jam at sound checks (when a band checks its equipment, house amplification, stage monitors, and lighting, usually a few hours before a performance). I'd always have my cassette player rolling (some bands record every sound check through the mixing console) to catch any brilliance that might just happen to be flowing through the band that particular day.

— JIM PETERIK, WRITER OF 18 BILLBOARD TOP 10 HITS INCLUDING THE PERENNIAL FAVORITE "EYE OF THE TIGER" FEATURED IN ROCKY III

If you're a songwriter with aspirations to write in the rock genre, put together a kind of songwriter's jam band, not necessarily to become a recording act (hey, you never know — crazier things have happened!), but to immerse yourself in that environment to write songs in the rock genre for other artists.

Pop

Pop, or popular, music sometimes overlaps with rock (*pop-rock*, *pop-punk*, and harder-edged pop) because it originally began as a softer alternative to rock 'n' roll back in the mid-'50s — but it's also a style all to itself that is basically commercial in nature. Pop music includes the subgenres of *dance-pop* and *electro-pop*, as well as the *fusion* genres (a music genre which combines two or more genres) of *pop-rap*, and *country-pop*. As you can see, there is a lot of crossover potential in this genre.

Usually what separates the rock from the pop is a sense of imminent danger that rock possesses and pop lacks. Rock songs walk terrain that pop songs often fear to tread (or choose not to). On the other hand, you'll probably not choose "Pit of Zombies" by Cannibal Corpse as your wedding song. Take a look at several of the modern-day subgenres — and the radio formats that define pop.

The term *Top 40* (contemporary hit radio), originally coined by Radio & Records magazine, was used to describe a radio format that primarily plays music that's charting in the top 40 songs — this includes several subcategories that mainly focus on rock, pop, and urban music. Think Miley Cyrus, Alicia Keys, Taylor Swift, Beyonce, Justin Timberlake, Britney Spears, Maroon 5, Black Eyed Peas, All-American Rejects, Lady Gaga, Rihanna, and Jay-Z when describing top 40 artists.

Contemporary pop

Evolving from the form called traditional pop (Barbra Streisand, Nat "King" Cole, Frank Sinatra, Barry Manilow), contemporary pop has been the songwriters' gold mine for a number of years. Usually represented by artists strong in the visual and performing arts (and not necessarily strong in the songwriting craft), it's an industry constantly searching for great songs to extend the careers of its stars. Artists such as Mariah Carey, Celine Dion, Whitney Houston, Enrique Iglesias, Kelly Clarkson, Katy Perry, and Marc Anthony have supplied the voices and talents to inspire (and feed) hundreds of songwriters.

Memorable melodies and catchy hooks are highly prized in this category, and ageless themes such as love, regret, faith, dedication, and family are the norm. Instrumentation can be innovative, but never harsh, and is subservient to the voice of the singer and the message they want to convey.

TIP

When writing a contemporary pop song, it's important to keep your lyrical themes fairly broad and universal if you want to be considered by the widest number of artists. If you're writing with a particular artist in mind, put yourself in their shoes, and see if you can picture your words and melodies emanating from that artist.

Dance-pop

Songs for this category are based around the almighty groove. If a song just happens to possess a memorable melody, relatable concept, and interesting chord progression, all the better — but getting an entire dance floor pulsating to the diva gyrating on the stage is much more to the point. Madonna is the *grande dame* of this genre, with the likes of Janet Jackson, Britney Spears, Paula Abdul, Kylie Minogue, and Lady Gaga following her lead.

TIP

Keep your lyrics very simple in this genre — also positive and young in feel. Reflect on experiences appropriate and relatable to your target audience — males and females in the 10- to 25-year-old range. A lot of the depth and complexity you put into your pop and soul songs may get lost on the dance floor in this genre.

Lyrically, this genre tends to be on the risqué and suggestive side, but it's not generally explicit or filled with foul language — call it X-rated innocence, if you will. The female singers love to seduce you and then tell you that they're "not that kind of girl." The guys, for all their strutting and posturing, would like nothing more than to "promise forever" to the girl of their dreams.

As a songwriter, your demo for the dance-pop field will be especially important in getting your song cut. Slicker is better, and the more like the finished product it can sound, the better your chances are. This is truly a genre where sound is as important as content. Use a good programmer to do the drum track for you. Treat him well; he's worth his weight in gold records. (You might even consider making him a part of your songwriting team in exchange for his services.) There are many rhythmic devices he'll know that'll keep your song cooking along even if it's a mid-tempo tune or ballad. Those inner rhythms will fool the ear (and the feet!) into thinking it's a much faster tempo.

OFF THE RECORD

I didn't quite get the whole dance-pop phenomenon until I took my nine-year-old son to see the, at that time, up-and-coming 'N Sync open the show for urban diva Janet Jackson. They took the stage in space suits and soon stripped down to their multi-colored, chick-magnet uniforms. The screams were high pitched and deafening (as opposed to the more muted din for Janet which seemed to be voiced about an octave lower because of the slightly older demographic of her segment of the audience). Each member had a distinctive persona and their own legion of fans. The songs, which seemed a bit clichéd and overly simplistic on the radio, took on a whole new power live when combined with the razor-sharp choreography and million-watt sound system. I gained a whole new respect for this genre — just make sure you don't have a "wardrobe malfunction" when performing these tunes!

— JIM PETERIK, WRITER OF 18 BILLBOARD TOP 10 HITS

WARNING

Don't skimp on hiring the right singer for your song. This is one genre where the A&R representative (A&R stands for artist and repertoire — the person responsible for not only finding talent but also finding songs for the acts he brings in) will cut no slack for a "charming" rendition by a non-singer-songwriter. Bite the bullet — spend the extra bucks on a great session singer to increase your odds of landing a giant cover of your song. A great singer will most assuredly elevate your song.

WORDS OF WISDOM

I just arrange my dance songs when I demo them as if I was doing a record for an '80s rock band. Many of the songs in this category like "Shape of a Heart" by The Backstreet Boys are like Journey, sideways. I then take it and add current sounds, effects, and rhythm patterns to make sure it keeps up with what is currently on the radio. A great song is a great song — it's mainly the arrangement that changes from genre to genre.

— KURT HOWELL, NASHVILLE WRITER/PRODUCER AND MEMBER
OF SOUTHERN PACIFIC

Adult contemporary

The Carpenters of the 1970s, with songs like "We've Only Just Begun" (written by songsmiths Paul Williams and Roger Nichols originally as a jingle for a savings and loan company), Neil Diamond, Barry Manilow, and the music of Bread helped define the genre known as *adult contemporary (AC)* — ballad heavy with varying degrees of rock influence intended for a more adult audience. This style, sometimes referred to as *soft rock*, takes its adjectives from being easy on the ears and not particularly controversial — either lyrically or musically — and that's not a musical slight. Sometimes the lighter side of rock is exactly what you need to help unwind and sooth your jangled soul. It's a genre short on story songs and long on first-person observations on the trials of life and love. Today it has found expression in such adult contemporary and hot AC (the more modern, hipper, and slightly edgier version of the adult contemporary genre) acts like the following:

>> **Five For Fighting:** Actually the creation of one man, John Ondrasek (the name was derived from the five-minute penalty for fighting in a hockey game), this piano-heavy music with its textures of acoustic 12-string guitar, upright bass, viola, B3 organ, and other pleasing sounds that certain unusual or unexpected instruments make goes easy on the ears and tough on the soul.

>> **Lifehouse:** Originally a "praise and worship" group at their church, this group relies on gruff, raspy vocals to offset its "soft core" instrumentation — and the guitars, even when distorted, are smooth and pleasant sounding. The drums are never overbearing.

>> **Train:** Although often a hard-rocking unit, Train's most popular songs, "Meet Virginia" and its Grammy-winning 2002 smash "Drops of Jupiter," are really hot adult contemporary due to their emphasis on acoustic guitar, piano, and real strings — they crossed over into the mainstream from the alternative charts.

In terms of arranging, guitars are heavily layered and fairly polite (as opposed to the raunchy distortion of the rock genres, such as hard rock and heavy metal). Keyboards and strings are a staple, and vocals are on the smooth side and often doubled. Drums are not bombastic, and they are used mainly to keep the groove as opposed to creating sonic effects.

OFF THE
RECORD

Since the 2000s, *adult contemporary (AC) radio* plays mainstream music that now includes hip-hop and hard rock, as well as youthful-oriented R&B, pop, and rhythmic dance tracks — even though this format typically is intended for a more adult-oriented market. Artists primarily played on AC (or it's subgenres of hot AC and soft AC) include Elton John, Celine Dion, Sheryl Crow, Josh Groban, Michael Buble, and Dave Matthews Band.

The genre known as adult contemporary is as much a function of treatment as it is of substance. The soft-rock Monkees hit "I'm a Believer" from the '60s (written by the soft rock king himself, Neil Diamond), was given a raunchy reworking by pop-rock czars, Smashmouth. Catapulted back onto the airwaves by its inclusion in the animated motion picture *Shrek*, it proves not only the staying power of a great song, but how it can be "painted to suit" the modern palette of tastes.

TIP

When producing a demo of your latest song, you may want to try multiple versions. If your song started its life as a soft rocker, try a radical treatment putting it fiercely into the hard rock or alternative category. Likewise, if you started out hard, you can tone it down to a softer version.

R&B, urban, hip-hop, and rap

All these genres are united by one word: *soul.* This is music that touches the heart at the gut level, reaches inside of you, and twists. This music seems to touch on something through shared expression (or oppression) that brings its emotions explosively to the surface.

REMEMBER

Although songs of R&B, urban, and hip-hop have carved out (and are frequently classified in) a genre unto themselves, there is still a tremendous crossover appeal into the realm of pop music (and for that matter within these three). Determining where to draw the line between classifying the two genre groupings can become a bit hazy — as *urban contemporary hits* (another mainstream radio format) have dominated the U.S. pop charts since the '90s, and urban contemporary refers to music that is a crossover of rap and contemporary R&B as seen in examples such as "Crazy in Love" by Beyonce and Jay-Z (written by Beyonce Knowles, Rich Harrison, Shawn Carter, and Eugene Record) and "I'm Real" by Jennifer Lopez and Ja Rule (written by Jennifer Lopez, Troy Oliver, Cory Rooney, and L.E.S.).

Rhythm and blues — R&B

This genre, derived from work songs and field chants, became commercialized in the '50s by artists such as Jackie Wilson, Ray Charles, and Solomon Burke. They paved the way for rhythm and blues artists of the '60s like Stevie Wonder, The Four Tops, Martha and the Vandellas, Smokey Robinson and the Miracles, and The Temptations, then later by contemporary R&B artists of the '80s like Michael Jackson, Prince, Luther Vandross, and Mariah Carey. These acts, in turn, passed the baton to Usher, Boyz II Men, Alicia Keyes, Joss Stone, and John Legend in the present day. R&B is generally heavy on the backbeat (the second and fourth beats of the musical measure). The vocalists of R&B songs often approach a melody in an interpretive or soulful manner, often straying from the written melody. Check out Stevie Wonder's soulful reworking of "For Once in My Life" (originally written by Ronald Miller and Orlando Murden), the standard made popular by Tony Bennett, and the R&B remake of the George Gershwin classic (co-written by DuBose Heyward) "Summertime," written by Billy Stewart. With these two songs you can clearly see the line where pop stops and R&B begins.

Urban

This seems to be the genre (although it's actually more descriptive as a radio format than a genre) that many in dance-pop gravitate to. It reflects the sound of the city: the fads, lingo, styles, habits, priorities, and sensibilities of the young, hip, and tuned-in generation. Destiny's Child, Ja Rule, Michael Jackson, Pink, Janet Jackson, Mary J. Blige, Jennifer Lopez, and Ginuwine typify the direction many of the dance-pop acts such as Christina Aguilera, Britney Spears, Backstreet Boys, and 'N Sync moved towards within their music — looking for that sound and image to give them street credibility with their hipper-by-the-day audience.

A hallmark of this style is an extremely simple chord structure (often just one or two chords) with a simple, often two- or three-note melody that varies a bit from section to section for delineation. The grooves themselves are actually quite basic as well (light years from the complex counter-rhythms of dance-pop and Latin). The kick drum (bass drum) samples used in the rhythm beds are big and bassy — think of the low-end sound that threatens to shake your muffler loose when that certain car pulls up next to you at the stoplight.

Lyrical themes in urban music are all over the map, but they are united by the casual slang lingo of the urban streets and a defiance that almost always burns through ("What Have You Done For Me Lately," written by James Harris III, Terry Lewis, and Janet Jackson).

TIP

If you aspire to write for the urban market, get to know the genre. Hang out at the clubs. Listen to the right stations and keep your ear to the street in terms of what is being said and how it's being expressed. This genre is all about street credibility — if your song lacks it, it will never get cut.

WARNING

Never assume you are writing urban just because you have developed a good groove for your song. Urban is all about attitude, and if it ain't got that, then maybe you should switch gears or just give it up!

Hip-hop and rap

In the beginning, rap was associated with break-dancing — amazing dance movements achieved by only the limber and soul-filled rhythm enthusiasts. The word *rap* originated from a '60s slang word for conversation, for example "my wife was on the phone rapping all day with her friends." The music consists of chanted, often improvised, street poetry — complemented by samples of well-known recordings, usually from the disco, funk, or rock genre.

In the late '70s, *hip-hop* was born from rap — a genre that tears down recognizable sounds and songs and rebuilds them as entirely new, unpredictable songs. Whereas rap is mostly spoken word, hip-hop is mostly sung lyrics. Rap is more aggressively rhythmic, whereas hip-hop is based more on sensuous, hypnotic grooves. Though the beats of hip-hop and rap might sound the same to an untrained ear, there are a number of different levels to add rhythmic contrast to even the simplest song. Rap originally started with DJs playing drum loops and *scratching* (the rhythmic sound of the phonograph needle going against the groove) the records while rapping to rhythms. As the form evolved, the techniques used by rappers became quite varied in style — some were more extreme and complex using instruments such as hard-rock guitars, while others smoothed out the rough edges and emphasized the lyrics.

OFF THE RECORD

In the OutKast debut release, 1994's *SouthernplayalisticadillacMusik* ushered in a new period of hip-hop — southern style. 2000's *Stankonia* received universal acclaim and garnered the duo a handful of Grammy nominations. With a tip of their hat to the funk of Parliament and Funkadelic, OutKast's thought-provoking lyrics, clever phrasings, and incredible fashion statements vaulted them to the forefront of the hip-hop scene.

Rap music has been criticized as a boastful promotion of violence and negative attitudes towards women, whereas others admire it as an imaginative manipulation of cultural idioms and credit many rappers with a heightened social and political awareness. Hip-hop features as many women as men (take a good listen to Fergie, Mary J. Blige, Lil Kim, Missy Elliot, and Queen Latifah), and it appeals to a broad range of ages, races, and social strata. A great example of someone who fuses hip-hop and rap together is Common, an artist who truly captures the authenticity and social commentary of hip-hop. His content is politically and culturally charged with African-American social issues, and he is a multi-Grammy Award winner to boot.

If hip-hop or rap is your calling, take a look at the lyrics and listen to the current songs that are hitting the charts. See if you can identify just what separates the styles of some of the more popular artists such as Snoop Dogg, Eminem, The Notorious B.I.G., Outkast, 50 Cent, Busta Rhymes, Ludacris, Gnarls Barkley, Kanye West, and Jay-Z.

TIP

When writing in other genres such as rock, R&B, and dance-pop, get creative and start experimenting by injecting rap sections and hip-hop rhythms into your arrangements. Listen to how Shaggy blends traditional smooth soul and reggae with rap ("It Wasn't Me," written by Orville Burrell, RikRok, Shaun Pizzonia, and Braun Thompson), and how Kid Rock mixes rap with rock 'n' roll ("Bawitdaba" written by R. J. Ritchie, Matt Shafer, and Jason Krause).

Country

This broad and popular genre prides itself in being the heartbeat of the working class. Its common messages and plain language ("Write it like you talk it" is a popular saying among country songwriters) have been the benchmark of a form that started in the rural south and spread like a wildfire to all points north, east, and west. Nashville, Tennessee, has been this genre's launching pad since the '30s and is now Music City to practically all types of music. We break this category down into two primary types:

>> **Traditional country,** which includes hillbilly, country and western, and bluegrass music

>> **Pop country,** also known as *alternative country,* which is where pop rock arranging meets the more traditional style of country

WARNING

If you live and breathe traditional country and it feels as comfortable as a broken-in pair of cowboy boots, then by all means, follow that old dusty road, no matter where you hail from. But if you don't really feel natural or are just trying to "cash in," you'd better know that no one can spot a wooden nickel quicker than country folk.

Traditional country

If you want to write country songs, it's good to know your roots — the flowers of today come from seeds of yesterday. The following segments will fill you in on the parts (or seeds) that can help you create your country song. Find some of the songs by the people or groups we mention, and pick them apart to see what made them so successful.

REMEMBER

Traditional country's appeal lies in its simplicity. It can be clever and intelligent, but it never aims over the head of the common man — nor does it talk down to him.

Traditional country music originally came from the Appalachian Mountains where people sang and played fiddles (violins), guitars, autoharps, and banjos. During the '60s, Johnny Cash became a superstar, followed by Willie Nelson; and George Jones is considered to be one of the greatest, if not *the* greatest, traditional country singer around. One of the most popular traditional country artists today is singer-songwriter Alan Jackson. In 2002, he won three Academy of Country Music awards including Top Male Vocalist of the year, and his song "Where Were You (When the World Stopped Turning)" won Song of the Year and Single of the Year.

WARNING

Alan Jackson brought in a new producer and sound to his '06 release, "Like Red on a Rose," which was unsettling to some of his fans — many whom believed he was abandoning his traditional past and aiming toward a more mainstream pop sound (despite the fact that it was labeled country music or bluegrass). Needless to say, Jackson quickly went back to his country roots for his next studio album, "Good Time."

There are two types of traditional country:

>> **Country and western:** *Western* music came about when country musicians, many from Oklahoma and Texas, started using western themes (cowboys, life on the range, horses and cattle, and, of course, the girl who waits back home) in their music and began wearing colorful western clothes. The biggest stars were Gene Autry and Roy Rogers. Country music grew dramatically in the '40s. To market both country and western music in the same genre, the record industry came up with the name "country and western" to include both genres.

>> **Bluegrass:** This type of music is acoustic (meaning they use no electronically amplified instruments). Typical instruments used are the upright bass fiddle, acoustic guitar, *Dobro* (the metal-bodied guitar-like instrument usually played with a metal or glass slide), banjo, fiddle (violin), and mandolin (the small-bodied instrument composed of four pairs of strings). With a continued up-shift in popularity of bluegrass music, you may want to consider songwriting in that genre. To become successful, it's necessary to immerse yourself in the music, especially in its roots. There are fine anthology CD sets available from Bill Monroe and the Stanley Brothers, and that's a good place to start. Then familiarize yourself with recent artists, especially Allison Krauss who finds herself regularly on the country charts, Ricky Skaggs, ex-Stanley brother Ralph Stanley, and the "new grass" sensation Nickel Creek — three talented songwriters-performers from California.

OFF THE RECORD

The bluegrass soundtrack for the movie *O Brother, Where Art Thou* won the Best Album of the Year Grammy award in 2002, to the shock, surprise, and delight of many in the industry.

Pop country (or alternative country)

Pop country is a wayward cousin of country that came to visit for the weekend and somehow became a permanent member of the household. In doing so, some of the rough edges of country were knocked off and substituted with some of the slick chord changes and production values of pop and rock.

Pop country is quite a different genre than traditional country. In traditional country, the songs are simple, using three-chords, and deal with real-world issues. Pop country songs, on the other hand, are often simple pop songs with a country feel and usually use more chords than the typical three-chord traditional song (like using the 2, 6 and 3 chords more frequently and even other more tantalizing chords such as the diminished, half-diminished, and sustained fourth chords). The hit song "Amazed" (written by Marv Green, Chris Lindsey, and Aimee Mayo; performed by Lonestar), which crossed over into the pop charts, actually uses three separate keys: one for the verses, one for the pre-chorus, and another for the chorus.

The fact is that there is little difference in the structure of many pop country ballads and those sung by boy-band groups such as the Backstreet Boys and 'N Sync. The songs "I Can Love You Like That" (written by Steve Diamond, Maribeth Derry, and Jennifer Kimball) and "I Swear" (written by Gary Baker and Frank Myers) were both #1 country hits for John Michael Montgomery as well as hits on the Top 40 when they were sung by the group All-4-One. The song "(God Must Have Spent) A Little More Time on You" (written by Carl Sturken and Evan Rogers) was recorded not only by 'N Sync (reaching #8 on the pop charts) but also by the country group Alabama (featuring 'N Sync), which hit the country charts as well.

WARNING

When you're writing for the alternative country marketplace, remember that songs with a negative theme will have trouble finding a home. Also, blatant "lost my baby and I'm gonna drown my sorrows in Jack Daniels" weepers go in and out of style — refer to today's music charts for reference.

OFF THE RECORD

Coming to Nashville for the first time to collaborate back in 1996 was kind of scary. Nobody seemed to care about my rock-and-roll resume. I was asked by one prominent publisher if I really thought I could write country. I answered honestly that I wasn't sure, but I told him I could write a good, simple song from the heart and that's really what country is all about anyway. Well, I guess I passed his pop quiz because he hooked me up with one of his top country writers who I continue to write with to this day — Mr. John ("Third Rock from the Sun") Greenebaum.

— JIM PETERIK, WRITER OF 18 BILLBOARD TOP 10 HITS

Arrangement-wise, many stylistic elements have been added in country's quest to cross over to the general populace. In the mix, there are now rock electric guitars (more distorted and hotter in the blend) and nontraditional elements like strings (Chet Atkins turned the country world on its head when he started adding string sections to country songs in the '50s), synthesizers, and even drum loops like the ones found on urban tracks. You can even hear the gimmick of misusing the pitch correcting devices to create the robotic vocal effect heard on Cher's hit, "Believe" (written by P. Barry, M. Gray, B. Higgins, S. McLennan, T. Powell, and S. Torch). Certain elements from traditional country are often added to put in the "down home" elements listeners are accustomed to hearing, such as fiddle and *pedal steel* (that's the unit that sits on four legs in front of the player and is picked with finger picks, chorded with a steel bar, and pitch-shifted by manipulating levers with the player's knees — it supplies the "crying guitar" sound you hear on many country songs). Also incorporated are the banjo, *Dobro* (the steel-bellied guitars you see on the cover of the *Brothers in Arms* album by those English hillbillies, Dire Straits), and harmonica.

REMEMBER

Sometimes a song can straddle more than a single genre by changing the arrangement, instrumentation, and vocal style. Producers can sometimes change a song from pop to alternative country with the addition of certain key Nashville instruments like pedal steel and fiddle. "I Swear" (written by Gary Baker and Frank Myers) was not only an R&B hit for All-4-One, but a country hit for John Michael Montgomery as well.

Seeking a Road Less Travelled: Other Notable Genres

When it comes to musical genres, one thing is for certain — there are a zillion of them in existence when you take into account all of the subgenres and fusion genre hybrids (really there are — just do a Wikipedia search if you don't believe us). Not only is it sometimes hard to get a clear handle on the entire scope of the subject of genres, but there is also much debate as to which, or how many, genres many artists and songs fall into (take a look at Amy Winehouse, for example). All that aside, there are several more genre groups we'd like to mention here, even though they perhaps currently fall outside the umbrella of the commercially recognized mainstream. Genres such as smooth jazz, new age, and reggae certainly have an audience — we'll save that discussion for another time — however, there are several more (significant ones) we would like to highlight in this section.

Christian

The Christian genre, like many others, is based on authenticity. Just as a true country aficionado can spot an insincere attempt at down-home songwriting, and the hip urban crowd can see a poser from down the block, writing in the Christian field requires true commitment and belief in Jesus Christ.

WORDS OF WISDOM

There's a well-documented story circulating about the rock artist who released a Christian-slanted song to Christian radio. When the programmers went to his website, as directed, they found foul language and un-Christian attitudes. That was all that was needed to put the kibosh on his Christian crossover ambitions.

— JIM PETERIK, WRITER OF 18 BILLBOARD TOP 10 HITS

This rapidly expanding genre covers practically all styles of music from soft rock to heavy metal. Groups like Creed (who during the new millennium were one of America's top-selling acts in *any* category and actually won a Grammy in a non-Christian category), Jars of Clay, Lifehouse, Switchfoot, and P.O.D. are part of the movement in Christian music where a spiritual message has entered the mainstream and is being programmed by not exclusively Christian radio as well as by Christian-only stations. (The group Stryper paved the way for metal music in the Christian genre, and Amy Grant was the first Christian act to make a major impact on the general pop charts.) Joining the more traditional Christian acts like Steven Curtis Chapman, Michael W. Smith, and Bill and Gloria Gaither on the contemporary Christian charts, this new breed of artist is helping to spread "the Word" to a broad marketplace.

REMEMBER

It's not always necessary to use the words "Jesus" or "Christ" in every song in order for it to be Christian. The message and spirit of your song is the most important element.

A trend towards more "positivity" is being heard on the radio. Contrasting the doom and gloom of the grunge era, a new message of hope is taking shape from Christian groups like P.O.D. and Audio Adreneline. Other acts, such as Lifehouse and Creed (though not marketed as Christian) began spreading good values and positive, life-affirming messages — the audience is often getting "the word" in between the lines.

OFF THE
RECORD

Blessid Union of Souls used fairly subtle Christian themes in many of their songs — by using the word "love will find the way" rather than "God will find a way," songwriter Eliot Sloan was able to get across the message without making it sound too preachy.

WARNING

If you're a singer-songwriter breaking through to the Christian world from rock, there may be some resistance and skepticism about letting you in. Just as the country world is hesitant to let "just anyone" be a part of country, the Christian market wants a high degree of proof that the artist is truly committed and walks the path of the Lord.

Gospel

Today's contemporary gospel music combines jazz, R&B, and hip-hop with words of praise and worship. Some of today's top gospel singers are Yolanda Adams, Mary Mary, CeCe and Bebe Winans, Trin-I-Tee 5:7, Hezekiah Walker, and Kirk Franklin.

Like most other genres, the borders of gospel music have been blurring in recent years to embrace more nontraditional musical styles. For every Shirley Caesar (more traditional), there is a Yolanda Adams (hip-hop gospel). Acts like Donnie McClurkin and Mary Mary are holding the gospel torch high while blazing new trails.

Stylistically, southern gospel has remained truer to its roots than any other genre of music excepting bluegrass. A tradition of family groups continues today with such groups as the McKameys and the Singing Cookes (both of which are Appalachian Mountain–style groups) and The Crabb Family. Groups such as the Isaacs Family and Jeff and Sheri Easter represent the bluegrass gospel tradition.

Music (the lyrics and the melodies) in all of the genres has a profound effect on our emotions. Many people believe that listening to songs about Jesus Christ is healthy for the spirit, and oftentimes, certain Christian and gospel songs, especially when performed live in church or in concert, can take people into a state beyond description — where the audience shouts with joy, feeling goose bumps all over while tears roll down their faces. Take a look at the lyrics of the following song, and imagine being in a crowd of people filled with the spirit:

"From the Depths of My Heart" written by Ben and Sonya Isaacs

It hasn't been a bed of roses since I've started on my way

And Lord you know I'm not complaining

There's just something I should say

For I've reached desperation and I've stumbled since my start

I've grown weary through the years, now I'm crying bitter tears

From the depths of my heart.

Chorus

From the depths of my heart, Lord, I'm calling out to you

For I need you here to lead me, I've done all that I can do

Lord I'm trying to do my part to see that others make it through

And though I know I don't deserve you

Still I'm trying hard to serve you from the depths of my heart.

It's not a prayer just from the lips, it goes much deeper than words

It's not a worthless expression, I just need to be heard

For Lord, I need to reach your throne, I know exactly what I'll do

I'll just fall down on my knees, I know you will hear the pleas

From the depths of my heart

Words and music by Ben and Sonya Isaacs © Isaacs Family Publishing (BMI)

TIP

If you're interested in writing for this genre, there's an excellent resource called the *Singing News* magazine that can point you in the right direction. The monthly magazine features tour schedules of (and articles about) all the major artists.

Blues and folk

Blues and folk music are considered by some to be the original soul music because they exist to document the trials and heartbreaks of the human condition. This was music created not for commercial gain. The music was created by people who needed to tell their story and vent their souls through simple and heartfelt songs.

Blues pioneers like Robert Johnson, Blind Lemon Jefferson, and Memphis Minnie inspired Howlin' Wolf, Muddy Waters, Big Mama Thornton (who performed the original version of the Presley smash "Hound Dog," which was written by Jerry Leiber and Mike Stoller), and T-Bone Walker, who lit the path for later blues greats like B.B. (Blues Boy) King, Buddy Guy, Albert King, Freddie King, Etta James, and Elmore James. They, in turn, inspired a new generation of blues journeymen starting with Eric Clapton, Bonnie Raitt, Stevie Ray Vaughan, and Robert Cray, and extending to current blues upstarts like Jonny Lang, Anthony Gomes, Shannon Curfman, and Kenny Wayne Sheppard.

TIP

For the ultimate guide to the blues, check out *Blues For Dummies* (published by Wiley Publishing, Inc.). You'll love Cub Koda and Lonnie Brook's insight and humor.

As a songwriter, there are always plenty of blues and folk artists looking for good, simple, and honest material. Blues is one genre where it's okay to bitch and moan. But as you listen to the great blues songs, you realize that it can also be very vibrant and uplifting. For every song about a lost love, you'll find one about a found love. Often it's the juxtaposition of the jumping blues shuffle beat that energizes an otherwise mournful lyric.

Writing for the folk market is mainly a matter of colorfully documenting events and telling a good story, as was done by the folk pioneers of America like Huddie Ledbetter (known as Leadbelly), Woddy Guthrie, and Pete Seeger. Remember to keep the chord changes simple and the language fairly plain.

TIP

Every genre has specific ways of expression. In the blues and folk categories, avoid flowery and overly poetic phrases. Speak to the heart of the matter and tell the story clearly and honestly. Listen to the early albums of Robert Cray for a textbook example of how to weave a great story around an immediately recognizable hook ("Smoking Gun," written by David Amy, Robert Cray, and Richard Cousins) in the context of a blues song.

Jazz

Songwriting in this genre is perhaps one of the most influential styles for many reasons. Not only does it hold unforgettable artists such as Ella Fitzgerald and Louis Armstrong, but Jazz also holds in its theoretical makeup the birth of blues, gospel, rock 'n' roll, and rhythm and blues. Jazz in essence created a bridge between classical forms and contemporary songwriting. The songs "I Got Rhythm" and "Embraceable You" (written by George Gershwin and Ira Gershwin) are two songs from the Broadway musical *Girl Crazy* that did just that.

With the chord progression referred to as "rhythm changes," "I Got Rhythm" set the tone for bebop music and other jazz forms — with a 1, 6, 2, 5 chord progression — and was expressed in a way that pioneered jazz songwriting. This was a critical time in western music history. Our conception of all contemporary styles would be completely different without jazz pioneers such as Duke Ellington, George Gershwin, Billie Holiday, Ella Fitzgerald, Tony Bennet, Frank Sinatra, Sarah Vaughn, and others.

Practice Makes Perfect

For the fun of it, experiment by trying your hand at several different styles of music, following the guidelines set up in this chapter. Keep in mind what you're most passionate about, and focus on what genre you're most comfortable with because this is most likely where your best material will be created. In the case of sports, there are not many athletes who can compete at a very high level in more than one sport (you can probably count them on one of your hands). The same goes for songwriting — very few songwriters can write hit songs in all genres. Do what you can to find your passion and direction, and let that be your ticket to the level of gold and platinum status.

IN THIS CHAPTER

» **Understanding the terminology of a songwriter**

» **Knowing the basic fundamentals of the verse**

» **Getting a handle on the various song formats**

» **Building the mood and telling your story**

» **Getting "under the hood" of your favorite songs**

Chapter **3**

Working It Out: Getting Your Song into Shape

When you hear a new song on the radio, you probably don't turn to your friend and say, "Wow, awesome pre-chorus — I love how it sets up the hook!" Nonetheless, every song has a structure that it's built upon. The framework can follow any of several tried-and-true patterns, or it can break the mold and go where no song has gone before. Knowing basic song forms, also referred to as *form*, will help guide you as you're constructing a song. It'll also help identify what you are already doing instinctively. It's important to understand the basics of song structure even if you choose to stray from it in certain instances. There's something reassuring in the use of familiar song organization that can help a songwriter sound immediately more professional and commercial.

In this chapter, we look at many of the most commonly used and successful song forms. We break down a song into its basic modular components and show how to organize the various sections to create a synergy that is greater than the sum of its parts.

Talking Shop about Song Form

Before we start looking at song forms, it's important to understand the terminology songwriters use when they're talking shop. You've heard most of these terms, but now we give a definite meaning to them:

» **Intro:** This section, which is where the song typically starts, reveals the melody of the chorus, or sometimes the verse, in instrumental form. Its purpose is to get the ear ready and introduce all that is to come. Listen to any radio station. Most of the songs you hear have some form of intro, and your "tune-out factor" is directly affected by how effective the writers and arrangers are at catching your attention right off the bat.

» **Verse:** The purpose of the verse is to reveal the storyline and melody of the song. It helps propel the listener to the chorus while conveying the song's basic mood and message. The words, or lyrics, of the verse tend to expand from verse to verse, with new information added to move the story along. The melody and chord pattern of the verse are usually the same from verse to verse, except for minor variations in melody usually to make a lyric fit.

» **Chorus:** The chorus is the "money section" of a song — if you've done your job well, this is the part people will go around singing as they plunk down their hard-earned money to own a copy for themselves. This section usually contains the title or "hook" of the song, at either the beginning or end of the chorus. The chorus features a signature phrase or musical figure that's repeated throughout the song and that serves as the main identifying portion of the song. Musically and lyrically, choruses tend to be identical except for minor variations. (One exception to this generality is the song, often a country song, that saves the surprise lyrical payoff for the last chorus and is therefore very different.) In most cases, songwriters like to keep their choruses identical — so it's harder for the audience to muff a line in the big sing-along!

» **Pre-chorus:** Sometimes a short section of a song precedes the chorus. It provides a little "fresh terrain" both lyrically and melodically before pressing on to the chorus. It's usually no more than eight bars in length and sometimes contains the identical lyric each time it comes around. It might even be just a single line. The pre-chorus isn't *essential,* but it can add a nice twist when it's used.

» **Bridge:** The bridge, sometimes called *middle eight* (referring to the eight musical measures the bridge tends to occupy), comes after the second chorus in the majority of pop songs. It's not a necessity in all songs. It can either contain lyrics or be instrumental in nature. Regardless of whether the bridge contains words, its main function is to give the listener a break from the established verse and chorus, providing a different melody and harmonic progression. A lyrical twist may also be exposed here. The name refers to the bridge between the halves of the song.

>> **Coda:** A special ending section, also called an *outro* or a *tag,* can be added to the end of a song. It's typically a kind of grand finale.

Now that you see the various components that make up a song, take a look at the different ways of organizing them. Again, there's no right or wrong way — only what *sounds* right or wrong to the ear.

In other songwriting guides (including the first edition of this book), you may see references to a system that assigns letters to sections of a song, like "AABA" and so on. We're not going to go that route in this book; instead, we opt to use the terms just listed. Plus, you will encounter a similar system for rhyming schemes in Chapter 6, and we don't want to confuse or overcomplicate things for you here.

REMEMBER

As you read this chapter (and the rest of this book), don't hesitate to flip back to this list of terms so that you know for sure what we're referring to.

Dealing with Verses

The basic fundamental section for any song is the verse. We start out by talking about songs that consist of nothing but verses.

The single-verse form

In this verse form, different lyrics are placed over the same music and are repeated in close succession. The chorus and bridge are often eliminated in this form, so the title typically appears in the first or last line of the verse. This form works when a story is being told, using each verse to propel the action forward. Church hymns usually fall into this category, as do many folk songs. Many of the songs of Bob Dylan, Joni Mitchell, Joan Baez, and Judy Collins use this form as well.

It's especially important for your melody to be interesting in this form so that it can withstand the repetition of identical sections. Often a musical section can come between verse sections to add interest. Sometimes a writer throws in a section that is choruslike, but doesn't contain the title hook of the song. Songs like this are generally considered a variation of the single-verse form.

The number of verses in a song written in the single-verse form varies widely. Jimmy Webb's song "By the Time I Get to Phoenix" (Glen Campbell's breakthrough hit) takes only three verses to tell the story.

Each well-crafted verse presents a location that the singer is thinking about as he embarks upon his journey away from his former lover in California. The song is about what she'll be doing when the singer arrives at each of three destinations: Phoenix, Albuquerque, and Oklahoma.

The title of the song is mentioned only once, in the first line of the first verse. That's because each verse describes a different location, which Webb has cleverly shown in his first lines. Webb cleverly uses lyrics elsewhere in the song — for example, "She'll just hear that phone keep on ringin' off the wall" is followed by a simple "That's all." True to the verse form, the song tells a story that progresses from verse to verse.

"Closer" (written by Caleb Followill, Jared Followill, Matthew Followill, and Nathan Followill), the opening track on the Grammy-nominated *Only By The Night* album by Kings of Leon, uses the repetitive single-verse form to build a brooding intensity to the track. Through synth sound effects and droning vocal, the listener enters into a near-trance state. The writers obviously felt that to throw in another section or two not only would be unnecessary, but would destroy the momentum of the mood being created in this song:

"Closer," performed by Kings of Leon

Verse 1

Stranded in this spooky town
Stoplights are swaying and the phone lines are down
This floor is crackling cold
She took my heart, I think she took my soul
With the moon I run
Far from the carnage of the fiery sun

Verse 2

Driven by the strangled vein
Showing no mercy I do it again
Open up your eye
You keep on crying, baby
I'll bleed you dry
The skies are blinking at me
I see a storm bubbling up from the sea

Chorus

And it's coming closer
And it's coming closer

Verse 3

You, shimmy shook my bones
Leaving me stranded all in love on my own
What do you think of me
Where am I now? Baby where do I sleep
Feel so good but I'm old,
2000 years of chasing taking its toll

And it's coming closer

For another example of the single-verse form, check out "All Along the Watchtower," by Bob Dylan, made famous by Jimi Hendrix. It consists of three verses and is a good example of the style of lyric writing Bob Dylan introduced during the 1960s.

If you listen carefully to these well-crafted words, you'll be hard pressed to find a hook (see Chapter 4 for more on hooks) in the song at all — until you realize that the entire song is one big hook. The title, "All Along the Watchtower," is introduced in one place only, as the first line of verse 3. Notice, however, that it's probably the best candidate in the song for a title. Dylan could have called the song "Two Riders Were Approaching" or "There Must Be Some Way Out of Here," but neither of these phrases comes close to "All Along the Watchtower" as its great title. Look up some (or all) of the songs in Table 3-1 for more help with this form.

TABLE 3-1

Single-Verse Song Examples

Song Title	Songwriter(s)	Singers/Performers
"Closer"	Caleb, Jared, Matthew, and Nathan Followill	Kings of Leon
"Doves Cry"	Prince	Prince
"Subterranean Homesick Blues"	Bob Dylan	Bob Dylan, Red Hot Chili Peppers
"Born in the U.S.A."	Bruce Springsteen	Bruce Springsteen
"So What"	Pink, Max Martin, and Shellback	Pink

The two-verse form

In the classic songs written by American composers for film and Broadway from the 1940s through the 1960s, the *two-verse form* became popular. Because of its lack of chorus, it isn't used much in the pop music of the '70s and beyond, but songwriter Lionel Ritchie used an extended two-verse form for his hit '80s song "Hello."

This form consists of, as its name implies, only two verses, but it tells a complete and tidy story. Each verse is traditionally 16 bars long (check out Chapter 8 for more on bars). The second verse is usually a musical repeat of the first, but in some songs, the second verse resembles the first, beginning the same way but wrapping up differently musically.

Okay, we admit, the songs from the '30s and '40s might be a little square, but they're great to study because they are usually very, *very* well written. The lyrics get right to the point and the melodies *are* memorable. You can learn a lot from Irving Berlin, Hoagie Carmichael, and George Gershwin, among others. If you want to study the two-verse form in more detail — both old, new, and some in between — take a look at this list of songs in Table 3-2.

TABLE 3-2 **Two-Verse Song Examples**

Song Title	Songwriter(s)	Singers/Performers
"Good Riddance"	Billie Joe Armstrong	Green Day
"In My Life"	John Lennon, Paul McCartney	The Beatles
"White Christmas"	Irving Berlin	Most of us, made popular by Bing Crosby
"Love Song"	Simon Gallup, Roger O'Donnell, Robert Smith, Porl Thompson, Lol Tolhurst, Boris Williams	The Cure, 311, Death Cab for Cutie, Good Charlotte, and many others

The "Standard" Form

The form of choice in the first half of the twentieth century consisted of two verses followed by one of those "variations" that we discussed in the single-verse section. This form is still used today in songwriting.

Learning about the standard form

In the *standard form*, two verses are followed by a section that has a new melody. It's not quite a chorus, and it's not exactly a verse. Some writers call this a *change part* because it offers a change from the verse, but doesn't work the same way as a chorus. In this form, another verse follows the change part. The title is usually placed in either the first or last line of each verse and is in the same place each time it comes around.

This change part provides a contrast to the verse sections by using different chords, a different melody, and sometimes a shift in the focus of the lyrics. It provides an interlude between verses, which can be effective if done well.

In the classic standard song, the verse sections are usually eight bars in length and constitute the main melody of the song. Each of the three verses has a different set of words, although the last verse section can be a repeat of the first, as is the case in John Phillips's "Monday, Monday," performed by The Mamas and The Papas. In fact, all three verses can be the same, as in John Lennon and Paul McCartney's "Do You Want to Know a Secret?" But these are exceptions to the rule, and you won't find many songs that repeat verses like that. Songwriters usually compose three separate sets of lyrics for the verse sections of a standard form.

The standard form continues to be used today in many styles of music — country, gospel, Christian, pop, jazz, theater, and film — but not as often as it once was. The form can be used to provide effective emotional satisfaction: The first two verses establish the main melody of the song, and the change part provides a different feeling with its contrasting quality. Thus, the return to the last verse offers an emotionally satisfying return to what was presented before.

Every rule has exceptions — that's what makes life (and songs) interesting. Some standard songs don't introduce the title in the first or last line of each verse. "The Christmas Song" (written by Mel Torme and Robert Wells) is an example of this. Everyone knows this song ("Chestnuts roasting on an open fire . . ."), but the title, "The Christmas Song," doesn't appear in the lyrics at all. The title describes what the song is about, and it's not a phrase that would sound good in the song itself.

Another example of different placement for the title is George Gershwin and Ira Gershwin's famous song "I Got Rhythm." The title appears at the beginning of the first verse and then gets transformed in the next two verses. In the second verse, it becomes "I got daisies," and in the third verse, it's "I got starlight." This is a great trick, the same one used by songwriter Jimmy Webb in "By the Time I Get to Phoenix" (although this song is single verse in form). Take note of it — you may want to do the same thing in a song of your own someday.

In the following sections, we steer you toward a few standards that illustrate what the form is about.

A real classic by Harold Arlen and E. Y. Harburg, "Over the Rainbow," was sung by Judy Garland in the film *The Wizard of Oz* and has been covered by many other artists since.

This is a great example of a standard song with an added section at the end called a *coda.* The verses have a flowing feeling to them with the expansive quality of the words ("Somewhere over the rainbow, bluebirds fly"). This is perfectly contrasted by the quick movement of words in the change part ("Where troubles melt like lemon drops away above the chimney tops"). The bridge provides a perfect interlude between the second and third verses.

The following list includes songs written in the standard song format. Table 3-3 shows some great songs for you to explore to discover more about the form.

TABLE 3-3   **Standard Song Examples**

Song Title	Songwriter(s)	Singers/Performers
"Hey Jude"	John Lennon, Paul McCartney	The Beatles
"Something"	George Harrison	The Beatles
"Forever and Always"	Taylor Alison Swift	Taylor Swift
"Save the Last Dance for Me"	Doc Pomus, Mort Shuman	The Drifters
"Just the Way You Are"	Billy Joel	Billy Joel

Taking the standard form further

Beginning in the 1960s, some songwriters began using an extended version of the standard form. This is the standard form with an additional change part and a final verse. This final verse may be a repeat of a previous verse or even just a part of one of the previous verses.

John Lennon and Paul McCartney's song "Yesterday" uses an extended standard form. The title appears as the first line in each verse except for verse 2, where the word *suddenly* is used instead. The title also appears in the last line of each verse and in the last line of the bridge, and the final verse is just a repeat of verse 3.

This extended standard form is also used in other Beatles songs (written by John Lennon and Paul McCartney), including the following:

>> "I'll Follow the Sun"

>> "I Want to Hold Your Hand"

>> "Hard Day's Night"

>> "Long and Winding Road"

>> "I Call Your Name"

**OFF THE
RECORD**

Things get a little more complicated in a few of McCartney's songs. "Michelle," for example (also credited to Lennon/McCartney), has four verses and three change parts. The fourth verse is not sung but is instead played as an instrumental. The words in the second verse are repeated in the third and fifth verses, so all these verses are the same. All three change parts have different words, however. This is an unusual and innovative formal structure. Because the formal structures in *many* of the songs written by McCartney and Lennon are advanced, you can get a lot out of studying them. (Don't you wish your school work was this much fun?)

The Verse-Chorus Form

The verse-chorus form is the most common in today's pop, rock, gospel, R&B, and country music. In the *verse-chorus form*, verses alternate with a chorus section. The chorus is always the same except, perhaps, at the end, where you can extend it to make a really great ending for the song.

The story that the song unfolds is contained within the verses. When the chorus is sung, it usually proclaims the title as the hook. Pop or rock songs that work well usually start out with a line that people relate to; then the words of the verse pull the listeners in and get them hooked. The power comes when the chorus is sung. Listeners take notice of a good chorus and imprint the song in their minds.

Throughout this section, we take a closer look at the verse-chorus form, starting with "Goodbye Yellow Brick Road," by Elton John and Bernie Taupin.

This song has two verses that tell the story about a person who is tired of the high life and wants to return to his life on the farm. The chorus emphasizes his feelings, bidding farewell to the "yellow brick road" and stating that he's going back to his former life on the farm. No matter how many verses a song has, the chorus always applies because it describes the main topic of the song. Notice that it starts and ends with the title, which helps it stick in the listener's mind as the song's hook.

TIP

The best place to put a title in a verse-chorus song is in the first line of the chorus. Some songwriters place the title in both the first line and the last line (as in "Goodbye Yellow Brick Road").

Another great verse-chorus song comes from Alicia Keys, the first artist to be released on legendary producer and Arista Records founder Clive Davis's new label, J Records. Her song "Fallin'" is a great example of a simple verse-chorus song elevated to high art by a smoldering vocal and a brilliant arrangement. Two chords make up the entire song, using the basic blues progression found in the classic song "I Put a Spell on You," by Screamin' Jay Hawkins (covered by The Animals in the '60s). The progression that alternates between E minor and B minor has never sounded more elegant. The structure is the verse-chorus form with a simple chorus. The song gains its momentum through repetition and the swelling of strings and background vocals in the arrangement. The song begins with a gospel-drenched *a cappella* (group or solo singing without musical accompaniment) opening line — "I keep on falling in and out of love with you" — and continues with the verse supported by piano:

"Fallin'," written and sung by Alicia Keys

Verse 1 (A)

I keep on fallin' in and out of love with you
Sometimes I love ya, sometimes you make me blue
Sometimes I feel good, at times I feel used
Lovin' you, darlin', makes me so confused

Chorus (B)

I keep on falling in and out of love with you
I never loved someone the way that I love you

Verse 2 (A)

Oh, oh, I never felt this way
How do you give me so much pleasure
And cause me so much pain
Just when I think I've takin' more than would a fool
I start fallin' back in love with you

Chorus (B)

I keep on fallin' in and out of love with you
I never loved someone the way that I love you

Coda

I, I, I, I'm fallin'
I, I, I, I'm fallin'
Fallin', Fallin'
I keep on fallin' in and out of love with you

I never loved someone the way that I love you
I'm fallin' in and out of love with you
I never loved someone the way that I love you
I'm fallin' in and out of love with you
I never loved someone the way that I love you

Words and Music by Alicia Keys ©2000 EMI April Music, Inc., and Lellow Productions (ASCAP)

"Goodbye Yellow Brick Road" and "Fallin'" stick to the verse-chorus form exactly. Sometimes, however, a verse-chorus song presents two verses before the first chorus is sung. You can look up the lyrics to some (or all) of the songs listed in Table 3-4 to learn about two verses before the chorus. This approach is sometimes an effective way to get into the feel of the song before the chorus arrives.

TABLE 3-4

Verse-Chorus Song Examples

Song Title	Songwriter(s)	Singers/Performers
"Daniel"	Elton John, Bernie Taupin	Elton John
"Helpless"	Neil Young	Crosby, Stills, Nash & Young
"My Hero"	Grohl/Smear/Mendel	Foo Fighters

If you want more examples of verse-chorus songs, you may want to study the songs listed in Table 3-5. As you're reading the lyrics or listening to these songs, pay close attention to the placement of the titles and ask yourself what title placement accomplishes.

TABLE 3-5

More Verse-Chorus Song Examples

Song Title	Songwriter(s)	Singers/Performers
"American Pie"	Don McLean	Madonna
"The Wind Beneath My Wings"	Larry Henley, Jeff Silbar	Bette Midler
"Foolish Games"	Jewel	Jewel
"Amazed"	Marv Green, Aimee Mayo, Chris Lindsey	Lonestar
"If You Ever Have Forever in Mind"	Vince Gill, Troy Seals	Vince Gill
"American Idiot"	Billie Joe Armstrong/Green Day	Green Day

YOUR VEHICLE TO SUCCESS

In Jim's opinion, his first #1 song, "Vehicle," performed by The Ides of March, is probably the simplest song he's ever written. The verse just merges seamlessly with the chorus, as opposed to being set up by a pre-chorus:

Verse

I'm the friendly stranger in the black sedan
Won't you hop inside my car
I got picture, got candy, I'm a lovable man
And I can take you to the nearest star

Chorus

I'm your Vehicle, baby
I'll take you anywhere you wanna go
I'm your Vehicle, baby By now
I'm sure you'll know
That I love you (love you), need you (need you)
Want you, got to have you, child
Great God in heaven you know I love you

Words and music by Jim Peterik © 1970/1999, Bicycle Music (ASCAP)

As a songwriter, Jim admits that he tends to devalue the simple songs he writes, but those seem to always be the ones that turn out to be the biggest hits. In this example, every section has a hook, climaxing with "Great God in heaven you know I love you." It took Jim years to figure out what he was doing right in his more successful songs, but it usually boils down to simplicity, relatability, and a killer beat.

The verse-chorus form using a pre-chorus

As mentioned, a *pre-chorus* — the short section that leads up to the chorus — is a great device that you can use when writing a verse-chorus song.

The Beatles' "Lucy in the Sky with Diamonds" is an excellent example of a song that uses a pre-chorus with great success. If you don't know the song well, listen to it while reading the words so you can get a good idea of what the pre-chorus sounds like and what it accomplishes.

You'll notice that Lennon and McCartney create a pre-chorus (each with different words) before the first two times the chorus is sung, but not before the last time it is sung.

TIP

Think of the pre-chorus as a mini bridge. Like an actual bridge, it takes your listeners' ears and minds into some new territory. It also allows the lyricist to build the story before hitting the chorus.

The next time you're writing a song, ask yourself whether your chorus would have more impact if it were set up by a pre-chorus. Often a good pre-chorus has some fresh chord changes that the verse hasn't used, especially if the chorus is in the same key as the verse.

Songwriter Chad Kroeger and the band Nickelback created a powerful hit song using the verse–pre-chorus–chorus form. The innovative element of the song "How You Remind Me" is the placement of the title in the pre-chorus instead of the chorus. The pre-chorus leads to a powerful sing-a-long chorus.

In the second verse, the singer tells about how he has failed in the past. The pre-chorus is restated with the title and thesis of the song, then the chorus.

The final verse is simply the first verse, but this time a completely stripped-down version using only the vocal and electric guitar, using just the first two lines. The pre-chorus then repeats and leads into a full-stride version of the final chorus, accentuated by dramatic breaks from the entire band. In this song, the pre-chorus, like the chorus, uses the same words each time.

The verse-chorus form using a bridge

The purpose of a bridge is to provide an interlude between other sections. Verse-chorus songs with bridges are very much a part of today's world. In this section, we look more closely at a verse-chorus song that makes use of bridges.

Vertical Horizon is one of those bands that took many years and multiple albums to become an overnight sensation. Released in 2000, "Everything You Want" (written by Matt Scannell) became their big breakthrough. In a mere 4 minutes and 17 seconds, it defined what modern rock sounds like — intelligent, concise, catchy, cryptic, and extremely well crafted. The song is basically written in a verse-chorus form, with the writer using two verses before hitting the chorus. Starting with a telegraphic electric guitar figure and soon joined by acoustic guitar and bass, the very "in-your-face" vocal starts the verse and immediately pulls you in.

After the first two verses, the song hits the very catchy and repetitive chorus. This is the part you remember most when you first hear the song. Next comes the third verse, which treads some of the same emotional ground already covered, but in a slightly different way. The chorus now repeats. Following is the bridge — and it's everything a bridge should be: Its chord progression blazes new thematic ground and raises the stakes as the singer reaches for higher notes. Finally, the song enters the fourth verse — the kind of nostalgic looking back that's a perfect wrap-up for this song. Following this is a double chorus, the first a clone of the other two choruses. The repeat chorus changes into the first person, however. Weaving in and out of the song is a magical, moody guitar motif. It's probably as important an element as anything else in the song.

If you like bridges and want to know them better, check out the songs in Table 3-6 and see how bridges created some pretty big hits.

TABLE 3-6   **Verse-Chorus with Bridge Song Examples**

Song Title	Songwriter(s)	Singers/Performers
"Here Comes the Sun"	George Harrison	The Beatles
"Rehab"	Justin Timberlake, Timothy Mosley, Hannon Lane	Rihanna
"I Turn to You"	Diane Warren	Christina Aguilera
"I Want It That Way"	Max Martin, Andreas Carlsson	Backstreet Boys
"Hands"	Jewel Klicher, Patrick Leonard	Jewel
"Un-break My Heart"	Diane Warren	Toni Braxton

The verse-chorus form using both a pre-chorus and a bridge

This popular song form pulls out all the stops to convince the listener that a song means business. This form includes not only a pre-chorus before every chorus, but also a formal bridge at the center of the song, usually after the second chorus, before the *out chorus* (as the final chorus is sometimes called). The truly daring can further test the audiences' attention span by adding a third verse after the bridge, before the out chorus.

This form expands the author's chances of getting his lyrical point across, gives him the opportunity to make additional musical statements, and challenges the programming directors at radio stations across the country with songs longer than their formats allow. When using this form, make sure it doesn't collapse under the weight of too many sections.

"Hold on Loosely," the Top 10 hit by .38 Special (written by Jim Peterik, Don Barnes, Jeff Carlisi, and Frankie Sullivan), is an example of a song that just flat out works in this form, as validated by its continued airplay. Take a look at how the song builds as you sing along, and you'll see why it has become a staple on classic rock radio:

"Hold on Loosely," written by Jim Peterik, Don Barnes, Jeff Carlisi, and Frankie Sullivan

Verse 1

You see it all around you
Good lovin' gone bad
And usually it's too late when you
Realize what you had

Pre-chorus

My mind goes back to the girl I met
Long years ago, who told me

Chorus

Just Hold On Loosely
But don't let go
If you cling too tightly
You're gonna lose control
Your baby needs someone to believe in
And a whole lotta space to breathe in

Verse 2

It's so damn easy
When your feelings are such
That you overprotect her
That you love her too much

Pre- chorus

My mind goes back to the girl I met
Long years ago, who told me

Chorus

Just Hold On Loosely
But don't let go
If you cling too tightly

You're gonna lose control
Your baby needs someone to believe in
And a whole lotta space to breathe in

Bridge

Don't let her slip away
Sentimental fool
Don't let your heart get in the way
Yeah, yeah, yeah

Verse

You see it all around you
Good lovin' gone bad
And usually it's too late when you
Realize what you had

Chorus

So Hold On Loosely
But don't let go
If you cling too tightly
You're gonna lose control
Your baby needs someone to believe in
And a whole lot of space to breathe in

As you may have noticed, the last verse bypasses the pre-chorus and heads right to the final chorus. By this time in the song, the writers felt the pre-chorus was no longer necessary and that it was more important to get to the main hook.

OFF THE RECORD

One of Jim's favorite songs that he cowrote is "I Can't Hold Back," a hit for his band, Survivor, back in 1985. It starts with Frankie's intricately picked guitar intro figure, then hits the first verse ("There's a story in my eyes . . ."), then goes into the pre-chorus ("I can feel you tremble when we touch . . ."), then into the chorus ("I can't hold back — I'm on the edge . . ."). From there, it goes unexpectedly into an instrumental version of the pre-chorus, then slides into a spacey bridge ("Another shooting star goes by . . ."), then glides straight into the pre-chorus. Next, instead of going into a chorus, the song returns to a reprise of the verse, "There's a story in my eyes . . ."); then it skips the pre-chorus and goes directly to the out-chorus. Whew-boy! When Jim's writing partner, Frankie Sullivan, and he were sitting at the piano at the Record Plant recording studio in Los Angeles with their producer, Ron Nevison, throwing around ideas, they weren't sure this unorthodox structure was going to work, but the next day when they recorded it, it was magic! The experience taught Jim not to be afraid to play around with song structure. Take a look:

"I Can't Hold Back," written by Jim Peterik and Frankie Sullivan

Verse 1

There's a story in my eyes
Turn the pages of desire
Now it's time to trade those dreams
For the rush of passion's fire

Pre-chorus 1

I can feel you tremble when we touch
And I feel the hand of fate
Reaching out to both of us

Verse 2

I've been holding back the night
I've been searching for a clue from you
I'm gonna try with all my might
To make this story line come true

Pre-chorus 2

Can ya feel me tremble when we touch
Can you feel the hands of fate
Reaching out to both of us
This love affair can't wait

Chorus

I can't hold back, I'm on the edge (I can't hold back)
Your voice explodes inside my head
I can't hold back, I won't back down
Girl it's too late to turn back now

Bridge

Another shooting star goes by
And in the night the silence speaks to you and I
And now the time has come at last
Don't let the moment come too fast

Pre-chorus 3

I can feel you tremble when we touch
And I feel the hand of fate reaching out to both of us

Verse 3

There's a story in my eyes, turn the pages of desire
Now it's time to trade those dreams
For the rush of passion's fire

Chorus

I can't hold back, I'm on the edge (I can't hold back)
Your voice explodes inside my head
I can't hold back, I won't back down
Girl it's too late to turn back now

Pre-chorus 4

I can see you tremble when we touch
Oooh, And I feel the hand of fate reaching out to both of us
This love affair can't wait
I can't hold back, I can't hold back
I can't hold back, I can't hold back

Words and music by Jim Peterik and Frankie Sullivan III © 1984 EMI Virgin Music, Inc., Easy Action Music and Rude Music. All rights for Easy Action Music controlled and administered by EMI Virgin Music, Inc. All rights reserved. International Copyright secured. Used by permission.

TIP

Listen to the songs of Lennon and McCartney and the various Motown writers. It's a great way to learn about the variations of song structure.

Even though the songs in Table 3-7 are older, they set the template for much of the new music you currently hear every day and demonstrate some nonstandard song forms.

TABLE 3-7

Structure Variations

Song Title	Songwriter(s)	Singers/Performers
"Standing in the Shadows of Love"	Holland/Dozier/Holland	The Four Tops
"My Girl"	Smokey Robinson, Ronald White	The Temptations
"I'm Looking Through You"	John Lennon, Paul McCartney	The Beatles
"We Can Work It Out"	John Lennon, Paul McCartney	The Beatles

"Drops of Jupiter" (written and performed by Train) is one of those songs that makes an immediate impression. Usually with brilliant songs like this, you remember where you were and what you were feeling when the song first hit your ears. "Drops of Jupiter" is an example of a song that takes a standard tried-and-true song form and twists it here and there to make it sound unusual and fresh, a pop/rock masterpiece. The song starts with the piano figure of the verse. The first verse contains the only reference to the song's title. So much for the traditional wisdom of driving the hook into the ground — but that didn't seem to hurt sales at all.

OFF THE
RECORD

By the way, the music charts, such as *Billboard, Radio and Records,* and so on, have taken to putting the words ("Tell Me") after the song's title for those of us who can't identify it by its cryptic title, "Drops of Jupiter."

The chorus comes next, although it's not a traditional type of chorus, in that the title is never stated. After the chorus, a significant instrumental signature is created by a string section. We now hit the second verse. It follows the same structure of the first verse, except that the last line before the second chorus is extended for extra impact. The song cleverly uses modern-day references such as "tae-bo" and, later, "soy latte." What's unusual in the second chorus is that although the rhythm of the words and melody stay the same, practically all the words are different. The hook "Tell me" is about all that stays the same. Moving the action along in a chorus as opposed to marking time is unique.

A bridge follows the second chorus, although not in the traditional sense in changing keys and mood. It's more chantlike and modifies the action by changing up the rhythm of the words. The arrangement then breaks down to just piano and voice again, and the song enters the final chorus. Again, the writers break form by combining elements of both earlier choruses into one. The song ends with the infectious "Na, na, na" refrain with alternating vocal ad libs lifted from various sections of the song. The last line is a brand-new variation on an earlier passage. The lyrics in this song are very open to interpretation. The majestic tone of the music matches perfectly the broad scope of the lyric.

REMEMBER

Some great songs out there don't play by the rules. The writers have ignored the standard forms to create something truly unique. "Drops of Jupiter" can be corralled, kicking and screaming, into some kind of traditional form, but it's really a maverick. As an experiment, try challenging the listener by shifting your sections around to make your song stand out from the pack of cookie-cutter tracks. If your song becomes confusing and unfocused when playing it for others, it's time to go back to the drawing board!

Practice Makes Perfect

Often the best way of learning a craft is taking the best examples you can find and tearing them apart to see what makes them tick. Pick five of your favorite songs — anything from a '40s standard to the latest by Nickelback. Listen to the song and analyze its structure by writing out the lyric in its entirety (you can find accurate transcripts of lyrics on many music sites on the Internet). You'll then be able to note the song's various sections by verse, pre-chorus, chorus, bridge, out chorus, and whatever other spare parts you encounter. See if the songs you like the most follow any particular pattern — if so, you may want to pattern your song after that form.

TIP

When analyzing the structure of your favorite songs, notice how the great ones push the boundaries of song craft for maximum impact. As you are listening and making notes, take an especially close look at the following areas:

>> **What is it about each section that sets it apart from the rest of the song?** For instance, notice how the story builds verse to verse as the song unfolds, how the chorus lifts the song to new heights, and how the bridge does its job by giving the listener some fresh chord changes and some new emotional ammunition.

>> **What is truly unusual or original about the structure or composition?** Most songs you encounter that have survived the test of time have one or more elements that elevate it above the pack. "We Built This City" (written by Bernie Taupin, Peter Wolf, Martin Page, and Dennis Lambert), the '80s hit for Starship, starts right out with the sing-a-long chorus. Certain songs defy logic by shifting their key signature down, instead of up, on the last chorus. Find those special elements in the songs that really get your attention.

>> **Where do the titles appear in your favorite songs?** Daring writers often disregard the traditional practice of placing the title at the beginning of the chorus. Notice songs that position their title at the end of the chorus or in the verse or pre-chorus, or that dispense with it altogether.

2

Unleashing the Lyricist in You

One of the first elements people notice when they hear a song are the words. Without effective words, also known as *lyrics*, it's hard for someone to care about the music underneath the song. In this part, we look at the art of writing a catchy, yet meaningful, lyric. (Yes, the two *can* co-exist!) We examine some of the great songs of our time to see how lyrical devices helped these songs scale the charts and stay in people's memory banks. Then we show you ways to develop your own lyrical power.

Chapter **4**

Snagging Your Listeners with a Hook

W hen a fisherman casts his lure, he waits — sometimes all day — for some unsuspecting fish to find the hook. As a songwriter, you don't have the luxury of having a listener wait that long for the *hook,* the catchy part that sticks in the listener's' mind and just won't let go. You have to hook your listener right away so that they'll want to hear the rest of the song — and keep listening to the song time and time again. In this chapter, we look at this important element of a song, see what types of hooks are in the songwriter's tackle box, and show you how to use hooks in your creation to win fans and irresistibly reel in the listener.

Stocking Your Tackle Box with Hooks

A hook consists of a couple elements. At worst, it's a boring, repetitive phrase that listeners hear enough to remember. At best, it's the catchy, short melody — or, more specifically, the part that you can't stop humming or get out of your mind, no matter how hard you try! The hook is also typically the memorable part that sells the song and makes it commercially irresistible. Some people even suggest that the hook is "the single most important component of commercial songwriting." It's usually in the song's title and is most often found in the chorus. Basically, all the other parts of your song make up a great supporting cast.

From a musical perspective, the hook is the most dynamic part of the song. Many times hooks are lyrical lines that are usually followed by a musical figure to emphasize the lyrical line. This technique is illustrated beautifully in the "Sultans of Swing" by Dire Straits.

Bait your hook by allowing listeners to believe they know where you are going. Let them hear a simple chord progression once or twice. Give them a melody that would seem to have a predictable resolution. Feed them lyrics and rhymes that seem obvious. Lull them into a false sense of security. Then yank on that line and reel them in!

Some people may suggest that hooks are a musical ambush that lies in wait for a surprise attack, hidden from view until the right moment. Regardless of the type of hook you choose to use, the point is that it should be both unexpected and irresistible.

You'll find these types of hooks in your favorite songs:

>> Melodic hook

>> Lyrical hook

>> Musical hook

>> Rhythmic hook

>> Sound-effect hook

Sometimes you'll find more than one type of hook in a single song. In fact, most successful songs combine several types of hooks. However, usually one takes precedence over the others, to command your attention. Try to keep your hooks simple, and remember that less is more: Even if your listeners don't know what a chord is, you'll win them over if your hook is easy to hum along with and hits them emotionally right between the eyes. In the following sections, we cover each type of hook and show you how they work.

WARNING

Having too many hooks in one song is not a good thing. If every phrase is vying for the listener's attention, remembering the one or two key phrases may be difficult. Some lines in your song should move the action along and help tell the story, but they shouldn't call attention to themselves. In the same vein, make sure you don't have too many melodic hooks competing with each other in one song. Too many melodic hooks may obscure the main hook and leave the listener confused about which part is the really important part. As they say, "Too many *hooks* spoil the broth." (Well, at least, from a songwriter's point of view!)

The melodic hook

The melodic hook is perhaps the most persuasive element in a songwriter's tackle box. If you choose a melodic hook, your challenge is to have at least one section of your song instantly hummable, regardless of the words that accompany it. That section is the *melodic hook*. It should stick in your listeners' heads long after the song is over. It should be the part of the song that people listen for each time the song comes around, sort of like finding an oasis in a desert.

In the following sections, we take a look at a few songs that have made millions, in no small part because of their infectious melodic hooks.

Beethoven's Fifth

No, not the fifth of whiskey Beethoven may have carried around with him, but his famous Fifth Symphony written early in the nineteenth century. This piece contains perhaps the most famous series of four notes ever connected. These three short notes and one long one *(dum-dum-dum dhaaa)* have spanned generations with their timeless power. Some have called it the ultimate riff, because it needs no lyrics to convey the feeling of urgent emotion.

OFF THE RECORD

In World War II, the rally cry was the letter *V*, for "victory." And the legendary status of Beethoven's Fifth was only enhanced by this. Why? Because in Morse code, the letter V is "short-short-short-long," which just happens to be the melodic hook of Beethoven's Fifth.

"The Way"

Though hundreds of years and musical light-years away from Beethoven, this 1999 pop gem performed by Fastball (written by Anthony Scalzo) is defined by a super-infectious melody that greets its listeners at the chorus. The words that accompany this musical feast, "Don't you know the road that we walked on was paved with gold" are nice, but what you really remember is the exuberant mood of that particular series of notes. The song, which lacks a strong title or musical hook, relies on the chorus melody to make it stand out in high relief from the hundreds of other songs in the pop genre.

"Chasing Pirates"

This song by Nora Jones is an example of the "less is more" school of songwriting. The melodic hooks are perhaps the most vital part of the song in terms of its stickiness: "and I don't know how to slow down, my mind's racing from chasing pirates." The little eighth-note synth riff is the perfect palette to present this pop confection. The image of chasing pirates could be a childlike fantasy of being a young girl among the daring and dangerous world of pirates of old.

"Land of a Thousand Dances"

This trashy '60s gem performed by Cannibal and the Headhunters (written by Chris Kenner) defined the term *garage band*. Over one droning chord, the honorable Sir Cannibal enumerated the many cool dances in this mythical teen paradise. But the real hook didn't rely on words. It was a primitive, wordless chant: na, na na na na, na na na na, na na na, na na na — na na na na! This is when the tough guys at school would tie their bandanas around their heads at the dance and really get down and dirty.

The lyrical hook

Nothing can endear a person to a song more than a strong lyrical hook. When two people fall in love and ordain one song as "their song," they usually do so because of the strength of the song's message. And the *lyrical hook* is the part of the song that summarizes that message.

Often the title is a key part of the lyrical hook. A title is how people identify a song. Finding a particular piece of music is fairly difficult if you don't know the title. We once saw a woman go into a store and start performing the song she was searching for — the store clerk had no idea which song she was singing, and she left empty-handed. And that's part of why titles are so important.

Songwriters often refer to the title of a song as its lyrical hook because they can use the title in particular ways that'll hook the listener and imprint the song's title in the listener's mind.

OFF THE RECORD

It took Jim a while to get used to referring to the title as the hook of the songs. In his opinion, a song has potentially so many different kinds of hooks that you can't just give the title alone that distinction. Suffice it to say, you'll run into this terminology in the music business, so be prepared.

TIP

Try setting up a groove on your rhythm machine (see more on drum machines in further detail toward the end of this chapter). You can make one up from scratch simply through experimentation or use one of the preprogrammed settings. Try your hand at creating a simple chord progression that goes with the beat. Now try creating a melody on top of that, and then find a lyrical hook to go with the melody.

Often one word in a lyrical hook leaps out at you and becomes a permanent file in your cranium. In the following sections, we take a look at some great lyrical hooks, both in the title and in the song.

HOOKING YOUR LISTENERS WITH THE TITLE

Titles become hooks when they're repeated throughout the song. Titles, just like concepts and ideas, can come from anywhere — daily headlines, popular expressions, movie dialogues, book titles. Titles are practically everywhere, and because, except in rare cases, they can't be copyrighted, they can be a popular source of inspiration.

The title of a song is often carefully placed and repeated in the song. This is how a title is used to hook the listener. Titles can appear at the beginning or end of the chorus (and sometimes in both places) or at the end of each verse. Sometimes titles are repeated over and over. This placement and repetition drives the title home to the listeners so they can ask their friends, "Did you hear such-and-such on the radio?" But don't think that a title has to be unique or clever to be valid. A name may be the quickest way to identify a person, but it's only the entrance to what a person is all about. If a song title is like a person's name, then the song itself is like the soul and being of a person. Many times a common song title can be infused with new meaning through the insights of the song itself. Common words can suddenly seem profound, and clichés can be twisted and reinvented. In most cases, it's what you make of a title that separates an average song from a great one.

Sometimes the title isn't used as a hook at all. In fact, the title may never even be used in the song, although the song may be memorable: "For What It's Worth" (written by Steven Stills, performed by Buffalo Springfield), "Positively Fourth Street" (written and sung by Bob Dylan), and "Badge" (written by Eric Clapton and George Harrison, performed by Cream) are all examples of songs in which the titles never appear within the lyrics. (The song "Badge" got its name when George Harrison, who played guitar on the song, was reading the lyric sheet upside down and mistook Clapton's notation of *bridge* as *badge*.)

"Therapy"

Therapy has never been sexier than in the song by the same name by India Arie. The song starts out with an infectious "Wo-o, wo-o" that repeats throughout the song. It's an open secret among songwriters that often the "non-nutritional" sounds, like "wo-o," "da da da," "na na na," and "sh-boom sh-boom" are more vital to include than the actual words themselves. "Therapy" gives us a double whammy, with some excellent word play around the concept of a lover who treats each intimate tryst as a therapy session: "He lays me on the couch and says how has your day been." Hello! Striking on a relatable fantasy is a hook all unto itself. Possibilities for rhyming hooks are endless in this song — "hands on me," "weak in the knees," "boy I can't bear to leave" all precede the main hook, "I need your Therapy." So there you have it . . . the patient is cured for life!

"I Heard It Through the Grapevine"

This Motown classic (written by Barrett Strong and Norman Whitfield) made famous by the late, great Marvin Gaye (predated by a version by Motown label-mates Smokey Robinson as well as Gladys Knight and the Pips) encapsulates its powerful lyrical premise in the title itself. When you hear the title, you pretty much know what the song is about: the rumor mill of careless whispers that can sink a love relationship. The word *grapevine* in and of itself is a descriptive and colorful word that's unusual without being too obscure for the average listener.

TIP

Try to make your title a kind of condensed version of the song itself. When someone can read the title and have a clue to what the song is about, it piques the listener's interest to see how the idea is developed. Avoid generic titles that are too frequently used, unless you can truly pump new life into it in the context of the song. For example, if you title a song "I Love You," it had better be a whole lot different from the thousands of other songs with the same title. Make your title intriguing enough that the listener wants to hear it and experience more of the song that follows.

"She Loves You"

This classic from the early days of The Beatles (written by John Lennon and Paul McCartney) proves that the main lyrical hook of a song is not always the title. In this case, the three little words "Yeah, Yeah, Yeah" became the rally cry for the baby boom generation, and those words are now crossing all boundaries to future generations. If you're hung up on making your hook profound, all you have to do is look at "She Loves You" to find proof that it isn't a necessity when it comes to writing lyrical hooks.

When Jim first saw the phenomenon called The Beatles, it was on some grainy footage Jack Paar brought back from England with him for his *Jack Paar Show* audience, a full three months before The Beatles appeared on *The Ed Sullivan Show*. Jim felt he was hearing the future of rock 'n' roll, and he woke up the next day singing "Yeah, Yeah, Yeah." Jim immediately ran to the record shop and sang these words to the stunned lady behind the counter, even though he didn't know the title of the song — proving the power of an infectious lyrical hook within a song.

"Just the Way You Are"

This classic by singer/songwriter Billy Joel proves again that the strongest lyrical hook is not always the title. It probably drives Billy to distraction that so many people refer to this song as "Don't Go Changing." When a phrase that unique opens a song, there is a great likelihood that it'll take over the actual title when listeners identify it.

"Oops, I Did It Again"

This song (written by Martin Sandberg and Rami Yacoub), performed by Britney Spears, found itself at the top of the charts with this suggestive confection. The title immediately makes the listener want to know just what it is that Britney did, how often she did it, and with whom — well, at least we *used* to want to know that stuff, before overkill with the tabloids.

The musical hook

Often the musical hook, or *money hook,* the one that sells the song, is not technically an element of the songwriting itself, but a part of the song's arrangement. A musical hook can be a riff, like the guitar figure in the intro of "Daytripper" (written by John Lennon and Paul McCartney, performed by The Beatles), the rhythmic hook in "I Want Candy" (written by Bertram Berns, Bob Feldman, Gerald Goldstein, and Richard Gottehrer; performed by The Strangeloves), or anything instrumental that cries for the ears' attention. Many disagreements have arisen through the years between musicians and songwriters about where songwriting ends and where arranging starts. If a musical hook helps identify a song so well that it's used as an indispensable part in countless versions, many in the songwriting profession consider it an element of the song itself. Other terms that fall into the category of the musical hook include the following:

>> **Riff:** A repeated series of notes, often played on guitar or keyboard or by a brass section, that's positioned throughout the song

>> **Lick:** A throwback term from the old be-bop days; like a riff, only shorter

>> **Figure:** A catchall phrase that refers to any repeated series of notes, generally identical throughout the song

You may be thinking that it's the job of the studio musicians, or perhaps the arranger or producer, to create the instrumental hooks. Not necessarily so if you are looking to get the attention of that producer in the first place. Hooks sell the song, and you may need every bit of ammunition to presell it to the producer or the artist *before* your song ever gets its shot in the studio.

In the following sections, we use these terms as we look at some prime examples of musical hooks within tunes.

"Black Horse and the Cherry Tree"

Here's a smorgasbord of hooks — some where you least expect — and the use of a few different techniques. Traditionally, the hookiest part of a song is the chorus, but here the opening "woo hoo" is the first thing to stick in your head, and it stays throughout the song. Then there's the insistent acoustic guitar figure, which gets even more embedded when the vocal is introduced. The vocal line is a simple blues riff, but you pay strict attention to it (and immediately remember it) because it is supported only by a quarter-note bass drum riff. The *absence* of the guitar makes you want to hear that guitar rhythm again. In this case, the chorus is probably the least memorable part of the song; you'll come away from this song singing "woo hoo."

One of the sure signs of a hook appears when someone tries to describe a song to someone else but doesn't quite know the name of the song. In the case of this K. T. Tunstall song, you may ask a friend, "What's the name of that song that goes 'woo hoo'?" Bingo! There's your prime hook — line and sinker!

"Satisfaction" (Mick Jagger/Keith Richards)

If Keith Richards's only contribution to this Rolling Stones classic from 1965 was to create the fuzz tone riff at the opening of this song, he'd easily have earned his keep as a songwriter. The fact that he was far more helpful than that (appropriating the memorable title from a line in an old Chuck Berry tune) was icing on the cake. This riff, which Keith always heard as a horn figure (and which was done that way in subsequent versions, most notably Otis Redding's 1966 cover), was inspired by the great Motown hooks of the '60s, specifically "Dancing in the Streets" (written by Marvin Gaye, Ivy Hunter, and William Stevenson; performed by Martha and the Vandellas). You hear that riff and know exactly which song you're listening to.

"Vehicle"

The five-note horn riff that starts off this classic performed by Chicago's Ides of March (written by Jim Peterik) has to be one of the most recognizable phrases in horn-rock history. Setting up the lyrical hook "I'm the friendly stranger in the black sedan, won't you hop inside my car," the figure involves the listener with its urgency and power.

"Someone to Call My Lover"

This 2001 smash by the resilient Janet Jackson (written by Dewey Bunnell, James Harris, Janet Jackson, and Terry Lewis), *samples* (uses pieces of previously recorded snippets of music) the musical riff from the group America's 1972 hit "Ventura Highway" (written by Dewey Bunnell) and adds it to a brand-new tune. The result is a cutting-edge song with the added depth of musicianship that the guitarist from the group America was famous for.

It's important to note that the practice of sampling is prevalent in modern recording. However, please be aware that it requires the permission of the writer and publisher of the original work and commands a fee called a mechanical royalty or licensing fee to be paid for the privilege of *lifting* (the current term for *using*) such a sample.

Frankie Sullivan and Jim received a request from Busta Rhymes, the multi-platinum rapper, to sample their song "Eye of The Tiger." His version used much of the music they'd written but substituted lyrics with off-color language that fit the rap genre — but didn't fit the spirit of the song they'd written. Frankie and Jim independently decided to decline his request and forfeit a potentially lucrative payday to uphold the uplifting message of the song. On the other hand, when the enterprising rap group Strata III asked for permission to sample their song "Vehicle" for a good-natured interpretation called "Hop Dis," they gave it their full blessing.

The rhythmic hook

As Bob Dylan said in the '60s, "The times, they are a-changin'." Songwriting used to be rigidly defined as words and music. Nowadays, rhythmic elements often form the basis of a song, especially in the urban, hip-hop, and rap categories, and can be as integral to the song as any other element. Of course, the use of the rhythmic hook is nothing new: Many songs from the '50s and '60s were the predecessors of today's trends. The following shows how different rhythms add memorable punch to songs.

"Uprising" (Matthew Bellamy)

This song is an international hit by "overnight sensation" Muse (together since 1999!), using some pretty potent musical hooks to make this fist-pumper work its magic. Although many elements insinuate themselves into the listener's psyche, the first thing that grabs you is the rhythm. This alternative rock trio from England deploys the sledge-hammer power-boogie beat also featured previously in guilty pleasure songs such as "Spirit in the Sky" (Norman Greenbaum's 1970 hit) and "Call Me" (written by Debbie Harry and Giorgio Moroder) by the '80s Top 10 punk/new wavers Blondie. It is used in an even more powerful context here, fueled by an enormous buzzy synth bass and overlaid with a Telstar-like synthesizer doing a spooky faux-futuristic line (refer to the '60s hit by England's Tornados). To these musical treasures add the classical chords of the chorus (D minor to G minor to F major to A major to G minor to F major). Over this, Mathew Bellamy sings the long notes F F F F F – E E E G F. The way this melody works against the chords reflects his influences of romantic piano composers Rachmaninoff, Tchaikovsky, and Liszt. Often a synergy between the old and new creates a sturdy bridge that the new generation can cross safely.

"Hey, Bo Diddley"

The jungle rhythms of Bo Diddley set the stage for many artists to follow. Punctuated by Bo's distorted electric guitar, this song and many of his others played one chord into the ground and built momentum with the intensity of the rhythm. Many of the early Rolling Stones songs, such as their fierce reworking of Buddy Holly's (and Norman Petty's) "Not Fade Away," used Bo Diddley's work as a stepping-off point. Also showing this influence was "I Want Candy" (written by Bertram Berns, Bob Feldman, Gerald Goldstein, and Richard Gottehrer; performed by The Strangeloves) and "Bad to the Bone" (written by George Thorogood, performed by George Thorogood and The Destroyers).

"Wipe Out"

The surfer's classic by The Surfaris (written by Robert Berryhill, Patrick Connolly, James Fuller, and Robert Wilson) owes its success largely to the manic tom-tom sticking of their young drummer. The crazed laugh at the intro was nice, the guitar work tasty, but everything else existed to set up the rhythm hook.

**OFF THE
RECORD**

As Jim's high school band director used to say, "First there was rhythm." He was right. What was the first thing the contestants on *Dick Clark's American Bandstand* would say when they were rating a new record? "It's got a great beat. You can dance to it. I give it a 97!"

"Stayin' Alive"

This song is a first-class example of a rhythmic hook — showcased in the timing of the Bee Gees' "Stayin' Alive" (written by the Bee Gees) from the *Saturday Night Fever* soundtrack to the actual rhythm of John Travolta's steps as his character Tony struts down the streets of New York. The brothers' use of rhythmic breath ("hah-hah-hah-hah, stayin' alive, stayin' alive") is one of the most recognizable hooks of the entire '70s — whether you loved or hated disco.

The sound-effect hook

Though not technically a part of the song, sound effects have become an indispensable component in certain hit songs. When constructing your song demo, weigh the possibility of adding certain sounds, whether they're sampled real effects (sampled effects — everything from church bells to explosions — are available for sale as downloads online and on physical CDs, as evidenced in the back pages of countless musician and recording magazines) or sound effects generated on your synthesizer. Sound effects can add atmosphere and, at times, even become a hook in your song. When the effects are used artistically and correctly, you can create mood, evoke emotion, and solicit responses unlike with using pure lyric or melody.

One of the best ways to kick-start your songwriting chops is to use a drum machine, either physical or virtual. If your plans are to write in a certain genre, pick a beat and turn on the machine — you'll be amazed to see how the ideas flow. If you're in a rut, close your eyes, press a button, and see where the beat takes you.

Drum machines have been around for a long time, and modern dance music wouldn't be the same without them. The vintage Roland TR-808 immediately comes to mind. If you're writing hip-hop or modern R&B, a machine or a virtual equivalent is almost *de riguer*.

With the proliferation of software such as Sony's Acid, Ableton's Live, and Propellerhead's Reason, the drum machine has taken a step into the future by allowing a songwriter to manipulate prerecorded drumbeats (and other musical bits) called *loops* into arrangements that really snap creativity into high gear. Apple's GarageBand simplified the process even further and made it standard equipment on most new Mac computers.

For those who use a DAW, programs such as Fxpansion's BFD, Toontrack's EZdrummer, and Spectrasonics' Stylus RMX gave the songwriter perhaps the best tool yet by putting different (yet related) drumbeats under each key of a MIDI keyboard, giving instant access to beats, fills, intros, and endings at any tempo the writer chooses. You don't need to know how to play the piano to effectively use these programs.

When you get a loop or beat going and immerse yourself in it, you may start dancing (or at least tapping your foot), images may fill your head, and your mind may start "filling in the blanks" with a melody or riff. A chordal groove may appear. You never know what you're going to get, but you will get *something*. This is a great confidence builder, because you will surprise yourself. Not to get all New Age here, but when you focus on a beat, your body's rhythms take over and your mind has the freedom to roam. This is great training for a songwriter and a real shortcut to getting to places in your soul that you've either forgotten about or didn't know were there.

In the following sections, we provide a few examples of hits that use the sound-effect hook to their advantage.

"Fireflies"

Songwriting used to mean pen, paper and a guitar or piano. In the new millennium, technology is available to everyone. This means that recording techniques and tricks can become an intrinsic part of a song. In the underground hit by geek wizard Owl City (actually just one man, Adam Young, at his desktop computer), hook number one is the synth motif at the top of the song. If you already know the name of the song, you can "see" the fireflies, and regardless of what you remember about the rest of the song, you'll remember this as the "firefly song" because of it — the synth riff is that sticky! Next is the slight use of *autotuning* (the robotic overmodulation of the voice or instruments most notably heard on Cher's smash "Believe") that informs of the opening vocal line (which itself is a sturdy, tried-and-true pop melody) but embeds itself into your head because of its sonic signature. As in the K. T. Tunstall song described earlier, when the synth riff goes away, the vocal loses much of its instrumental support (plus the auto-tune trickery) and you are drawn back into the song, finding a reason to be interested again. When the opening motif returns, the singer rhymes "hugs" with "lightning bugs," which would be kind of lame in any other context, but the childlike singing and that autotune treatment somehow spotlight those words. Now you make an investment to pay attention to everything this singer has to say. Three quick and interesting turns in the first part of this song grab your ear and never let go!

"Let's Roll"

This song (written and sung by Neil Young) was sent out to radio in a plain brown wrapper soon after the tragic events of September 11, 2001. There was nothing plain about the response to this song that addressed the heroic passengers aboard Flight 93, who overthrew would-be suicide terrorists and crashed their plane into a field in Pennsylvania before it could reach its intended target. Neil uses the words that one of the passengers spoke before taking the plane down; "Let's Roll," as the song's title, and the chilling sound effect of three rings of a cellphone in the song's introduction denotes the passengers' last communication. In this case, the use of sound design enhances an already effective and poignant song.

"Reflections"

Motown producers like Holland-Dozier-Holland and Smokey Robinson were no strangers to the use of certain sound effects on their records. This song (written by Lamont Dozier, Brian Holland, and Edward Holland; performed by Diana Ross and The Supremes) uses the new technology (for the time) of the Moog Synthe-sizer to emphasize the emotion of the title. The ethereal sound of the Moog becomes like another voice filling the song with bittersweet feelings. Although the electronic sounds of the Moog have been elevated to high art since then, in "Reflections," the sound was used more to create an ethereal mood. Next time you hear the song, try to imagine it without the effects created by the Moog.

"Barbara Ann"

This Beach Boys cover of the hit (written by Fred Fassert; performed by The Regents) became a very big hit on its own as a part of the Beach Boys' *Party* album. What most people don't know, however, is that the party was added later! They call this *post-production* nowadays, which means effects are added after the song has been recorded. The sound effects of a crowd having an absolute ball added an element of fun to an already exuberant track. Thanks to Brian Wilson for producing this tune and adding the hook post production.

"Leader of the Pack," "Last Kiss," and "Teen Angel"

"Leader of the Pack" (written by Jeff Barry, Ellie Greenwich, and George Morton; performed by the Shangri-Las), "Last Kiss" (written by Wayne Cochran and first performed by Wayne Cochran and the C. C. Riders; later performed by J. Frank Wilson), and "Teen Angel" (written by Jean Surrey, performed by Dion and the Belmonts) all use the sound of automotive crashes to help tell their stories of teen tragedy. Next time you hear J. Frank Wilson's weeper "Last Kiss," listen for the background-singing angel who seems to expire on the high note along with the hero.

The songs of The Beatles

There's not enough room to mention all the songs The Beatles have used sound effects in to add atmosphere and hooks to their music, starting with their album *Revolver* and reaching a climax on *Sergeant Pepper*. Listen to the great circus sound effects on "For the Benefit of Mr. Kite" or the cacophony of sound created by the orchestra at the end of the first section of "Day in the Life." The Beatles, especially Paul McCartney (who was enamored by the sonic experimentation of Karlheinz Stockhausen), took every opportunity to include avant-garde sound samples in the mix. Their producer, George Martin, made available to them the vast sound effects library of the BBC (British Broadcasting Corporation) and its array of electronic devices for their experimentation. He also taught them techniques of slowing down and speeding up the tape machines to warp the tonality (or timbre) of the sound, and actually reversing the tape for even more otherworldly effects (like the backward guitar solo in "Taxman" by The Beatles).

The use of different types of hooks in one song

Of course, many examples point to different types of hooks used in one song. When you put them all together, you get a pretty compelling package. Using too many hooks of the same type is not a good idea, but using a variety of hooks constantly persuades the listener to hang in there until the end of the song. Love them or hate them, here are two good examples of songs with a well-stocked tackle box of hooks.

"Turn Out the Lights" (Turn Off the Light, 2001)

This 2001 hit for Canadian Nelly Furtado (which she also wrote) combines many different types of hooks to excellent advantage. The intro starts right off with what sounds like a Gregorian chant (a melodic hook) building into a backward cymbal (a sound-effect hook), then launches into the sparse hip-hop groove (a rhythmic hook) and then a hypnotic electric piano figure (a musical hook) — and Nelly hasn't even opened her mouth yet at this point! Accompanying the intro elements is the subtle disharmony of birds, crickets, and some indecipherable filtered voices. Nelly sings the verse and prechorus with understated charm — the perfect setup for the chorus, which contains the big melodic/lyrical hook of "They say that girl ya know she act too tough, tough, tough — well it's till I turn off the light, turn off the light." Everything about that line is a hook, from its sing-along melody to its rhythmic repetition of the word *tough*, rhyming with the thrice-repeated *rough* in the next line. She then ups the ante with the machine-gun repetition of the words "follow me" and "down." Nelly's bridge is what could be considered a rap section with melody. The final chorus closes out with the return of the nighttime choir of crickets and birds.

"Music"

Madonna's multi-platinum hit from the year 2000 (written by Miruais Ahmadzai and Madonna) is one of those songs from which every last ounce of fat has been trimmed, exposing nothing but the hooks. It opens with the main lyrical hook (even though it's not the title), "Hey Mr. D.J., put a record on, I wanna dance with my baby," spoken by a male in a cool, dry delivery. The song then hits the underlying musical hook (reminiscent of the organ riff in The Animals' '60s hit "It's My Life," written by Roger Atkins and Carl Derrico) combined with an unstoppable groove created by Miruais Ahmadzai. The song then hits the main musical hook performed on a synthesizer using the three notes D, B-flat, and C, with the last note repeated (the sound seems to be run through a voice simulator making what sounds like the words "Do You Like It?"). Madonna then takes center stage with the sung version of the earlier spoken words, "Hey, Mr. D.J. . . ." This lyrical hook is now combined with the secondary melodic hook (the main melodic hook will hit in the chorus) to create a double whopper. The setup to the haunting chorus is a filtered vocal (sound-effect hook) of the words to come. Now it's time for the main hook: "Music makes the people come together . . . ." It's a vaguely Eastern melodic motif combined with the powerful main message of the song. After the second verse and chorus, the song starts an instrumental section emphasizing electronic effects and sweeps leading into a severely *filtered* version of the song's verse (filtering is the practice of limiting the frequency response of a sound — the telephone effect is a good example). Now a third melodic hook enters for the very first time, a couple of minutes into the tune (hey, when you're Madonna, you can get away with anything!), and is soon counterpointed by the four-note hook introduced earlier in the song. As complex as this all sounds, like most smash hits, it comes across as elegantly simple — the real proof of a great song and arrangement. This is one song that tests the theory that too many hooks spoil the broth!

Having the Right Mindset When Working with Hooks

There's no such thing as a universal hook or one hook that always works with every listener. (If there were, it would be included in every song.) Each person is receptive to slightly different stimuli. Songwriters have the tendency to get discouraged if everyone isn't absolutely captivated by every hook they throw into the pond, but it's important to remember that *no* song is loved by everyone.

TIP

Don't be devastated if someone doesn't respond favorably to one of your songs. Even if after a record company president says straight-faced that he "must have his tin ears on this week because he just doesn't hear a hook," stay true to your beliefs. We have personal experience of getting an artist signed to a record deal with the same songs that evoked the former negative comments — although that "tin ear" comment will probably forever live in our memory banks.

The number of times you use a hook and the different ways you use it can affect the shelf life of your song. Everyone has heard songs that they love right away but that they're totally sick of after hearing them 50 or 60 times. This could be a result of what is known in the hushed corridors of publishing empires as *hook dysfunction.* To prevent hook dysfunction from happening to you (although it happens to us all from time to time), be careful that you don't drive the main hook into the ground (with too many repetitions) or that the melodic hook isn't so insipid (refer to "Yummy, Yummy, Yummy" written by Joey Levine and Kris Resnick, performed by the Ohio Express — a one-hit wonder from the '60s) that it haunts your nightmares.

Strive instead for a song that hooks you subtly at first, then takes hold and won't let go. If the lyrics have enough to say, they'll build in power with repeated listening and give your song staying power.

REMEMBER

Not everyone will listen to every word of your lyrics the first few times they hear them, so make sure you have a couple of easy-to-digest, hooklike phrases that sum up the *premise* (or idea) of the song.

Practice Makes Perfect

Check out the Top 10 songs on *Billboard's* Top 100 Chart and pick three songs you like. Listen to each song and figure out how many hooks are in each song. Remember, you're looking for melodic, lyrical, musical, and rhythmical hooks, as well as the use of any sound effects or other qualities that make the song memorable. By dissecting current hits, you'll really get a flavor for writing your own hooks. After you've picked out what different types of hooks are used in these songs, make a note of how many times each is repeated within the songs.

If you have a song already written or have one started, go through it and analyze the types of hooks you use, how effective they are, and how they can be sharpened and improved. If you haven't yet written your first song, try your hand to come up with what you feel is a good hook. It could be a potential title, a musical riff, an intriguing sound, a hypnotic rhythm, or a catchy series of chords. Hold on to it as you discover more about the mechanics of writing a song.

A great way to flesh out whether you're on to the makings of a great hook is to experiment on five of your closest friends or relatives — or those who will still love you in the morning. Play your song for them and then ask them each to write down what they remember the most about your song. If you find after reading the secret ballots that you're not voted off the island and that one element of the song seems to have been mentioned on all five sheets, you may just be on your way to having a good hook. If they call you in three days slightly irritated that they can't get that song out of their heads, you may have just "hit a home run" and developed that special quality that gives a song staying power.

Chapter **5**

Making an Impact with Lyrics

hink back to the very first song you can remember hearing as a child. What part of that song really made a connection in the developing synapses of your brain? It could have been the beat, the sounds, or a silly melody. But most likely, these parts wouldn't have had much impact on you if they hadn't been attached to words that somehow made an impression on you. The words you noticed were probably very simple at first, perhaps a part of a game ("ring-around-the rosie") and so on. As you grew up, you started gravitating toward songs that seemed to reflect the experiences of your expanding awareness. If you could turn to your friend and say, "Hey, that's me they're talking about," or "I've been wanting to say that myself," or "That's exactly what I'm going through, right now," chances are, you'd buy that song and play it till you wore it out. As a songwriter, it's the connection you make with a song's lyric and how closely you can relate to the feelings of your audience that put you in touch with them. Writing about what matters to you most is a great place to start.

In this chapter, we look at the various ways you as a songwriter can make an impact through lyrics. We break it down and discuss the various forms in which your ideas can be expressed, explaining the different devices the pros use to add impact and professionalism to their songs. Chapter 6 then dives into creating lyrics of your own.

Getting to Know the Different Lyric Types

Webster's defines a *lyric* as "the words of a song, as distinguished from the music." Well, that's fairly cut and dried. But when the word is defined as an adjective, things get interesting: "songlike; specifically, designating poetry or a poem expressing the poet's personal emotion or sentiment. . . ." Now we're talkin'! You can think of lyrics as thoughts with rhythm and rhyme — and on rare occasions, you can even dispense with the rhyme.

A great lyric is an idea with wings. Take a look at the different forms a lyric can take and see where some of your favorite songs took root before taking flight:

>> Concept-driven lyrics

>> Story lyrics

>> Love song lyrics

>> Current event and protest lyrics

>> Novelty and humorous lyrics

>> Parody lyrics

>> Inspirational and spiritual lyrics

OFF THE RECORD

When Jim sits down to write a song with other people, before writing even one note, he asks what's on their minds and tries to flesh out what really matters to them personally. He also suggests writing about something all of them know or are experts in (most people are good at something, even if it's about having a broken heart!). The conversation that springs from these questions can often be the jumping-off point for a song that actually has substance — because it's something that's important to the people writing the song.

In the following sections of this chapter, we describe each type of lyric in detail and give you some song examples to illustrate that point.

TIP

A great way to dive into this pool of songwriting is to take a look at the popular songs that are already out there. By dissecting the lyrics of other well-done songs, you may just find the inspiration you're looking for. No, we're not suggesting that you copy what's already been done, but this exercise can help you get into the flow of analyzing the words, looking at rhyme patterns, and seeing how emotions rise up from the page to make a song tick. You have a wealth of material at your fingertips by surfing the Net — just drop in the keywords "lyric search" and take a look at all the sites that pop up: songlyrics.com, metrolyrics.com, lyricsmania.com, lyricsmode.com, songmeanings.net, azlyrics.com, lyricsondemand.com, and so on.

Concept-driven lyrics

Behind most great songs is a great idea or concept. A concept is a lyrical blueprint for the song (and its authors) to follow. A strong concept usually equates to a great song.

TIP

Write down the concept of the song in prose (the un-poetry sort of writing down the simple points of a story) when you start the song, and refer back to it frequently to make sure your lyrics stay on course. The concept is also referred to as a song's premise — basically, a one- or two-sentence sum-up of what the song is about. If you can't distill your idea into one or two sentences, perhaps your idea is too complex for one song or you lack a clear idea of what you want to say.

WARNING

In many songwriting sessions, you may look back at the initial concept of the song and realize it has somehow morphed into something else. If this happens, you'll have to decide just which song you want to write. You may have two songs in one, and that's never a good thing. The focus of your song must be clear, or you run the risk of confusing the listener.

Don't let the word *concept* intimidate you. A concept can be extremely simple — in fact, most successful songs have simple ideas driving them. In the following sections, we take a look at a few notable songs driven by concepts.

"Missing You"

This '80s classic written by Charles Sanford, Mark Leonard, and John Waite (former lead singer for The Babys and Bad English) was a Top 10 hit and has been covered numerous times by other artists (most significantly by former Ikette Tina Turner in her soul-drenched version), largely on the strength of its telegraphic guitar figure and the underlying irony of its concept.

This song's concept revolves around the tortured hero who throughout the verses professes the many ways life is no longer the same now that the love of his life is gone. He's in a quandary as to why she left, and it sounds as though he's ready to stick his head in the oven when he's saved by the chorus.

The dichotomy between what he's saying in the verses (his gut-wrenching feelings) and what he's saying in the chorus (where he puts on a front for the world) is the unique concept for this song. No matter what his friends say, what he says, and how it may appear, he's not missing her at all.

TIP

Often the contrasts in life have the most impact — the difference between what our lips are saying and what our heart is feeling (for a good example, listen to "Tears of a Clown," written by Henry Cosby, Stevie Wonder, and Smokey Robinson), or the way you feel about her as opposed to how she feels about you.

"Good Vibrations"

This collaboration between songwriters Brian Wilson and Mike Love of The Beach Boys is a good example of a great concept that got better and more commercial (in other words, more people could relate to it, so it sold zillions) through the process of collaboration. Brian was initially intrigued by the notion of vibrations in the universe (both good and bad) that dogs and humans pick up on.

His initial lyric didn't contain any reference to relationships, and there was no romantic back story. Mike Love heard and loved the song but felt that an element was missing. He felt that by adding "that boy/girl thing," they could expand their market and still stay true to the original concept of cosmic vibrations coursing through the universe. "I'm picking up good vibrations, she's giving me excitations" became the catch phrase for the baby boom generation with the song's brilliant juxtaposition of heaven and earth.

TIP

When you find a lyrical concept that intrigues you, see how you can make it as easy to relate to as possible. If the listener can see himself or his situation in your song, you may have put something into words that he could never quite express on his own.

"Viva La Vida"

This smash hit recorded by Coldplay (written by Chris Martin, Guy Berryman, Will Champion, and Jonny Buckland) plays on the contrast of a royal past and a bleak future. This dude is seriously depressed. The listener doesn't know whether he is really a king or just suffering from delusions of grandeur: "seas would rise when I gave the word," "now I sweep the streets I used to own" — many of us can relate to this feeling. There's a fine line between a hero and a bum, and we walk it every day.

WARNING

The last thing you want as a songwriter is to be slapped with a copyright infringement suit — although, if you are a prolific and popular writer, somewhere in your career, it just may happen anyway. As the saying goes, "Where there's a hit, there's a writ!" In the case of this popular song by Coldplay, it must have been a very big hit, because it has been the subject of at least three infringement suits — a very rare situation, to say the least. In the most public of these suits, guitarist Joe Satriani alleges that Coldplay lifted elements of his song "If I Could Fly" for the song "Viva La Vida." The key element in resolving a case such as this is determining whether the members of Coldplay had access to this recording prior to writing their tune, whether the similarities constitute infringement of its copyright, and whether they perhaps "subconsciously" appropriated some of Satriani's song quite innocently. Plagiarism hit the big-time when George Harrison lost a suit in 1981 by "subconsciously plagiarizing" the musical essence of the Chiffons' "He's So Fine" on his #1 hit "My Sweet Lord." (See the section "My Sweet Lord" later in this chapter.)

Storytelling Lyrics

Songs that tell a story are as old as time itself. Even in days of old, songwriters realized that songs were a good way to put a relatively plain story into an attractive package and make everyone want to listen. Today great storytellers often write in the style of country, but no restrictions govern the genres the story song can cross.

Now take a good look at the lyrics to the story song "Just to Get High" (written by Chad Kroeger; performed by Nickelback). You can just feel the urgency and intensity of emotion rise in Chad Kroeger's tragic tale of his best friend's dance with the demon of drugs. His own mother stays silent even after he sells her rings. The specific imagery Chad uses — the sores on his lips, his melted fingertips — gives the listener a gruesome visual to go along with the narrative. The repeating mantra of "tell me what you know . . . tell me what you gone and done now" makes the listener wonder whether his friend is alive or dead — or just a part of the living dead. One can't help but suspect that this person actually exists in Chad's life; whether he does or not is immaterial, because he lives within this song.

"Just to Get High," written by Chad Kroeger

Verse 1

He was my best friend, I tried to help him
But he traded everything, for suffering
And found himself alone

I watched the lying, turn into hiding
With scars on both his lips, his fingertips
Were melted to the bone

Chorus

But I can still remember
What his face looked like
When I found him in an alley
In the middle of the night

Tell me what you know
Tell me what you gone and done now
Tell me what you know
Tell me what you gone and done now

A gun would do the trick, get it over with
You're better off to take all
You've got and burn it on the spot
Just to get high-igh, igh, igh (high-igh, igh, igh)

Verse 2

Three days no sleeping, he gave up eating
He sold his mother's rings, she said nothing
And pretended not to know

He started stealing, to supply the feeling
Found out he pulled a knife, on someone's wife
And held it to her throat

Extended Chorus

But I can still remember
What his face looked like
When I found him in an alley
In the middle of the night

Tell me what you know
Tell me what you gone and done now
Tell me what you know
Tell me what you gone and done now

A gun would do the trick, get it over with
You're better off to take all that
You've got and burn it on the spot
Just to get high-igh, igh, igh (high-igh, igh, igh)

Tell me what you did, where you gone and hid?
Show me, is what you really want, watching what you got?
Slowly circling the drain, throw it all away
Just to get high-igh, igh, igh (high-igh, igh, igh)
High-igh, igh . . . ooooh

Tell me what you know
Tell me what you gone and done now
Tell me what you know
Tell me what you gone and done now

A gun would do the trick, get it over with
You're better off to take all that
You've got and burn it on the spot
Just to get high-igh, igh, igh (high-igh, igh, igh)

Tell me what did, where you gone and hid?
Show me, is what you really want, watching what you got?
Slowly circling the drain, throw it all away
Just to get high, just to get high
Circle in the drain, throw it all away
Just to get high-igh, igh, igh (high-igh, igh, igh)

Love song lyrics

Love is one of those dishes that can be served up a thousand different ways and still be a lyrical feast. Like Bubba's shrimp list in the movie *Forrest Gump,* if you made a list of all the song titles that use the *L* word, it would reach from "here to New Orleans."

The love song can range from celebratory to suicidal and all points in between, and still be considered a love song. Because love is the driving force behind much of human activity, writers never seem to run out of inspiration. In fact, every generation seems to recycle some of the same emotions, situations, and predicaments that love seems to breed, each time around, totally unaware that it was said before by other generations.

Let's take a look at the variety of ways the subject of love can be treated in the following selections.

"Love Story"

This love song uses the age-old and very effective Romeo and Juliet theme — hey, it was good enough for Bill Shakespeare! Composer and artist Taylor Swift uses the effective flashback device to add the dimension of time. This adds a somewhat dreamlike mood to the lyric and makes the listener wonder, did it really happen like this, or is she living an illusion? Notice the quick rhymes as she baits the hook: "We'll make it out of this mess, it's a love story baby, just say yes" and "go pick out a white dress, it's a love story baby, just say yes." This song was a hit for many reasons: Taylor's vocal delivery, her persona, the strong melody, a hot video, and, more than any other element, the "relatability" to her target audience — a young audience that can relate to every word she says and can put themselves in the shoes of the modern-day Romeo and Juliet.

"Love Story," written by Taylor Alison Swift

Verse 1

We were both young when I first saw you
I close my eyes
And the flashback starts
I'm standing there
On a balcony in summer air

See the lights
See the party, the ball gowns
I see you make your way through the crowd
And say hello, little did I know

Pre-chorus

That you were Romeo, you were throwing pebbles
And my daddy said stay away from Juliet
And I was crying on the staircase
Begging you, please don't go, and I said

Chorus

Romeo, take me somewhere we can be alone
I'll be waiting, all there's left to do is run
You'll be the prince and I'll be the princess
It's a love story, baby, just say yes

Verse 2

So I sneak out to the garden to see you
We keep quiet 'cause we're dead if they knew
So close your eyes
Escape this town for a little while

Pre-chorus

'Cause you were Romeo, I was a scarlet letter
And my daddy said stay away from Juliet
But you were everything to me
I was begging you, please don't go, and I said

Chorus

Romeo, take me somewhere we can be alone
I'll be waiting, all there's left to do is run
You'll be the prince and I'll be the princess
It's a love story, baby, just say yes

Romeo, save me, they try to tell me how to feel
This love is difficult, but it's real
Don't be afraid, we'll make it out of this mess
It's a love story, baby, just say yes
Oh oh

Bridge

I got tired of waiting
Wondering if you were ever coming around
My faith in you is fading
When I met you on the outskirts of town, and I said

Chorus

Romeo, save me, I've been feeling so alone
I keep waiting for you but you never come

Is this in my head? I don't know what to think
He knelt to the ground and pulled out a ring

And said, marry me, Juliet
You'll never have to be alone
I love you and that's all I really know
I talked to your dad, go pick out a white dress
It's a love story, baby, just say yes

Oh, oh, oh, oh
'Cause we were both young when I first saw you

© Sony/Atv Songs d/b/a Tree Pubg Co; Taylor Swift Pub Designee

TIP

When writing a love song, try to find a fresh angle from which to approach this subject. Look at some of your favorite love songs and notice the ways in which the writers have set their songs apart from the thousands of others.

Like so many writers, you and I might be lost for words if not for the subject of love. (Desire is another staple in the writer's pantry.) The challenge, of course, is finding fresh ways to serve it up. When in doubt, follow your heart. If the sentiment rings true, you may have the start of a great new love (or *out*-of-love) song.

"I Don't Want to Miss a Thing"

This super-smash #1 hit by Aerosmith (written by Diane Warren) shows that top songwriters don't get much better — or more popular — than Diane Warren. She was asked by Aerosmith's A&R guy, John Kalodner, to come up with the main title for the soon-to-be-blockbuster film *Armageddon* — and what she came up with summarized the emotions of the film to a tee. It's touching without being sappy or maudlin, sentiments that would have destroyed the street cred of a hard-rock band like Aerosmith in one downbeat! In some future rock 'n' roll encyclopedia, if you look up "power ballad," this may be at the top of the heap.

"I Don't Want to Miss a Thing," written by Diane Warren

Verse 1

I could stay awake just to hear you breathing
Watch you smile while you are sleeping
While you're far away and dreaming
I could spend my life in this sweet surrender
I could stay lost in this moment forever
Well, every moment spent with you
Is a moment I treasure

Chorus

I don't wanna close my eyes
I don't wanna fall asleep
'Cause I'd miss you, baby
And I don't wanna miss a thing
'Cause even when I dream of you
The sweetest dream would never do
I'd still miss you, baby
And I don't wanna miss a thing

Verse 2

Lying close to you
Feeling your heart beating
And I'm wondering what you're dreaming
Wondering if it's me you're seeing
Then I kiss your eyes and thank God we're together
And I just wanna stay with you
In this moment forever, forever and ever

Chorus

I don't wanna close my eyes
I don't wanna fall asleep
'Cause I'd miss you, baby
And I don't wanna miss a thing
'Cause even when I dream of you
The sweetest dream would never do
I'd still miss you, baby
And I don't wanna miss a thing

Bridge

I don't wanna miss one smile
I don't wanna miss one kiss
Well, I just wanna be with you
Right here with you, just like this
I just wanna hold you close
Feel your heart so close to mine
And just stay here in this moment
For all the rest of time

Chorus

Don't wanna close my eyes
Don't wanna fall asleep
'Cause I'd miss you, baby
And I don't wanna miss a thing

'Cause even when I dream of you
The sweetest dream would never do
'Cause I'd still miss you, baby
And I don't wanna miss a thing

I don't wanna close my eyes
I don't wanna fall asleep
'Cause I'd miss you, baby
And I don't wanna miss a thing
'Cause even when I dream of you
The sweetest dream would never do
I'd still miss you, baby
And I don't wanna miss a thing
Don't wanna close my eyes
Don't wanna fall asleep, yeah
I don't wanna miss a thing
I don't wanna miss a thing

© Realsongs

"Ghost Story"

This story song from Sting's 1999 release *Brand New Day* takes the love song into fresh new territory. This song (written and sung by Sting), which examines a complex relationship, has the singer looking back at his denial of love throughout the years. The audience is never quite sure who Sting is addressing — perhaps his father or a former lover. What we do know is that his "indifference was my invention" and, through it all, "I must have loved you."

When you look up the lyrics, notice that as the story unfolds, the songwriter uses many devices (see Chapter 6 for more on devices): personification ("his icy sinews," referring to winter), metaphor ("the moon's a fingernail"), anaphora (the repetition of phrases like "the same," "I did not," and "you were"), the use of only perfect rhyme (suffer/tougher, stars/scars, measure/treasure), and others, such as the absence of a title as a hook and an innovative form. But as with most great songs, the devices all become invisible as the listener becomes intrigued with where the lyrics of this unique love song are headed.

You have so many different ways to treat the subject of love. Listening to Sting crooning the hook "I must have loved you" might get you thinking, "Leave it to Sting to find a unique way to use a song as a form of self-therapy." By getting the chance to peek inside his diary — his emotional journal — the listener becomes an insider, and that role makes a fan for life.

Lyrics that make a statement

What better way to make a statement than through a song? People are much more inclined to listen if an idea is attached to a catchy melody and a good beat — and as a songwriter, it's a great way to get things off your chest, raise awareness, and possibly even make a difference in the world. Certain artists have become well known for their ability to encapsulate world events into musical form and often sum up the feelings of the people. Take a look at a few examples of songs that use current events or social protests as their reason for being.

"Sunday Bloody Sunday"

In this archetypal song and mega hit by U2 (written by Paul Hewson, Dave Evans, Adam Clayton, and Larry Mullen Jr.), the sound of the band found its perfect and defining form in Larry Mullin Jr.'s mesmerizing and hypnotic drum beat, the nearly robotic sixteenth-note chording of The Edge, and the righteous indignation of singer Bono. This song documents the troubles in Northern Ireland focusing on that one bloody Sunday in Derry when British troops shot at civil rights marchers. Although it seems that the audience holds the final verdict on what the intention of a song really is, Bono has always claimed that Sunday Bloody Sunday is not about rebellion; it's about finding a peaceful solution to the violence between Ireland and Great Britain.

"Sunday Bloody Sunday," performed by U2

Verse 1

Yes

I can't believe the news today
Oh, I can't close my eyes and make it go away
How long, how long must we sing this song?
How long? How long?
'Cause tonight we can be as one, tonight

Verse 2

Broken bottles under children's feet
Bodies strewn across the dead end streets
But I won't heed the battle call
It puts my back up, puts my back up against the wall

Chorus

Sunday, Bloody Sunday
Sunday, Bloody Sunday
Sunday, Bloody Sunday

Verse 3

And the battle's just begun
There's many lost but tell me who has won
The trench is dug within our hearts
And mothers, children, brothers, sisters torn apart

Chorus

Sunday, Bloody Sunday
Sunday, Bloody Sunday

How long, how long must we sing this song?
How long? How long?
'Cause tonight we can be as one
Tonight, tonight

Sunday, Bloody Sunday
Sunday, Bloody Sunday

Bridge

Wipe the tears from your eyes
Wipe your tears away
Oh, wipe your tears away
Oh, wipe your tears away
Oh, wipe your blood-shot eyes

Chorus

Sunday, Bloody Sunday
Sunday, Bloody Sunday

Verse 4

And it's true we are immune when fact is fiction and TV reality
And today the millions cry
We eat and drink while tomorrow they die
The real battle just begun to claim the victory Jesus won on

Chorus

Sunday Bloody Sunday
Sunday Bloody Sunday

© Polygram Int. Music Publ. B.V.

"Ohio"

Neil Young's powerful response to the four students killed by National Guardsmen at an antiwar demonstration at Kent State University on May 18, 1970, became the protest song of choice for an America that was sick and tired of its troops dying in the Vietnam War. "Tin soldiers and Nixon's coming, we're finally on our own, this summer I hear the drumming, four dead in Ohio." The photos in the newspapers told the story of the horrific event, and this rock anthem became the soundtrack. ("Ohio" was written and sung by Neil Young; performed by Crosby, Stills, Nash and Young.)

"Youth of a Nation"

Who can forget the impact of this groundbreaking hit by rap metal band POD? So many times a great song is inspired by actual events — but it takes a sensitive antenna to pick up all the incoming signals. In this case, the band was on its way to one of the sessions for its *Satellite* album when the members were held up in a traffic jam. The reason: a school shooting. The song this incident spawned was strong enough to actually hold up the release date of the album, giving the band time to record this song. It focuses on three characters: the singer himself, little Suzy, and Johnny boy — three random lives claimed by a school shootist, with stories uniquely theirs. Spooky as it seems, the singer is communicating to us from the great beyond, where it seems he has found a divine perspective. The powerful chanted chorus "We are, we are, the youth of the nation" makes no real distinction between the perpetrator and the victims, both interwoven into the fabric of modern life. One waits for the chorus like someone in the desert searching for an oasis. The final lines assert the frustration of watching these incomprehensible acts — "There's got to be more to life than this, there's got to be more to everything I thought exists."

"Cop Killer"

This rap tune is the one that for several years caused all records to carry rating stickers (labels that indicate that certain language contained could be considered offensive and unsuitable for minors). The record was also banned by stores like K-Mart and Wal-Mart and incited many racial confrontations all over America. This song proved once again the power a song can have, whether it's used as a positive tool or a negative one. ("Cop Killer" was written by Ernest Cunnigan and Tracy Marrow; sung by Body Count.)

Novelty and humorous lyrics

One concept that is sometimes forgotten by "serious" songwriters is the element of a novel approach or humor in a song. A thread of wit running through an otherwise serious lyric can add a much-needed lift to a song. Bob Dylan is especially good at injecting humor into his songs — "the pump don't work 'cause the vandals took the handle" from "Subterranean Homesick Blues" is a good example.

Some songs, however, center most of their appeal on the novelty value of their concept. These "gimmick" songs have been around in various reincarnations since day one. They are often based on some current fad or craze, so their shelf life can be affected by the longevity of the craze they document. They are often based on current expressions or popular catch phrases. Some of these songs can actually outlive the phenomenon they describe. In the following sections, we take a look at a few examples of novelty songs that may or may not stand the test of time.

"The Thong Song"

This new-millennium smash by young urban artist Sisqo (written by Mark Andrews, Desmond Child, Marquis Collins, Tim Kelley, Joseph Longo, Bob Robinson, and Robert Rosa) shines a light on the current undergarment-of-choice of the club-hopping, hip-hop, woman on the go: the thong. Girls in the audience of Sisqo's shows have been known to toss these articles on stage during his performances, causing the Lycra police to do double duty. His follow-up to "The Thong Song" did not rely on a gimmick for its hook, perhaps in his desire to be taken more seriously and not be typecast as the "underwear guy." He also left out this song in some of his shows, to the bewilderment of many of his fans. Oh well, as they say, "The Thong Remains the Same." (We just couldn't resist!)

"I Kissed a Girl"

This song performed by Katy Perry (written by Lukasz Gottwald, Max Martin, Cathy Dennis, and Katy Perry) showcases the force of human nature to experiment with the unknown — in this case, kissing someone of the same sex. Noting that this is not her usual practice nor something she would ordinarily act upon, she admits, "I got brave, drink in hand, lost my discretion" and, from there, found the experience to be conflicted: "It felt so wrong, it felt so right . . . I hope my boyfriend don't mind it." This is a great example of a song that has a catchy or novel approach to something as common as kissing.

"Surfin' USA"

Brian Wilson of The Beach Boys certainly had his finger on the pulse of the youth of America when he wrote this song. He put the whole carefree West Coast feeling into songs like "Surfin' USA," "409" (his tribute to a hot Chevy with a 409-cubic-inch engine), and "Surfer Girl." (When you can combine a hot trend with a hot date, you've got it made!) Based on "Sweet Little Sixteen," by Chuck Berry, "Surfin' USA" proves that you don't have to actually experience what you write about in a song to capture authenticity. (Brian didn't surf!) An audience can sit back or hit the dance floor and live vicariously through the soft-focus lens of a song. Songs based on fads and crazes have been known to "surf" the generations and have enjoyed popularity long after the fads that inspired them have come and gone.

REMEMBER

The gimmick or novelty song is another form to experiment with as a songwriter. The popularity and the longevity of the subject matter, however, will affect the popularity and longevity of the song itself.

OFF THE RECORD

Being a huge fan of the comedian Mel Brooks and his masterwork (along with Carl Reiner) "The Two Thousand Year Old Man," Jim was inspired to write a series of songs based on this famous, largely ad-libbed, stand-up routine. One such song is sung from Mel's own perspective as he doles out hilarious health tips and wisdom from his alleged 2,000 years on Earth. The main hook of the song is, "Eat a nectarine every day." Although that song has never been commercially released, Jim got an enormous charge out of writing it (and playing it at parties), and he waits for the day when he gets to play it for "The Man" himself. Until then, "You've been a great civilization!"

Parody lyrics

A parody lyric is a (hopefully) comical reinterpretation of someone else's more serious lyric. Some parody songs have gone on to be hugely popular, a few even rivaling the popularity of the original. Many times a parody artist takes a popular song and writes a lyric that is often topical and sometimes even in direct contrast to the original. If you look at the world in a humorous light and tend to see the comic or ironic possibilities in every situation, writing song parodies may be right up your drainpipe. Right now, we'll take a look at a couple artists who've made a career out of spoofing popular songs.

"Weird Al" Yankovich

First breaking into Billboard's Top 40 in 1984 with a parody of Michael Jackson's mega-smash "Beat It," written by Michael Jackson (which Weird Al rechristened "Eat It," complete with a hilarious accompanying video in which he plays a guy with a serious food addiction), Weird Al has carved a wide niche for himself with his clever and well-crafted take-offs. Some of his popular parodies include "Lasagna" (a parody of "La Bamba," written and sung by Richie Valens), "Addicted to Spuds" (a send-up of "Addicted to Love," written and sung by Robert Palmer), "Like a Surgeon" (based on Madonna's hit "Like a Virgin," written by Thomas Kelly and William Steinberg), and "The Rye or the Kaiser" (a parody of Survivor's "Eye of the Tiger," in which, presumably, Rocky Balboa gets fat and weak and is a delicatessen owner offering his customers roast beef "on the rye or the Kaiser"). Al is a master at taking the grand statement of a song and cutting it hilariously down to size.

When Frankie Sullivan (co-writer of "Eye of the Tiger") and Jim were approached by their label and publisher to grant permission to a new artist named "Weird Al" Yankovich to release a parody of their then-current hit, "Eye of the Tiger," Jim admits he had his doubts. Two factors ultimately changed their minds: the excellence and wit of the comic concept and the fact that the "The Gloved One," Michael Jackson, had just given Al permission for parodies on a couple of his songs. That gave instant legitimacy in their minds to the notion of poking fun at their big motivational song.

Cletus T. Judd

Some would call Cletus T. Judd the undisputed king of the country music parody song. His send-ups (another term for parodies) of country hits include his hilarious parody of Deana Carter's hit "Did I Shave My Legs For This?" (written by Deana Carter and Rhonda Hart), entitled, "Did I Shave My Back For This?"; "If Shania Were Mine" (spoofing Shania Twain's hit "Any Man Of Mine," written by Mutt Lange and Shania Twain); "Cletus Went Down to Florida" (taking off from "The Devil Went Down to Georgia," written and performed by The Charlie Daniels Band); and, of course, "Third Rock from Her Thumb," his parody of Joe Diffie's hit "Third Rock from the Sun" (written by John Greenebaum, Tony Martin, and Sterling Whipple), boasting the lyric "Nothing else shines like a zirconium, don't tell her what it's worth, third rock from her thumb."

Inspirational lyrics

Lyrics of praise and worship, words of inspiration, and stanzas of belief have been the basis of many of the world's greatest and longest-lasting songs. A song is a powerful force that can change minds, shape nations, spearhead causes, and uplift the emotions. As a songwriter, it's a perfectly acceptable goal to make the listener want to wiggle ("Bootylicious," written by Beyonce Knowles, Rob Fusari, Stevie Nicks, Falonte Moore, and Frank Tai; performed by Destiny's Child), giggle (see "Parody lyrics" featuring Weird Al), or jiggle (". . . Baby One More Time," written by Martin Sandberg, sung by Britney Spears). When a writer can inspire, however, he's helping to change the world. As songwriters, we have the unique opportunity to get our message across to potentially millions of people. Here are a few noteworthy examples in this wonderfully crowded category.

"Don't Laugh at Me"

Although this hit single reached #2 on the Billboard country charts as recorded by Mark Willis (written by Allen Shamblin and Steve Seskin), it's hard to describe the experience felt during a live performance when composer Donna Michael performs this piece on the piano. There is not a dry eye in the audience when she sings, "I lost my wife and little boy when someone crossed that yellow line" — "the day we laid them in the ground is the day I lost my mind." Check out why this song is so effective for Donna in her work as a "radical forgiveness" coach:

Verse 1

I'm a little boy with glasses
The one they call the geek
A little girl who never smiles
'Cause I've got braces on my teeth
And I know how it feels
To cry myself to sleep

I'm that kid on every playground
Who's always chosen last
A single teenage mother
Tryin' to overcome my past
You don't have to be my friend
But is it too much to ask

Chorus

Don't laugh at me
Don't call me names
Don't get your pleasure from my pain
In God's eyes we're all the same
Someday we'll all have perfect wings
Don't laugh at me

Verse 2

I'm the cripple on the corner
You've passed me on the street
And I wouldn't be out here beggin'
If I had enough to eat
And don't think I don't notice
That our eyes never meet

I lost my wife and little boy when
Someone crossed that yellow line
The day we laid them in the ground
Is the day I lost my mind
And right now I'm down to holdin'
This little cardboard sign . . . so

Chorus

Don't laugh at me
Don't call me names
Don't get your pleasure from my pain
In God's eyes we're all the same
Someday we'll all have perfect wings
Don't laugh at me

Bridge

I'm fat, I'm thin, I'm short, I'm tall
I'm deaf, I'm blind, hey, aren't we all

Chorus

Don't laugh at me
Don't call me names
Don't get your pleasure from my pain
In God's eyes we're all the same
Someday we'll all have perfect wings
Don't laugh at me

"Change the World"

This mid-@'90s hit for singer Eric Clapton (written by Gordon Kennedy, Wayne Kirkpatrick, and Tommy Sims) centered on the ways we all can make a difference in this vast universe. It's a great example of how an old concept can be given a new lease on life through a fresh musical approach. The arrangement of this song is a unique combination of country-blues and soul.

"My Sweet Lord"

George Harrison was considered the Beatle "on a quest," and this song he wrote is a wonderful documentation of his journey. As he explored religions of all peoples, he came to the conclusion that they all had one thing in common: a belief in something greater than us all. This song reflects his wide-eyed allegiance to his "Sweet Lord" and sweeps us away with producer Phil Spector's lush bed of 12-string and slide guitars.

WARNING

In the '70s, George Harrison was involved in a lawsuit over "My Sweet Lord" when the publisher of the '60s hit "He's So Fine" sued him for copyright infringement claiming significant similarities between the two songs. In the end, George admitted that he had perhaps unconsciously incorporated a portion of the old song by The Chiffons into his song. When you're writing a song, be as sure as you can be that it's not too reminiscent of something that already exists. When in doubt, play it for your friends (and your publisher) to see if they experience a strong sense of déjà vu and feel as though they've heard it someplace before.

"With Arms Wide Open"

This 1999 hit by Creed (written by Scott Stapp and Mark Tremonti) taps into one man's boundless joy over learning that he is soon to become a father. We can feel his awe and uncertainty in the journey that lies ahead for him and the woman he loves. He's ready and eager to be the child's tour guide on this planet, but wants to inspire his offspring to be even more embracing of life and its spiritual riches than he is himself, to "greet the world with arms wide open."

Practice Makes Perfect

We've given you examples of the different lyrical types of songs in this chapter. As you develop phrases that work together with your general concept, take a look at what lyrical type your phrases are fitting into, and then drive your message on home with the rest of the song. Remember to keep checking back to see what form your song is taking so that the focus remains intact. Being aware of this form helps stay consistent throughout your song. If you're telling a story, then tell the story. If your lyrics are situation driven, don't lose sight of the situation that inspired the song in the first place.

Chapter **6**

Finding Your Voice in the Lyrics

Lyrics can make or break a great melody. But coming up with lyrics is often easier said than done. In this chapter, we fill you in on some tried-and-true techniques used by the pros when they're setting out to write lyrics. We also take you step by step and show you how to fit your lyrics into the common formats of songs.

Writing a Great Lyric

You've just bought yourself a brand-new laptop (the kind that weighs a couple of ounces and is paper thin). You've purchased a silver pen with your initials on it. You've rented a villa in the Caribbean. You also have your trusty digital audio recorder by your side, set to capture the cosmic overlap of words and music. The scene is basically set for one of those *Behind the Music* episodes seen on VH1.

You're ready to write a great lyric. But where do you start? Start at the heart. Find the subjects that matter to you most. Find the melodies that resonate in your soul. In this section, we show you some of the ways the pros get started on their journey to writing a great lyric. Take a look at using one of these suggestions as a starting point:

>> A title (from just about anywhere) that suggests a concept

>> An idea or concept that suggests a title

>> An experience you've had

>> A cause you believe in deeply

>> A storyline you've imagined (or lived)

>> A catchy phrase

>> A melody that suggests a lyric

REMEMBER

Much of the process of lyric writing is experimentation and trial and error. Many writers prefer to start a song with a co-writer and finish it up separately (often getting back together one more time to compare notes and finalize the song). Like viewing a painting, it's good to take a step back to see the whole picture clearly. There's no need to force a lyric. You'll find that if you just give it a little time (but not too much), the lyric will naturally come. It's great to come back after a break and get each other's fresh point of view.

Starting with a title

When you feel you have an intriguing title, the next step is to examine the possibilities of those words. Find unique ways to look at common words (or common ways to look at unique words!). Following is a list of some famous song titles. As a quick exercise, pretend you're seeing the title for the first time. Now imagine the storyline that the title may imply to you, as if you just stumbled across it in your own notebook. How would the concept of your song differ, and how would it be similar to the hit? How would you put your own life experience into the lyric?

>> **"Heart of the Matter"** (written by Don Henley, Mike Campbell, and JD Souther; sung by Don Henley)

>> **"My Life Would Suck Without You"** (written by Max Martin, Dr. Luke, and Claude Kelly; sung by Kelly Clarkson)

>> **"If I Were A Boy"** (written by B. C. Jean and Toby Gad; sung by Beyonce)

>> **"Breakeven"** (written by Stephen Kipner, Danny O'Donaghue, Mark Sheenan, and Andrew Frampton; performed by The Script)

TIP

Oftentimes, a good title is a stepping-off point for a lyric and song. At its best, a title can literally sum up what you're going to say in the song itself. Jim is constantly jotting down potential titles from the words people say, things he sees in newspapers or magazines, and phrases that seem to come to him out of thin air. "The Search Is Over," "Vehicle," "High on You," "Hold on Loosely" . . . in fact, most of the hits he's written or co-written have started life as ink stains between the lines of a spiral notebook, as a title he jotted down or one that someone suggested to him.

Example step #1: Developing a title idea

There are many ways to achieve a goal, and although in this example we're suggesting one particular method of writing lyrics from scratch, we encourage you to find a style you're comfortable with and one that works best for you.

If you start with only the title in mind, you'll want to develop that title into an idea. If you're not sure what the song is going to be about, then sit down and create a list of different ideas that could be expanded and covered by your title. Just for an example, we'll say you had a dream last night; the title "Deep in the Heart of the Night" jumped right out and you're convinced that this title was sent to you from the ethers to use in your next song. Your mission now, should you accept it, is to go about discovering just what the song will be about in relation to your title.

As you think about your title, "Deep in the Heart of the Night," make a list of all the things that you can imagine happening deep in the night. Your list may look something like this:

>> Falling in love *deep in the heart of the night*

>> Fantasizing that you're falling in love *deep in the heart of the night*

>> Looking back at falling in love *deep in the heart of the night*

>> Thoughts and feelings that only come to you *deep in the heart of the night*

>> Waking up from a dream *deep in the heart of the night*

>> Getting a phone call *deep in the heart of the night*

>> Driving your car or truck *deep in the heart of the night*

You get the point. Now, after thinking over those ideas, you decide to use "Driving your car or truck deep in the heart of the night." Maybe this is because you just bought some new wheels or you're craving an escape to somewhere — anywhere. It's most likely that what you choose from your list will be one with which you feel the strongest connection. That affinity for your subject will become the fuel for your brain that will help you maintain your creative flow.

REMEMBER

A title doesn't have to be clever or even unique to be effective. Sometimes a generic title can be infused with new life by using a different camera angle or shedding a new light on an old subject. Notice how one of the most common titles of all time, "I Love You," is presented in a fresh light in the context of the song performed by Martina McBride (written by Tammy Hyler, Adrienne Follese, and Keith Follese) of the same name. By using edgy, similar sounding words to set up the title hook like "electrically," "kinetically," "erratically," "fanatically," and "magically" the songwriters are adding contrast to the simple closing line of the chorus, "sure as the sky is blue, I love you."

Finding a place for the title within the song

TIP

After you hit on a good title, experiment by placing it in different spots within your tune to see where it works the best. Many successful songs place the title in one of the song's power spots to help hook the listener. Take a look at the following examples in Table 6-1.

TABLE 6-1

Power Spots for Titles

At the end of each verse	Songwriter(s)	Singer/Performer
"Bridge Over Troubled Waters"	Paul Simon	Simon & Garfunkel
"Blue Eyes Crying in the Rain"	Fred Rose	Willie Nelson
"The Times They are A-Changin'"	Bob Dylan	Bob Dylan
At the beginning of the chorus	Songwriter(s)	Singer/Performer
"By the Way"	Tyler Connolly/music by Theory of a Deadman	Theory of a Deadman
"Valentino"	Diane Birch	Diane Birch
"Lucky"	Jason Mraz, Colbie Caillat, Timothy Fagan	Jason Mraz
At the end of the chorus	Songwriter(s)	Singer/Performer
"Second Chance"	Dave Richard Bassett, Brent Smith	Shinedown
"Love the One You're With"	Stephen Stills	Stephen Stills
"Something in Your Mouth"	Mutt Lange, Chad Kroeger	Nickelback

In both the first and last lines of the chorus	Songwriter(s)	Singer/Performer
"Human"	Brandon Flowers, Dave Keuning, Mark Stoermer, Ronnie Vannucci Jr.	The Killers
"Apologize"	Ryan Tedder	Timbaland featuring OneRepublic
"Half of My Heart"	John Mayer, Taylor Swift	John Mayer (with Taylor Swift)

In various sections of the verse	Songwriter(s)	Singer/Performer
"Never Say Never"	Joseph King and Isaac Slade	The Fray
"Breakeven"	Stephen Kipner, Danny O'Donaghue, Mark Sheenan, and Andrew Frampton	The Script
"Different Name for the Same Thing"	Benjamin Gibbard	Death Cab for Cutie
"Superstition"	Stevie Wonder	Stevie Wonder
"Try Sleeping with a Broken Heart"	Jeff Bhasker, Alicia Keys, Patrick "Plan Pat" Reynolds	Alicia Keys

In both the chorus and the verse	Songwriter(s)	Singer/Performer
"If You Only Knew"	Dave Richard Bassett, Brent Smith	Shinedown

So where should you put your song title? In as many places as you can without going overboard. Some songs take the concept of the title as a hook to the extreme and really hammer it home in this way. In the song "Let It Be" (written by John Lennon and Paul McCartney; performed by The Beatles), the title appears 42 times!

TIP

Don't force a title into numerous places within your song because you feel you have to — unless it really makes sense to do so. A good title has a way of sticking in your head even if it's only used a few times. There are also instances where the title does not appear anywhere at all in the song, such as in "For What It's Worth" by Stephen Stills, "A Dustland Fairytale" by The Killers, "Superstar" (written by Bonnie Bramlett and Leon Russell), which is best known for The Carpenters' version of the song (but was also covered by many others including Ruben Studdard and Luther Vandross), and "Chasing Cars" (lyrics by Gary Lightbody;

music by Snow Patrol) — okay, so the title was mentioned just once in the last verse in "Chasing Cars" — but you've got the picture now.

WARNING

There is no need to panic if you find out that someone else has already beat you to the punch and used that amazingly creative and catchy title you just slaved over for nearly two weeks — because titles cannot be copyrighted, you are free to "move about the cabin" and allow your title to take flight by embarking upon a totally new and different direction the second (or third) time around.

Starting with an idea or concept

Whenever the process of songwriting seems to become more of a craft and less of an art — more of a puzzle and less of a passion — it's good to throw the tricks away (at least temporarily) and go back to the theme and concept. Some of the greatest lyrics are remembered more for their idea or story rather than for their clever rhyme schemes, hooks, twists on the title, plays on words, or expanded clichés. A theme that matters to you can draw out some amazing emotions in, and often as, a sidelight. As a bonus, it helps you come up with some incredible titles, rhymes, and hooks.

Harnessing a concept

WORDS OF WISDOM

Just as I have reams of pages of hooks, phrases, and titles, I have nearly as many pages of potential concepts for songs. Many times in a co-writing session with another person (or co-writing with myself on an old idea), the idea of the song actually suggests the title of the song, the tone of the lyric (angry, sad, happy, nostalgic, and so forth), and an appropriate musical hook. In a songwriting world often driven by title and hook, it's refreshing to go back to concept and work the rest from there. Some writers say they write great songs when they're in the depths of depression, but it sure doesn't work for me. Even a great idea holds little appeal for me when I'm in the dumps. However, when I finally pull out of the trenches, I draw from the experience of having been there. You can learn to create from your sorrow, but for most songwriters, only after they've experienced it. Similarly, some writers insist on getting high before attempting to write a song. All I can say is that from what I've learned through the years it's extremely easy to be fooled into thinking you have a brilliant idea or song only to say, "What was I thinking?" once you get sober.

— JIM PETERIK, PERFORMER, SONGWRITER, AND MULTI-INSTRUMENTALIST
FOR BOTH IDES OF MARCH AND SURVIVOR, PLUS WRITER OF HITS
FOR .38 SPECIAL, SAMMY HAGAR, AND OTHERS

Example step #2: Expanding the concept

After you have a concept — what the song is going to be about — you'll want to elaborate on that concept and develop it into a story. Let your imagination run free. Going back to our fictitious example of "Deep in the Heart of the Night," try to picture yourself being deep in the night, and take note of all the emotions you might be feeling in the seat of your vehicle as you drive the night away. Make note of all that your imagination dictates to you — the stars, the clouds, the terrain, the glow of your dashboard dials. These are the images that will illuminate your lyric.

For "Deep in the Heart of the Night," you may decide that the song is going to be about driving to Tulsa late at night. Perhaps you chose Tulsa because you liked the way the word sounded. Maybe it was the wide-open plains of Oklahoma that held the attraction for you. Perhaps there is someone waiting for you in Tulsa. Maybe Tulsa somehow represents a fresh start for your life. Or it could be that Tulsa is just a random point on the map, and you're thinking "anywhere's better than where I am right now." When you're expanding on the idea of driving deep in the heart of the night to Tulsa, ask yourself questions such as the following:

>> What is the motivation for driving?

>> Why is the destination Tulsa, Oklahoma?

>> Am I writing from a personal perspective, or am I telling a story about someone else or from another person's point of view?

>> Am I writing about the trip in the present tense, looking back at a past trip, or dreaming of one in the future?

>> What is going through my mind as I'm driving?

>> What emotions am I feeling as I drive along?

>> Who or what is waiting for me when I finally reach my destination?

Asking these questions and making these decisions will influence the tone your lyric will take — angry, tender, excited, full of longing, full of remorse, and so forth. These decisions will also influence the style of language you use from formal to hip or slang.

There are plenty of things to think about when developing your concept. When writing a screenplay for a movie, one of the tips in training is to decide how the story will end up before you even begin. And so it goes with developing the story for your song — think your concept through to the end of that drive to Tulsa — deep in the heart of the night.

Telling a story

Much like starting with a concept, putting a story into lyrical form has been the basis for many memorable songs. Story songs (see Chapter 5 for a definition of story songs) can be very involving for the listener because, for one reason, the listener is waiting to the end to hear the story's outcome. The effectiveness of songs as divergent as "Stan" (written by Eminem, Paul Herman, and Dido; sung by Eminem), which is the story of an obsessed fan of the artist himself, and "24 Hours From Tulsa" (written by Burt Bacharach and Hal David; sung by Gene Pitney), which is the tale of a man who was unfaithful to his wife just 24 hours before he was to come home to her, depends on how interested the audience is in the story the songs are telling. In the case of these two smashes, the answer is clear.

Find a story that interests you from current events, fictional accounts, or history books. Now try to put the story into verse form using your own style.

Using a melody that suggests a lyric

Sometimes as a songwriter you get very lucky and hear a melody in your head. Other times, you noodle around on your keyboard, guitar, mandolin, or trombone and stumble upon a series of notes that sound good together. Then there are times when you're even more blessed and your vocal chords produce some primitive utterances that actually resemble words. In this way, a melody can literally inspire a lyric — as opposed to the other way around.

On occasion, when Jim hits upon an interesting melody, he'll sing it out with what he calls *creative gibberish* — in other words, nonsense syllables that sound remarkably like words. (Another widely accepted term for such gibberish is *vocable*.) He once sang a new but unfinished song for a friend with nothing but gibberish for words. Afterward, the friend told him it was one of his best lyrics. When Jim told him it was nothing but nonsense, he still insisted it was one of his most meaningful lyrics! (When Paul McCartney played the yet unfinished "Hey Jude" for John Lennon, he told John that the lyric "The movement you need is on your shoulder" was just a nonsense lyric to indicate the sound of the words and to fill the musical bars until something permanent was created. John insisted the lyric stay and stated that it was one of the best lines of the song!) The amazing part is that often, when you listen to tapes of these artificial lyrics, you hear sounds that you can actually develop into real words. And if you become adept at the art of gibberish, it can be a tool to your lyric writing. The trick is that when you're unencumbered by the English language (or whatever tongue you speak), you are freer to concentrate on the naturalness of the sound and the rhythm of the words without being hung up on their meaning.

REMEMBER

When starting a song, try to put yourself in the most receptive mood possible. Many a song never got past the first verse because the writer was convinced it wasn't any good. Try to be as patient and caring with yourself as you would be to a friend in whom you're trying to bring out the best. Let yourself go and let the words flow — without judging whether or not they are any good.

Finding the Format for Your Lyrics

Different sections of a song serve different purposes. Sometimes it takes a great deal of experimentation to find the best format for your song (see Chapter 3 for more on song forms). In the following sections, we cover ways that you can use lyrics to help differentiate the sections, as well as the lyrical techniques you can use to build and shape your song.

OFF THE RECORD

Jim Morrison of The Doors used to love to write poetry. He would sit in with a young local band that he liked and recite his poetry during their sets. He loved to use the rhythm of the music to move his words. (By the way, this band later changed its name to Kansas and went on to have a multiplatinum career of its own.)

Verse lyrics

Songwriters generally use the verse to set up the idea or premise of the song. The *verse lyric* conveys the meat of the meaning of the song. First it draws the listener in with a catchy opening statement or question, and then it sets up the song's premise or idea as it leads to the chorus. Each subsequent verse adds new information to the story — often looking at the premise from a different perspective. One popular technique is to start with a general or nonspecific idea in the first verse and get more situation-specific in subsequent verses as the song develops. You may also want to set up your scene geographically ("In the town where I was born . . .") as to where the action takes place, or set the time perspective as to when the situation occurs ("Many, many years from now . . ."). The verses serve to set up the chorus of the song. In story songs, the verses are all-important, drawing the listener in as the tale unfolds. Tell it as simply and interestingly as you can, embellishing it with poetic devices such as rhyme, word rhythm, alliteration, imagery, personification, simile, metaphor, assonance, and anaphora (a-NA-phor-a). (See the section "Using Poetic Devices in Lyrics" later in this chapter for more information.) You might also draw the listener in by posing a question in verse one, making him an interactive member of the song — as in "Is there anybody going to listen to my story?" which is the first line of "Girl," or "Roll up, roll up for the mystery tour" from "Magical Mystery Tour" (both of these songs were written by John Lennon and Paul McCartney and performed by The Beatles).

Example step #3: Developing the verse lyric

On the fictitious song we are collaborating on, "Deep in the Heart of the Night," we've chosen one of most common forms in popular songwriting, the one that uses verse, pre-chorus, chorus, verse, pre-chorus, chorus, bridge, repeat chorus (for other options of song forms, refer to Chapter 3). *Note:* We can always change it later as the song develops.

Now that we've decided on the basic concept or premise for the song, it's time to start brainstorming some verse lyrics. Because this is a chapter about words, we'll start with the lyrics, as opposed to the melody or chords (not that a melody or chord progression can't pop into your head as you're working on the lyrics). We'll suggest the opening two lines and you can take it from there. These lines can of course be substituted for others as you develop the song but it'll at least give you someplace to start:

» "Do you wonder why I'm sittin' here behind this wheel?"

» "'Nowhere' circled on the map, 300 horses at my heel?"

These lines can serve as the setup to 100 different expandable scenarios. Whatever concept you've chosen to illuminate the title "Deep in the Heart of the Night," make sure every line sticks to that concept and moves the action of the plot along. Try to use some descriptive words and intriguing visual images if possible (maybe "moonlight" in Line 3?). You may only want to work on the first verse for now and wait to write your second verse until after you've written your chorus (often the chorus will suggest where to take the second verse). You can also decide at that point if you need a third verse or a bridge.

Letting the verse express the concept

TIP

The opening line of your song is all-important. Try to capture the listeners' imagination and curiosity as to where your song is heading.

By looking at John Lennon and Paul McCartney's song "Eleanor Rigby," we see an excellent example of verse progression. The song consists of three verses and a chorus and uses the verse-chorus form. The concept of the song (loneliness and the basic futility of life) is shown through the interwoven lives of an elderly spinster named Eleanor Rigby and the town preacher, Father McKenzie.

The concept unfolds over the course of three verses. The first verse presents Eleanor Rigby picking up the rice at the church after a wedding. We immediately get a feel for the careful, prayerful type of person she is. In the second verse we're introduced to Father McKenzie, who writes the "words to a sermon that no one will hear" and clandestinely darns his socks late at night as if it were somehow a sin.

These two lonely people are joined in the final verse when Eleanor Rigby dies ("nobody came" to her funeral) and Father McKenzie buries her "Wiping the dirt from his hands as he walks from the grave." The good father accomplishes nothing in his life ("no one was saved"). The writers did a great job in telling a sad story and developing two memorable characters in a few short minutes of the song.

The verse is really where you first set up your concept and then expand upon it as the verses progress.

TIP

After you have your first and second verses written, try flipping them around. It's amazing how often the second verse sounds better as a first verse and vice versa.

Pre-chorus lyrics

If you feel your song needs a pre-chorus (see Chapter 3 for more details on pre-chorus), make sure it's doing its job lyrically. A pre-chorus can give the song some fresh chords to differentiate the verse and chorus. Lyrically, the pre-chorus (or *B section* or *channel*) is a place to further set up the action in the chorus. If the verse is very specific — mentioning names, dates, and locations — you may want to make your channel more conceptual for contrast as you set up the hook. If your verse is general in nature (talking about love as a concept as opposed to jumping in bed with someone), your pre-chorus can get down to specifics before hitting the chorus.

Example step #4: Developing the pre-chorus lyric

In our fictitious song "Deep in the Heart of the Night," we have our title, have considered many concepts and chosen one, picked a potential song form, and started a verse. Because the form we've chosen includes a pre-chorus, it's now time to look at that element of our song. The specifics of where you've taken the verse will influence where you go on the pre-chorus. If your verse talks in very specific terms about the trip you are taking (the lyric, "*Tulsa* circled on the map," indicates a certain goal), then perhaps your pre-chorus could be very conceptual (perhaps something about your innermost thoughts as you are driving). If your verse is in the present tense, another approach might be for your pre-chorus to shift to a retrospective outlook, thinking about the events that led up to your decision to drive. For instance:

>> "Wish that I could change your mind"

>> "And claim the love we left behind"

This two-line channel could be expanded to four if you have more to say, but generally four-measure pre-choruses are an appropriate length (refer to Chapter 8 for an explanation of measures). A good example of the two-line, four-bar pre-chorus would be "You're trying hard not to show it (baby), but baby, baby you know it" ("You've Lost That Lovin' Feeling" written by Barry Mann, Phil Spector, and Cynthia Weil; performed by the Righteous Brothers).

Putting the pre-chorus to work

REMEMBER

It's often the lyrical contrast between sections that keeps a song moving. Feel free to change your perspective from general to specific and past to present in a given tune. It's also okay to change the location of the action — and move the listener around from place to place.

Sometimes you may be laboring for hours on a second verse or bridge, and when done, realize that it just doesn't flow with the rest of the song. Be sure to keep referring to your lyrical premise. Don't be afraid to go back to the top and read the lyric again and again to make sure all your lyrics belong in the same song.

Chorus lyrics

The chorus lyric is really the money lyric (the one that people remember first and that motivates them to buy the record — that in turn makes the songwriter money!). When you've done a great job in your verse (and pre-chorus, if necessary), you want to sum it all up as simply and infectiously as possible in the chorus. This is generally where the hook of the title is placed. The chorus is sometimes just one or two words chanted over and over as in "Mony, Mony" (written by Tommy James, Bo Gentry, Ritchie Cordell, and Bobby Bloom; sung by Tommy James), or it can really expand and crystallize all that was said in the verse as in "Because You Loved Me" (written by Diane Warren; sung by Celine Dion). Whether the listener is hit over the head with the lyrics of the chorus or seduced by it, it must be something they want to hear again (and hopefully, again and again).

WARNING

There is no law that says the lyrics in a chorus have to be exactly the same each time the chorus comes around. Sometimes when writing a chorus, you have a few variations that are hard to choose between. If you can't decide on the one best option (at the risk of confounding a sing-a-long), use them all in unfolding choruses. Just make sure the title doesn't change too radically.

Example step #5: Developing the chorus lyric

In our future hit, "Deep in the Heart of the Night," our next step is to work on the all-important chorus of the song. We should consider keeping the chorus extremely simple, emphasizing the (quite lengthy) title, "Deep in the Heart of the

Night." This is the area of the song where we emphasize the premise of the song in its most basic terms. Depending on the concept you've chosen, the chorus could be as simple as, "Deep in the heart of the night, I see you, deep in the heart of the night, I touch you." This section needs to be the part that people are compelled to sing along with.

Having the chorus make your point

TIP

Very often, the chorus is the first thing to be written because it can spring right out of the title and lyrically sum up the point of the whole song.

If you want to write a memorable song, one that people will fall in love with and sing forever — write a great chorus. The chorus presents the main point of the song, while the verses describe the details. This principle can be seen in many verse–chorus songs such as:

>> **"Goodbye Yellow Brick Road"** (written by Elton John and Bernie Taupin; sung by Elton John)

>> **"Amazed"** (written by Marv Green, Chris Lindsey, and Aimee Mayo; performed by Lonestar)

>> **"Live Like You Were Dying"** (written by Tim Nichols and Craig Wiseman; sung by Tim McGraw)

>> **"Circle of Life"** (written by Elton John and Tim Rice; sung by Elton John)

>> **"The Wind Beneath My Wings"** (written by Larry Henley and Jeff Silbar; sung by Bette Midler)

>> **"Un-break My Heart"** (written by Diane Warren; sung by Toni Braxton)

>> **"I'm in Love"** (written and performed by Geoff Byrd)

The chorus can be similar in tone to the verses, blending in with them, or it can become a surprise or a climax, such as we find in "The Night They Drove Old Dixie Down" (written by Robbie Robertson; performed by The Band).

Bridge lyrics

The bridge of your song can be an important element for a variety of reasons. It can serve to sum up, in broad terms, the main idea of the song. It can expand upon or amplify the lyric's main theme, or it can simply be a respite or oasis from the intensity of the rest of your song. At the bridge of "What a Girl Wants" (written by Jenny Bicks and Elizabeth Chandler; sung by Christina Aguilera), the song's feel shifts from its intense groove to a light, syncopated rhythm that adds contrast. It is the singer's chance to give her loved one a heartfelt thanks for being there for her. The bridge is also your chance to reflect on what you've already said in the song and say it a bit differently — as in "Don't let her slip away, sentimental fool, don't let your heart get in the way," in the song "Hold on Loosely" (written by Don Barnes, Jeff Carlisi, and Jim Peterik; performed by .38 Special).

In our opinion, The Beatles wrote the book on great bridges. Often, John Lennon and Paul McCartney would supply each other with bridges for their songs (they called it the middle eight, referring to the standard length of a typical bridge — eight musical measures long). The lyrical shift from one writer to the other was usually enough to make the bridge a welcome section of the song, both musically and lyrically. John added the "life is very short" bridge to the otherwise optimistic tone of their song "We Can Work It Out," and in doing so added a much-appreciated contrast.

Example step #6: Developing the bridge lyric

In our imaginary song "Deep in the Heart of the Night," it's time to *build a bridge* to the end of our song. Having nailed down the concept in the verses, taken it to some contrasting ground in the pre-chorus, and laid out the title boldly in the chorus, now it's time to change things up and shift the mood a bit. We need to give the ear something fresh to ponder and the emotions some new land to wander. If our verses and choruses are filled with a lot of words and fast syllables, it might be time to relax the pace of the words to supply contrast. If the verses and choruses unfold at a leisurely pace, it may be time to step up the frequency of the words. From a "meaning" point of view, it's time to perhaps reflect on the scenario that's been painted in the verse, pre-chorus, and chorus. You may also want to look ahead to what may be waiting down the road "deep in the heart of the night," before heading into the third verse or the final chorus.

TIP

One of the best ways to learn about bridges, what they are and what they do, is to study them in a variety of different popular songs.

Using a short form bridge in your song

If you have inserted your bridge in its most common location — after the second chorus, the listener has already had to process a heck of a lot of information. Many current pop songs are using extremely short bridges (often two or three lines) to change the pace without extending the song too dramatically. Many writers are taking a cue from the "bridge masters," Lennon and McCartney, and from their songs such as "I'll Be Back" — "I love you so, I'm the one who wants you, yeah, I'm the one who wants you, oh, oh, oh, oh." Writers such as Richie McDonald, Gary Baker, and Frank Meyers, who wrote the goose bump rendering 2001 release "I'm Already There" for Lonestar, make use of a simple, but triumphant, two-line bridge to sum up the message of the song: that even when the father and child are a thousand miles apart, the father is with him every minute and every mile in a thousand different ways. Similarly, the bridge in "This I Promise You" (written by Richard Marx; performed by 'N Sync) is short and sweet, adding a little new information and some fresh chord changes (starting on the 2 minor), and revealing that, "Over and over I fall, when I hear you call, without you in my life baby, it just wouldn't be living at all." And onward to the out chorus!

Moving Beyond Format to Sound

Building your lyrics around established song forms is a vital aspect of lyric writing. But making the words sound attractive and professional within that form is an art in and of itself. In this section, we give you some concrete tips for making sure your lyrics have the right sound for the song.

Paying attention to the rhythm of the words

Whatever section of your song you're writing, you need to consider not only the meaning of your words but their rhythm as well. This often-overlooked element of the mechanics of lyric writing is the secret weapon of many successful songwriters. Frequently, the beat of the words is accelerated in a certain section of a song to add excitement. (Check out the chorus of the 2009 hit "Boom Boom Pow" written by William Adams, Stacy Ferguson, Jamie Gomez, and Allen Pineda; performed by Black Eyed Peas.) Other times, just a few words are stretched over vast expanses of measures for a romantic or passionate effect, such as in "You Are So Beautiful" (written by Bruce Fisher and Billy Preston; sung by Joe Cocker) and "Without You" (written by Peter Evans and Tom Ham of Badfinger; most notable covers by Harry Nilsson as well as Mariah Carey).

A couple more songs to check out where the syllables are spread over a vast landscape are "Pride in the Name of Love" (written by Bono; performed by U2) and "Doesn't Mean Anything" (written by Alicia Keys and Kerry Brothers, Jr.; sung by Alicia Keys).

The rhythm of the words in a song can be as important as the rhyme scheme and the meaning. This is a large part of the feel and appeal of rap music. In the smash rap-meets-melody "Empire State of Mind" sung by Jay-Z and Alicia Keys (written by Alicia Keys, Al Shuckburgh, Sean Carter, Jane't "Jnay" Sewell-Ulepic, Angela Hunte, Bert Keyes, and Sylvia Robinson), the entire song depends on the rhythm of the words for its engine. The success or failure of any rap song depends not only on the cleverness of its rhymes and the lyrical content, but to an even larger extent on the "danceability" and catchiness of the rhythm of its words.

The original opening line for the song "Vehicle" (a #1 hit for The Ides of March back in 1970) was "I got a set of wheels, pretty baby, won't you hop inside my car." It wasn't until it was changed to "I'm the friendly stranger in the black sedan, won't you hop inside my car" (a line inspired by one of those well-intentioned, but corny, government-issued anti-drug pamphlets) that the tune really started to move. Not only was the new version a much more visual line, but it also had a rhythm all its own that cut across the backbeat and the choppy rhythm guitar figure.

WORDS OF
WISDOM

I had no idea what was so special about that line at the time — so much of what we do when we're just starting off is purely instinctual. It took me years to know what I was doing right on the songs that became hits. I realized much later that the first line of "Vehicle," when spoken, is similar to the rap rhythms that came into vogue some years later.

— JIM PETERIK, WRITER OF 18 BILLBOARD TOP 10 HITS

TIP

Even if you're not a great singer, try to sing the song you're in the process of writing to see whether the words flow rhythmically. Certain lyrics read well but sing lousy. If your tongue trips over a word or phrase time after time, you may want to consider modifying that portion. Is there too much room for certain words, and not enough for others? Is there enough contrast between sections in the rhythm of the words? Reading a lyric over is a good first step, but road-testing it with a singer can really reveal a lyric's true strengths and weaknesses.

Paying attention to the sounds of words within a lyric

Another often-overlooked element of lyric writing is the actual *sound* of the words themselves. Certain words and phrases roll off the tongue, and others just don't. The most popular songs are ones that people love to sing. If the words sound odd and awkward, it doesn't matter how deep the meaning of your lyric is, the message won't be delivered effectively. Sometimes a great writer will throw in an unusual word or an unconventional pronunciation as a special effect — listen how Elton John delivers the word *discarded* in his power ballad, "Don't Let the Sun Go Down on Me" (co-written with Bernie Taupin).

Example step #7: Making the words sound right

In our fictitious song, "Deep in the Heart of the Night," we've chosen our title, expanded on our concept, chosen our song form, and developed our verse, pre-chorus, chorus, and bridge lyrics. Now it's time to make sure our words *sound* right. Notice that, going back to our starter opening lines, "Do you wonder why

I'm sittin' here behind this wheel; 'Nowhere' circled on the map, 300 horses at my heel," we have already made some poetic and sound choices that make them sound professional. Notice the repeated "w" sound in the words "wonder" and "why" (this is alliteration, which is explained later in this chapter), the exact rhyme of the words "wheel" and "heel," and the rhythm of the syllables as they roll along (much like the rhythm of the wheels of the car).

Making the words flow

As you develop your lyric, try to include lyrical and poetic devices like these (and the many others we explore in this chapter) in your lyric. As these lyrics start finding a melody, be sure to try out your lyrics to see how comfortable they feel being sung.

TIP

One way to help ensure that the sound of your words will be an asset to your song is to write as you would talk. If a lyric is conversational and informal, it's more likely to be easy to sing and sound natural.

OFF THE RECORD

Baby is a word you'll find a lot in songs, yet few people still use it in conversation. Some popular writers would sooner die than use this word. Yet, others have made a career out of using the word *baby*.

Noticing a lyric's point of view

Another important element of a lyric is the point of view from which the lyric is sung. Hit songs have been written from every imaginable perspective. "A Day in the Life of a Tree" (written by Brian Wilson and John Rieley; performed by The Beach Boys) is sung from the point of view of an endangered species of tree. In "I Am the Walrus" (written by John Lennon and Paul McCartney; performed by The Beatles), John Lennon takes on different personas as the song develops.

First person

The first person perspective is perhaps the most popular of all the forms. This is where the story is told from the singer's point of view — it's also the most personal of all the points of view. Take a look at this list of songs that illustrate the first person point of view:

>> **"Every Little Kiss"** (written and sung by Bruce Hornsby)

>> **"Pretty Wings"** (written by Hod Davis and Maxwell; sung by Maxwell)

>> **"Superman (It's Not Easy)"** (written by John Ondrasik; performed by Five for Fighting)

The first person approach to a lyric is many writers' favorite point of view. Maybe that's because so many of us use songwriting as a way of expressing what's in our hearts — getting things off our chests. The singer/songwriter era in the '70s spawned many songs from this perspective when the buying audience seemed fascinated by the innermost feelings of the introspective artists of that time — such as Dan Hill, Cat Stevens, and Jim Croce.

TIP

Even if you write a lyric from a personal perspective, before you finalize it, try changing the perspective to third person (see the next section) to see how you like it. Changing the perspective can sometimes add needed depth to a lyric.

Third person

The third person point of view is a powerful vantage point because the songwriter becomes the reporter, if you will, of the events taking place in the song. He's the storyteller, and the whole world wants to hear his tale. Though not as personal as first person, third person is an extremely effective point of view because, as a semidetached observer, the singer is able to express feelings, comment, praise, and criticize without having to take complete responsibility. In "Well-Respected Man" (written by Ray Davies; performed by The Kinks), the singer documents the hypocrisy of England's class system — while staying out of the line of fire, because he's just reporting the issues. The Rolling Stones like to mix their first-person songs ("I Can't Get No Satisfaction," written by Mick Jagger and Keith Richards) with third-person songs ("She bitches 'bout things that she's never seen, look at that stupid girl"). Songs like "Dirty Laundry" (written by Don Henley and Daniel Kortchmar; sung by Don Henley) draw their power from the writer's ability to satirize and criticize the world of sensationalized journalism from a vantage point just left of center stage.

Example step #8: Setting the point of view, tone, and perspective

In the fictitious song, "Deep in the Heart of the Night," it's time to make sure we keep our perspective in mind and consider issues such as point of view and the tone of the lyric. In our dummy lyric, so far we have the beginnings of a verse, "Do you wonder why I'm sitting here behind this wheel, 'Nowhere' circled on the map, 300 horses at my heel." This is a story being told from the first person point of view; in other words, the story is unfolding in the life of the person who is singing. The lines that follow this can either stay in that point of view or change to the third person point of view. We might want to shift to the feelings of the woman who perhaps broke his heart and made him take to the highway. In the pre-chorus, we switch to a looking-back perspective with "Wish that I could change your mind, and claim the love we left behind." In the chorus, we go back to the present tense, "Deep in the heart of the night, I see you, deep in the heart of the night, I touch you." Also, whether you use these lyrics or not, when you're practicing writing this song, make sure the overall tone of the lyric is consistent throughout. An overly hostile lyric, for instance, would be at odds with the wistful tone that we've set up so far in this song.

Experimenting with point of view

Sometimes a lyricist can change the point of view within a single song. In "Hold on Loosely," by .38 Special, the pre-chorus starts in first person — "my mind goes back to the girl I met some years ago who told me." But when it hits the chorus, "Hold on loosely, but don't let go," the message now comes from the woman's point of view. When the words hit, "who told me," it's now the advice of the woman we're hearing — even though the singer is delivering her message. Until Jim, who was a co-writer on that song, stumbled upon this technique, the chorus was sounding "preachy," as if the singer was expounding this piece of wisdom. In any "advice songs" or songs where you'd like to be a step away from the action, consider placing the words in someone else's mouth (or quoting the words as if from a billboard or a magazine).

TIP

Experiment with changing the point of view of your lyric after you feel you've completed it. "She Loves You" (written by John Lennon and Paul McCartney; performed by The Beatles) wouldn't have been nearly as involved lyrically if John and Paul had chosen to call it "I Love You." By making the point of view third person, you allow the listener to be an observer of the situation alongside the singer — and most everybody loves being an insider.

Getting some perspective

The perspective of a lyric refers to whom a song is directed and who will deliver it. It also refers to the song's timeframe. As a songwriter, you may have someone specific in mind to perform the song you're writing. As you're creating, you're putting yourself in the mindscape of that artist and, depending on whether your target is male or female, rough or gentle, political or apolitical, religious or agnostic, or sarcastic or sincere, you are tailoring the perspective of the lyric to fit.

TIP

Find out all you can about an artist before you begin writing a song with him or her in mind. Try to write a lyric that stays within the boundaries of that artist's persona. Discover the marital status, hobbies, passions, and philosophical leanings of this person by reading interviews and listening to other songs he's written or chosen to perform.

When you're writing a lyric, also be aware of the time perspective or tense in which you're writing. The present tense is very prevalent in popular songs because it's here and now and immediate. There's no time like now to get an urgent message across — a good example is "Survivor," written by Anthony Dent, Beyonce Knowles, and Mathew Knowles; performed by Destiny's Child. The past tense in a lyric looks back on a time or situation. The reflective nature of past tense encourages songs about what could have been and what should have been, but it can also celebrate the good times of the past. Bob Seger is an artist who found a future in the past with powerful songs like "Night Moves," his bittersweet ode to coming of age in the heartland of America, and "Against the Wind" (both written and sung by Bob Seger). Future tense is also popular in lyrics. People love to fantasize and futurize. "We'll Be Together" (written and sung by Sting) is a good example of future tense.

OFF THE RECORD

Jim sometimes likes to combine past and present tenses in the same song. In "High on You," (written by Jim Peterik and Frankie Sullivan; performed by Survivor), the lyricists describe a scenario from the night before — "There you stood, that'll teach ya, to look so good and feel so right." In the pre-chorus, they then move to the present tense — "Now I'm higher than a kite, I know I'm getting hooked on your love." The combination of tenses adds movement to the action of a song. You can even add what Jim calls a *someday section* to bring the story into the future. Songs that come around full circle get me every time.

Tuning in to the lyric's tone and style

Many factors weigh into the overall tone of a song. Musical factors are perhaps the biggest influence on the mood of a song. The lyric, however, has to match whatever emotional tone the music sets (or vice versa). The images you choose for a sad, tragic, or moody song are going to be very different from the images you use for a joyful, giddy, or humorous one. Images of light and color seem to infuse positive songs, while images of darkness and shadow permeate the more negative songs. However, it is sometimes appropriate to mix the hues of emotional color and create a new shade.

If you choose informal language in a particular song (complete with slang, intentionally bad grammar, and colloquialisms), make sure you don't suddenly become a Rhodes Scholar at the third verse and blow your cover! If your tone is formal and intelligent (listen to Don Henley's song "Heart of the Matter," written by Don Henley, Mike Campbell, and JD Souther; sung by Don Henley, for a good example of this), try not to slip into a John Mellencamp kind of style, which is far more "down home" than "downtown."

Most of the songs I write tend to be on the positive side. I've always been more of a "half-full" guy than a "half-empty" guy, and my lyrics reflect that. Even when I write a sad song, there's usually a light at the end of the tunnel (and it's not the lights of an oncoming train!). You'll probably have more luck writing lyrics that reflect your personality rather than attempting to write "against type."

— JIM PETERIK, WRITER OF 18 BILLBOARD TOP 10 HITS

The musical marketplace you're targeting with a particular song does, to some extent, determine the style of your lyric. Certain words, expressions, and phrases are appropriate for a rock song, but they just won't work for a country song. Many lyrics are genre-specific. For instance, the country market by and large doesn't tolerate any word that resembles a swear word or a coarse or crude reference (better to change your *damn* to *dang* and your *lust* to *love*). There's no such ban, however, on words like this in hard rock (good examples are Limp Bizkit, Korn, and Slip Knot). Certain phrases in country, Christian, and easy listening are not going to sound appropriate against a balls-to-the-wall Linkin Park track or the latest by My Chemical Romance.

Using Poetic Devices in Lyrics

Many times people ask what the difference is between poetry and lyrics, and they often get one of a number of stock answers. People may tell you that poems are usually read and not heard, yet if that were always the case, we wouldn't have poetry readings. In reality, poetry is a kind of music on its own. If you look up the word *lyrics* in Webster's dictionary, you'll find that it means "words expressing a writer's strong and spontaneous feelings in a poem or a song." The truth is that the principles of poetry apply to lyrics as well.

Through the centuries, poems have been set to music by composers. Some poems can be set to music virtually unaltered, while others must be tailored to fit the form of a popular song. Factors such as song form, rhyme, rhythm, song length, and singability all come into play.

Some songwriters are as much poets as they are songwriters. When you read the lyrics of songwriters such as Leonard Cohen, Bob Dylan, Joni Mitchell, and Jewel, it's obvious that these lyrics have considerable power even without musical accompaniment. This is the hallmark of the poet who also happens to be a songwriter as well.

OFF THE RECORD

Bob Dylan changed his last name to Dylan as a tribute to the poet Dylan Thomas. (Bob Dylan's given name was Robert Zimmerman.)

There is much to be learned by the songwriter from reading and analyzing great poetry. We'll now take a closer look at some of the poetic devices that'll serve to enhance the sound of your lyric and song.

Using repetition

Repetition is an important component in both poetry and songwriting. A kind of poetic music can be created using the repetition of sounds. The repetition of words, phrases (such as a title), verses, and choruses can help get the point of your songs across to your listeners.

Applying word and phrase repetition

In our discussion of repetition, we'll start with the repetition of words and phrases, the most obvious example being the title.

Titles can be repeated frequently in a song. An example is "Hey Jude" (written by John Lennon and Paul McCartney; performed by The Beatles). The title in this song is repeated at the beginning of each verse and over and over again in the song's lengthy outro (outro is the opposite of intro). The repetition of the "na na na na" phrase in that same outro forms a hypnotic backdrop to the instrumental chaos that is mounting.

Certain words can be repeated for emphasis or to adapt to a melody. Sometimes this occurs in the title, as in "Say, Say, Say" (written and performed by Paul McCartney and Michael Jackson) and "Hi, Hi, Hi" (written and sung by Paul and Linda McCartney/Wings). Sometimes parts of a song are built using a single word (often its title) such as in the song "Hero" from the hit movie *Spider-Man* (written by Chad Kroeger; sung by Chad Kroeger of Nickelback and Josey Scott of Saliva).

Utilizing verse repetition

Repetition can also be used effectively with entire sections of a song. Verse repetition is fairly common. This usually occurs when the first verse is repeated at the end of the song. An example is "California Dreamin'" (written by John Phillips and Michelle Phillips; performed by The Mamas and the Papas). Sometimes the songwriter does this because he just cannot come up with another verse. Other times it's because the verse is really worth repeating, or perhaps the songwriter wants to emphasize something that was said earlier in the song.

Utilizing chorus repetition

The verse–chorus form lends itself to chorus repetition just by its very nature. A strong chorus can benefit from multiple repetitions in the song, or by being repeated over and over at the end of the song.

Examining poetic devices

Using poetic devices in your lyrics is kind of like seasoning your food. The right spices in the perfect amounts can add flavor, excitement, and romance to a dish, but using too much can mask the flavor and make the food inedible.

Viewing different poetic devices

Look at some of the following spices that gourmet songwriters use to enhance their lyrics, either suggesting alternate meanings in words or evoking an emotional or sensual response:

» **Rhyme:** A regular recurrence of corresponding sounds, especially at the end of lines. Rhyme is one of the most basic spices that can bring out the flavor in any dish (or song). (Rhyme is covered in Chapter 7.)

» **Alliteration:** The repetition of the same sound, usually of the *consonant* (everything except A, E, I, O, and U) at the beginning or within two or more words immediately succeeding each other. "I turned stranger into starman in the Sunday New York Times . . . like Anne Sexton and her star rats working backward till it rhymes . . ."("Stranger into Starman" by Aimee Mann). The following are songs that use strong alliteration, sometimes even in the title:

  • **"Umbrella"** (written by The-Dream, Tricky Steward, Kuk Harrell, and Jay-Z; sung by Rihanna and featuring Jay-Z)

  • **"Silent Lucidity"** (written by Chris DeGarmo; performed by Queensryche)

  • **"She Sells Sanctuary"** (written by Ian Astbury and Billy Duffy; performed by The Cult)

» **Imagery:** Those magic words and phrases in a lyric that impress images into your mind, the descriptive words that help drive home lasting impressions, mental pictures created with words. Who can ever forget the "tangerine trees" and "marshmallow skies" of "Strawberry Fields Forever" by John Lennon and Paul McCartney? Imagery is the indelible stamp of a truly great phrase. For a wonderful example of the use of imagery (and many other poetic devices such as simile — "like Sinatra in a younger day"), call up the lyrics to "A Dustland Fairytale" (written by Brandon Flowers, Dave Keuning, Mark Stoermer, Ronnie Vannucci Jr.; performed by The Killers) — "saw Cinderella in a party dress . . . I saw the Devil wrapping up his hands. . . ."

>> **Personification:** When a poet or lyricist refers to a thing, quality, or idea as if it were a person and ascribes human characteristics to inanimate objects. Good examples of this poetic device would be "They Call the Wind Mariah" (written by Alan Lerner and Frederick Loewe; sung by Sam Cooke) and the great line from "Mrs. Robinson" (written by Paul Simon; performed by Simon and Garfunkel), "Where have you gone Joe DiMaggio, *the nation turns it's lonely eyes to you*." Nations don't really have eyes except in wonderfully creative songs like these.

>> **Simile:** Comparing one thing to a dissimilar thing by the use of *like* or *as*. "I'm in Love" (written and performed by Geoff Byrd) is a good example, as are "you love me like a dollar bill" in "Phoenix" (written and performed by Aimee Mann) and "Like a Virgin" (written by Tom Kelly and Billy Steinberg; sung by Madonna).

>> **Metaphor:** This is a figure of speech where one thing is compared to another thing, as if it were that other thing (without using *like* or *as*). A perfect example of this is in the song "Save Me From Myself" (written by Matt Scannell; performed by Christine Aguilera), which is filled to the brim with metaphoric references. Check out "I Am The Walrus" and "Happiness Is A Warm Gun" (written by Paul McCartney and John Lennon; performed by The Beatles) for some more tasty morsels.

TIP

A good example of a lyric that skillfully combines metaphor, simile, and imagery is the song in John Mayer's debut release *Room For Squares* — "Your Body is a Wonderland," written and sung by John Mayer. The title of the song is the *metaphor,* "Your skin like porcelain" is a *simile,* and "Swim in a deep sea of blankets" is where *imagery* comes to play.

>> **Assonance:** A partial rhyme within phrases or sentences where the stressed vowel sounds are alike, but the consonant sounds are not alike, as in *late* and *make*. In the Simon and Garfunkel classic "America" (written by Paul Simon), the long *o* sound is used three times in the wonderfully descriptive line, "The moon rose over an open field." The use of assonance basically makes your lyric easier to sing.

WARNING

Always go for a perfect rhyme when you can find one, but never eliminate a great line simply because it doesn't rhyme exactly. Assonance in two words is a perfectly acceptable substitute for rhyme in most situations.

>> **Consonance:** According to *Webster's,* "a pleasing combination of sounds simultaneously produced." This word covers a lot of ground in lyric writing and harkens back to what we said on the subject of words sounding good and flowing well together.

Example step #9: Using poetic devices

We're at the final fine-tuning stage of our lyric for "Deep in the Heart of the Night." It's time to make sure we use enough poetic devices to invigorate the imagination. Again put yourself into the driver's seat of that car and take inventory of every emotion you might be feeling. Look around and observe the landscape as it goes rushing past. Look up in the stars that light the plains and feel the pull of the moon on your heart. Now take these feelings and observations and see how you can apply the various poetic techniques to your lyric writing. It'll help to make your song linger in people's memories long after the sun has risen on Tulsa and our solitary driver has found some peace of mind.

Practice Makes Perfect

At this stage in the game, you've probably got the itch to get going with writing some great lyrics, so start now by writing down the theme or concept that's buzzing around in your head at this very moment. Go ahead and have some fun putting phrases together.

As a starting point, you might want to take a stab at writing a lyric by going back to the song form you came up with from Chapter 3, as well as the hook you created in Chapter 4, and combining them with your lyric work in this chapter. Try not to get bogged down or frozen. Very often, songwriters are afraid of writing something that sounds pretty stupid, so they hold back from the freedom of just writing whatever comes to mind.

The more you free yourself to just let go with the words, the more of an opportunity you've provided yourself to lay down something that works great in your songs. Always remember that the more times you allow yourself to practice writing down phrases and thoughts that fit a burning concept inside of you, the more opportunities you give yourself to "hit the mark" and write some great lyrics.

Chapter **7**

Using Rhymes in Your Songs

N othing puts the final coat of shellac on a song better than a well-constructed rhyme scheme. The careful and often clever use of exact or similar sounding words is the spice behind the meaning of the words that helps market the emotions of a song. Without rhymes (unless purposely not used to create a specific unschooled effect), songs tend to sound unfinished and amateurish in nature.

Although finding these clever rhymes can be a challenge, many writers consider this to be the fun part of the songwriting process — think of the art of rhyming as similar to solving a brainteaser or putting together a jigsaw puzzle.

In this chapter, we fill you in on some rhyming techniques and show you how to use a few helpful tools to find and create rhymes for your own songs. As we've said before, there really is no right or wrong way to write a song — if it sounds good to *your* ear and expresses what you want to say, lyrically and musically, then it's "right."

Identifying the Rhyme

In some songwriting tutorials (and even in the previous edition of this book) rhyming schemes are meticulously detailed, giving names to the types of rhymes, like masculine, feminine, and so on. This analysis technique was derived from classical poetry, and it still has its definite place there. But trying to learn all these terms and the classical protocol of using them can be somewhat confusing — even counterproductive — to your songwriting progress. So instead of getting into all that, in order to identify what rhyming means for the songwriter, we'll look at examples of the clever rhymes that powered some very big hits and at the processes the writers used to get there.

Getting the basics of rhyme structure

Knowing full well you might get a laugh or two from some of the examples used in the following, we'll give them to you anyway to simplify and illustrate the point, and provide you with the confidence required to master the almighty art of rhyme. If you are old enough to read, you most likely know the simple children's song "Twinkle, Twinkle Little Star" (published as a poem by sisters Ann and Jane Taylor in 1806) and can easily recall the lyrics:

> Twinkle, twinkle little *star*
> How I wonder what you *are*

The words *star* and *are* are the rhymes. They have the same sound at the end of them because of the *ar* sound — pretty simple stuff, eh? This is rhyme at its most basic. You might chuckle at this example, but think about it. You remembered this couplet the second you heard it as a child, and can recite it today as if it were second nature. There are many songs referenced in these chapters, and you probably don't know all of them, but we'll put our money on the fact that *every person* who picks up this book will know "Twinkle, Twinkle Little Star." It's the rhyme of this little piece that you remember, and that's what renders it unforgettable. This is the perfect example of how powerful rhyme can be!

REMEMBER

When you sit down to compose a song, you're basically writing a poem and setting it to music. At its basic foundation, simple poetry has words that have a "beat" to them — and the last word of every line sounds the same.

As in "Twinkle, Twinkle Little Star," the words *star* and *are* share the same sounds — about as perfect of a rhyme as you can find. Chances are good that your first-ever attempt at songwriting had a rhyming scheme that was similar. Perfectly legit, but if you have three verses of a song that all feature the same rhyme, it's going to get really boring really fast! Or will it? Check out this sample from The Killers in their short song "Enterlude" written by Brandon Flowers:

> We hope you enjoy your *stay*
> It's good to have you with us, even if it's just for the *day*
> We hope you enjoy your *stay*
>
> Outside the sun is shining, it seems like heaven ain't far *away*
> It's good to have you with us, even if it's just for the *day*
>
> © Universal-Polygram Int'l Pub Obo Universal Music Pub. Ltd.

The Killers made the simplest of rhyme schemes work — and so can you! At the risk of beating a dead horse here, take a look at yet another nursery rhyme favorite to reinforce the point and highlight simple rhyme structure variations:

> Mary had a little lamb
> Its fleece was white as *snow*
> And everywhere that Mary went
> The lamb was sure to *go*

Here we find the rhyme occurs in every other line with *snow* and *go*. This is the rhyming scheme to more hit songs that you can count on the arms of an octopus! What was said about "Twinkle, Twinkle Little Star" goes for this example as well — this child's song is memorable *because* of the rhyme.

In "Mary Had a Little Lamb," the rhymes come at the end of every other line. It's perfectly acceptable to have the rhyme come at the end of the first line, and then have it hit on every other one. You can double it up, as well, having the odd lines rhyme in one way, and the even lines rhyme in another. As you can begin to see, the possibilities of rhyme are endless.

Starting with the alternate line method

A very common rhyme pattern occurs when the words rhyme at the ends of alternating lines. This is the scheme of the verses of "Heavy Metal," the movie-driven '80s hit for Sammy Hagar, co-written with Jim Peterik:

> Head bangers in *leather*
> Sparks flying in the dead of the night
> They all come *together*
> When they shoot out the lights
> Fifty thousand watts of *power*
> And it's pushin' overload

The beast is ready to *devour*
All the metal they can hold

Each line leads perfectly to the next as a night at a heavy metal show is described. Also note how the rhyming words in italics *(leather, together, power, devour)* tell their own story — there's no doubt why this is a song entitled "Heavy Metal." Very often the rhyming words offer essential points to a song, and the rhyme itself becomes another hook.

WORDS OF WISDOM

When Jim wrote the song "Heavy Metal" with Sammy Hagar, they put themselves into the moment of the concert and started to draw from their own experience of attending and performing big shows. The rhymes just kind of came naturally from the conversation they were having at the time. It's not like either of them said, "Let's construct an ABAB-type of rhyming pattern." They just started with the lines "Head bangers in leather, sparks flying in the dead of the night," and those lines seemed to dictate where the rhymes went from there.

This rhyming pattern is one of the oldest in pop-lyric writing. No matter what's being said, what sentiments are being reflected, and what style of language is popular at that particular time, this form has resilience in every era. In "Vehicle," a '70s hit written by Jim Peterik for The Ides of March, notice that the same rhyming scheme is also used:

I'm the friendly stranger in the black *sedan*
Won't you hop inside my car
I got pictures, got candy, I'm a loveable *man*
And I can take you to the nearest star

If you haven't already figured this out, it's perfectly acceptable if the rhyming words aren't *exactly* in the same "shape." In the previous examples, the rhyming words have the same makeup: *sedan . . . man, night . . . tight,* and so on. If your ear is tuned in, you'll notice that in "Heavy Metal" the even lines rhymed, but not in the same way as the odd lines. There are plenty of rhymes to be found where the dominant sound of the word is matching, even though the construction of the word is different.

In "Superman (It's Not Easy)" by John Ondrasik of Five For Fighting, this rhyme scheme is used to good advantage on its verse:

. . . stand to *fly*
. . . that naïve

. . . out to *find*

. . . part of me

The rhyme here is the "long i" sound of *fly* and *find*. It opens up a universe of possibilities, doesn't it? If a rhyme sounds clumsy, it probably is, but then again it might just work. Your ear will guide you — *trust it!*

TIP

When you're learning anything, it's a good idea to take a look at history. The great pop songs of the '30s and '40s can teach you a lot about how to construct rhymes. They might not get big play on your iPod, but they are worth checking out, right alongside the hits of today.

Looking at other basic rhyming patterns

Helping to make rhyme work for you, here is an example where the first and second lines end in similar sounding words and the third and fourth lines end in a different set of rhymes. Take a look at how one of America's most descriptive songwriters, John Mellencamp, uses this form in the verse of his 2001 release entitled "Peaceful World:"

. . . world is a *wreck*

. . . being politically *correct*

. . . didn't at *first*

. . . made it worse and *worse*

"All Fall Down" is a modern-era example by the group OneRepublic. Check out this gem from the pens of Ryan Tedder, Andrew Brown, Zack Filkins, Brent Kutzle, and Eddie Fisher:

Step out the door and it feels like *rain*

That's the sound, that's the sound on your window *pane*

Take to the streets but you can't *ignore*

That's the sound, that's the sound you're waiting *for*

© Sony/ATV Tunes Obo Midnite Miracle Music

Another song in this pattern is "Night of the World Stage" by Jim Peterik's ensemble group, World Stage. The second verse goes like this:

You're sittin' at the phone with your everyday *frustrations*

I'll take you to the zone for mood *elevation*

There's a whole rhythm section bangin' in your *head*

Your heart could be my drummer, let's run it in the *red*

For more examples of basic rhymes, check out the songs in Table 7-1.

TABLE 7-1 ## Songs with Basic Rhyming Patterns

Song Title	Songwriter(s)	Singers/Performers
"Uprising"	Matthew Bellamy	Muse
"Waiting on the World to Change"	John Mayer	John Mayer
"If You Ever Have Forever in Mind"	Vince Gill, Troy Seals	Vince Gill
"Marrakesh Express"	Graham Nash	Crosby, Stills, and Nash
"Your Song"	Elton John, Bernie Taupin	Elton John
"All Along the Watchtower"	Bob Dylan	Jimi Hendrix
"Because You Loved Me"	Diane Warren	Celine Dion

Trying out trickier forms of rhyme

Another type of rhyme scheme is where the last line of four lines rhymes with the first two lines instead of the third. For an example of this, check out the verse in the '80s Survivor song, "I Can't Hold Back" (written by Jim Peterik and Frankie Sullivan):

> There's a story in my *eyes*
> Turn the pages of *desire*
> Now it's time to trade those dreams
> For the rush of passion's *fire*

The third line adds just enough sound variation to keep the whole verse sounding fresh. You can see how monotonous it would get if the pattern was identical by inserting the fake line *Now it's time to trade those lies* in place of the third line. In the original line, the long *e* sound of *dreams* is a welcome relief from all the long *i* sounds.

Oftentimes you can get away with a minimum of rhyming and still have your song sounding top notch. The lyric to the classic hit recorded by Elvis Presley, "Can't Help Falling in Love with You" (written Luigi Creatore, Hugo Peretti, and George Weiss), has an interesting back story. The song, originally titled "Can't Help Falling in Love with Him," was then tailored to fit Elvis when he showed interest in the song. If you read through the lyric, it's apparent that all the rhymes were crafted to fit the original title. Look at these lyrics and read it the way it turned out, then try substituting in your mind the word *him* for *you* each time it comes around to see the difference it made.

"Can't Help Falling in Love with You" performed by Elvis

Wise men say, "Only fools rush in"
But I can't help falling in love with you

Shall I stay?
Would it be a sin
If I can't help falling in love with you

Like a river flows
surely to the sea
Darling, so it goes
Some things are meant to be
Take my hand
Take my whole life, too
For I can't help
falling in love with you

Like a river flows
Surely to the sea
Darling, so it goes
Some things are meant to be
Take my hand
Take my whole life, too
For I can't help
falling in love with you
For I can't help
falling in love with you

WORDS OF WISDOM

When Jim was working on the lyrics for "Eye of the Tiger" (co-written with Frankie Sullivan), more emphasis was put on telling Rocky's story than rhyming up a storm. The word *rival* was originally there as an exact rhyme to the original working title, "Survival." When the (extremely wise) decision was made to make the hook "Eye of the Tiger," the word *rival* came along for the ride and became an "approximate rhyme" for the word *tiger*. Even though it may have been more desirable to find an exact rhyme for either *rival* or *tiger*, the emotion of the lyric was well worth the trade-off. It's fascinating to look at the rough drafts of famous lyrics to see their raw beginnings, before they were refined and merely scrawls on a notebook page. Figure 7-1 shows one of the rough drafts of "Eye of the Tiger" taken from Jim's work notebook.

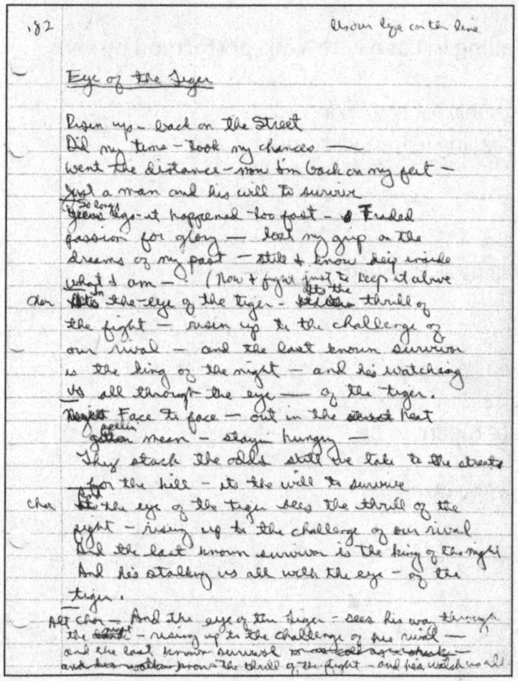

FIGURE 7-1: Lyric draft for "Eye of the Tiger."

Now look at an excerpt from the lyric of this ode to the human spirit to illustrate its lack of traditional rhyming techniques:

> Rising up, back on the *street*
> Did my time, took my chances
> Went the distance, now I'm back on my *feet*
> Just a man and his will to *survive*
> So many times, it happens too *fast*
> You trade your passion for glory
> Don't lose your grip on the dreams of the *past*
> You must fight just to keep them *alive*

Notice how the rhyme pattern actually spans two verses with the last line of each verse containing the rhyming word.

The chorus then shifts to the following pattern:

> It's the eye of the tiger
> It's the thrill of the *fight*
> Rising up to the challenge of our rival
> And the last known survivor stalks his prey in the *night*
> And he's watching us all with the eye — of the tiger

REMEMBER

Sometimes you can fool the ear with an approximate rhyme. *Tiger* is such a strong word that it more than justifies the lack of exact rhyme.

Like many songs, the rhyme scheme on this one varies from section to section. This variance, in fact, further helps separate sections and makes them more distinct from one another.

As you can see, there are many different rhyme patterns used in popular songs. Here are some more patterns and some corresponding sample songs:

» **AAAA patterns** (where the first four lines rhyme):

- "Fortunate," written by Robert Kelly; performed by Maxwell

- "American Pie," written and sung by Don McLean

- "Every Breath You Take," written and sung by Sting

» **ABCB patterns** (where the first and third lines don't rhyme with anything, and lines two and four do):

- "My Girl," written by Smokey Robinson and Ronald White; performed by the Temptations

- "God Must Have Spent a Little More Time on You," written by Carl Sturken and Evan Rogers; performed by 'N Sync (pop hit) and Alabama (country hit)

- "House of the Rising Sun," written by John Sterling and Eric Burdon; performed by the Animals

- "In My Life," written by John Lennon and Paul McCartney; performed by The Beatles

The only real criteria for the validity of a rhyme pattern are not how many hits it's been used in, but how it sounds to the ear. Not coincidentally, most of the patterns used on the biggest hits happen to be the most pleasing to the ear.

Adding internal rhyme

Rhyme isn't limited to the ends of lines. It can occur within a line or in the midst of two successive lines. "Internal rhyme" is a common element in many of our favorite songs. Without knowing it, the audience is getting a nice portion of ear candy. It may not be nutritious, but it sure is tasty!

This line from the second verse of Survivor's "The Search Is Over" (written by Jim Peterik and Frank Sullivan) is a good example of internal rhyme used within a single line of a lyric: "You followed me through changes and patiently you'd wait"/"Till I came *to* my senses *through* some miracle of fate."

Lyrical touches like this tend to be rather subliminal, but they have the effect of making a song sound professional and "finished."

In the song "Long Day" by Matchbox Twenty (written by Rob Thomas), the band uses the technique of internal rhyme that occurs not only within a single line but within successive lines: ". . . sitting by the overcoat . . . second *shelf*, the *note* she *wrote* . . . can't bring myself to throw away." The word *note* is an inner rhyme to the word *wrote* in the same line (which is an end rhyme to *overcoat* in the first line). *Shelf* is an internal rhyme to the word *myself* in the following line.

In John Mayer's song "No Such Thing" (co-written with Clay Cook), he adds internal rhyme in the very first line of the song: ". . . she said to *me* condescendingly." He uses the technique again a few lines later: ". . . the *dreams* of the prom *kings*."

Using Other Rhyming Techniques in Your Song

When writing a lyric, you can use various techniques to make your job a whole lot easier. Also note that it's not cheating to use inexact rhymes and play games like working backward from an end line and shifting pronunciations to make a rhyme work. Now look at a few of the methods that the pros use to complete a song.

Working with perfect rhymes

A "perfect rhyme" is when the syllables of two or more words contain the same vowel and final consonant sounds, but begin with different consonant sounds (such as *boat* and *coat* or *bullet* and *pull it*).

It doesn't matter how the word is spelled as long as the sound of the word is the same. For example, *fight* and *ignite* are exact rhymes even though they're spelled differently (*night* and *ignite* are not rhymes because the two sounds are identical even though they are spelled differently). Conversely, *love* and *prove* are not perfect rhymes because even though they are spelled the same (other than their opening sounds), they're not pronounced the same. Even the addition of an *s* at the end of a word technically prevents two words from being considered perfect rhymes. On the other hand *night* and *ignite* would not be considered rhymes because though the end of the word is identical, the preceding consonant needs to be different to be considered a rhyme.

Practically speaking, there is no compelling reason that I can see for insisting on perfect rhymes throughout an entire song. It's good work when you can get it, but don't sacrifice meaning and emotion for lack of a perfect rhyme.

— JIM PETERIK, SINGER AND SONGWRITER — SURVIVOR AND IDES OF MARCH

Sometimes there are nuances between words that put their status as perfect rhymes in question. In the David Pomeranz and David Zippel hit "Born for You" (sung by Cathy Lee), they rhyme *stars* with *ours*. Though there's a slightly different vowel sound between the words, they sound virtually identical when sung.

Some writing teams of the past, such as Richard Rodgers and Oscar Hammerstein II, always used exact rhymes in their lyrics, otherwise they wouldn't write it. Look up the lyrics to "My Favorite Things" from *The Sound of Music*, and check out the wonderful perfect rhyming schemes.

The argument for this perfection is the absolute neatness of all the phrases, similar to the way the military demands its beds be made or the way the woman down the road keeps a perfect lawn. It sure looks nice, but you can decide for yourself if it's mandatory.

Even if you are writing with a very successful songwriter in Nashville, don't let them insist on using perfect rhymes all the time. You might end up writing a few good songs, but you also might just sacrifice some great emotion on the altar of perfection if you do. Sometimes the *perfect word* for a line does not happen to be a *perfect rhyme*.

Getting it close with near rhymes

"Near rhymes" are words that are close enough in sound to be similar but not exactly the same. They are used extensively in all types of musical styles and seem to be getting more and more popular as rhymes are getting further and further apart. In "Take the Money and Run" (written and sung by Steve Miller), the line that you may remember most is his wonderful mangling of the English language when he rhymes *Texas* with *facts is*. This is a great example of the near rhyme taken to its extreme.

You'll find this kind of rhyme prevalent in hip-hop. Here's an example from Jay-Z in "Empire State of Mind," featuring Alicia Keys — this song stretches near rhyme almost to the extreme, but it works for Jay-Z:

> All of my *Dominicanos*
> Right there up on Broadway
> Brought me back to that *McDonald's*
> Took it to my stash spot

© EMI April Music Inc. "Empire State Of Mind" by Al Shuckburgh, Janet Sewell, Burt Keyes, Alicia Augello-Cook, Shawn Carter, Jane't Sewell, Sylvian Robinson, Angela Hunte

OFF THE RECORD

In "Can't Say It Loud Enough," Johnny Van Zant, Robert White Johnson, and Jim were stuck for a rhyme for the word *window*. Here's how they got around it:

> I see the eyes of a child barely five
> In a photo right next to my *window*
> I see the shadow of a man at my side
> Feel his spirit each time the *wind blows*

Notice the inner rhyme of *eyes* and *five* in the first line.

WORDS OF WISDOM

No matter how good a line or a thought is, if it doesn't please the ear in the context of the music, it's not gonna do what it's supposed to do, which is to make the listener enjoy the song. Poetry has to read well — lyrics have to sing well. Music is based in time and meter. A good lyric blends with melody; it doesn't fight it. It should be as ear-pleasing and interesting as possible. I use sound-alike words as much as possible. Bouquet/day, problem/solve 'em, God/job; these were all in hit songs I've written. A good exercise is simply practicing rhyming words that don't easily rhyme; the ultimate being "orange." There is no perfect rhyme in the English language for "orange," but there are plenty in songwriter-ese: i.e., "storm," "born," "torn," etc.

— JOHN GREENEBAUM, NOTED NASHVILLE SONGWRITER — CO- WRITER OF "THIRD ROCK FROM THE SUN" BY JOE DIFFIE AND MANY MORE

Working backwards with rhyme

When working up a lyric, you often have one key line, perhaps the first, to build up from. It would then be a good idea to create a *dummy lyric* for the next three or four lines (or however long your verse might be). As noted in Chapter 1, a dummy lyric is not intended to stay as a permanent fixture of the song; it exists mainly to block out the mechanics of the verse, marking parameters such as the amount of syllables per line and possible rhyme schemes.

TIP

Being a big fan of the dummy lyric (Hey — how about a book called *Dummy Lyrics For Dummies!*), when Jim writes with someone else, he'll say, "Let's just come up with a dummy lyric for now to help us remember the melody." It's a great way to beat the writer's block that comes from thinking that everything you write down has to be brilliant. Almost invariably what happens next is that you'll come up with at least one or two lines that are pretty darn cool in the climate of lowered expectations.

In creating your mock-up section (this technique works equally well for all sections of the song), you may hit upon a last line that is actually a keeper. Your next step may be to work back from that line to find appropriate rhymes for the rest of the verse.

WORDS OF WISDOM

When I was writing the lyric to "Can't Say It Loud Enough" for the Van Zant album with Robert White Johnson and Jim Peterik, all we had was a great second line, "My daddy said that the truth is the truth and there just ain't no space in between it." We worked backward all day long to find the right line and the right rhyme for the first line. We finally came up with, "Some people think that a lie ain't a lie if you find enough fools to believe it." Working backward on a lyric, you can sometimes come up with some great stuff you never would've otherwise.

— JOHNNY VAN ZANT, LEAD SINGER OF LYNYRD SKYNYRD
AND MEMBER OF VAN ZANT

Changing pronunciations to help rhyme

Sometimes, merely how a singer pronounces a word will dictate if a word will rhyme. *Thinking* is a perfect rhyme for *drinking*. If you're writing a country tune, however, you could easily rhyme *spankin'* with *drankin'*, which is country past-tense for *drinkin'*.

WARNING

You can stretch the language only so far in search of a rhyme. When rhyming *pain*, it would be out of fashion to pronounce *again*, so as to rhyme exactly.

Rhyming across verses

Take a look at this old standard, "In the Chapel in the Moonlight" (written and sung by Billy Hill), to see how the rhymes match up across the verses.

Verse 1

How I'd love to hear the organ
In the chapel in the moonlight
While we're strolling down the aisle
Where roses ent*wine*

Verse 2

How I'd love to hear you whisper
In the chapel in the moonlight
That the *lovelight* in your eyes
Forever will *shine*

Bridge

Till the roses turn to ashes
Till the organ turns to rust
If you never come, I'll still be there
Till the *moonlight* turns to *dust*

Verse 3

How I'd love to hear the choir
In the chapel in the moonlight
As they sing "Oh Promise Me"
Forever be mine

Words and music by Billy Hill, 1936 Shapiro, Bernstein & Co., Inc. New York Copyright Renewed/International Copyright Secured/All rights reserved/Used by permission

Notice the use of *lovelight* and *moonlight*, and the technique where the same word or words are repeated at the beginning of succeeding verses or lines: *How I'd love to hear . . .* (1) *the organ,* (2) *you whisper,* (3) *the choir . . . in the chapel in the moonlight.* A picture is painted here: moonlight, the choir, the silence. Then the bridge provides the counterbalance: *rust* and *dust.* There is no rhyme scheme in the verses, the whole thing is tied together by the repeated lines and the cross-verse end rhymes: entwine, shine, and mine. What a well-crafted gem this song is — no wonder it reached the #5 position and spent one third of the year on the charts in 1954.

To Rhyme or Not to Rhyme?

That is the question — you must decide! Since the '60s, the use of rhyme in popular, rock, country, and R&B songs has changed greatly, with less and less of an emphasis on rhyme in many cases. Near rhyme is used more as an embellishment nowadays — the same trend **that** poetry took at the beginning of the twentieth century when free verse came alive.

Looking at songs with little rhyme

It's interesting to note that there's only one rhyme in the Paul Simon-penned song "Bridge Over Troubled Water," again proving the point that there are a lot of choices when it comes to using rhyme. Take a look at the following song, "Wild-Eyed Southern Boys" (written by Jim Peterik and performed by .38 Special), as another example of this — we've noted the few words that actually do rhyme:

Verse 1

It's a hot night at the juke joint
And the bands pumpin rhythm and *blues*
Gonna spill a little rock and roll blood tonight
Gonna make some front page *news*

Pre-chorus

And the ladies hate the violence
Still they never seem to look away
Cause they love those

Chorus

Wild-eyed southern boys
Wild-eyed boys
Wild-eyed southern boys

Verse 2

It's a southern point of honor
You got a get right in on the *act*
You can hear the outlaws holler
Fightin' for the lady in *black*

Pre-chorus

And she's just one in a million
But she's all I need tonight
Cause she loves those

Chorus

Wild-eyed southern boys
Wild-eyed boys
Wild-eyed southern boys

Another song with very little rhyme scheme going on in the lyric is "Happy Endings" by Jason Mraz. There are a few rhymes in there, but it's a hard look to find them — *feet*, *weak*, . . . and *anyway*, *grey*, which is a little more on point — proving that overall, the absence of rhyme is not a show-stopper to writing a great song:

> You are naked
> Standing at the other end of this
> Poison arrow
> I am William tell
> And you are the girl with the golden apple
> And you are hungry to be swept off your *feet*
> You wanna do this out in the open
> But my aim is often *weak*
> And you fear my shoulders sloping
> Your split ends will end up falling *anyway*
> Before the weight of the apple world
> Gets to turn them all *grey*
> And your eyes they need
> Calming down
>
> © *Goo Eyed Music ASCAP*

Check out some of these other hit songs with very little to offer in the rhyming department:

>> "Let's Make Love," written by Chris Lindsey, Marv Green, Bill Luther, and Almec Mayo; sung by Faith Hill and Tim McGraw

>> "Shape of My Heart," written by Max Martin, Rami Yacoub, and Lisa Miskovsky; performed by The Backstreet Boys

>> "White Flag," written by Dido Armstrong, Rollo Armstrong, and Rick Nowels; performed by Dido

>> "You Don't Have to Cry," written by Stephen Stills and Gold Hill; performed by Crosby, Stills, and Nash

Bringing it all together

Songwriting has a bunch of rules that can be broken at will — and you never need to feel a bit of guilt about it — but remember what Shakespeare said: "To thine own song be true" (Shakespeare did say that, didn't he?). Here's an example of a lyric that illustrates almost every part of this chapter on rhymes.

Analyze "Roses for No Reason" by Jim Peterik and Lisa McClowry to see how rhymes can work for you, too.

Verse 1

Lying on my bed, overtired, uninspired
Paging through a book of far off islands
Wondering who I am
Where I belong
I search for songs
To soothe my soul
And help me find the inner silence

Pre-chorus

Then just when I'm about to give up hope
When nothing in this world
Can help me cope

Chorus

He brings me roses for no reason
Orchids out of season
Love right to my door
And he sends me
Where no one dares to travel
I'm taken by the man who comes to call — with roses for no reason at all

Verse 2

I wonder if he knows
To what degree he means to me
Sometimes I'm overtaken
By emotion
And what I thought was love
Is so much more — I know for sure
Never has there been a sweeter potion

Pre-chorus

I'm just about to call this night a day
When I hear the knock
That takes my breath away

Chorus

He brings me roses for no reason
Orchids out of season
Love right to my door

And he takes me where no one dares to travel
I've finally found the softest place
To fall — and roses for no reason at all

Bridge

A gift without occasion
The taste of sweet persuasion
A celebration of just being alive
A love without condition
My whispered premonition
These roses could be just the start
Of sharing secrets heart to heart
Of special moments just like these
Until the end of time.

Practice Makes Perfect

For this exercise, try looking at the rhyme schemes of ten of your favorite songs by writing out the lyrics line by line and determining what method was chosen. You'll start to see the various patterns of the rhyme schemes and the tricks writers use to make a lyric sound good while they're telling a story. Now go to a song you're currently writing and see how you might improve upon it by using more exact rhymes, rhyming variations, inner rhyme, and dissimilar-sounding vowel sounds. Look at how your rhyming words draw attention or add emphasis to enhance the final piece.

Next, again choose one of your favorite songs and make a note of all the rhyming devices you find: internal rhyme (both within lines and between lines), perfect rhymes and imperfect rhymes, and also the instances where a singer's pronunciation affects its RQ (rhyming quotient). Is it believable, conversational, or is it just plain sappy? Then take a look at your own finished or work-in-progress songs to see the workings of what you probably accomplished on pure instinct. Now figure out how the lyric could be made more "ear-pleasing" by the addition of some inner rhymes or some closer rhyming.

Pay attention to the effective rhyming methods that are used to hold the listener's attention and how good rhyming techniques make the lyrics seem so easy to remember. Also keep track of which songs were able to make the rhymes sound effortless, and use those to model your own efforts at perfecting the art of rhyme.

3
Creating Memorable Music

Although you probably don't analyze a song when you're on the dance floor or cruising in your car, the elements that create the music are what makes the song powerful and are important to understand when you're doing your own songwriting. In this part, we show you those musical elements that combust spontaneously to create magic. We take a look at how the synergy of rhythm, melody, and chords combine to help your song take flight, and show you how new shortcut technologies can help you write songs quicker, better, and easier than ever before.

Chapter **8**

Feel the Rhythm, Feel the Ride

Have you ever noticed how, in certain songs, the words seem to dance across the music like they have "happy feet"? Or you are driving down the highway and your "peddle hits the metal" as the song you're listening to hits the chorus? It's practically a given that some of the biggest songs in pop history came right out of the box with a grabber-word rhythm. Think of "Hot town, summer in the city, back of my neck gettin' dirty and gritty" ("Summer in the City," written by John Sebastian, Steve Boone, and Mark Sebastian; performed by The Lovin' Spoonful) or "Sir or madame won't you read my book, it took me years to write, won't you take a look" ("Paperback Writer," written by John Lennon and Paul McCartney; performed by The Beatles).

In addition to the lyrical pulse, there is the musical rhythm of a song. In ancient times, messages were sent to distant villages using simple drum patterns to signal the news (the use of "talking drums"). Even today, to get the message of your song across, you may need the persistent pulse of rhythm (drums, loops, and percussion effects) to communicate the intensity more effectively. From the off-beat style of reggae music to the intricate rhythmic interplay of African music, you can add flavor and interest to your song by interweaving divergent rhythm patterns (also known as *grooves*) into your song.

In this chapter, we look at how rhythm becomes the heartbeat — the cadence of the words, the meter of musical phrasing, and the underlying groove of the drums — that impacts your song. We show you some very basic examples on which you can expand as you write your song.

Looking at the Rhythm of Words

When you listen to people talk, you'll notice a natural rise and fall in their voices as they express themselves in words. If not for this variety of speech, we'd all speak in monotone, and much of the nuance and expressiveness of language would be lost. The same is true in song. The *rhythm* of the words is the lilt or groove that the words possess even without the music. It's the beat you're left with if you were to substitute all your words for nonsense syllables like "ba ba, da da, do." The dynamics of a lyric can convey even more than the spoken word because lyrics have the added bonus of music underneath them to add even more interest. Such a deal!

Accented and unaccented syllables

When the voice rises in a phrase it's called an *accented* or *stressed* syllable. When the inflection of the voice lowers, it's called an *unaccented* or *unstressed* syllable. Take a look at some of the following lines of a lyric and notice the natural rise and fall in the patterns of speech. (The accented syllables are in capital letters.)

MAry HAD a LITTle LAMB

When you say that line, you can hear your voice rising on the accents (natural to the English language). The line has seven syllables and four accents.

To match this line *accentually* (counting the number of accents) and *syllabically* (counting the number of syllables), you'd create a second line following the same template:

Its FLEECE was WHITE as SNOW

This famous example then goes on:

And EVEryWHERE that MAry WENT

The LAMB was SURE to GO

Just how Mary obtained the lamb and why the lamb in question was so eager to follow her has been the subject of heated debate throughout the years and is frankly outside of our field of investigation.

Lines one and three now match each other and lines two and four match each other. You may have noticed, however, that line one has seven syllables, but there are eight syllables in line three. How do these lines match if they don't have the same number of syllables? They match because the first line is missing the first unaccented syllable shown in the third line, starting out with the accented MA syllable instead. Unaccented syllables at the beginning of lines can be dropped without affecting the meter of that line.

The pattern of a set of four lines with the four accents in the first and third lines and three accents in the second and fourth lines is called *common measure*. This particular pattern is often found in hymns. Now notice the common measure in the timeless hymn by John Newton, "Amazing Grace":

aMAzing GRACE, how SWEET the SOUND

That SAVED a WRETCH like ME

i ONCE was LOST, but NOW i'm FOUND

Was BLIND but NOW i SEE.

Now take a look at the cadence of the lyric of "Alcohol" (written by Stephen Page and Stephen Duffy; performed by Barenaked Ladies). Notice the stressed and unstressed syllables.

ALcoHOL, my PERmaNENT acCESsory

ALcoHOL, a PARty-TIME neCESsity

ALcoHOL, alTERnaTIVE to FEELing like yourSELF

o ALcoHOL, i STILL DRINK TO YOUR HEALTH

Notice how, even without the music, you start feeling a little tipsy due to the ups and downs of the accented and unaccented syllables.

Before you write lyrics to your song, try mapping out the rhythm by creating a dummy lyric (see Chapter 1 for a detailed explanation) or blocking out the lines with nonsense syllables like "da dum, da dum, da dum" or "dum da dum dum, dum dum da dum dum," or whatever sounds good against the beat. For practice, find a lyric or poem by someone else and reduce it to its "dum da dum" pattern to expose the rhythm's raw structure. Or, you can use the "scrambled eggs" method (the use of words that may be real words or just sounds to simulate the words) — just like Paul McCartney did when he used the temporary phrase, "scrambled eggs" in place of what later became one of his signature classics "Yesterday" — good move on Paul's part.

When people think of rhythm in a pop song, they generally think of the beat — the dependable pulse you dance to. But that's only part of the story. Rhythm can also be used to make the melody more interesting or bring greater emphasis to aspects of the lyric. For instance, when in West Side Story, Anita sings, "I like to be in America . . ." the composer, Stephen Sondheim, uses rhythm to punch up and highlight the word "A-me-ri-ca" from the rest of the thought. Looking at the subject of creative rhythm, we're really dealing with a combination of predictability and unpredictability and the artful mix of the two. I love a song that takes you for a predictable stroll down the street and all of a sudden takes a left turn — only to return to the familiar path again. Burt Bacharach, of course, is the master of this and, to me, this is why he and Sondheim are among the finest pop composers of our time. His use of rhythm is singularly unique. In "The moment I wake up, before I put on my make-up . . ." from "I Say a Little Prayer For You," he sets up Hal David's wonderful lyric with a predictable 4/4 pattern and on the words "on my," he throws in a 2/4 bar! Completely unpredictable, but it works to excite because of Bacharach's setting the first lines up straight and returning back to 4/4 time. Essentially, rhythm not only makes a song groove, but at its creative best, can also make it an adventure.

— DAVID POMERANZ, MULTI-PLATINUM RECORDING ARTIST AND WRITER
OF SUCH HITS AS "TRYING TO GET THE FEELING AGAIN"
AND "IT'S IN EVERY ONE OF US"

Notice the rise and fall of speech patterns in the #1 hit classic by Night Ranger, "Sister Christian," written by drummer/vocalist Kelly Keagy:

SISter CHRIStian, oh the TIME has COME

And you KNOW that you're the ONly ONE to SAY

oKAY.

WHERE you GOin' what you LOOKin' FOR

You KNOW those BOYS don't wanna PLAY NO MORE with YOU Its TRUE

WORDS OF WISDOM

I must have performed "Sister Christian" thousands of times throughout my career, but it always feels like the first time for me. I enjoy singing it partly because it's written from personal experience and partly because of the conversational tone of the verses. The inflections of the words are just like talking to the audience.

— KELLY KEAGY, FOUNDING MEMBER, DRUMMER, AND VOCALIST
OF ROCK BAND, NIGHT RANGER

Songs can also get their power from a succession of long, equally stressed words where every word carries an equal emphasis.

OFF THE RECORD

Many of the songs I write vary lyrical rhythm patterns from section to section. This is another way to create dynamics in a song. However, I like to try to keep corresponding sections as identical as possible in terms of the stressed and unstressed words and the length of syllables.

— JIM PETERIK, PERFORMER, SONGWRITER, AND MULTI-INSTRUMENTALIST
FOR BOTH IDES OF MARCH AND SURVIVOR, PLUS WRITER OF HITS
FOR .38 SPECIAL, SAMMY HAGAR, AND OTHERS

Syllable length

Another parameter that affects the rhythm of the words besides accented and unaccented syllables is the length of the syllables themselves. Short, fast words and syllables followed by long, slow words and syllables create interest by adding dynamics to a line and giving the ear some variation.

In the lines "We really NEED TO see this through" and "We never WANTED to be abused" from Blink 182's "Anthem Part II," we can see good examples of syllable length variations.

Notice the quick *pickup notes* (the unaccented notes that occur before beat one, the downbeat, of the musical bar — these terms will be explained later in this chapter) of "We really" contrasted with the long phrase "need to" (four beats to each word), then the mid-tempo "see this through" (one beat to each word). The next line follows the identical form with the quick "We'll never," the long "wanted," and the mid-tempo "be abused."

Looking at the classic Motown hit, "My Girl" (written by Smokey Robinson and Ronald White; performed by the Temptations), you can see the effective use of long and short syllables. When you know the devices of word meter, you suddenly start noticing elements that you previously took for granted.

> I've got SUNSHINE on a cloudy day
>
> When it's COLD OUTSIDE
>
> I'VE got the month of May
>
> **Pre-chorus**
>
> I GUESS YOU SAY
>
> WHAT can MAKE me FEEL this WAY
>
> MY Girl, talkin' 'bout MY GIRL
>
> *Words and music by William "Smokey" Robinson and Ronald White © 1964, 1972, 1973 (Renewed 1992, 2000, 2001), 1977 Jobete Music Co., Inc./All rights controlled and administered by EMI April Music Inc./All rights reserved/International Copyright Secured/Used by Permission*

Notice how the word *sunshine* is stretched to match the vibrant feeling of the word. Also note how the pre-chorus section uses evenly stressed syllables (known as *spondaic rhythm*) to create a relaxed, peaceful feeling ("I guess you say"). When the song hits the hook, the rhythm of the words changes to the quick, punchy quarter notes of "My Girl" (and those wonderful background vocal echoes of "My Girl, My Girl") to drive the title home.

Looking at the Meter of Music

As important as the rhythm of the words is, it wouldn't mean much without the backdrop of the meter of the music. The *meter* of music is based on "beats" — the basic pulse of a piece of music. A *beat* is a recurring, regular pulse that defines the song's *tempo* (the speed or beats per minute at which the pulse or groove is played). Beats are arranged into sections called *measures* or *bars* — with a particular number of beats in each bar.

Even the silences between notes help create the pulse of what we hear. When combining music with words, rhythm is a vital unifying element. When creating melody and harmonies, the force of rhythm helps shape what we come up with. Applying musical meter to lyrical rhythm is one of the most important facets of songwriting.

THE NOTES

Musical meter is written using a system of notes of different length values:

- **A whole note** has a length of four beats. It occupies a full bar in common time.

- **A half note** has a length of two beats. Only two of these can appear in a bar of common time.

- **A quarter note** has a length of one beat. Only four of these can appear in a bar of common time.

- **An eighth note** has a length of one-half beat. Only eight of these can appear in a bar of common time.

- **A sixteenth note** has a length of one-quarter beat. Only sixteen of these can appear in a bar of common time.

There are also dotted notes. When a dot is placed after a note, the value of that note is increased by 50 percent. A dotted half note therefore equals three beats instead of the two beats of a normal half note.

If no sound is to be made, then a *rest* is used instead of a note. Rests are the funny-looking symbols that we have shown in the figure. There is one that coincides with each of the notes (a whole rest, a half rest, a quarter rest, and so on). Also, rests can be dotted just like notes to increase their value by half. A rest in a piece of music simply indicates that no sound is made for the duration of the rest.

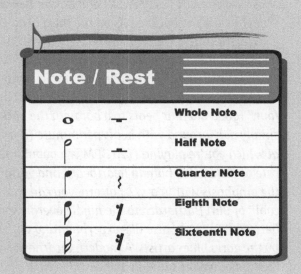

Placing beats in a bar

The pattern of four beats to a bar and eight bars in a section is the most commonly used of all beat structures. Four beats to a bar is called *common time* (or 4/4). In these four-beat bars, the first and third beats are the strongest and usually receive an accented word from the lyrics (we call these *on beats*). The second and fourth beats are weak, usually receiving an unaccented word (we refer to these as *off beats*). When a song is "in four" (or 4/4), it means there are four beats in each bar and each quarter note receives one beat. If a song is "in two" (also called *cut time* or 2/4), there are two beats to a bar with a quarter note getting one beat. A song "in three" (also called *waltz tempo* or 3/4) has three beats to each bar with a quarter note receiving one beat.

In each bar of music, you'll find notes of different value — a whole note in a bar of 4/4 will last for four beats (the whole bar), a half note for two beats (one half of a bar), and a quarter note for one beat (one quarter of a bar). A quarter note can be subdivided further into two eighth notes (the notes coming twice as fast as a quarter note), four sixteenth notes (twice as fast as an eighth note), and eight thirty-second notes (you guessed it — played twice as fast as sixteenth notes). It's this variation of note values that gives a melody its rhythmic movement.

WORDS OF WISDOM

Sometimes before I write a song, I'll pick a rhythm template to work off of. Perhaps I'm in a mellow mood and choose a waltz tempo — this is the signature of three-quarter time where there are three beats to every bar with the backbeat landing on the second beat — or a variation like in the song "Go Now" (written by Larry Banks and Milton Bennett; performed by The Moody Blues) where the backbeat is on the third beat. Or maybe I'll try noodling over a six/eight time signature where there are six beats to each bar with the backbeat landing on either the second or fourth beat — like on "Take It to the Limit" (written by Glenn Frey, Don Henley, and Randy Meisner; performed by The Eagles). Or, if I want to rock or write a big pop ballad, I'll usually stay "in four" (good old four beats to a bar with the backbeat falling on two) and simply play around with beats per minute (BPMs), which indicates the tempo at which you're playing (120 BPM is a popular tempo reflecting the average rate of the excited human heartbeat), and various rhythm patterns. By varying the emphasis within a 4/4 pattern, you can change the feel from the "samba cool" of Burt Bacharach to the jungle overdrive of Bo Diddly and all points in between! In four, I also like experimenting with the "shuffle" feel pioneered by the early blues artists. A modern incarnation of this feel would be "Everybody Wants to Rule the World" (written and performed by Chris Hughes, Roland Orzabal, and Ian Stanley; performed by Tears for Fears) and

"Revolution" (written by John Lennon and Paul McCartney; performed by The Beatles). Sometimes the beat will give you just the needed direction for you to create a new song.

— JIM PETERIK, WRITER OF 18 BILLBOARD TOP 10 HITS

Applying notes to common time

Now we take a look at how notes and rests can be used to rhythmically notate music — with seven bars of common (4/4) time shown in Figure 8-1.

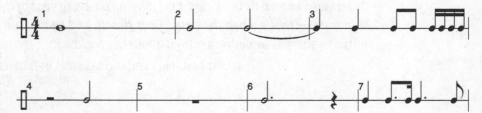

FIGURE 8-1:
This example shows how notes and rests can be used in 4/4 time.

The example in Figure 8-1 starts out with the "time signature" of 4/4, meaning that there are four beats in each bar, and a quarter note is equivalent to a beat. In the first bar of Figure 8-1, there is only one note: a whole note, which lasts four beats — the whole bar. In the second bar there are two half notes, each lasting two beats. But the second note has a *tie* to the first quarter note in bar three. When notes are tied together, that means that they have been joined to a single note: in this case, a note that lasts three beats.

In bar three, there are two quarter notes (the first tied to the half note in the bar before), followed by two eighth notes, and those in turn are followed by four sixteenth notes. The quarter notes each have a value of a beat, the eighth notes a half beat each, and the four sixteenth notes occupy a full beat for themselves, the fourth beat of the measure.

In bar four, the first rest is presented, a half-note rest, and in bar five, a full-note rest (also commonly referred to as a "whole rest") is presented, which makes the entire measure soundless. Bar six introduces the dotted note. Remember, a dot following a note increases its value by one half. In this case, the dotted half note equals three beats. It's followed by a quarter-note rest, which yields one beat of silence. The seventh bar shows how dots can be applied to quarter and eight notes, and *dots* all there is to it!

Especially in rock music, there is a heavy emphasis on the backbeat (in a 4/4 time signature the backbeats land on the second and fourth beats) — in fact such a premium is placed on the sound of this backbeat that producers have been known to spend an entire week just creating the ultimate snare drum sound. In a song like "She Drives Me Crazy" by Fine Young Cannibals, most listeners can identify the song just by hearing the unique sound of the snare drum (the snare drum is the one in the middle of the drum kit that relies on the thin wire strands on the bottom of the drum for its buzzy and percussive sound). To highlight the significance of the backbeat in rock, just listen to the song "Human" by The Killers. The first chorus is set up with merely the bass drum (also known as the kick drum) playing on every beat of the 4/4 time signature — that's when the dance floor fills up and people start writing to the music — there is something primal about the backbeat.

— KHARI PARKER, CHICAGO SESSION DRUMMER AND TOURING
DRUMMER WITH BOZ SKAGGS

Putting Rhythm and Meter to Use in Your Songs

We've shown how lyrics have accents and syllables. Now take a look at how lyrics are applied to the meter of a song. For this we'll turn again to the familiar "Mary Had a Little Lamb" nursery rhyme, and adopt it to 3/4 time. (We could've chosen 4/4, or even 5/4 — 4/4 will work, but the 5/4 rhythm will feel awkward). Figure 8-2 shows how we set the lyrics to the rhythm.

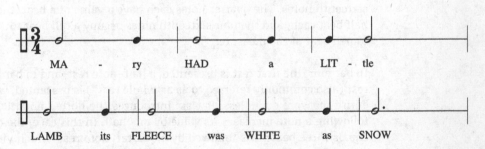

FIGURE 8-2:
In this example of "Mary Had a Little Lamb," we apply the words to three-quarter time.

"Mary Had a Little Lamb" has the honor of being the first words ever recorded on a phonograph! In 1877, Thomas Edison spoke these famous words into the first recording machine ever made in his laboratory in Menlo Park, New Jersey.

The observant reader will notice that the strong accents of the lyric (capitalized) have been placed on the strong (first) beat of each bar. Matching accents with strong beats, as we have pointed out, is what marries the meter of lyrics with the meter of music. It's the natural way that the two come together, although variations and exceptions will always be found — this is not a hard and fast rule, just a basic guideline.

Now take a look at Figure 8-3 to see how one of the great songwriting/lyricist teams dealt with setting lyrics to meter using the opening of "All the Things You Are" by Jerome Kern and Oscar Hammerstein II.

FIGURE 8-3:
This is how Kern and Hammerstein applied lyrics to meter at the beginning of the song "All the Things You Are."

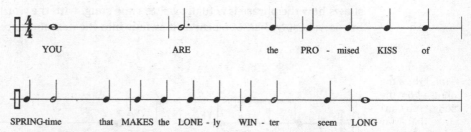

First of all, notice how all the strong syllables fall on strong beats (1 and 3). The opening words *you* and *are* are both strong and the songwriters wisely placed them both on the first beat of a bar (called the *downbeat*), giving them both a strong emphasis. *You*, the first word in the song, has a nice vowel sound (*ou*), therefore creating a nice effect when extended for a whole measure (which wouldn't have happened if the first word in the song was *zeke*).

Songwriting with Syncopation

Syncopation is the shifting of a note from a strong beat to a weak beat — in other words, this term describes a deviation or interruption of the regular flow of your song's rhythm. For some reason, the subject of syncopation is often overlooked in songwriting books, but it's important to understand when writing today's songs.

Syncopation entered the mainstream with swing music in the '30s. Arrangements were created where some of the notes of the song were shifted slightly to anticipate the *downbeat*, or to come just after it (listen to the string section hook in the song "1000 Miles," written and sung by Vanessa Carlton, to hear a modern day example of syncopation). We'll take a look at how this works using an excerpt from George and Ira Gershwin's "You Can't Take That Away From Me" with normal *straight* rhythm as shown in Figure 8-4.

FIGURE 8-4:
In this phrase from the song, "They Can't Take That Away From Me," you see that the accented word "hat" falls on the downbeat.

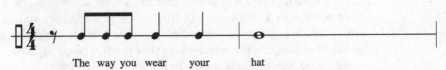

The way you wear your hat

Notice in Figure 8-4 that the word *hat* falls on the downbeat. If the Gershwin brothers had written it like this, with a strong syllable *hat* landing on the strong beat, it might have sounded too formal and a bit stiff for the song. Figure 8-5 shows how the phrase is actually written and sung, with the word *hat* anticipating the downbeat by half of a beat as it swings into the next measure.

FIGURE 8-5:
This is how the phrase from the song, "You Can't Take That Away From Me," shown in Figure 8-4, is actually sung, with a syncopated downbeat.

The way you wear your hat

The word *hat* now appears a half-beat in anticipation of the downbeat. This syncopation helps give the melody a swing feeling. In fact, it's this trick of syncopation that gave swing music its swing, and hence its name.

The next example shows how John Lennon and Paul McCartney similarly used syncopation in the song "I'll Be Back" (see Figure 8-6).

FIGURE 8-6:
This is how John Lennon and Paul McCartney used syncopated downbeats in the song, "I'll Be Back."

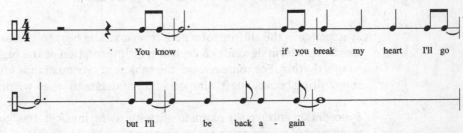

You know if you break my heart I'll go

but I'll be back a - gain

Syncopation is a standard feature in pop, R&B, jazz, country, and rock music, and it's a major part of many songs not just as downbeat anticipation, but as a continual singing of words on the off-beat. Take a look at an excerpt from "Genie in a Bottle" written by Pamela Sheyne, David Frank, and Steve Kipner and sung by Christina Aguilera (see Figure 8-7).

FIGURE 8-7:
In this example of syncopation, from the song "Genie in a Bottle," every beat is syncopated.

I feel like I've been locked up tight for a cen - tu - ry of lone - ly nights

TIP

Words and music working synergistically to create interesting rhythms is one of the hallmarks of a good song. Try syncopations in your lyrics so they cut across the beat as opposed to landing right on the beat. Consider if each word of the opening line from "Dance Hall Days," written by Chris Hues and Ross Cullum and performed by Wang Chung, "Take your baby by the hand," had landed squarely on the beat — sounds pretty boring, doesn't it?

Some genres, especially country and pop country, tend to insist on consistent word rhythm between corresponding sections of a song from their writers. For instance, if a verse has a certain number of syllables and accents per line, it should be exactly the same when the second verse comes around. Traditional Broadway songwriting is just as sticky about this rule as they are about exact rhymes. The theory is that this consistency makes a song more natural for the singer and easier to remember for the audience. This general rule isn't nearly as strictly enforced in other genres such as soul and rock. In fact, rap music thrives on the constant shifting in the accents of the syllables. Again, referring to the example of "My Girl" by The Temptations, the first line of the first verse — "I got sunshine on a cloudy day" — is replaced by a whole different word rhythm in line one of the second verse — "I got so much honey, the bees envy me" — even though the musical chords and rhythm remain identical. This technique provides fresh interest for the second verse — I can't even imagine it any other way!

Practice Makes Perfect

"Feel the rhythm. Feel the ride. Get on up. It's bobsled time." Do you remember this great chant from the popular movie about a Jamaican Olympic bobsled team entitled *Cool Runnings*? It's what those unlikely athletes chanted to get them into the rhythm and working together in harmony and with the same beat.

Isn't it amazing how rhythm is such a big part of our everyday lives? That's why it plays such a big role in the heartbeat of the song. How many times have you heard an athlete who's just accomplished major success say, "I just got in my rhythm," or how many times have you yourself said, "I'm really in a groove" when everything was going just right for you?

When I played professional tennis, sometimes my heart would be racing seemingly out of control. To counteract this, between points I'd take a deep breath and create, in my mind, a slow steady beat that would keep me from rushing and losing my rhythm. Today, when I work with singers in the studio, I'll have them take a couple of passes at the song, then typically we'll have a talk and I'll ask them to take some deep breaths, relax, and just feel the rhythm of the music. The more the singer gets connected with the rhythm, the greater the chance for pure magic to take place.

— DAVE AUSTIN, MENTAL PERFORMANCE COACH, FORMER WORLD-RANKED TENNIS PROFESSIONAL AND RECORD INDUSTRY EXECUTIVE

Now it's your turn as the songwriter to let yourself go, get into the groove, and let the rhythm in you come rising up to the surface. Lay down a basic beat on your digital recording device using your "mouth percussion" (simply doing the beat with your lips, like "paa, pa pa paa, pa paa, pa pa" — mimicking the sounds of a drum kit). Now sing a dummy lyric over the beat letting it dictate the rhythm of the lyrics. When you come up with something compelling that inspires you to write more, go back to all those great phrases you've previously written down and cataloged. Pick an idea that fits the rhythm of the song, and start replacing those dummy lyrics with great ones that tell your story. Even though we might not have been able to shed any light as to why the little lamb followed Mary home, we hope the rhythm has gotten a hold of you.

Chapter **9**

Making Melody Magic

You've plunked down your hard-earned money to buy this book, and chances are you have some songs stirring in your soul already and a melody or two percolating in your brain. At this point, maybe you just want to know a little more about how to encourage and capture these "notes in conversation" and how to organize them into a song.

But what exactly is a melody? According to *Webster's,* a melody is "an agreeable succession of sounds, a sequence of single tones." (Fine, now if only you could look up "platinum smash hit" and get a definition for that, too!) The melody is the ultimate "ear candy" of a song. It's the series of notes that transports the lyrics along, or, in a musical piece without words, it's the "tune" that the main instrument plays. Where do melodies come from? Perhaps they are just out there, waiting to be harvested. Perhaps a melody comes "from nowhere" into your head. Perhaps you are the type to experiment on a musical instrument until a series of notes sounds good to you. Maybe writing various successions of notes on music (or staff) paper and playing them back is what works for you.

However you create a melody, the proof is in the beauty of the result. One of the measures of a great melody is its *hum-ability* (can the listener remember it after he hears it, and how long does it stick with him?). Another is durability. Try to come up with melodies that wear well. The melodies that last, the ones people never tire of, are usually simple, but they have something unique about them that keeps folks coming back for more.

Exploring the Basics of Melodies in Music

How do you create a great melody? Writers have been trying to pinpoint a way for years. Just what is the "Melody of Love" that you've heard so much about, and how do you write one of your own? The process is part technical and part divine — inspiration and perspiration, if you will! The following sections show just how important the melody is and how to come up with a melody of your own.

WORDS OF WISDOM

Melody is the thread that ties a song together. If done poorly, every seam will be apparent and it will not hold together for long. When sewn together carefully, a song becomes a melodic whole with one section flowing seamlessly into the next.

— DAVID POMERANZ, WRITER FOR BARRY MANILOW ("TRYING TO GET THE FEELING AGAIN") PLUS MANY OTHERS

Knowing the power and emotion of a melody

If rhythm is the backbone of a song, chords the muscle and lyrics the heart, then surely melody is the soul. Melody is the element that transcends all else and is remembered before the words are fully comprehended and long after they are forgotten.

When listening to, for instance, Christina Aguilera's Latin album, released in 2000 and entitled *Mi Reflejo*, notice that she sings all her hits in Spanish. Whether you know that language or not, the power of the music comes through based on the rhythm and, most of all, the beauty of the melodies. You don't have to know what she's saying to feel the emotion.

Similarly, check out this song by Portland singer/songwriter, Geoff Byrd, who is best known for being the first artist to emerge into mainstream recognition via the Internet (more on Internet opportunities in Chapter 13). "When I Fall From Grace" is a song about guilt, self doubt, and poor choices made — but it's also about forgiveness, hence the line "but the sun still shines on my face." It's about being honest with an assessment of your own poor choices, yet still knowing there is hope going forward. The true brilliance of melody is when you are able to blend the mood of the lyric with the magic of the melody. In this particular example, you can literally feel the swing from being in the depths of despair with the darker vibe of the melody up to the positive feelings of when forgiveness is found. The key is blending the right melody with the emotion and feeling you want to get across in your song's message.

GIVING GOOSE BUMPS

There are many ways to gauge the impact your song is having on the world — how many weekly downloads you are getting, how many requests you are receiving for co-writes and interviews, and how many local bands are doing your song at the club (and we won't even go into the burgeoning Karaoke scene). But arguably the best indicator of the true soul-connection your song is having on other members of the human race is its ability to raise that involuntary response known as goose bumps. Almost always it seems to come at some point of the chorus when words and melody intersect like the confluence of rivers and create that moment of realization. Whether it has to do with galvanic skin response, heart rate, blood pressure, intervention from above, or simply too much caffeine, there are specific spots in certain songs that never fail to provide chicken skin. You can't write it into your song any more than you can tell the sun when to break through the clouds. It just happens when all conditions are right. As a songwriting "lifer," it's the highest honor to bring about this response in others. It means you have connected at a level deeper than words and higher than music. This intimacy between writer and listener is a songwriter's greatest responsibility and most sacred privilege.

WORDS OF WISDOM

When people ask me what my forte is in songwriting, I tell them I'm a melody man. Writing lyrics has been a craft I've worked hard on and have steadily improved at. The longer I live, the more stories I gather and the more grist I have for the lyric mill. Melodies just tend to enter my head from nowhere. However, the more you listen to and practice writing melodies, the luckier you get at spinning gold from thin air. Just as no one has to teach a bird to sing, it's much easier to write a melody than to tell someone how.

— JIM PETERIK, PERFORMER, SONGWRITER, AND MULTI-INSTRUMENTALIST FOR BOTH IDES OF MARCH AND SURVIVOR, PLUS WRITER OF HITS FOR .38 SPECIAL, SAMMY HAGAR, AND OTHERS

Understanding the basics of a melody

TIP

Analyze the melody of one of your all-time favorite songs. Get a hold of the sheet music, if it's available, and learn it on an instrument — a guitar or piano would be ideal because you could then track both the melody and the way it works against the chords. Notice the intervals between notes, how many are jammed into one measure, the *range* of the notes (the distance from the highest note to the lowest), and each note's relationship to the chord (in the key of A, the note A is the root or dominant note of the chord). If the chord is changed to D, the same A note is now the fifth of the chord (five notes above the dominant) and, therefore, takes on a whole different mood. Notice also how the melody shifts between musical sections and how the minor or major mode of the melody is used to emphasize the mood of the song.

As a songwriter, your goal is to develop:

» **A keen sense of melody:** The more you listen to and analyze great songs, and the more you nurture your own melodic sense through constant experimentation, the sharper it will become.

» **A method for creating a melody:** Whatever works for you is the best way. It could be *noodling* around on an instrument until a melodic pattern emerges, meditating in a quiet place and letting the melodies find you, or creating beautiful melodies in the midst of total chaos. Discover what the wellspring of melodic ideas is for you and visit it often.

» **A way to collect and remember melodies:** Whether you record your melodies on a pocket recorder (if you forget your recorder one day, try the quick fix of leaving the song idea on your cell phone's voice mail) or notate them in note or number form in a notebook or on staff paper, it is vital that you formulate a way to freeze in time your melodic tidbits.

» **An ability to incorporate melodies into a cohesive song:** The more you experiment and practice setting your melodies to music (finding just the right words that fit), the better songwriter you'll become. Don't be afraid to try a hundred different variations of your original chord pattern for your melody — you can always go back to your original if the others don't pan out. Try different lyrical approaches until the mood of the melody and lyric is a perfect match.

Just as with lyrics and chord patterns, the great songwriters have a unique melodic signature that signals who you're listening to before you even know for sure. The influence of melody masters such as Burt Bacharach, Paul McCartney, Elton John, Kenny Loggins, Todd Rundgren, Brian Wilson, and of course the classical geniuses like Mozart, Bach, and Chopin can be heard in many writers' melodies. Billy Joel seems to have taken melodic cues from Paul McCartney, whose melodies were influenced by the "rockin' fifties" and traditional Vaudeville and dance-hall classics. Modern alternative bands such as Coldplay and Snow Patrol seem to favor melody over any other element of the song. Whoever your influences might be, your goal is to assimilate them into a unique sound that is all your own.

Finding your melody

There's no right or wrong way of hitting upon a melody. Some people write their best melodies while doing something else — washing the car, shopping, driving, working in the yard, working out, hiking, or any activity that is *not* songwriting. It seems that in casual, unguarded moments like these, the unconscious mind is free to do some creative play on the side. Often it's when you're not really trying to write a melody that your mind becomes a clear channel and starts picking up some strong signals. This is when you need to be ready with your recording device (or staff paper if you know how to notate) to capture those often fleeting glimpses of inspiration.

WORDS OF WISDOM

Sometimes cool melodies enter my head when I'm not really trying to write one. It is often when I am doing something I enjoy, like driving — maybe that's because when we drive we have that wonderful feeling of being in control of our own destiny — eating, riding the Tube subway in London, exercising, or doing something nice for others. Certain seasons tend to bring out different melodies in me, different times of the day and different weather conditions. I also have my "rainy day" melodies, which are often bittersweet or reflective, and my "sunny day" melodies, which are more expansive and optimistic — to me the melody is the first step to a great song; it's in most cases the first thing you hear, and the last thing that you remember.

— KELLY KEAGY, WRITER OF NIGHT RANGER'S SMASH HIT "SISTER CHRISTIAN"

There are melodies all around; you just have to listen for them. Sometimes the vocal inflections of someone talking can suggest a melody. Other times, the sound of the ocean (remember "Sailing" written and sung by Christopher Cross) or the chaos of the city can spark a mood that inspires a melody (listen to "Summer in the City," written by John Sebastian, Steve Boone, and Mark Sebastian; performed by The Lovin' Spoonful). Other times, the simple sounds of nature can be the beginnings of a song. The late great Otis Redding and his co-writer Steve Cropper began writing "(Sittin' On) The Dock of the Bay" while doing just that!

OFF THE RECORD

The first time Jim wrote with Bill Chase — the virtuoso trumpet man whose cutting-edge, high-pitched wail helped define the sound of Woody Herman's Thundering Herd when he was a fledgling member — Bill told Jim an amusing story. One early Canadian morning while he was camping, he was awakened from his slumber by a particularly persistent bird chirping the same series of five notes over and over again. He shook himself out of a peaceful dream, grabbed some staff paper, dutifully notated the riff, and fell right back to sleep again. Of course, Jim loved the riff immediately once Bill played it for him — it became the signature horn riff and verse melody to "Run Back To Mama," perhaps the most requested song from Bill's Epic Records release, *Pure Music.* Even though Jim and Bill didn't donate a portion of their songwriting royalties to the National Audubon Society, they'd like to take this opportunity to thank that little bird and all of his fine feathered friends for inspiring our senses and routinely filling the skies with songs that brighten even an average spring day.

TIP

Many writers have the most luck coming up with melodies as they're experimenting at the piano or guitar, trying out the sound of different series of notes as chords are played. If you've come up with an intriguing chord progression, record it on your laptop, iPhone, or handheld recorder. Then play it back, experimenting with different melodies over the chords. Be sure to record the combination of music and melody on yet another recorder or on a separate track. After many repetitions, you will inevitably land on one melody that seems to work the best (which is usually the one you keep going back to in the first place).

Switching up instruments can be extremely helpful in finding new melodies. Try writing with just a bass guitar in hand or even a ukulele. Roger Cook presents his biggest hits such as "Long Cool Woman" and "You've Got Your Troubles" on a humble baritone uke when he plays writer's rounds in Nashville — and somehow it sounds like an orchestra. Also check out what's new on the technological side of things. Yamaha has a cool instrument called the Tenori that produces a huge variety of unique and musical sequences to inspire a whole different range of melodies.

OFF THE
RECORD

Lenny Kravitz presented Mick Jagger with a nearly complete track over which Mick added lyrics and melody. The song "God Gave Me Everything." became the first single from Kravitz's *Goddess in the Doorway* solo album.

Many successful songwriters have learned the concepts of good melody writing from some of the courses taught at the various music colleges around the world — where classes are often conducted by masters at the craft. You can also enroll in other various songwriting workshops and seminars to learn the art of melody writing and melody appreciation.

Making a Song More Memorable

Certain songwriters can make you feel a certain way, and the true masters always seem to have a very specific mood. Burt Bacharach can make you feel happy in a bittersweet way. Certain Paul Simon songs bring a sense of calm and introspection. Mick Jagger and Keith Richards are filled with the danger and recklessness of rock 'n' roll. Chris Martin of Coldplay brings a certain contemplative energy through his melodic gift.

Diane Birch recalls the simpler times of the '60s when the brilliance of the Brill Building sound became influential and their stable of writers (such as Carole King and Gerry Goffin, Burt Bacharach and Hal David, Neil Diamond, Ellie Greenwich, and Jeff Barry) were churning out hits. What's especially intriguing about melody is the intimacy the listener is experiencing with the artist by sharing the mood the artist was in when he or she wrote a particular song. Their brain chemistry at the time becomes *your* brain chemistry.

The next time that you hear and really feel "Goodbye Yellow Brick Road" by Elton John and Bernie Taupin, or "Try Sleeping with a Broken Heart" by Alicia Keys, Patrick Reynolds, and Jeff Bhasker, you are, in effect, tuning into the masters as they were creating. You are becoming one with the composers — feeling and experiencing the distilled essence of what they were feeling at the time of creation. The intimacy of that connection is really what gives power to a melody.

To get more specific on the art of writing a melody, we look at how melody can affect the mood or atmosphere of the song you're writing. We also give examples of how genre can determine the scope of your melody, and look at the different melodic requirements of the various sections of your song.

Finding a melody that fits the mood

Maybe you've been experimenting (creative noodling) at the piano for the last three hours and have come up with a sturdy set of chord changes that really sound cool. You've searched through your notebook and found a title or a lyric phrase that reflects the mood of the music. It's now time to experiment with melodies that best highlight the mood of the chord changes and the mood of the words:

>> **Use a major key.** If the chord changes are based around a major key, and the title and concept are upbeat and optimistic, you'll probably find yourself gravitating toward an uplifting melody to complement your chordal and lyrical choices.

>> **Use a minor key.** If your chord progression is in the minor mode, you'll probably choose a darker lyrical theme and experiment with blues-ier and more mournful melodies.

>> **Use a combination of major and minor.** One great technique in songwriting is the shifting back and forth between major and minor mode. Perhaps the verse is contemplative and sad — minor key mode. Then the chorus explodes

with optimism and change — a shift into major key mode — or vice versa. Sometimes a song can go from major to minor in just a matter of a measure. In the brilliant song "Ghetto" by India.Arie (written by India.Arie Simpson, Shannon Sanders, and Drew Ramsey), the chorus goes from minor mode to major for just one measure when it hits the lyric "Look around." This move creates a welcome oasis for the ear and makes you take notice of the directness of the lyric imploring us to take some responsibility for world poverty.

>> **Make the melody complex.** If your music bed is extremely simple, you may have the luxury of making your melody more complex, using fast flurries of notes — it's here that the rhythm of the words really shines.

>> **Make the melody simple.** If your music bed contains rapid and complex chord changes, it may dictate a more relaxed, simple, and sweeping melody to give it some needed contrast.

You may want to try experimenting with an optimistic set of chord changes with a dark and evocative melody that is emotionally at odds with the mood of the music. There are also many songs with a dark, minor key mood in the verse that benefit from the contrast of a shift to an optimistic, major key mood at the chorus (or the inverse — mournful minor chords in the chorus and a melody with an upbeat lyric). With this technique you can achieve a sense of irony.

**OFF THE
RECORD**

Jim and Brian Anders co-wrote the song "Empty," where they set up a dark reflective mood in the verse as the singer describes his sense of alienation from self and those around him ("Now the fields are bare, I feel I'm breathing without air"). The key is minor and the melody is narrow and low in range. As soon as the song hits the chorus, it suddenly shifts into the major key (from D minor to D major), and the melody starts to soar. This move supports the lyrical shift from the singer's desolation in the verse to his search for truth in the chorus. As he reaches for answers, his voice reaches for higher and higher notes.

Figure 9-1 shows the song "Empty" notated musically and lyrically to illustrate how the words, chords, and melody work together to create the drama of the song.

Finding a melody to fit the genre

In the same way that every genre has certain lyrical tendencies and arrangement styles, so too do they have different melodic leanings. In the following sections we take a look at the melody trends prevalent in a few of the most popular genres.

FIGURE 9-1:
The song "Empty."

Rock 'n' roll

Melodies sung over the blues-based chord changes of rock 'n' roll, are usually very simple and often *mono-tonal* (variations of only one or two notes). Charting the melodies of rock 'n' roll classics like "Johnny B. Goode" (written and sung by Chuck Berry) or a few of their latter-day offspring like "Travelin' Band" (written by John Fogerty; performed by Credence Clearwater Revival) or "Rock-and-Roll Never Forgets" or "Old Time Rock and Roll" (written by George Jackson and Thomas E. Jones III; performed by Bob Seger) looks like a flat line of dots due to the linear, nonmelodic nature of the vocal. Variation is achieved by vocal inflection (for example, when a vocalist changes his sound from smooth and calm to raspy and agitated) and chordal changes — the same note over a different chord gives the note a whole different mood and is often as effective a device as changing the note.

WORDS OF
WISDOM

I'm a sucker for the big, soaring melody. Some of my favorite songs like "Waiting for a Girl Like You" by Foreigner (written by Mick Jones and Lou Gramm) have amazingly rangy melodies. This particular song achieves its range by changing keys upward from verse to pre-chorus and again to chorus. However, one of my biggest hits, "Vehicle," uses a narrow five-note range, similar to the early rock 'n' roll and blues songs, and achieves its impact through the changing chords (E flat minor to B flat minor) to give the melody its variety.

— JIM PETERIK, WRITER OF 18 BILLBOARD TOP 10 HITS

WARNING

When you are writing a song, make sure it's singable. If it spans over two octaves, you are severely limiting the number of singers out there who can pull it off (as was the case in the above song "Empty"). Try singing it yourself to make sure it's in the realm of possibility. If the range is too wide, experiment with modifications of the melody. If you're writing for the country market, you may want to limit the note span even more. This genre is noted for sincerity of the singer's delivery — and if they're too concerned about vocal gymnastics, the message could easily be lost.

Pop rock

Melodies in the rock genre range from the blues-based, two- or three-note wails (some call it screaming on key) by Robert Plant of Led Zeppelin ("Whole Lotta Love," written by Willie Dixon and Led Zeppelin, and "The Lemon Song," written by Led Zeppelin and Chester Burnett) to the octave leaps of Steve Perry, lead singer of melodic rock pioneers Journey ("Open Arms," written by Steve Perry and Jonathan Cain, and "Faithfully," written by Jonathan Cain). The later pop bands and solo artists like Fastball ("The Way," written by Tony Scalzo), Guster ("Barrel of a Gun," lyrics by Ryan Miller; music by Guster), and Barenaked Ladies ("Brian Wilson," written by Steven Page) take their melodic cues from The Beatles and The Beach Boys, who practically wrote the book on catchy melodies. For an example of a wide-ranging melody, listen to the jump of one octave when John Lennon sings "I Wanna Hold Your Hand," (written by John Lennon and Paul McCartney).

REMEMBER

In every genre, you'll find a broad spectrum of melodic styles.

Urban and rap

To generalize, this genre is short on melody and long on attitude and vibe. The melodic nature of rhythm and blues (R&B) and soul with songs like the sweet "You Send Me" (written and sung by Sam Cooke, who, by the way, was a major melodic and stylistic influence on Steve Perry of Journey) and "Try a Little Tenderness" (written by James Campbell, Reginald Connelly, and Harry Woods; sung by the immortal Otis Redding) did not seem to make the transition to the gritty, urban streets because of the sophistication and craftsmanship of the song. Whether helping to set the style through choice or necessity, artists like Joss Stone and Duffy sing songs whose melodies toggle back and forth between essentially three or four notes. The songs gain their momentum through their insistent grooves and the vocal shadings and sexual nuances of the vocal delivery.

Obviously, rap being a spoken genre, any melody added occurs in brief interlude sections. When Will Smith reworked "Just the Two of Us," the great old Bill Withers tune, he created a rap for the verses and switched to the traditionally sung chorus. It was an extremely effective blend of old school and new. In the mega smash song "Empire State of Mind," master rapper Jay-Z takes the verses and Alicia Keys takes over with the soaring melodic chorus (sampled from her completely sung version "Empire State of Mind Part II") — the wildly optimistic in tone and melody, "Baby I'm From New York," — she's spreading the news, indeed!

OFF THE RECORD

Jim has endured occasional criticism that the songs he wrote for the urban marketplace had too many chord changes and were "too melodic" for the genre. When he listened to the radio, he understood what they meant. It's very attitude based, where too much melody and too many chord changes can serve only to break the hypnotic groove of this type of music.

Finding the right melody for each section of the song

Take a look at how the element of melody can help you help your song be all it can be — section by section:

>> **Finding the right melody for the verse:** The melody of this vital setup section is crucial to the impact of the chorus and whether your audience will continue to listen or press the Delete key.

>> **Finding the right melody for the pre-chorus:** The melody of this "gateway to the chorus" has to build from the verse, yet not eclipse what is soon to follow.

>> **Finding the right melody for the chorus:** The mother lode of your song — the importance of the right melody in the chorus — cannot be emphasized enough.

>> **Finding the right melody for the bridge:** As we cross the bridge, it's important to change up that melody, and often the chord changes, to give your listeners a taste of something new — some fresh "real estate" that makes your song a better investment.

WARNING

It's not unusual for a writer to work on a song all day only to realize at midnight that the melody was written "on top of" another song (Nashville-speak for "you inadvertently ripped it off from another song, you hack!"). Instead of panicking or scrapping the song altogether, the next day, try modifying the melody to remove any similarities and make it your own. Sometimes if you keep a positive attitude, you can actually improve on what you had and avoid a lawsuit at the same time.

The verse

The verse of a song is your chance to set up the premise, or idea, of the song. Because that is its primary mission, try to keep your verse simple melodically. With too many notes, or too varied and unusual a melody, you run the risk of overstepping the purpose of the verse and distract from the lyric. That's not to say it should be boring or bland — just not too wacky — letting the upcoming sections steal a little thunder from the verse, and giving your song a *build* (the continual rise of momentum, which is the hallmark of many great songs). If you fire all the cannons melodically at once, you won't have any ammo left for the real battle — the chorus.

In Sheryl Crow's '90s smash "If It Makes You Happy" (written by Sheryl Crow and Jeff Trott), it's difficult to identify the song until it hits the chorus. The catchy chorus is what you remember. The verse, however, is never a tune-out factor (when your hand involuntarily goes reaching to find another station or song on your iPod); because even though it's short on melody, it's long on intriguing images ("scrape the mold off the bread and serve you French toast again"). The relatively tuneless verse also makes for a stunning contrast to the melodic feast of the chorus.

In the opening cut of Connecticut native John Mayer's major label debut, *Room for Squares*, entitled "No Such Thing" (written by John Mayer and Clay Cook), he teaches a master's class in effective melodic build. The verse melody is sparse and conversational, pulling the listener in with the promise of the lyric, interesting intervals between notes, and nice spaces between phrases to give us time to process the previous phrase. The verse is followed by a nearly singsong pre-chorus, which cycles its five notes over shifting chords. When the chorus hits, the runaway melody mirrors the action on the set, "I wanna run through the halls of my high school, I wanna scream at the top of my lungs." When John sings "top of my lungs" he does so at the top of his lungs (and vocal range) for emphasis. All the wonders of the pre-chorus and chorus, however, would never have been revealed to his listeners if not properly set up by the verse.

Even with my early attempts at songwriting, I always tried to keep it interesting and colorful. . . . I think because I began as a guitar player, my criteria for what was interesting was a bit more involved in what's happening on the guitar. I approached everything from the guitar neck up. . . . So I think by default, the music that I sang over was already a little more involved and interesting on its own.

— JOHN MAYER, HIS MAJOR-LABEL DEBUT, ROOM FOR SQUARES, SHOWCASES HIS SINGER/SONGWRITER TALENTS AS HE TAKES AN ACOUSTIC ROCK BASE AND FUSES IT WITH JAZZ OVERTONES; © PERFORMING SONGWRITER, ISSUE #59

Think of the melody of the verse as the appetizer — a bit of intrigue for the palette to get you in the mood for what is to follow. Too much, though, may spoil your appetite for the rest.

The pre-chorus

The purpose of the pre-chorus is to set up the chorus lyrically with a little different approach than the verse — and chordally — often injecting some fresh chords to come between a verse and chorus that happen to start on the same chord (if the verse and chorus both start in G major, try starting your pre-chorus in E minor or F major). The pre-chorus or channel (also known as the B section) melodically serves to further get everyone ready for the chorus. The melody of this section usually ascends higher in range (but not as high as the chorus) and changes up the rhythm of the words from the verse rhythm.

In Elton John's classic song from 1992, "The One" (Elton John and Bernie Taupin), the pre-chorus sounds suspiciously like a chorus the first time you hear it ("In the instant that you love someone, in the second that the hammer hits"); as the suspended chords of the verse resolve to the major chords, the melody starts to soar. It's only when the song hits the chorus ("And all I ever needed was the one"), that we realize Elton has upped the ante again with an even more majestic and compelling section.

A pre-chorus can be as good as you can make it, but make sure that the chorus is even more memorable.

One of our producers (who also worked with Jefferson Starship, Led Zeppelin, The Who, and Bad Company) would always push Frankie Sullivan and me to write pre-choruses for the songs we were working on. He felt melodically it gave a song more build and created a further sense of anticipation for the chorus. In "High on You," we inserted a melodic pre-chorus in the relative key of E minor (the verse is in G) and elevated the melody ("Now I'm screaming in the night, I know I'm getting hooked on your love"). Each time this section comes around, it's like a mini-chorus due to the repeated words and the hookiness of its melody.

— JIM PETERIK, WRITER OF 18 BILLBOARD TOP 10 HITS

There may be times when the mesmerizing lyrics you've just written don't really fit with the infectious melody you want to pair them up with. When this happens, you need to ask yourself these questions: "Do these lyrics convey something so powerful that they simply can't be changed?" and "Is keeping the melody line more important here?" If you keep asking these questions, the answers will undoubtedly be revealed. You'll either keep the melody line that is just too gorgeous to change and adjust the lyrics with a new word that means basically the same thing, or you'll adjust the melody to retain those perfect lyrics that can't be touched. By being disciplined and open to making a change to either the melody line or the lyrics, you won't be saddled with two ideas that aren't in harmony and unison.

If a melody just isn't coming, don't "beat it into the ground" or try to fit a "square peg into a round hole." Leave it alone and come back to it after dinner, tomorrow, next week, or next year. If it's meant to get written, it'll happen at exactly the right time.

The chorus

If songwriting were an athletic event, the chorus would be the Olympics. It's every songwriter's chance to win the gold (pun intended). The chorus melody is generally what we go home singing after attending a concert, play, movie, club, or fest. It's the main course after you've been teased by the appetizer (verse), and eased by the salad (pre-chorus) — after the chorus is our palette cleansed by the bridge sorbet?

The chorus melody is generally the climax of the song, featuring the highest notes and often the widest intervals between notes. (Certain songs like Van Halen's "Love Walks In" actually take an opposite approach and come down dynamically at the chorus to add contrast.) Power ballads pride themselves on the big, melodically soaring chorus, such as:

>> "All By Myself" (written and sung by Eric Carmen)

>> "How Do I Live" (written by Diane Warren; sung by Trisha Yearwood as well as LeAnn Rimes)

>> "Uprising" (written by Matthew Bellamy; performed by Muse)

>> "Lucky" (written by Colbie Caillat and Timothy Fagan; sung by Jason Mraz)

In "Day of Freedom" (written by Cindy Morgan, Brent Bourgeois, and Chris Eaton; sung by Christian artist, Rachael Lampa), the song features an Eastern-influenced melody in the verse (complete with sitar and tabla arrangement touches) and a brief two-bar channel (pre-choruses need not be long to be effective), and then hits its sprawling chorus featuring long notes stretched over the four minor chord to the five seventh, and the words "We're all children of the faith, and though we walk in different ways, let's live our lives to celebrate the day of freedom." The power of the chorus comes from many factors: the deceleration of the velocity of the words (the verse is quite choppy and busy), the anthemic and universal nature of the lyric, and the melody, which sounds more unusual than it really is due to the unique chords underneath it. Try singing the same melody over the dominant chord of the key and see how common the melody now sounds.

REMEMBER

When writing a chorus melody, make sure it's the high point of your song. If your pre-chorus or verse is more memorable than your chorus, keep working on it until it is the musical peak.

Certain songs use other melodic devices at the chorus to achieve impact. "One Week" (written by Ed Robertson; performed by the Barenaked Ladies) is a wonderfully twisted example of unorthodox song form. Basically the verse is a stream of non sequiturs spouted by the temporarily deranged lead singer at the breakneck speed of a nervous auctioneer. When it hits the chorus, the beat relaxes to half time and the lyrics drape lazily over the melody. The chorus derives its power from repetition of its three-note melody, the slowdown of the velocity of the words, and the staggering groove of the drums. If you read through the lyric of this song, and sing it to yourself, notice how the changing melodic patterns keep the song moving from section to section.

TIP

Here's one little-known trick of the trade that you can try: If you can't seem to find a chorus that is stronger musically than your verse (or channel), maybe your verse is strong enough to pull a flip-flop and become your chorus. If that works, go back and rewrite the verse and pre-chorus to lead up properly to the new chorus.

In a song Jim co-wrote with Don Barnes and Don Chauncey of .38 Special entitled "Fade to Blue" (contained on their 1997 release "Resolution"), they found it had this wonderfully melodic pre-chorus leading into this really lame chorus. Finally, Danny Chauncey of the band suggested they just make that section the chorus and write another pre-chorus. Jim thought he was nuts until they tried it and the idea worked like a charm.

The bridge

Just what is the right melody for the bridge? Well, that would be dictated by the road leading up to that bridge. A bridge provides whatever is required to give the ear a change of pace. That change of pace could be rhythmic or chordal. In addition to these elements, the bridge can also change melodically. The bridge is your last chance to say anything lyrically, chordally, and melodically that has been left unsaid.

If you have nothing left to say in your song, you don't really need a bridge. It's one area of the song that's truly optional. When it works, it's something the listener waits for. When it doesn't, it's excess baggage that makes your song seem long and cumbersome.

Often an instrumental bridge is all your song needs. An *instrumental bridge* is where a solo instrument improvises or restates the melody. (The way the classical guitarist on Sting's "Fields of Gold," written by Sting, interprets the musical theme.) Other times, a simple extension of the chorus is precisely what is needed. Listen to how the writers of Jo Dee Messina's Top 10 country hit "Burn" (written by Tina Arena, Stephen Werfel, and Pamela Reswick) use some chord substitutions to extend the chorus and create an effective bridge.

When you finish your verse and chorus, try to see where the song could flow in terms of a bridge. Try a melody that's similar to the chorus, but try different chords underneath it. Or try changing keys and really reinvent the wheel. When you feel you have the bridge nailed, play the song in its entirety to see if it feels like it's needed.

When Jim had the pleasure of co-writing in Nashville with pop ace David Pomeranz and gifted Nashville writer Tammy Hyler, they had the music finished for the entire song one day, when David then came up with a wonderfully melodic and inventive bridge. Three hours and seven cups of coffee later, they still couldn't find the right lyric for that section. Finally, as the trio was just about to give up and admit defeat, Jim said, "Let's try it without the bridge." "Blasphemy!" everyone shouted, but when they played the song through, there was plenty of music without it — and more time to do some creative arranging on the last chorus.

Evaluating your melody magic

After you have created your melody masterpiece, go back and review some of the important elements that it contains to see if it successfully incorporated the new tools that you've stored away in your melodic toolbox. Is it easy to remember and easy to hum along to? What about the words and use of your title — do they fit nicely and are they in a range that most singers can achieve? Does your song have that "magic" moment when something unexpected shows up to break up the potential of becoming boring to listen to? Are the lyrics being forced into anywhere they shouldn't be?

The easiest method of evaluating your song's melodic hit quality is to listen to it without benefit of the lyric. Record your song without the words by using either the humming method or nonsense syllables like "la, la, la" to get the true feel and melody of the song. You will quickly sense if there are areas within your masterpiece that have extra notes crammed in to make the lyric fit or if notes or syllables are missing entirely. Then if it's good to go, you are on your way to having a hit song in the making — otherwise it may be time to make some minor tweaks here or there.

Practice Makes Perfect

In sports, when a baseball player is on a roll and is hitting everything in sight, he'll often say that the ball looks as big as a watermelon and that it's coming towards him practically in slow motion. In contrast, when a player can't hit anything, you might hear a comment like, "Boy, that pitcher is really throwing BB's today." Likewise, when a professional tennis player can do no wrong and is always in the right place at the right time, the ball actually feels so good making contact on the strings of the racquet that the player feels that it can be hit to any spot on the court. This is called being "in the zone," and those who have experienced it know how incredible it feels. It's where all that preparation and hard work hit home effortlessly and you don't even have to think about all the little technique issues that you've worked so hard to develop over time — you basically "just do it."

With most songwriters who've written hit songs, you'll hear similar comments about their sensational melodies that so captivate the masses — "It just comes out of nowhere," or "I was in such a groove, it just wrote itself." Know that for all the hard work you spend in creating songs, you're helping yourself to be prepared so that moments of "being in the zone" are allowed to take flight. An athlete can't ever know what it's like being "in the zone" unless he's practiced his craft over and over again, so he's prepared for those moments when preparation meets inspiration. The same goes for the songwriter — keep working at melodies that float in and out of your head. Maybe it's just a great start to a melody and you can't, at that moment, find the right direction for it. Write it down, or better yet, record it so that the next time you're driving around doing errands and you're least expecting it, the melody just takes flight in your mind. When you bring out the old notes or recordings, you can see how it's all connected and you're now in the groove to allow the song to soar to new heights.

Go ahead. Jot down or record the little melodies that are bouncing around in your head — no matter how small. Too many songwriters wait until it's more formed before they start writing down anything. Don't wait. The little notes you capture might just be the catalyst later on that helps you get "into the zone."

OFF THE RECORD

I have a good friend (and very successful songwriter) who's really fun to be around, but seemingly out of nowhere he'll get a melody idea for a song, and disconnect from the outside world. I always know when this happens because all of a sudden he doesn't hear a word I'm saying and he seems to be way off in the distance. I know him well enough to realize that some magic melody idea just hit and he's repeating it over and over again in his mind until he can get to his recorder before it's lost forever. Don't discard any thoughts or ideas because you think you'll be able to remember them later on — stop and write them down before it's too late.

— DAVE AUSTIN, MENTAL PERFORMANCE COACH TO PROFESSIONAL
ATHLETES, FORMER RECORD COMPANY EXECUTIVE AND
INDEPENDENT MUSIC LABEL OWNER

Chapter **10**

Using Chords in Songwriting

G iven the fact that you're reading this book, you may already have a basic grasp of chords on the instrument of your choice. You can use this knowledge of chords to your advantage and actually play the songs for others while you're in the process of writing them to receive some valuable feedback. But, even if you're strictly a lyricist, you can use what you learn in this chapter to speak intelligently about chords with your co-writer. The more you understand the underlying chord structures of a song, the more appreciation you'll have for them when you hear a great song on the radio or Internet. The next step will be applying that knowledge and appreciation into your own songs. Putting chords to work within the context of a song is what this chapter's all about.

Using Chords to Write Songs

Just like the concrete that forms the foundation of your house, think of chord structure as the foundation of your song. If the chord structure is solid, you can build a masterpiece on top of it; if it's weak, everything you lay on top of this foundation runs the risk of collapsing.

So what is a chord? A *chord* is a combination of three or more musical tones played simultaneously. Chords are constructed of different combinations of the half step intervals between the notes. You can locate these intervals by going to a piano and finding your way up and down the keyboard, including the black keys. The specific intervals between the notes determines the colors of the individual chord you use. The color of your song will depend upon the chordal intervals you choose. It's perhaps the most overlooked element of a song because it does its job more or less invisibly. (When was the last time a friend came up to you and said, "Wait till you hear the chord progression on "Uprising" by Muse. It's almost Bach-like.") Nonetheless, great songs need great chords and interesting progressions. They do their work "behind the notes," influencing a song's mood and where it'll turn melodically. A particular note or series of notes can sound entirely different depending on the chord it's played against.

TIP

If you have very limited know-how on an instrument, check out *Guitar For Dummies*, 2nd Edition by Mark Phillips and Jon Chappell, *Rock Guitar For Dummies* by Jon Chappell, or *Piano For Dummies*, 2nd Edition by Blake Neely (all published by Wiley Publishing, Inc.) for additional great tips and information.

WORDS OF
WISDOM

When I'm listening to a new song on the radio, my ear usually focuses on the melody first and the lyrics second — the chord pattern is just the delivery medium. However, when a writer is daring enough to throw in an unexpected chord or two along the way, I take special notice and gauge whether it was a risk worth taking.

— JIM PETERIK, PERFORMER, SONGWRITER, AND MULTI-INSTRUMENTALIST
FOR BOTH IDES OF MARCH AND SURVIVOR, PLUS WRITER OF HITS FOR
.38 SPECIAL, SAMMY HAGAR, AND OTHERS

Believe it or not, your choices of chords can dramatically affect the commerciality of your song. Throwing in *odd intervals* (unexpected jumps between chords) can be too jarring for simple pop tunes, but it's practically required for grunge and alternative rock. *Diminished chords* (in which a musical interval is reduced by a half step) are hardly ever used in country music, but they're commonplace in jazz-oriented songs. Knowing what genre your song fits into is a big part of choosing the right chords.

REMEMBER

You can't copyright a chord progression; if you could, the estates of the pioneers of the 12-bar blues progression would be overflowing! So unless you're particularly inventive with your chord progression, you're building melodies over ground laid by others. This is not to say you can't vary the changes and substitute chords to make them your own. Just don't be too surprised when someone else comes along with the same variation.

Getting started with chords

As a songwriter, even if your focus and strength lie primarily in lyrics, having a working knowledge of a chordal instrument like keyboard or guitar can help you find the proper chords for your song — or at least help you guide your co-writer. Learn some of your favorite songs on piano or guitar to see the chord sequences used and to notice the moods being set. Songwriters start as fans of different writers and songs, and then as they learn those progressions, they start to adapt and modify them to their own style.

OFF THE RECORD

The first song I ever learned on the guitar when I was nine years old was the hit "Tom Dooley" by The Kingston Trio. With the sequence of just the two simple chords, A major to E major, suddenly I was making music — not to mention impressing my relatives and members of the opposite sex!

— DON BARNES, .38 SPECIAL

The most basic and useful thing to learn when studying chords is that each key has seven different notes. From each one of these notes, you can build a chord — one through seven. When you hear someone refer to a "1, 4, 5 progression," he's talking about the one chord, the four chord (four notes up in the scale from the first), and the five chord (five notes up in the scale from the first).

Knowing your scales in every key will be an enormous help for you as a songwriter. In every key, you have three major chords, three minor chords, and one diminished chord. In a major key, the chords built off of the first note, the fourth note, and the fifth note will give you a major chord. This is the 1, 4, 5 progression of so many great rock 'n' roll and blues tunes. The chords built off of the second note, the third note, and the sixth note will give you a minor chord (a 2, 3, 6 progression). And a chord built off of the seventh note will give you a diminished chord. As long as you know what key you're in and what notes are in that key, you can begin to base your major and minor *triads* (three-note chords starting with the *root* — or basic note — of the chord) off of each respective note. Technically, you can arrange them in any order (this is where personal taste and style come in) and they'll all sound reasonably good together, because they contain notes from that key that you've chosen.

WORDS OF WISDOM

When I'm writing a very simple pop-oriented tune, whether on guitar or piano, I definitely try to use the three major chords in a particular key — so if you're in the key of G, you'd have G, C, and E minor to give it a little color. G, E minor, C, and D are often called "ice cream changes" because this chord pattern harkens back to the '50s and many of the doo-wop and rock 'n' roll songs heard in the old-fashioned ice cream parlors. This is kind of a cool way to start — just knowing the basics of which chords are major and which chords are minor in a major key.

— MIKE AQUINO, NOTED CHICAGO SESSION GUITARIST

Blues and blues-rock chords

Blues and most forms of rock 'n' roll use a premise of a major key for the most part, using the 1 chord (the root), the 4 chord (the fourth), and the 5 chord (the fifth), which are the major chords. If you are in the key of A, you'd have an A major, a D major, and an E major. What blues and some rock do is to make each chord a *dominant* (the namesake of the key — if you are in the key of E, then E is the dominant — also referred to as the *root* or *tonic* of the chord) seventh chord. Your A will become an A seventh — an A major chord with a G natural on the top of it to give it that grindy or bluesy sound. To the D, you'll also add a dominant seventh of a C natural on top. The E will be an E major chord with a D natural on the top. When you're adding sevenths to your chords, you're actually going outside the notes contained in the major scale of that key and dipping into the notes of the minor key. It's that minor sound on top of that major chord progression that gives you the bluesy sound.

The minor blues progression is also a popular form from which to base your song. In the key of A, your 1 chord is now an A minor (lowering the second note of the triad from C sharp to C natural) with a G on top making it an A minor seventh chord. The D or 4 chord becomes a D minor chord with a C on top to make it a D minor seventh. Theoretically, your 5 chord — the E in the key of A — should also be a minor chord in a minor key, but often writers will make it a major or even a seventh to give it a more definite resolution back to the 1 chord. Songs like "Ball and Chain" (written by Willie Mae "Big Mama" Thornton; sung by Janis Joplin) feature the minor seventh on the five-chord turnaround and it sounds great.

REMEMBER

Chord progressions don't have to be complex in order to be powerful. In fact, often a simple two-chord sequence can sometimes be the most powerful of all. Listen to the two minor chords (E minor to B minor) of "Fallin'" (written and sung by Alicia Keys) as a good example.

Pop- rock chords

Pop and rock chord progressions are all over the map in terms of style. The minor-key sound, however, may take the prize for being the most popular. The sound of classic songs like "Separate Ways" (written by Jonathan Cain and Steve Perry; performed by Journey) and "Eye of the Tiger" (written by Jim Peterik and Frankie Sullivan; performed by Survivor) are good examples of how the minor key mode can be used in the rock genre. In "Eye . . . ," you start with your C minor (the first degree of the scale) then move to G-sharp major (the sixth degree of the scale), still keeping the C note in the bass. Then you move to A-sharp major (the seventh degree of the scale), also with the C in the bass, and then back to home base, C minor. You can see that even though there are more major chords than minor, the verse still has a minor-key sound because of how that first chord sets the tone for the rest and how the common bass note C casts the minor mood on even the major chords.

Another popular progression in rock would be 1 to 4, 7 to 3, and 6 to 5. In the key of A minor, this would translate to A minor to D minor, then G major to C major, and finally F major to E major for your 6 to 5 change. Each of these chord pairs is all a fourth apart, just down one step from the previous pair.

Jazz chords

In jazz, instead of the 1, 4, 5 progression that you find so often in pop, rock and blues, you might use a repeating back and forth cycle of the 1, 6, 2, 5 chord progression. In the key of A major, this would be A major or A major seventh or sixth (adding the seventh or sixth note of the scale to the chord) to F-sharp minor to B minor to E seventh.

In the swing era, to make this jazzy progression less "white bread," songwriters substituted an F-sharp dominant seventh for the F-sharp minor. Instead of B minor, they used a B dominant seventh and also kept the E as E seventh. In this cycle, there are always two notes in each chord that are a half step away from the next chord — known as *leading tones*. These leading tones help create smooth transitions from chord to chord. Tricks like these make things a little more interesting — adding color and opening up other notes from which to write your melody. Whenever you change a chord from minor to major temporarily, you're obscuring the actual key you are in.

TIP

There may be times when you are driving and are without a musical instrument in your hands (I know, I know — you're still threatening to build a synthesizer into your dashboard), and there's a certain chord buzzing around in your head, but you don't know its name. Try singing the notes of the chord into your digital recorder or cell phone, and when you get home, pick the notes out on your keyboard.

Moving forward with chords

It's now time to get inspired by chords and to move forward. Get out your big acoustic guitar (the one with the low action and deep ringing tone), and sit in your favorite part of the house or under that tree in the backyard. Perhaps you'll want to plug that electric guitar into an amplifier and even hook up one of those inspiring effects pedals like a *flanger* (units like the Electric Mistress flanger by

Electro-Harmonics give your chords that shimmering 12-string effect you heard on those Tom Petty and Rush records), so that each chord sounds profound. If you're writing hard rock, dial up some heavy distortion on an overdrive effects pedal (like a Ratt pedal by Pro-co). You could combine many effects into one by plugging into a Pod effects unit (made by Line 6 Electronics), which digitally models the sounds of classic effects pedals and devices from vintage fuzz boxes, Leslie speaker effects (the rotating speaker sound that simulates the classic Hammond organ), phasers, wah-wahs, and other sound-warping mischief to get your juices flowing. Or sit behind your electronic keyboard and find an inspiring *patch* (one of those factory programmed settings that you fiddle around to find — as a last resort, refer to the manual!). A good suggestion would be a piano setting combined with a touch of strings or choir to give it a little cushion and grandeur.

Now play a nice big C major chord. Voice it fairly low on the keyboard or fret board so it sounds big and rich. Hold it for four beats. Now play a G major. Hold it for four beats. Play four beats on A minor, and then go with F for four beats. Next time around add a *second* (the term for a note just one note above the basic or tonic note of the chord) to the C chord (in this case a D). Sounds cool doesn't it? No charge! You just played a chord progression as good as the best. Next, close your eyes as you play these same chords and just let your mind drift. From nowhere often come fragments of melody, words, and even where to go next from that basic three-chord beginning — this could be called a meditative state. Your unconscious mind is now in the driver's seat — and there are no wrong turns! Rhythm will almost invariably suggest itself as you wander about mentally and emotionally. You become a member of the audience — and yet you are at the same time also the performer!

Play these chords over and over, experimenting with different tempos and different styles of chording from *staccato* (choppy and short) to *legato* (long and connected). Next try substituting a few of the chords for others to see if you like the sound of the progression even more. Perhaps it may spark a different melody. After the C major and the G major, try a B-flat major instead of the A minor, and then move to F major as before. Notice the edgier mood the chords now convey. Want edgier still? Follow the B-flat major with an A-flat major. Now, instead of changing your left hand with the chords (it had been changing with the root note of the chord), let that hand stay on the C root through all the chord changes (this technique will radically change the mood of the chords to a much darker perspective). Now go back to your original C, G, Am (abbreviation of A minor), F progression. What a difference! You can experiment endlessly with any number and sequence of chords till you come up with one that inspires you to find the perfect melody (or motivates you to call the perfect co-writer to help complete your vision).

REMEMBER

The instrument you choose to write on and the sound you dial up can markedly affect not only your attention span of concentration on any given day but also the style of song you'll be inspired to write.

When coming up with a basic chord progression, try not only substituting one chord for another but experimenting with different voicings of chords. For instance, a basic C major chord is the notes C, E, and G. To give the chord a little more uplifting sound, make the lowest note of the chord the E and then add the G next and make C the top note of the chord. Also, a trick from the arranging style of Brian Wilson is to use a note other than the root. If you play a C major chord on the right hand, try playing an E on the left hand instead of a C. Notice how nicely that configuration slides into F major.

WORDS OF WISDOM

I love fooling around with substitute bass notes when I'm working on a progression. If a chord pattern is sounding a little commonplace, I'll search around with my left hand to see what color I can add to a chord. On "I Can't Hold Back," a song I co-wrote with Frankie Sullivan for Survivor, tension is added to the first chord of the chorus ("I can't hold back, I'm on the edge") by putting the third of the chord on the bottom instead of the tonic (the chorus is in E major, so the third of the chord would be three notes up — a G#). The last of three times the E major, A major, B major chord progression is repeated, the root of the chord is used for that extra solidity the last time around. This trick makes the chorus of this song much more unusual sounding. Go ahead and try this on the next song you're writing.

— JIM PETERIK, WRITER OF 18 BILLBOARD TOP 10 HITS

Now try a minor key progression. Start with an A minor chord, and stay there for two beats. Move to C major for two beats. Now to D major for two beats, then to F major for two. Sounds really cool and smoky doesn't it? Kind of like "House of the Rising Sun," written by Eric Burdon and John Sterling and made popular in the '60s by The Animals. Now try a few substitutions. Start with the A minor, then move to the C major like before, then to F major and to E seventh. Notice how the mood is retained, but you avoid the inevitable comments like "It sounds just like 'House of the Rising Sun.'" Now really shake things up and try A minor to D minor to G-sharp seventh to G major. Wow! How cool is that? Just keep experimenting with different progressions and combinations until you have something you can't wait to come back to every day.

WORDS OF WISDOM

Substitute chords are a staple in a songwriter's larder. For instance, instead of using an A major chord, which contains the notes A, C sharp, and E, you can find another chord within that key or outside of that key that contains one or two of the same notes. If I want to stay in the key of A major and find a sub for the A major chord, I go to the sixth degree of the scale — F sharp — the notes in that chord are F sharp, A, and C sharp — which contains the A and the C sharp just like the A major chord. These substitute chords help add variety and create a different mood under exactly the same melody notes.

— MIKE AQUINO, CHICAGO SESSION GUITARIST

OFF THE RECORD

A while back Jim learned a valuable lesson about substitution chords when listening to "Private Dancer," the hit for Tina Turner written by Mark Knopfler. At the end of the chorus under the lyric "and any old music will do," where it could've been totally predictable and gone to the one major of the key, it goes instead to the minor six chord. This technique is called a *deceptive cadence* because you expect it to go home to the root, but it goes to the relative minor. It creates an unsettling and unresolved mood that's in keeping with the bittersweet message of the lyric. Now, when Jim writes, before he changes a melody, he experiments with the underlying chords to see if a simple substitution will add the needed interest.

TIP

Learn as many chords as you can on the instrument of your choice. If you're a guitarist, you can't do better than the old Mel Bay chord book: *Rhythm Guitar Chord System* (published by Mel Bay Publications, Inc.). Countless rock, pop, and jazz guitarists have cited this book as their primary source of self-learning. Basically, if a chord isn't in this book, you've probably just invented it. Another great online source is at chordbook.com where you make up your own virtual chords and store them for later use. The more chords you have in your arsenal, the more options you give yourself.

Many writers will find interesting ways of linking chords together by keeping certain notes within the chords the same whether they are at the bottom of the chord or the top of the chord — keeping the main note of the key common to at least two or three of the chords. This technique has the effect of holding things together. The chords are moving in a certain direction, but there's an element behind the chords that says, "We are all connected."

TIP

A course or two on music theory is a good idea for the aspiring songwriter. You'll come away with a better idea of why things work and don't work in chord sequences. But if you are in a hurry, you may want to take an hour or two and learn the following six chords: C major, D minor, E minor, F major, G major, and A minor. With these six chords you're basically on your way towards writing your first mega-hit — heck, most of the top-charting songs use only three or four chords, so with six in your arsenal you've got more than enough to write your masterpiece!

Choosing Your Style of Chordal Instruments

The type of instrument you choose as you write your song may influence the direction your song will take. Conversely, if you are attempting to write a song in a particular style, the appropriate instrument will help inspire the results you need. Take a look at the following sections for various chordal instruments and their stylistic strong suits.

Picking the guitar

Depending on the type of guitar, this instrument can run the gamut of musical styles. For folk, country, light rock, and certain types of pop, a good acoustic guitar (also called a folk guitar) might be your first choice. With its airy, transparent sound, it's a beautiful texture to use to experiment with the chords needed in those genres of music. Interesting to note is Corinne Bailey Rae's self-titled debut release, which relies heavily on acoustic guitar to give it its organic, personal, and soulful quality — quite unique in her adult contemporary rhythm and blues genre.

When you want to write hard rock (or the various styles of alternative, punk, grunge, melodic, and so on), choose an electric guitar run through an amplifier that's overdriven to various degrees. To make sure your landlord doesn't kick you out of your house, amp manufacturers have come up with a master volume control, which allows you to dial in all the distortion your heart desires even at low volumes. You can write hard rock on an acoustic guitar, but it takes a lot of imagination to hear it differently. Also an acoustic guitar lacks the sustain of a distorted electric that helps extend the chords and create the signature riffs of this genre.

TECHNICAL STUFF

If you happen to be in your home studio, you may just want to access your Amp Farm (Line 6) or your Sansamp Software and scroll through the various sounds that these fine companies have *modeled* for you (the art of manipulating sine waves, wavelengths, and other electronic content to precisely mimic the signature sound of these classic amplifiers) — everything from a distant mic'd Marshall stack (the classic British rock amp used by Pete Townsend of The Who, Duane Allman, and countless others) to a shredding Soldano tone to a bone-clean Fender Twin Reverb.

For Latin songs, a nylon-stringed guitar (also called a classical or flamenco) may be your ticket to inspiration.

TIP

Using a capo on the neck of your guitar can be a useful technique while writing a song. A *capo* is a device that you clamp onto the neck of your guitar to change the key you are playing in without changing the way you form a chord. (For example, if you place the capo on the third fret of the guitar and play an E major, the chord will now become a G major without changing your fingering.) By wrapping a capo around the neck of your guitar at various fret positions, you can vary the key signature you're working in without changing the voicing of the chord. This is great when trying out various keys for a singer, but it also inspires different emotions from a songwriter because the chords take on a very different perspective and color when moved up and down the scale.

WORDS OF WISDOM

I'll use the capo device (good ones are available at any music store for about $15) especially when I'm writing country and folk. I'll place it generally on the third or fourth fret. I love the chimney, almost mandolin, texture it adds to the chording — it makes the song sound fresh. When I'm writing rock, especially alternative, I enjoy tuning the whole guitar a whole step down to give the instrument a grungy sound. I also enjoy tuning the low E down to D — this is the sound of the guitars on Aerosmith's "Draw the Line."

— JIM PETERIK, WRITER OF 18 BILLBOARD TOP 10 HITS

You might want to buy one of several books on alternative tunings. Whether they are the tunings of Joni Mitchell on acoustic guitar or the tunings of Keith Richards of The Rolling Stones on electric and acoustic guitar, these alternatives to the standard E, A, D, G, B, A tuning can elicit totally unique chord progressions and accompanying melodies. Also, take a look at how the group Creed based their chordal sounds on the D, A, D, A, D, D tuning, which gave their chords an ominous power and droning quality.

TECHNICAL STUFF

Fender came up with a newer version of their iconic Stratocaster model that gives you many alternative tunings electronically with just the turn of a knob — amazing but true!

Pecking at the keyboard

The keyboard (any instrument based on the piano) is one of the most versatile and widely used chordal instruments for the songwriter. For everything from power ballads to old-fashioned rock 'n' roll (Jerry Lee Lewis was perhaps the king of the rock 'n' roll piano), the acoustic piano would be the weapon of choice. Nowadays, we have electronic pianos that rival the sound of a real acoustic piano at a fraction of the size and cost. The majesty and honesty of a good piano (or sampled grand — the name that refers to the electronic variety) is second to none.

For extra inspiration, you can purchase a keyboard such as the Yamaha S90 that not only contains a reasonably good grand piano patch, but also includes terrific electric piano — the sound of the Wurlitzer immortalized in "These Eyes" (written by Randy Bachman and Burton Cummings; performed by The Guess Who) or the Fender Rhodes piano featured in "You Are the Sunshine of My Life" (written and sung by Stevie Wonder). In addition, you'll find synthesized brass patches — useful when writing '80s style rock — listen to "Heat of the Moment" (written by John Wetton and Geoff Downes; performed by Asia for reference), woodwinds, and a vast collection of strange and wacky synthesizer and bass sounds. R&B, gospel, jazz, new age, urban, and dance pop are all primarily the divinity of the keyboard.

Because urban music is so simple chordally (generally one or two chords throughout the entire song), the texture of the keyboard sound becomes especially vital in setting the mood and creating variation throughout the song.

TECHNICAL STUFF

Many of the classic synth (some refer to these sounds as "retro") keyboards are now sampled and available in the newer instruments — formerly impossible to find sounds of the classic Jupiter 8 by Roland, the Oberheim, the Yamaha DX 7 and even the much maligned Mellotron. This wonderful British keyboard — heard most famously on many recordings by The Moody Blues — employed a series of magnetic strips of recording tape that contained first-rate recordings of real violins, cellos, flutes, and vocals. Unfortunately it had a penchant for not working. For instance, no sooner did Neil Young buy one for his band (at a then very pricey ten grand!) than it was transported *on its side* in the equipment truck instead of upright, thereby spilling all the strands of tape much like ticker tape on the floor of the van — and that was the end of that!

TIP

As fun as it is to experiment with chords on a keyboard or guitar, it's also interesting to call up a bass patch on the keyboard (perhaps synth bass or electric bass) or plug in an electric bass guitar and work with the simple primary notes of each chord. It gives your imagination plenty of room to wander when not encumbered by a lot of chords.

REMEMBER

Although you can write any genre on practically any chordal instrument (death metal on mandolin and acid rock on banjo being possibly the only exceptions), certain instruments seem to have a connection to certain genres. The more you experiment with different instruments, the more you'll find your true direction as a songwriter.

Practice Makes Perfect

Now that you've found some amazing chords and great ways of joining them in progression from reading this chapter, go back to some of those great melodies you came up with in Chapter 9, and experiment with laying down different chord patterns beneath them. Who knows? Maybe you'll create a chord pattern that creates a color of its own and takes the song to new heights.

Chord theories and progressions are certainly the more technical side of songwriting — and if it flows easily for you, great! But, if not, don't get discouraged. Keep practicing and experimenting, and allow yourself the freedom to create and to also make mistakes. Review (over and over if necessary) the material presented here until you get comfortable with the nuts and bolts of chords. Then get in the groove and let your creative juices flow and see what magic can happen. Never judge your work in progress, and allow yourself to be a songwriting "Dummy," if that's what in fact it takes to get the inspirations flowing.

Regardless of what anyone says, when it comes right down to it, you'll need to rely heavily on your gut instincts and inner intuitions to find just the right chords. Just try to remember not to go overboard and add too much in the way of chord progressions, or you might just lose your audience — basically because they can't quite keep up with your creative moves.

Chapter **11**

The Cheating Side of Town: Shortcuts and Cool Technologies

Ah, welcome to the twenty-first century, where the impossible now seems commonplace and practically anything you can imagine seems possible. With the advent of the Internet, we have seen a major shift in not only how we access our information but the speed in which it comes to us as well.

In this chapter we look at some cool new technology tools that are available to the songwriter. These tools can assist in creating everything from writing lyrics to recording melodic ideas, from creating commercial-sounding demos to organizing and archiving your document files.

Creating Songs Quicker, Better, Easier

Unless you have been hiding somewhere under a rock on some distant and deserted island, you have noticed that the ol' music business just ain't what it used to be. Much of the last decade has been in a state of managed chaos, and the playing field has been greatly leveled with cool new technological advances. Even though this may be bad news to the major labels and traditional music stores, this is certainly good news for the songwriters and independent artists of the world.

The #1 question remaining seems to be this: With all these new gadgets that are supposed to make life easier, do we actually end up with more or less free time? It's now possible for us to get instant access to just about anything we can imagine — a phenomenon that also allows our grandmothers to find us anytime and anywhere with their sweet little cell phones that are now attached directly to their ears — a highly distracting thing during one's creative sessions! It seems that quite often, we are running around like chickens with our heads cut off, doing more things in less time. This, my friend, is the beauty and power of new technology.

Doing stuff quicker with gadgets

You are probably in favor of getting work done more quickly and efficiently. The same holds true for songwriters as it does for any other business professional. The sooner you get your inspirations written, recorded, and out there in the world, the better. The following are some of our favorite time-saving methods, devices, and gadgets:

» **iPhone (or another smartphone):** Whether it's taking pictures of guitars, recording quick audio ideas for songs, navigating to gigs or meetings, or managing your contacts, the iPhone is a super valuable tool that can help you get tasks done faster.

» **Skype (or iChat and Google video):** This technology is great for making cheap international calls and collaborating with folks overseas — very helpful when booking international tours. So why waste time with e-mail or "snail mail" when you can get the deal done with a one-on-one conversation. It's a great tool to becoming "big in Europe."

» **Dropbox:** This is virtual storage where you can store and share with others pretty much any type of file. The great part is that you can then access your files on any computer at any time; so if you don't have your laptop, no worries. And it's super easy to use because you just drag and drop — it saves you time, and you can skip the burning to CDs and "snail mail" method of getting your music delivered.

» **Filezilla FTP Client:** FTP stands for *file transfer protocol,* which translates to "moving big files quickly over the Internet" — in other words, it's a program for file uploading and downloading to and from your songwriting buddies. Another one to try out is "cyberduck" — it's great and user friendly!

>> **Cardioid condenser microphone:** This is a USB mic that is plug-n-play so you can quickly connect the microphone to any laptop on the go and put down your ideas with a decent sound. It's also great for *podcasting* (podcasts are a way to distribute media files over the Internet for playback on mobile devices, often in MP3 format).

If you seriously want to set your songwriting sessions at warp-speed, try using our favorite timesaving methods:

>> Have any reference materials, like a rhyming dictionary or thesaurus, close by.

>> Have a "template" ready on any digital workstation you may use, and set it up for a microphone and any instruments you may use — or have a portable recorder at hand (if it's a cassette, have a blank cassette available), but make sure the batteries are fresh!

>> If you use a pencil, get the "click" ones that don't need to be sharpened — there's nothing worse than getting involved in a song and having a point break, and then having to look for a sharpener.

>> Turn off your cell phone and silence the ringer on any land lines — and if there are other people in the house, ask them to act like you're not at home. Make sure all your obligations are looked after — a clear mind is a creative mind.

Becoming the expert . . . instantly

Gone are the days when you needed to hire experts to do anything and everything for you. With the advent of new technologies, we can become experts in our own rights at just about anything — without spending a half dozen years training for it and spending a ton of dough in the process. Today we can use "expert" tools that help us shorten any of our learning curves of the past. The following are some of the areas that, not so long ago, were reserved for the experts:

>> **iMovie:** A Mac software program that is very handy if you need to quickly cut together video clips. It offers great transitions and effects to quickly crank out content for YouTube and other video sites.

>> **ReverbNation (or Constant Contact):** All you need to start building your contact list and begin sending out news and updates to your fans. A simple way to manage your database and social networking from one spot. It also has an easy-to-use widget that allows you to put a "Sign up" button on your website so you can stay in touch with new fans.

>> **WordPress:** Want to share your ideas with the world and become a hit on search engines? WordPress is a great way to set up a *blog* (more on blogs in Chapter 13) that can also be used as your website. If you want to easily update content on your site, a blog site is the way to go.

>> **Google:** Google offers more than just search engine capabilities — although in some cases a quick "Google search" can make you an instant expert. But you can also set up an e-mail account, manage your contacts, update your calendar, and keep tasks and documents online for easy access anywhere — a one-stop organizational system that keeps your details straight, so when you go to thank San Diego for a great show, you won't accidently say "Thank you Cleveland" and look like a dummy.

When nothing less than genius level is your goal, try the following "expert in the making" tips:

>> Know how to work the software you use — that includes word processors, digital audios workstations (DAWs, like Pro tools), and any hardware items (like drum machines, and so on). If the technology comes with an electronic manual on pdf format, download it, print it out, and *read it!* Also, there might be a *For Dummies* book about your software, and you know how easy those books are to read!

>> Get a system to organize your lyric ideas — it could be as simple as a spiral notebook or index cards; or you may use a database on a computer. *Keep* everything that you write, even if you think it's lame. As you write, these archives will become more valuable than you can imagine — refer to them often. . . .

>> Get a small portable micro-recorder that you can throw in your briefcase, purse, daybag, or "man-bag." You never know when the muse will strike. That killer melody hook or lyric line that just popped into your head on the way to the store will slip away faster than a greased eel every time. Best to seize the moment as it happens!

>> Be surprised. Don't let personal tastes quash your muse. If you fancy yourself a heavy metal writer, and a country-type tune pops into your head — follow it! Write it! Demo it! It's your art. The experts know to "let it flow" — and fortunate for you, now you do, too!

More tools for making life simpler

The idea of a simpler life is near and dear to everyone's heart — or so it would seem! What would life be like if you had more time to do the things you really enjoy doing? Even if you're doing what you love to do, anything that makes the job simpler to accomplish seems like a great idea to most of us. What's the point of being a songwriter if you're always weighed down with dozens of time-consuming activities in the process of creating? Wouldn't it be more fun to have the time to enjoy your life and the music you have thus created? The following list highlights some of the tools that quite possibly will make the art of songwriting a simpler task for you:

>> **YouTube:** This site offers a quick and easy way to locate and watch music videos and video-taped live performances to keep abreast on what's new.

>> **Pandora:** Simply by listening to the music you like on this free Internet radio station, this site will suggest other music that you might also like. This can be a great help to hone a particular sound you are looking for.

>> **Recording apps:** Got a quick idea or thought? Quickly flip open your phone and sing it. Later you can download it to your computer. No need for a notepad or digital recorder when a cell phone will do.

>> **Tuning apps:** There are portable tuners available; however, now you can download applications for your phone to help you tune your instruments on the go.

Getting back to the simpler things in life can be a daunting challenge to some. Perhaps your nature is to overcomplicate things and attempt to manage the chaos you have conveniently made for yourself. When you need a break, and a breath of fresh air is calling your name, try out one or two of the following methods we highlight below to make your day a little less complicated:

>> **Relax.** Clear your mind. Turn off the lights and sit in the dark for awhile. Imagine you're listening to the radio and hearing the song you're about to write — you'll be amazed at how many times a lyric or riff will pop out, and that's enough to get you started!

>> **Don't judge.** Not everything you write is going to be a gem. Don't be embarrassed — certainly *don't* toss the stuff you don't like. Every writer has 100 pieces of junk for every keeper. Join the club!

>> **Don't share (at first).** The problem with asking someone their opinion is that they may give it to you. Remember, you are your own expert. Unless you're collaborating with another writer, keep your work to yourself. An unkind word may put you off your game. When your song is finished to your satisfaction (and copyrighted), then go ahead and share it with the world.

>> **Be strong.** Keep going. Take praise and criticism lightly and seriously. The truth is that your songs are your art. Don't stop!

THE MP3: THE 21ST CENTURY'S 45

Music has traveled an interesting journey from the single to the long-play format and then back again to the single. Only this time, it's on steroids. Where video may have killed the radio star, the Internet was the conduit that freed music. The MP3 occupies space in today's portable devices the same way 45s filled jukeboxes in the 1940s and '50s.

Gone are the days where listeners have to wait for a radio station to break a new artist. The latest music can be heard and downloaded with the click of a button. We now have global access to the latest creation by a garage band no one has ever heard. Can't get interest from a label? No problem. Self-released music is no longer taboo. Can't get a retailer to stock your disc? Make it available online. Today, an artist can write, produce, market, and distribute songs in the way he envisioned.

Is this Nirvana or a Pandora's Box? Maybe a little of both . . .

When a song is digitally bouncing around the world, you can't get it back. And unless you have a seemingly bottomless well of cash for legal fees, there is a lack of power to enforce your "FOR SALE ONLY" intent. Just as 45s, LPs, and CDs are a physical collection of sound, the MP3 is still recorded music, something someone has put time and effort into creating. Consequently, until these ones and zeros are treated with respect and given the value they deserve, future generations will continue the current trend of ripping and swapping with little thought to the artist's well-being.

With the music industry's decaying old-school business model and the rise of the Internet, "360" deals (otherwise known as "multiple rights deals," which allow record labels to receive royalties on the artists' merchandise sales, concert sales, and endorsements) became the fashion to help labels recoup losses. A series of lawsuits punctuated how labels really felt about illicit MP3 use. And they had that well of cash to feed their pain.

While labels reacted, in glacial and extreme manners, brick and mortar music stores and journalism were next in line to take on the full brunt of this colossal shift. Major chains even became challenged by iTunes, P2P networks, and online retailers. Their focus shifted from the music itself to its delivery — with more interest appearing to be given to the latest MP3 device than to the contents. The music is now considered an accessory, like a set of earbuds.

Respectable music critics have been replaced by the blog. There appears to be no end to the vast number of sites dedicated to music reviews where the reader is subjected to an individual blogger's tastes — where "I'm their biggest fan" trumps actual journalism. Unfortunately, this could be the tale wagging the dog as the industry looks to mirror its releases to capture the disposable income of the "tween" market.

Is it all worth the hassle?

As this is the only system available at the moment, the default answer has to be "yes."

Access is easy. There are few barriers so (almost) everyone has the ability to participate. A computer, the proper software, and your respective instrument — these are all the basics for a DIY recording studio. Creative control is something artists have longed to possess. As previously stated, an artist can write, produce, market, and distribute songs in the way he originally envisioned. Collaborations can be done inexpensively with recorded tracks being sent via e-mail so the layers can be assembled. Imagine carrying around in your pocket a résumé which allows you to present your latest creations.

Once recorded, the MP3, whether a sample or an entire song, can be loaded onto a web page where the masses can hear your newest offering. And if a social network site like Facebook or MySpace is chosen, feedback can be received almost immediately. The web page address can be sent to booking agents, labels, and publishing companies and even blogs for the purpose of furthering one's career. Is your band better live? Record a show, edit it, and post it on YouTube for downloading.

When the band Radiohead self-released *In Rainbows* in 2007, their website was set up to "pass the hat" among those who downloaded the album as compensation to the band. Pay what you want? Something? Nothing? The choice was yours. Music, technology, and e-commerce all came together in harmony that day for Radiohead.

Before an independent songwriter can pitch a song, they must record a demo of it. The function of the demo is to introduce the song to interested parties — publishers, artists, and producers. It stands to reason that the demo should portray a song in its best light, but now that demos are taking on a life of their own, a rebellion has begun. . . .

— CHRISTOPHER HORN, INDIE ARTIST MUSIC MANAGER

OFF THE RECORD

Radiohead drew inspiration from the success of their 1992 single "Creep" to write "My Iron Lung" (written by Thom Yorke). Although "Creep" cracked the Top 40 across the pond, the British band (and more specifically Thom Yorke) did not feel the song was a true representation of the band's sound. The same can be said for their image that was perpetuated on MTV. Their response to that was "My Iron Lung."

"My Iron Lung" written by Radiohead

Suck, suck your teenage thumb

Toilet trained and dumb

When the power runs out

We'll just hum

This, this is our new song

Just like the last one

A total waste of time

My iron lung

© 1998 Melanie Howard Music (ASCAP)/Pugwash Music Inc. (BMI)/Waterdance Music (BMI). All Rights Reserved. International Copyright secured. Used by permission.

The initial release of *Pablo Honey*, from which "Creep" is taken, sold poorly and garnered less than stellar reviews from the British press upon its debut. Ironically, it was the success of "Creep" that gave the band a stay of execution from the "here today, gone later on today" music industry.

Discovering Songwriting Software

Do you ever feel like the information highway is passing you by? Maybe you've just been reluctant to try any "new-fangled" gadgets — or perhaps you haven't even heard of them yet. Well, now is the time to jump in that Ferarri of yours and put the pedal to the metal — to once and for all see what this "high-tech" song-writing stuff is all about.

Need rhyming software?

Here is a partial list of some cool rhyming tools and a brief description of what each of them do:

>> **Rhymesaurus:** This is the ultimate collection for the songwriter who wants to find "just the right word." This computer reference software tool has more than 120,000 words and provides 21 different rhyme types including perfect rhymes, reverse rhymes, assonance, consonance, and "sounds-like" references.

>> **Rhyme Wizard:** With over 100,000 words, phrases, and cross-references to near rhymes, this is an indispensable tool that is easy to use. Just type in a word or phrase and you're off to the races.

>> **Rhymer:** This software is available in a free version or an expanded version that contains a 93,000 word dictionary that's compatible with Microsoft Word. The phonetic dictionary software lets you find words that have whatever sounds you want in whatever order you want.

>> **A Zillion Kajillion Rhymes:** Possibly the mother lode of rhyming software, this program claims to find more rhymes than anything else out there, and instantly finds single, double, and triple rhymes for literally thousands of words.

Other software and tracking tools

Here is a partial list of additional software programs that will help you with the task of songwriting and a brief description of what each of them does:

>> **Lyricist:** This program combines everything you need for both lyric writing and archiving. No longer having to worry about a bunch of unorganized document files or shift through piles and piles of paperwork looking for the perfect word or rhyme — this may just be the ultimate songwriting tool you've been looking for.

>> **MasterWriter:** This may be the priciest of these sorts of tools, but you're sure to get a complete collection that includes a rhyming dictionary with phrases, idioms, clichés, sayings, and word combinations, combined with an amazing database that keeps track of your lyrics, melodies, and any other info you might want to keep in order.

>> **GarageBand:** You'll get a big bang for your buck here. By combining CD-quality samples, recording features, and canned rhythm tracks in one package, this software can turn the inspirations of a true beginner into a pretty decent commercial-sounding demo.

>> **Band In A Box:** This program helps to get the ball rolling — and at a fairly decent price. If you want to create a solid scratch melody with original chord progressions, rhythm tracks, bass lines, titles, and melodies in any of the genres from country to pop, this is the one for you.

TIP

For those of you who are visual learners, Visual Thesaurus may just be your ticket to paradise. It's an interactive tool that allows you to discover the connections between words in a visually captivating way. Using word maps, this program lets you search for just the right word and then explore related concepts, revealing the way words and meanings relate to each other. It has more than 145,000 words and 115,000 meanings organized in an innovative way, making it a great resource tool for those who could use a road map in finding just the right word or phrase to convey the feeling of your song.

Recording in Your Own Home Studio

Okay, so there aren't flying cars or jetpacks, and the only place you'll see a moving sidewalk is at the airport. But the twenty-first century has nothing but good news for the songwriter who wants to make a record (and yes, you can still call them that) at home and on their own terms. There are still big (and expensive) recording studios in most large cities, and it's easy to find storefront studios with modest rates in practically every town on the map. For most songwriters, the home studio is the way to go — and it is far, far easier than you think to afford, get started with, and get good at in a relatively short time.

WORDS OF WISDOM

When I first started making music way back in the olden days, the thought of having a recording studio in your home was unheard of except for the super-rich. Now, thanks to the computer, everybody has one! We live in an amazing time, when musicians can write, record, design, duplicate, and market their music to the world, all via one little gray box.

— AARON CHENEY, SONGWRITER, MUSICIAN, AUDIO ENGINEER, AND PRODUCER

Creating commercial-sounding recordings

Like everything, there's good news and bad news, and the bad news ain't so bad — so we start with that. You need to learn basic recording skills because you'll be the engineer, producer, mixer, and mastering artist along with being the songwriter, singer, and instrumentalist (if you're playing your own stuff). There are terms and procedures you have to know, plus you need to learn the hardware and software you acquire — you also have to learn a little about mic technique — that's the sum total of the bad news.

The good news is that there are a ton of books out there (including a bunch of *For Dummies* books) that put all of this in perspective and make it easier for you to focus on your music instead. Trust us, if you apply yourself for a very short time, you can learn the basics of recording.

Microphones

To start, you should probably buy a decent microphone. Don't skimp on this — plan to spend at least $100. Just about any pro you meet, if asked to have *one* mic for that "desert island" you always hear of, would choose a Shure SM 58 — the workhorse of workhorses. No other mic does so many things so well. They have cost about $100 forever, and there's no reason to think that's going to change any time soon. You also need a stand — get a "boom," if you can.

Recording equipment and software studios

Now the news gets even better. Whatever your budget can bear, there's a pretty good selection of recording equipment available — and you may already own some! If you have an Apple computer like an iMac, MacBook, or Mac mini, you probably already have the iLife bundle installed. Look for a program called "GarageBand" — that nifty little program is a complete recording solution. Besides multitrack recording, it has built-in instruments, audio processing like reverbs and EQ, and a great tool for songwriter called "Apple Loops," which are backing tracks, beats, and just about everything else you need to flesh out a song.

There are tons of "software studios" (or as they're called in the biz, Digital Audio Workstations or DAWs) out there at every price range for both Macs and PCs — and they'll do just about everything. We won't talk about models or versions here because they change so quickly and might be obsolete or replaced by a newer version by the time you get to this chapter, so we'll talk mostly about manufacturers. Go to their websites and explore.

Two really great companies are Digidesign and Propellerhead. Digidesign makes the industry-standard Pro Tools range of or DAWs — there's your first bit of modern recording and editing lingo). These go from a few hundred bucks all the way to a king's ransom. What's cool about Pro Tools is that all the levels pretty much share the same basic operation — and the files are compatible among all platforms and levels.

This means you can do a basic track in your bedroom, and take the files to another musician or studio that has Pro Tools and continue working. Or, better still, you can do your basic tracks at home and then take your files to a big-deal studio (that has Pro Tools) to have a seasoned engineer record your vocals, or do your mix and mastering. Pro Tools is the most widely used recording suite. It's a *very* complex program if you want to go deep, but it's surprisingly easy if you want to do basic recording — in short, there's room to grow, even on the most basic Pro Tools system.

TIP

Two very popular beginning level programs that offer drum looping and such are Acid and Logic. Something else I came across in my work was Digi Designs M-Audio — which is very affordable and a great song writing tool. I use it on a daily basis.

— STEVE "SKILLET" KILLEN, SINGER-SONGWRITER, GUITARIST, SESSION PLAYER, AND FOUNDER OF HERON BLUE RECORDING WORKSHOPS

Another great DAW that will run on your Mac or PC is Propellerhead's Reason and Record. Reason is primarily a digital instrumental studio, with samplers, drum machines, loop players, and synths, whereas Record takes care of stuff that uses a mic or a pickup. Together, they are a formidable pair — the software is amazingly comprehensive, with great sounds, and the price is shocking. Shocking because it's so *low!!* Even though the price is easygoing, this is serious software that countless pros use and swear by.

Recording hardware boxes

If you're not a computer person and want a hardware machine to do the job, there's good news for you, too! Like the software studios, there are scads of boxes available at every price range from less than $100 all the way to "hope you won the lottery." But we won't use the word *cheap* because the inexpensive ones do a really good job.

Also like the DAWs, the hardware models change like the weather. Look to companies like Zoom, Korg, Roland, Yamaha, and Tascam. They all produce fine multitrack digital recording equipment. A word to the wise, however — if you buy a DAW, you're usually kosher for at least a few software updates, and you'll mostly get a break if you want to move to a higher level. When you buy a hardware machine, that's it.

Finding the deals and techies

At this point your head might be spinning. Don't get discouraged just yet — there's *more* good news. Most of the major retailers have folks on their staff in a "pro audio" department. Don't let the "pro" title spook you — these are the folks you really do want to talk to! Don't be embarrassed saying that you're new to the game, and don't forget to say that you only have so much money to spend. Give them your pre-thought-out budget, and you should go home with what you need at a price that won't bust your wallet.

The online retailers are also a great resource — high on our go-to list is Sweetwater Sound in Ft. Wayne, Indiana, because of their deep commitment to customer service before, during, and after the sale. Send for one of their catalogs (or for one from Musician's Friends, Sam Ash, or Zzounds). All of these online retailers offer "bundles" in all price ranges that'll give you plenty for your money — and remember to stop at the bookstore for the corresponding *For Dummies* books!

OFF THE RECORD

The best news of all is: Hits have been known to come from home studios. In 2007, a fellow named Adam Young made and recorded music in his parents' basement in Owatonna, Minnesota, using gear similar to that discussed earlier in this chapter. He put his tunes up on MySpace, and before long he was getting a lot of attention, which turned into a big-deal recording contract. Now when you hear "Fireflies" by Owl City (the name Young records under), you're hearing the fruit of DIY recording.

Old School vs. Home Schooled

Many who pursue a career in music spend years learning the trade. Budding artists dream of attending Julliard, and boatloads of very talented students audition for acceptance all around the globe. There are awesome schools out there that cater to the best and brightest talent, and we commend those who have traveled down that road. The very good news is that for all the rest of us perhaps not so awesomely talented souls, there are now other options.

Take a brief visit searching the Internet for music schools and training options, and you will find a never-ending supply of leads. In the following sections, we highlight just a few to get you pointed in the right direction.

Instrument playing: 101

Have you ever wished you could master the guitar or piano like the greats? What if it took no more than a few weeks, days, or even hours? Sounds pretty tempting, doesn't it? There are some really cool tools and software programs that teach you the basics of playing just about any instrument. One example of this is Piano Wizard (or Guitar Wizard for all of you rock gods), an amazingly simple video game that teaches you how to master the piano. Even though you might think that video games are for kids, this one is great for really big "kids" as well.

Check out Piano Wizard — or the other software programs out there that are similar — to assist you with your instrument of choice. Using a tool such as this to get up to speed quickly and proficiently so you can at least get your songwriting ideas and concepts put to music is . . . what do they say? Priceless!

Is it live or is it Memorex?

Okay, so everyone seems to be striving for perfection, but when do we take that obsession too far? The great benefit of a really good song is that it can reach way deep down and touch a chord in your soul. There is a human element that cannot be performed by machines or technology that literally speaks to you and brings forth an emotion. And sometime that element comes in the form of our imperfections — God forbid we ever hit an off-key note! Having that duly noted, there are some really cool devices that are now being used by more artists than you'd expect.

Whether it be the use of such high-tech tools as compressors or delay units to enhance vocals, it's now becoming more difficult to discern whether what you are listening to is live or Memorex — can you recall those old Memorex commercials of years ago? One such tool is the audio processing software known as Auto-Tune. The use of Auto-Tune (a high-tech vocal pitch-correcting tool) has jumped into high gear on pop records around the world ever since Cher used it on her hit single "Believe" in 1998 (written by Brian Higgins, Stuart McLennen, Paul Barry, Steven Torch, Matthew Gray, and Timothy Powell).

Virtual song recordings

If you are comfortable and fairly proficient with a computer, and you enjoy the new opportunities that the Internet has brought us in the twenty-first century, you are likely a "new school" candidate for virtual songwriting collaborations and recordings. You don't have to be a *millennial* (the generation following the baby boomers, who are especially adept in the use of and are familiar with communications, media, and digital technologies — yes that's why teenagers can grasp the functions of a cell phone light years faster than their parents!) to get on this "virtual" bandwagon.

Let's put it this way. How would you like to find and communicate with top professional talent, negotiate agreements, share (and protect) files, and make payments — all the things you would normally do in a studio — online, from anywhere, at any time of the day or night? What if you could go online and find a website that allows producers, mixers, and musicians, regardless of geographical location, to create, collaborate on, and manage musical recording projects? Wouldn't that be a cool service to provide to a fresh, new songwriting talent? Well, that's exactly what the creators of Virtual Recording Studio, eSession, and other virtual song recording websites have set out to do for songwriters across cyberspace.

It is no longer a pipedream to imagine a day when you can sit with your laptop in the comfort of your home and collaborate with the best musicians, engineers, mixers, vocalists, and songwriters in their area of expertise. What does that do to your Rolodex file potency? All that's needed to get started is create your own *sketch* (a rough beginning of a finished masterpiece) with a program like Apple's Garage-Band, then hook into one of these songwriting services, and off you go into the World Wide Web of virtual collaboration. Some music software programs even enable you to use audio/video plug-ins so that two people in two different locations can record, produce, and collaborate in real time from any operating system, Mac or Windows, and in perfect sync and harmony.

Think of iChat or AOL Instant Messenger (AIM) meets Pro-Tools and you get the idea. The result? Beautiful music to any songwriter's ears.

OFF THE RECORD

It's been my career mission to help songwriters move into the digital age without the intimidation factor of technology and to let them know it's possible to learn this stuff without wanting to take a sledgehammer to the computer. For example, ASCAP's Collaborator Corner 2.0, hosted and powered by eSession, lets you search for and interact with thousands of songwriters, composers, musicians, engineers, and producers. You can then negotiate, contract, and collaborate online from the comfort of your home studio, or anywhere you have Internet access. This is the power of technology.

— GINA FANT-SAEZ, SONGWRITER, HOME STUDIO EXPERT, AUTHOR OF PRO TOOLS FOR MUSICIANS & SONGWRITERS, AND CEO OF ESESSION.COM

REMEMBER

New technology seems to change so rapidly nowadays that it almost makes your head spin — just don't let fear of the unknown get in your way of trying out some of these new cool tools. Instead, celebrate and embrace them and treat them as your new best friend.

4

Cooperation, Collaboration, and Community

IN THIS PART . . .

In this part, we explore online marketing methods
and how to use the art of social networking to your
advantage. You get to see how the right collaborator
can help you complete your musical vision, and how
you can perfect these strategies of cooperation and
community to build a solid base and examine the
networking possibilities that can increase your creative
and business powers exponentially. We also give you
directions for how to write and submit your songs
for television, movies, and theater, plus provide the
whole low down on making your demo stand out in
a competitive market.

IN THIS CHAPTER

» **Recognizing your strengths as a songwriter**

» **Collaborating with others to write a song**

» **Splitting up the writers' share**

» **Getting to know the famous songwriting teams**

» **Being in the right place at the right time**

» **Raising the level of your networking circle**

» **Finding your inspiration in harmony**

Chapter **12**

Bringing Talent Together: Collaboration and Networking

Y ou may be one of those rare individuals who can literally do it all when it comes to the creation and presentation of your song. But more than likely, you're like most mortals who, in the process of bringing their songs to fruition, need to team up with other talented people. If so, you've come to the right place. This chapter is all about the fine art of collaboration — an all-important element of songwriting. This chapter also covers networking places, where you can reach out to other songwriters and music industry people.

Finding Your Strengths and Weaknesses

Collaboration is a great way to write a killer song. When a team gets hot — look out! The sparks (and hits!) can really start to fly. But before you call your potential Paul McCartney on the phone, do a thorough self-inventory and ask yourself, "What are my strengths?" Take a look at these specific areas of songwriting to help define your own role in the process:

>> **Melody:** If you're the kind of person who goes about your business every day with a tune in your head, whether it's your own or another's, your talent may lie in the area of melody. A strong melody is an important element in practically every style of songwriting, so your talents will be well put to use as a member of a collaborative team.

>> **Chord structure:** The chords are often called the *foundation* of a song. If chord progressions are your specialty, this talent will be a useful tool as you become an effective member of any songwriting partnership.

>> **Lyrics:** If you're the kind of person who is very observant of life and who loves jotting down ideas, philosophies, insights, and so on — even putting these inspirations in some kind of poetic form — your strength may lie in the field of lyric writing. In every collaboration, at least one of the partners must excel in this area.

>> **Rhythm:** Maybe you're the kind of person who is constantly pounding out a beat on your desktop or steering wheel. Perhaps you love to spend hours on end programming exciting beats on your electronic rhythm box. Writing teams can surely use this type of talent because many songs are actually built up from these rhythmic grooves.

>> **Musical hooks and riffs:** An often-underrated element of a song is the repeating musical series of notes known as a *riff.* Everyone remembers the signature fuzz-tone guitar figure at the beginning of "Satisfaction" (written by Mick Jagger and Keith Richards; performed by The Rolling Stones), the guitar part at the top of "Day Tripper" (written by Paul McCartney and John Lennon; performed by The Beatles), or the intro horn riff of "Vehicle" (written by Jim Peterik; performed by The Ides of March). If riffs are your musical forte, you can undoubtedly be a valuable asset to any writing session.

>> **Editing and overview:** Knowing what's good and what isn't is a talent in itself. In many great songwriting teams, there is one great overview person who acts as a kind of sounding board for all ideas that are flying around the room. Not that they don't have creative ideas of their own, but the main strength here is

knowing what's hot and what's not. It's certainly a good idea to have a person with this talent on your team.

>> **Some combination of these talents:** You may be one of those unique and lucky people who have all the preceding talents (or some combination of them in varying degrees). All the better! However, try to be honest with yourself and spend time doing what you do best — knowing there are others available who can help round out the team.

TIP

A great writing team is one of balance — where one partner is especially strong in certain areas, the other one is weak (and vice versa). If your talents skew toward the music side, find a brilliant lyricist (many poets are simply songwriters without a melody). If your passion runs to expressing your heart through words, but you only have a passing acquaintance with a musical instrument, track down that guy that you heard jamming down at the local Guitar Center — the one who made everyone's jaw drop.

Perhaps you hear rhythms in your head and you're dying to set them to music. Or maybe you're just one of those people who has that gift of knowing a great musical idea when you hear one, and you just need to be around the right inspiration to bring all the pieces together. Whatever your strengths and weaknesses, the right collaborator can be the missing piece in your songwriting puzzle.

OFF THE
RECORD

I've had experiences where two excellent songwriters who attempt to write a song come up short because their strengths, shortcomings, and attitudes are too similar. They basically are two of the same and end up canceling each other out. Sometimes a skeptical way of looking at things can actually complement someone else's positive outlook. When Paul McCartney wrote the words, "It's getting better all the time," in the Beatle's song of the same name, John Lennon chimed in, "Can't get no worse!" It was the bitter mixed with the sweet that made their collaborations so rich in texture.

— JIM PETERIK, PERFORMER, SONGWRITER, AND MULTI-INSTRUMENTALIST FOR BOTH IDES OF MARCH AND SURVIVOR, PLUS WRITER OF HITS FOR .38 SPECIAL, SAMMY HAGAR, AND OTHERS

TIP

Songwriting workshops are a great place to locate other songwriters with whom to collaborate. The Internet is a great source of songwriting associations that can lead you to such workshops in your area.

Seeking the Chemistry of Collaborative Songwriting

OFF THE RECORD

Many times publishers will often put writers together in a see-what-happens, blind-date sort of way. This process often seems very impersonal and cold, so it's a good idea, before writing even one note, to go out for a cup of coffee to get to know each other a bit and find out a little about what makes the other person tick. In doing so, a better song may be the result.

Collaborative songwriting is as much about the chemistry between people as it is about individual talent. Take note of other factors that enter into a session and affect the vibe, such as the writing environment, the time of day, the weather conditions, and the mental and physical conditions of the various partners. At the end of the day, though, if a song is meant to be written, it'll happen — even under the worst possible conditions.

As a good collaborator, knowing when to step forward with an idea and when to "wait in the weeds" and let the talents of others shine through is important. Also, try to stay open about where the session goes, and don't be too strict in following the agenda that you may have planned out. Accommodating all the possibilities of the moment may yield a song that is totally beyond the boundaries you create on your own. Always expect the unexpected and allow for the possibility of pure musical magic to break through.

WORDS OF WISDOM

The most important lesson I've learned through the years is to let go of preconceived notions. We can be so ingrained with being in control of our lives that we're afraid to let a writing situation run wild. On one particular occasion, I had the pleasure of writing with Henry Paul and Dave Robbins of the platinum country-rock act Blackhawk. I came armed with my usual sheaf of ideas earmarked for the band. But as the three of us sat behind our guitars and keyboards in the warm glow of the neon beer sign in Hank's studio, the brotherhood between us suddenly seemed a lot bigger than any idea I had intended on showing them. As we sat talking, just idly strumming our guitars, chords started lining up, words started flowing, cassettes started rolling, and the first of two songs started emerging — "Brothers of the Southland," a sincere ode to the brotherhood of southern rockers past and present. It was not a song we had planned to write, but it was the right song for that day. On the following day, guided by the same patient muse, we wrote "Spirit Dancer," a tribute to Van Stephenson, one of the founding members of Blackhawk, who had succumbed to cancer at the age of 47. A brilliant songwriter himself — he wrote "Bluest Eyes in Texas" (co-writers: Van Stephenson, Dave Robbins, and

Tim DuBois), "Every Once in a While" (co-writers: Van Stephenson, Henry Paul, and Dave Robbins), "Modern Day Delilah" (co-writers: Van Stephenson and Jan Buckingham), and many more. We used references from some of his best-loved songs and even used the Native American translation of "I love you, I miss you," which became a chant throughout the song. I have learned that letting go of what you think you know about songwriting is as important as knowing the craft itself.

— JIM PETERIK, WRITER OF 18 BILLBOARD TOP 10 HITS

TIP

Be honest with your co-writers. If they show you an idea that you have absolutely no affinity for (or if you literally think it stinks!), let them know diplomatically. You could say, "That's a great idea, but it's really not my style. Let's hear what else you have." Songwriters can exchange ideas all day long before they find one that strikes both of their fancies. Don't settle until you find that common ground. Find a writing partner who can challenge, inspire, push, and sometimes annoy you into being the best you can be.

Making sure you're in harmony with your team

Have you ever heard the saying "what goes around, comes around?" The same holds true when looking for collaborators and co-writing partnerships. To find the perfect partners, you need to put yourself out there and offer your services to others in your songwriting community — as they also say, "the more you give, the more you receive," so based on these philosophies, the best way to get what you are looking for is to provide your talents and wisdom to others *before* you expect theirs in return.

WORDS OF WISDOM

Take the lead given by the "king of collaboration" himself, Carlos Santana. This master musician demonstrates how far you can stretch the limits — evidenced by his amazing collaborative efforts. Just how many Grammys or hit records does it take to get that message across? Hmm lemme see!

The other part of the equation comes after you've found the perfect partner; make it a major priority to maintain that harmony as best you can. You never know where your paths will take you — or how often they may cross with your peers.

For instance, take a look at an example of cooperation and collaboration at its best when the Dave Matthews Band performed their hit "You and Me" at the 2010 Grammy Awards. Imagine how amazing a feeling it would be to have 45 musicians and singers bring your "intimate" song creation to life in front of millions of people around the globe — it's almost as if Dave Matthews came right out of his body during a interlude in the song as he began dancing to "a different beat" while mingling with his peers and fellow performers. That performance basically took on a life of its own — add to that the imagery of flowing water in the river of life backdrop, the song's message of "you and me together," an assortment of cultures, instruments, and ages blended together in harmony, and you get an even deeper meaning of the art of collaboration!

OFF THE
RECORD

Another notable Grammy moment was when Blink 182's Travis Barker, Lil Wayne, Eminem, and Drake all took the stage in a performance collaboration that blended their talents while expressing their unique individualities. It was a powerful combination where their mutual admiration was evident, but would someone please explain how they were able to keep those pants up anyway? And what about all those "bleeps" during their telecast! We're just relieved and lucky there weren't any wardrobe malfunctions!

Finding strength in numbers

How many geniuses does it take to write a hit? There are no hard-and-fast rules as to the optimum number of collaborators on a songwriting team. For The Beatles, the magic number was two; out of the many songs Lennon and McCartney wrote, only 27 of them were written together (even though they shared credit on their entire catalogue), but their undeniable chemistry seems to be present on all their tunes, even in each other's absence. For the Brothers Gibb (better known as The Bee Gees), the writing was split three ways no matter how much each brother may or may not have contributed. In the following sections, we outline some popular writing configurations, along with the pluses and minuses of each.

The two-way split

The image of two songwriters in a dingy room with a broken-down upright piano somehow creating musical magic is one of the most enduring and inspiring images in movie memory. The fact is, however, that this mythical image has plenty of basis in truth. Duos throughout the years such as Rodgers and Hart, Bacharach and David, and Jagger and Richards have proven that, as in the words of Harry Nilsson, sometimes "one is the loneliest number you can ever do," and as Nick Ashford and Valerie Simpson crooned, "What two can easily do, is so hard to be done by one." It's hard to argue with the statistics (songwriting duos have had more success than any other combination — three can truly be a crowd especially if the chemistry is not right). Duos, in general, may be so successful simply because there aren't too many ideas being generated in the room, and it's therefore easier to focus on the good ones. Too many opinions can lead to "a camel" — a horse designed by committee — and camels are just not as sleek and beautiful as a well-groomed thoroughbred.

The three-way split

There are times in songwriting when three is not a crowd, however — in fact, it's the perfect number. If each person in a three-way split has a particular strength, it can become a triple threat. Also, if two of you are deadlocked on the validity of an idea, the third wheel can break the tie and act as a kind of arbiter over the proceedings.

WARNING

When a three-way is bad, it's really bad, with three times the disagreements of doing it alone. If the third member of the team is a negative influence (perhaps there's a "my way or the highway" type or someone who's not open to the others' ideas), he'll more than likely suffocate the creative process. In that case, three really are too many, no matter how brilliant his ideas may be.

More than three

Sometimes when you're part of a band, or are writing for a band, three, four, five, or even more people will be in a room attempting to write a song. Though this arrangement can sometimes work, getting a consensus in the room with everyone fighting for their own idea can be extremely difficult. And, from a business point of view, a collaboration like this splits up the publishing pie into sliverlike pieces and makes it difficult for anyone to make any real money (unless the song becomes a mega hit). On the other hand, you should never limit the size of a writing party merely to maximize each person's individual share. Just make sure that everyone is pulling their weight and that no one is just taking up space. Having coffee with everyone is nice, but it's not necessarily great in songwriting.

OFF THE RECORD

On several occasions I have had the honor of sharing the stage with a master hit songwriter, Eliot Sloan of Blessid Union fame, and each time during our presentations we actually created a song by collaborating with the entire audience — among more than a thousand people in the room at once. Yes it was only the seeds of those songs that were birthed during these inspired sessions and the finished songs were crafted later in the privacy of his home studio, but these songs were initially created using the hundreds of random thoughts that were floating around in the room when the creative atmosphere was created. This is the same environment we create in our Creative Expressions Workshops, where Eliot and I also collaborate. So even though it is not the norm, there are times when great songs can be born of the masses.

— DAVE AUSTIN, MENTAL PERFORMANCE COACH, PROFESSIONAL ATHLETE, PLUS THE NATIONAL ACADEMY OF RECORDING ARTS AND SCIENCES (NARAS) PRESIDENTIAL MERIT AWARD RECIPIENT AND FORMER RECORD LABEL EXECUTIVE

REMEMBER

Take notes after each session as to who did what and whom you'd consider writing with again. If there were any bad working habits displayed, make note of those as well before these memories fade into the night.

Collaborating with a band or an artist

Knowing how to write with a band or an artist is an art in itself. It means becoming like an extra member of the group or an extension of the artist you're working with. Every band or solo performer has a style of his own; the outside writer's challenge is to adapt his style to that of the artist. It's not that you can't bring your personality and vibe to the party, but you should never obscure or try to change what the artist is all about. And try as you might, most artists won't allow you to tamper too much with who they are. It's also important to be a statesman and discover the politics of each situation. Every band has a unique dynamic, and the more you can find out about who does what, the better. Also, if they're new to the outside-writer game, taking it slow and easy is best. Get to know each other personally and musically. Here are some tips on how to work with a band or artist:

>> Listen to as much of a band's or artist's recorded work as you can prior to your writing session to get familiar with their sound, direction, and flavor. It's also a good idea to see them perform live, to get a feel for their style and the kind of audience that they attract. (This applies especially if you are writing with a new act that has limited recorded work.)

>> Learn as much about the artist or band members as you can so you feel as if you know something about them before you even meet (we're not talking about doing background checks — we're talking about reading their interviews and getting info off of their website).

>> Arrange a meeting with the artist or band to scope out their dynamic, individual strengths as songwriters, and to determine their objectives for the project you're writing for. Discuss whether they would like to stay with their current sound or try to break some new ground.

>> Find out what they hope to accomplish with their new project and what they're hoping you'll bring to the writing table.

>> Ask to hear their ideas first, when you're at the writing session, before suggesting that they work on one of yours.

>> If they're open to hearing your musical or lyrical ideas, have confidence in your presentation, but avoid being too pushy. If they reject an idea, try not to sit there and sulk for the rest of the session!

- ›› Don't be afraid to offer constructive criticism regarding their songs. But be a good statesman and make sure you present it in a diplomatic way. For instance say, "It might be better if we came up with a memorable hook for this song," as opposed to, "Hey you morons, haven't you ever heard of a hook?"

- ›› Don't belabor a song that you don't all have a mutual affinity with. It's okay to say, "This is a good idea but I might not be the guy to help you with this one." Make sure they know to be just as upfront with you.

OFF THE RECORD

Years ago, I had the opportunity to write with one of my favorite artists, Sammy Hagar, the "Red Rocker." He picked me up at the airport in San Francisco and whisked me off to his Mill Valley spread in his brand-new Ferrari Daytona. After a few cups of high-octane coffee, we picked up our guitars and proceeded to stare awkwardly at each other for about an hour. He finally broke the silence and told me he'd never written with anyone face to face before and was afraid he'd say something dumb or play something that wasn't absolutely brilliant. He was used to messing up only in private! I eased his mind and told him that we were both bound to lay out some pretty embarrassing stuff — and I proceeded to prove my point. After that, things started to fly — and in two hours, we'd written and recorded a demo for what became the main title for the animated classic Heavy Metal. Sammy obviously got rid of his jitters permanently and went on to collaborate on countless hits as a member of the band Van Halen.

— JIM PETERIK, WRITER OF 18 BILLBOARD TOP 10 HITS

Collaborating with a script

Though not a true collaboration, many writers consider the script of a movie to be a silent member of the writing team. The songwriter often uses the storyline, characters, language, and style as an inspirational stepping-off point for the song.

OFF THE RECORD

Frankie Sullivan and I were lucky enough to have the nearly finished *Rocky III* movie to watch as we wrote its theme, "Eye of the Tiger." Having those powerful visuals to inspire us and the motivational story to guide us, it's no wonder we came up with a lasting song. The movie footage was like a third person in the room. Similarly, when we wrote for *Rocky IV*, we worked from the finished script and were able to find key phrases in the dialogue to help us flesh out the lyric. The result was the song "Burning Heart."

TIP

You can try your hand at writing for film by picking a movie that you really like and can get into. If you don't already own it on DVD, rent it so you can see it over and over if necessary. Use the storyline or script as your writing partner, and let the feeling and emotion of the movie inspire a song or two within you. Use some of its dialogue as a starting point and go from there. If nothing of substance materializes, pick a different movie — one that may give you more to work with for your practicing purposes.

Collaborating with yourself

Though not technically a songwriting team (unless you happen to have a split personality!), you can often make use of the popular writing technique known as *self-collaboration*. If you're having a case of writer's block in a given week (and it happens to the very best), it's a good idea to go through your stockpile of notebooks and files to find the gems that maybe you couldn't quite finish before. Often, so much time has passed that you can barely remember writing what you were working on back then, and it almost feels like you're collaborating with someone else — plus, you have the advantage of gaining perspective on an idea that you couldn't quite bring home the first time around.

Interestingly enough, with the passage of time and a fresh outlook, you can almost always tell why you were unable to finish a song in the first place. You're able to gain the perspective a collaborator usually has, but on your own work. With the gift of time elapsed, you can often see the flaws, the missing pieces, the lack of focus, and poor organization that you couldn't see before, and you're now able to take steps to correct those problems. This is known in production as "having fresh ears."

Dividing Up the Credits

When a song is finally finished, it's a good idea to decide then and there how the songwriting credits will be divided. At the risk of blowing the mood, while everyone's memory is fresh, put down on paper who did what. If you want to make it more official, you may want to consider a songwriting contract between the collaborators that everyone signs to make the splits official. The Songwriters Guild of America can supply you with various standard forms to use. Some writers use their ASCAP or BMI forms to make the writers' splits official.

WARNING

In the absence of an agreement, any of the writers technically could claim an equal share of the song regardless of their contribution, so putting it all in writing is a really good idea.

There are many philosophies as to how the writing credits should be split up, but there is no standard method. In the following sections, we provide some guidelines as to the most common ways to cut up the pie.

The Nashville method

Nashville is to some the songwriting capitol of the world. It's the town where practically everyone you run into is there for one thing — to be where the action is in the field of songwriting. Whether they're waiting tables, playing at the local bar, or showcasing at The Bluebird Café (*the* happening showcase room for songwriters, often hosting roundtables where three or four of the world's most successful songwriters will take turns playing each other's hits), the Rutledge, or the Listening Room, they're all there for the same reason.

Nashville is also the mecca for collaboration. The way it usually works is that one of the many publishing companies will hear about a particular artist who is looking for material for his or her next release. The publisher rounds up its best writers and plays cupid, putting different writers together (usually two-way writes, but sometimes three-way). Sometimes a publisher will call another publisher if there is someone in that stable they feel could bring something unique to the party. The established writers in town are very familiar and comfortable with this kind of roulette, where they might write with three different groups of writers on any given day. It's not unusual for a writer to have completed five or six songs by the end of the week and have them demoed by Wednesday of the following week.

In the Nashville method, whoever is in the room actively writing a song gets an equal share of the writer's credit. This has been the etiquette in Nashville for many years because its writers have learned that they would rather be writing the *next* song then arguing about who did what and for how much on the *last* one. If someone ends up getting equal credit when they didn't pull their weight, they just won't be asked back.

WARNING

No matter how the seasoned pros do it in Nashville, it's better to write one great song than five mediocre ones. However, they're not all going to be gems no matter what you do. Sometimes you'll find one great song in ten you've written. Don't be afraid that the songs you're writing won't live up to the hits (either yours or others). Try your best to leave judgment at the door and not let past successes (or failures) affect the present. Keep a positive outlook and stop comparing everything you write to other successful songs. The art of letting your inspirations fly takes a clear and open mind.

The honor system

The honor system is where, after a song is finished, the splits are discussed with all partners present. Besides the common 50/50 split, it isn't unusual for percentages to be divvied up 60/40 or 70/30 for a two-way collaboration. In a situation where one person wrote all the music and the other wrote all the lyrics, it's practically always a 50/50 split. For a three-way write, it's not unusual to see 50/25/25, 40/30/30, and other variations. Try to avoid goofy fractions that will make accounting a nightmare (and will mean next to nothing in the long run), and make sure the percentages don't add up to more than 100. (Don't laugh — it happens!)

The Spinal Tap system

The Spinal Tap method basically happens after the song is done, when everyone has a few drinks and starts arguing about who did what. One guy might start counting the words he contributed and try to affix a percentage to every word. The other guy will claim 50 percent on the strength of the riff he created for the song — until the bass player reminds him that it was actually *his* lick from another song. At that point, the roadie comes in and reminds everyone that it was his girlfriend who inspired the song and that he should get a piece (of the song, that is!). He's cut short by his girlfriend, who just arrived and recognizes the belly ring described in the song as hers and demands payment for the procedure from future royalties. Scenes like these really do happen, and they can take the fun out of songwriting and create bad feelings all the way around, not to mention driving up everyone's blood pressure!

REMEMBER

If a song is successful, there'll be lots of money to go around. If it's a stiff, then all the nitpicking you do won't matter anyway.

WARNING

It's hard to make any generalizations on the differences between writing with men and writing with women. You can't necessarily say that women are more sensitive writers than men or any other such stereotypical nonsense. There are songs written by guys with the heart of a poet just as there are some women who are as tough as nails — it really doesn't seem to matter if you're an X or you're a Y — both bring something valuable to the mix.

Looking at Famous Songwriting Collaborations

Musical sparks can ignite when there's an open flow of ideas between like-minded individuals and a free exchange of information. These conditions have paved the way for various creative wellsprings that have emerged through the years such as the hit factory known as the Brill Building in New York City in the '50s and early '60s, which spawned writers such as Gerry Goffin and Carol King, Neil Sedaka, Neil Diamond, Barry Mann and Cynthia Weil, and more, plus Motown (Berry Gordy's creative Camelot in Detroit in the early 1960s that grew into a multi-million-dollar entertainment conglomerate that's still active decades later). These were situations in which people weren't afraid to help one another, knowing full well that by combining creative juices they could achieve more than they could on their own.

In the following sections, we take a look at a few notable writing teams to see who does what and what makes their songs tick.

John Lennon and Paul McCartney

John Lennon and Paul McCartney were the main writing force behind The Beatles. John and Paul were both equally gifted in words and music. In the early days of The Beatles, they wrote in the same room (or van), each one bringing to the party the start of an idea for the other's input, until they had something good enough to show the rest of the boys. Oftentimes, the other one was there to add a bridge to an otherwise complete song. Later in The Beatles' career they would write more on their own, only showing each other their songs for comments after they were practically finished. By nature of their original songwriter's agreement, however, they always shared their copyrights 50/50, figuring (correctly so) that their individual contributions would even out in the end.

What made their collaborations truly special were the different ways John and Paul looked at life. John's cynical nature made a good counterpoint to Paul's oftentimes Pollyanna optimism. When The Beatles broke up and they no longer wrote as a team, John's songs often seemed abrasive and a bit defensive — with some notable exceptions, like "Starting Over" and his master-work, "Imagine" — while Paul's sentimental streak dominated songs like "Silly Love Songs" and "My Love" (co-written by Linda McCartney), which might have benefited from a dose of John's clarifying wit. After ending their collaborative efforts, they both continued to write great songs on their own, even without the contrast provided by each other's own unique worldview.

Burt Bacharach and Hal David

The hits of this gifted team just go on and on with "What the World Needs Now," "Alfie," "Do You Know the Way to San Jose," and "I Say a Little Prayer for You." Their songs have been recorded by countless artists and are constantly being redone and updated by contemporary artists.

In the case of Bacharach and David, their duties were well delineated: Burt supplied the music and Hal wrote the words. The integration of words and music would take place in any number of ways. In some instances, Burt would supply a portion of the music and Hal would write the words to that section with the two of them collaborating in the same room on the next part. Other times Hal would supply Burt with a lyric or a portion of a lyric and he would set it to music. Basically every means of combining music with words was used in creating the classic songs of Burt Bacharach and Hal David. Not that there weren't some successful misunderstandings in the process, like when Hal received a tape from Burt with the music that would become "Magic Moments," a big hit for Perry Como. Hal wrote the extremely busy lyric — the part about the hayride and the sleigh ride — over the section the Burt had intended to be the intro! The chorus was then written where the verse was supposed to go. A happy accident indeed, yielding a song perhaps more unique than Burt had originally imagined.

Bernie Taupin and Elton John

You'd be hard pressed to find a more prolific and successful writing team in popular music than these two. Like Lennon and McCartney, who mainly wrote with The Beatles in mind, Bernie and Elton exist mainly to supply a steady stream of hits to one artist: Elton John. Answering Bernie's ad in the personal column of a London newspaper, Elton John (Reginald Dwight at the time) found his partner of destiny with one fortuitous phone call.

Bernie was a poet without a song, and Elton was a brilliant piano player and songwriter in search of words. Usually, Bernie would drop off a few sheets of lyrics and Elton would put them on his piano and go through them one by one until something struck his fancy. Often the song was completed in 45 minutes or less (to this day, if it takes Elton more than half an hour to finish a tune, he'll move on, often never to revisit it). Songs like "Your Song," "Goodbye Yellow Brick Road," and "The One" are all timeless testimony to the power of their collaborations. They both have written successfully with other partners (most notably the songs Elton has written with lyricist Tim Rice for *The Lion King*, *Aida*, and other works), but the songwriting team of Bernie and Elton will probably define each of them for years to come.

Elton John is not only a master of songwriting collaboration, but also a master in his live performances. Notable Grammy telecast moments include a duo performance with Eminem, and then years later in the Lady Gaga medley — arguably the greatest showman and show-woman in the music business paired up together for a musical and visual feast — you just gotta love it!

Networking for Songwriters

There are zillions of places where you can reach out to songwriters and others in the music business — making yourself available for others to reach out to you. We suggest that you check out the places below to get a healthy exchange of ideas (plus e-mail addresses!) and see how great music cannot only be created, but where it can find an audience as well. Some main sources for networking (covered in more depth later) include the following:

>> **Writers' nights:** Intimate club-type gatherings where you can interact with songwriting associates, watch or perform new songs live, and make new friends.

>> **Writers' organizations:** By researching the various organizations — big and small, international and local — you can find out which ones best suit your needs and budget.

>> **Writers' camps and cruises:** Getaway places in the woods (or out on the sea) for workshops that promise to be filled with inspiration and education for the aspiring songwriter along with instructional advice from songwriting pros.

>> **Internet roulette:** A place to get the ball rolling (the mouse ball that is) by surfing the 'net. There's an enormous amount of information — actually more than you'll ever need — at your fingertips that can be accessed by doing a keyword search through a search engine like Google. It's just a matter of finding enough spare time to use it.

>> **Seminars, workshops, conferences, and symposiums:** Educational and inspirational programs that offer opportunities to learn from and network with others. Get on their mailing lists and expand your horizons with these resources — the bonus is that some events are free.

Hanging Out at Writers' Nights

The writers' night is a phenomenon that came into form and popularity in the "beatnik" coffee houses of the '50s (along with usually avant-garde poetry readings) and has been gaining steam and prestige with every passing decade. They're usually held at fairly intimate (that's code for "cramped and smoky") clubs and sponsored either by the visionary club owner or a nearby writers' association. They generally take one of two forms:

>> Showcases where writers take the stage one at a time and perform a few of their songs (usually kept to around 20 minutes by a soundman with his eye on the clock).

>> Showcases where a group of usually three or four songwriters perform together (often in a roundtable formation) and take turns accompanying and harmonizing (even trading verses) with each other on their songs.

Even as a member of the audience, you can get a lot out of these nights. You can observe the songs that are and are not working, and then try to gauge your own songs and performing readiness against what you've heard. Be sure to introduce yourself to as many people as you can (including the club owner, sound technician, industry representatives, and all the performing writers). Network, network, network!!! And see if you can convince the organization to include you the next time there's a similar writers' showcase.

The exposure you can receive from word of mouth within the songwriting industry is perhaps more important than the exposure you get from the audience in general. At events such as these, as much activity takes place offstage as it does onstage, with phone numbers exchanged, co-writes planned, and ideas brainstormed.

REMEMBER

Make sure you follow up with the people you meet in these types of events. It's easy to make promises to call or get together in the glow of the night and after a few beers, but even more important is your following through.

TIP

If you can't find an existing writers' night or showcase in your area, why not organize your own? It's not hard to put a flyer up at the local music store or post it on your website. Just mention that you'll be hosting a writers' roundtable at your home (or convince a club owner that it'd be good for building business on an off-night). A $5 entrance fee should more than cover the snacks and overhead. Plus, a workshop of your own is a great way of making new contacts.

Joining Songwriting Organizations

Many organizations are designed to aid the songwriter in every stage of the game. Almost all major cities (and many smaller ones) have established songwriters' guilds and clubs to help develop and market your songs. Whether you live in Pittsburgh or Portland or any point in between, you'll find it relatively easy to locate those who share your same passion for songs. Here are a few organizations that can help you network your talents in the songwriting field.

Nashville Songwriters Association International

NSAI is a not-for-profit songwriters' organization based in Nashville, but it covers the United States and a few foreign countries and includes all genres of music. Besides being an effective defender for the rights of the songwriter (fighting for royalty protection and so on), it's a terrific resource for the songwriter at any stage of his development in the craft and business of songwriting.

In fact, after you become a member, you can take advantage of their song-critiquing service (where pros evaluate your song for you — free of charge) and attend symposiums, song camps, cruises, and workshops. You'll also benefit from their quarterly newsletters, special events, and use of their office facilities when needed.

WORDS OF WISDOM

NSAI's yearly Tin Pan South event is simply the biggest week-long celebration of the art of songwriting in the world. Every single club in Nashville is booked with celebrity songwriters, and celebrity artists show up too. Music City USA treats songwriters with the ultimate respect they deserve, especially because of the tremendous efforts of NSAI, working in concert with songwriters, publishers,and all the other performing rights organizations.

— DAVID PACK, GRAMMY AWARD–WINNING ARTIST, PRODUCER, AND THE FRONTMAN, VOCALIST, AND GUITARIST FOR THE ROCK GROUP AMBROSIA

Songwriters Guild of America

The Songwriters Guild of America (SGA, or simply the Guild) offers a wealth of information and services for its members, including sample songwriter's contracts, reviews of publishing contracts, and a copyright renewal service. SGA also offers its members online and offline classes in songwriting and the music business, plus in-depth song evaluations, royalty collection services, and other music industry resources — they even have Ask-A-Pro, which is an opportunity to get your questions answered my music industry professionals!

WORDS OF WISDOM

I only wish I had known about organizations like the Songwriters Guild of America years ago when I was starting out. Even now, they're a great source of knowledge when it comes to songwriting contracts, writer contacts, and performing (for a below-standard industry fee) many of the functions of a publishing administrator such as filling out and filing songwriting forms and other paperwork. Their song-critiquing service and rewrite workshops could've really shaved a lot of time off my craft learning curve if I'd been smart enough to take advantage of organizations like these — but as the saying goes, "it's never too late!"

— JIM PETERIK, WRITER OF 18 BILLBOARD TOP 10 HITS

Don't get discouraged by criticism, especially from the pros; consider it an opportunity to improve your songwriting. However, if you really believe in an idea, no one's opinion is more important than your own.

Attending Seminars, Workshops, Conferences, and Symposiums

Practically every writers' club, society, and organization puts together song workshops and seminars for their songwriting communities. This is where you can get together with other songwriters and hear lectures by great writers and industry hot shots and participate in roundtable discussions on the craft with other songwriters at all stages of development. There may be a talk from a lyricist, a composer, a producer, an A&R rep, a commercial writer, a film scorer, and a publisher. These workshops are an indispensable tool to the serious songwriter and a brilliant way to network.

There are virtually hundreds of these events around the world. Besides the most famous ones like the South By Southwest Music and Media Conference (SXSW) held each year in Austin, Texas, and MIDEM which takes place annually in Cannes, France, you can find many others on music sites on the Internet and in songwriters' resource books (such as *Billboard Musician's Guide to Touring and Promotion,* a Billboard publication, *The Musician's Atlas* published by Music Resource Group, and *Songwriter's Market* published by Writer's Digest Books).

When you mingle with like minds, you're expanding your opportunities exponentially. You've probably heard the saying, "It's not what you know, it's *whom* you know." Well, it's really both. It's just not enough to "have the gift," you've got to "work the gift." Workshops, seminars, writer's nights, and songwriting camps and cruises are your opportunities to combine forces with other gifted individuals, and to make the best music of your life. Who knows, that hot-looking songwriter you just met at your last workshop just may be searching for the perfect partner for the movie writing assignment he just landed — and he just may want to collaborate with you!

At the end of the day, it just may be a matter of being at the right place at the right time — it worked for Italian pop tenor, Andrea Bocelli, who became a huge success and crossover artist due in part to the successful duet he did with Sarah Brightman — which occurred after she heard him singing while dining in a restaurant, no less.

Practice Makes Perfect

One of the best ways to practice the art of collaboration is to dive straight in with your arms wide open — make a point of getting informed and involved in your craft. One such way is to combine business with pleasure and attend a camp workshop or cruise — Creative Expressions Workshop is a personal favorite that provides just the right atmosphere to get in touch with your inner source of inspiration. By attending an outing such as this, not only can you vacation and network at the same time, you may just come home with something more than a souvenir — you may be able to sneak away in your suitcase a duty-free hit song collaboration that was created during your stay!

Chapter 13

Online Marketing and Social Networking for Songwriters

The state of the union (musically speaking) is that nothing remains the same, and the recent evolution of our music industry (which has basically been turned upside down and shaken around like a rag doll) reminds us of that fact. And like anything else in its evolutionary process, a variety of new marketing and promotional opportunities for songwriters and musicians have come into play that weren't even in existence a short time ago. Not only are there new ways to sell music, for example, song by song on iTunes and as ringtones for your mobile devices, but Internet marketing sites such as MySpace, Facebook, Twitter, and others have opened up a whole new world for songwriters and musicians.

In this chapter, we focus on various avenues of social marketing, explore the new opportunities for the songwriter who want to broaden their network of friends and associates, and suggest ways to jump on the Internet bandwagon in order to expand their marketing reach.

Playing Internet Roulette

It's taken only a decade for most everyone to have Internet access. And those in the music business find that the Internet is a viable way to solicit songs and network with others. The World Wide Web is just that . . . world wide! Users aren't limited by geographical boundaries, and access is practically instantaneous. That's the up side.

The down side is that accessing someone via the Internet is really only the first step to human interaction, which still requires actual contact between parties where a person's mannerisms, vibe, and voice can come through. Sometimes it is difficult to generate chemistry between people by merely sending e-mails and sound files back and forth. Sooner or later, after initial connections are made, it's important to get in the same room with the contacts you've made online. Whether it's co-writing a song, networking a business plan, or testing out a song, there's still no substitute for in-person interaction.

That being said and done, take a look at the ways you can harness the power of the Internet to find information and opportunity, gain exposure, and help network your talents with others.

Creating your own website

One of the best ways to get the word out about what you're up to as a songwriter is to have your own website — actually, it's a necessity if you want to be taken seriously. If possible, use your own name as your *domain name* (the domain name is the part between the *www* and the *.com*), and do whatever it takes to get a professional-looking site up and running.

There are many resources available that can fill you in on how to set up an effective website yourself, including *Building a Web Site For Dummies,* 3rd Edition, and *Creating Web Pages For Dummies,* 9th Edition, both published by Wiley Publishing, Inc. But if you'd rather not take the time to create the site yourself, hire someone (at a reasonable price) to do it for you.

The goal here is to create a kind of virtual press kit for you and your music, complete with photos, biography, accomplishments, goals and aspirations, and strong suits. Let it be known what kind of people you're looking to connect with. In addition to this, include any songs that you feel best represent your work so that others can listen to them (or purchase a download on the spot). Remember to include all of your affiliations, contact material, and anything else you want to share with the world. This is not a case of "less is best" — be bold and toot your horn a bit about who you are.

Having the best website in the world will make no difference if no one sees it. Be sure to get the word out every way you can think of, including posting it on myriad musical networking sites (more about this later in the chapter). Also, whenever you send out an e-mail message, remember to include an automatic signature at the bottom of the message that mentions your website as well.

Your site can also be a useful forum for ideas. You can post *a blog* (a web log) and pose questions for your peers to answer; you can solicit critiques on the songs or lyrics you've posted (get ready for some very honest responses because people tend to be more candid online than they would be in person). You can also create a "members only" area to your site where you can interact privately with other writers and stream music back and forth for opinions and collaborations.

You must keep your site current and relevant. If visitors see no changes on the site after visiting a few times, they'll stop coming altogether. If inquiries go unanswered, you'll get a bad rap — rightly so! Consider incorporating a blog into your site and keep adding fresh entries on a daily (or at least weekly) basis. Not only will you keep your fans up to date, but this also helps get your website higher up in the search engine rankings.

I was the original "who needs the Internet," but once I had my first site created, my whole perception changed. Not only was it a great way for people to purchase my CDs, but it's also a way for them to get information on my past, present, and future. I get immediate feedback from around the world on what I'm doing right and wrong. And I can post bits and pieces of new things I'm working on as they occur. After I got over "web anxiety" and found a capable webmaster, I found this to be an indispensable component of my career.

— JIM PETERIK, PERFORMER, SONGWRITER, AND MULTI-INSTRUMENTALIST FOR BOTH IDES OF MARCH AND SURVIVOR, PLUS WRITER OF HITS FOR .38 SPECIAL, SAMMY HAGAR, AND OTHERS

Taking advantage of other people's sites

There are multitudes of music and songwriting sites that are helpful in creating awareness for your talents — not to mention a means to finding potential collaborators and contacts. You can cross-pollinate information between your site and other people's sites, and also post your music there for others to listen to and download. Just make sure you have filed the copyright papers for your songs before you share them with the world. You can also distribute your songs to generate revenue on a variety of these sites as well. A few highlights from some of the more popular sites include the following.

Online music stores

These are online businesses that sell audio files, usually in the form of MP3 files. The files are sold either per song or on a subscription basis. The top online music stores include

>> **iTunes:** A digital media player and online music retailer, not just for music, but also movies, TV shows, and more

>> **Amazon Music:** Another online music retail source offering more than 10 million songs for downloading to any device

>> **Napster:** Online music service with both a subscription service and a pay-per-track purchasing option with over 8 million songs.

>> **CDBaby:** Touted as the world's largest online distributor of indie music, and a company run *by* musicians, *for* musicians

Social networking

Web-based social networks provide users with the ability to interact with friends and fans while building a community of people with shared interests: Social networking sites include

>> **MySpace:** The original social networking website where you customize your own site for you or your band, post music for listening purposes, add friends, and create a fan base of gigantic proportions

>> **Facebook:** A social networking site similar to MySpace, but in a slightly different style and method of user profiling (and about several hundred million more subscribers at last count)

>> **Twitter:** A social networking and microblogging service that lets users send and read messages otherwise known as "tweets"

Specialty social networking sites

Some social networking sites cater to a specific user, such as musicians, songwriters, and other music-industry professionals. These sites include

>> **ReverbNation:** A social networking site for musicians, bands, producers, and venues to collaborate and communicate

>> **OurStage:** A social networking community made up of undiscovered artists, music lovers, and industry professionals who want to collaborate with others who share the same interests

- >> **iSounds:** Where both artist and listening fans hook up online for an easy way to discover and stream new music

- >> **Sonicbids:** A place where bands from any genre anywhere in the world can find and connect with industry professionals such as music promoters, licensors, or broadcasters — not to mention a great place to find songwriting competitions and book gigs

Music distribution networks

Services such as music distribution networks provide musicians with the opportunity to place their songs into digital retailers such as iTunes and Amazon. These networks include

- >> **TuneCore:** A digital music and video distribution platform that delivers your songs to the top digital stores (iTunes, Amazon, Rhapsody, and others), without taking a percentage of the sales

- >> **SongCast:** Another music distribution network where you can get your songs sold on iTunes, Amazon, Rhapsody, Napster, and so on

Video and music sharing

Some websites or software programs enable users to distribute their video clips, messages, and music videos through their own accounts or channels. These include

- >> **YouTube:** A place to post your songs and music videos for massive exposure potential (A very clever example is OK Go's music video "This Too Shall Pass," which within a short time had over 10 million views worldwide — heck, they even got a sponsor to pay for their production costs!)

- >> **Viddler:** An interactive online video platform for uploading, sharing, enhancing, tagging, commenting, and forming groups around videos

- >> **nValeo:** A virtual video delivery system that not only combines television, the Internet, and social media, but allows you to create and transmit high definition media content and music videos over the Internet and provide fan access for your live streaming events

Internet radio

Also know as web radio, this is an audio service transmitted over the Internet by means of webcasting and a continuous stream, much like *terrestrial radio* (the radio stations your transistor has been playing since the '50s). These include

>> **Pandora:** Personalized Internet radio service that helps you find new music based on your favorite songs or artists and creates a customized playlist; also has a very popular iPhone app

>> **Grooveshark:** A place where you can listen to practically any song you want for free, and where you can promote your own music, create ads, and share your songs for more exposure

>> **Live365:** Another Internet radio network where members can create their own station or listen to other Live365 broadcasters' online stations

REMEMBER

Not only is the Internet a great way for others to hear your songs, it's also a good way for you to check out what other songwriters are up to and what's new on the scene.

Locating resource, advice, and information sites

Besides being a means to get your songs and information broadcast to potentially millions of people, the Internet can be the ultimate source for up-to-date information, contacts, and those looking for what you've got. For example, The Muses Muse is a resource for both the beginner and the pro. Several other noteworthy networking sites include the following.

TAXI

This organization is basically an independent A&R company that helps independent artists, songwriters, and composers get record, publishing, and film/TV deals by providing the following services:

>> Pitch opportunities to major and indie record labels, top music publishers, and music supervisors — a great way to get your music heard

>> Critiques and written feedback on your songs, pitches, or any other questions — almost like having your own personal coach

>> Music hosting on your own TAXI web page to host your songs, photos, and bio information — cross promoted for greater exposure

>> Access to private, members-only conventions for you as well as your guest — in a networking smorgasbord setting

Song Catalogue

This site also connects publishers, labels, independent artists, and producers with companies looking to license music for commercial use, by way of

>> A music network that provides record labels, producers, and artists with a way to get exposure and license their music

>> An advertising network that provides ad agencies with a steady source of music that can be licensed for commercials

>> A film/TV network that provides music supervisors with an easy way to access good music to license for film or TV

Just Plain Folks

The Just Plain Folks Music Organization (JPF) not only serves as a community of songwriters, recording artists, and music industry professionals, but is also host to what's been known as the world's largest independent music awards — and also claims to be the world's largest grassroots music organization. Its aim is to provide the following:

>> A network community that promotes cooperation in sharing ideas and experiences from those who've been there to those who are on their way

>> Long-term relationships by collaborating with other industry professionals, whether a seasoned Grammy winner or a brand-new songwriter

>> A total freedom in communicating through the power of the Internet without corporate restrictions or boundaries

Songwriters Resource Network

This site is another great networking resource for songwriters, lyricists, and composers that provides reliable material from professional-level songwriters, recording artists, song publishers, music producers, songwriting educators, and music-industry professionals. This resource network offers

>> Informative articles on the art and business of songwriting and up-to-date education for the songwriter who wants help fine tuning their craft

>> Networking opportunities and events that help open doors to finding songwriting partners, publishers, producers, and recording artists

>> Contacts and resources that include song publishers who are seeking great songs and music, as well as advice on how to get your music heard.

>> Songwriter billboards and free ads to find producers and publishers, or for lyricists wanting to hook up with music composers and vice versa

WARNING

There often are subscription fees that come along with these various music sites, especially the ones that offer shopping services and song listings and that provide weekly or monthly *tip sheets* (exclusive listings of artists and producers looking for songs, writers looking for collaborators, and so on). Make sure you understand the fee structure, and decide if it can be justified as far as how it benefits your career.

Finding Friends and Building Your Social Networking Community

Unless you have been camping out in an igloo on some lonely iceberg in Antarctica, you have probably heard about the massive amount of friends and followers you can build through social media sites such as Facebook, MySpace, and Twitter. It seems that everyone is jumping on board to build their circles of friends and fans to gargantuan proportions. But something to think about is the quality of your friends. It might be a good stroke to one's ego to have hundreds of thousands of so called "friends" out there in cyberspace, but when it really comes down to it, best friends and loyalty are still high on the list of desired qualities.

In the following sections, we provide a brief overview of what's out there in the cyberworld of friends and family. Use this as a guideline as to where you might go to begin building your circle of friends and community. Start with what services feel right (and comfortable) for your lifestyle and personality. You don't have to keep up with the Joneses here and be like everyone else. As a songwriter, use the ever-expanding world of social media to enhance your community and build long-term relationships with them.

All-in-one social media networks

These sites feature an area for your bio, blogging, photo/video sharing, bulletins, and event calendars in an environment where you can become "friends" with others on the same network. All-in-one social media networks include

>> MySpace

>> Facebook

>> LinkedIn

>> Bebo

>> Xanga

>> Orkut

Specialty social media networks

These are sites and stand-alone blogs; leveraging "specialty" social media and communication sites are other great ways to increase exposure for musicians and songwriters. Specialty social media networks include

>> YouTube

>> Twitter

>> Viddler

>> Digg

>> Wordpress

>> Blogger

Social network sites for indie artists

The advantage of these music-driven specialty social network sites is that they are highly specialized and generally offer expanded functionality because they are dedicated to only one specific niche. Examples of these include

>> GarageBand

>> Reverbnation

>> Ourstage

>> iLike

>> iSound

>> Songalive

Online downloading music sites

Peer-to-peer music sharing sites took the industry by surprise, but proved that consumers were willing to buy songs on the Internet via sites such as

>> iTunes

>> CDBaby

>> Rhapsody

>> Napster

>> Artist Direct

Mobile device networking

Many new avenues of songwriter marketing and networking are popping up all over the place to interact with fans and generate new revenues for the artist specifically through your mobile devices, some of which include

>> Band text messaging

>> Mobs (mobile fan clubs)

>> Ringtones

>> Mobile marketing

Putting "Social Skills" into Networking

The art of blasting out message after message to your network and not providing value or relevant content at the same time is just plain spam in most people's opinion. Bringing social manners and etiquette into the music arena is not only prudent, it's simply good manners.

Connecting to your fan base and others

Always try to come from a point of view of what you would want from others when connecting to your network. In other words, give what you would like to receive and treat others how you would like to be treated. A great way to begin your relationship is to start blogging. You can keep your blogs to certain generic areas of a topic, such as your opinions on lyric writing, or you can provide product reviews or interviews with music industry people. Another option is to get more personal and begin blogging your thoughts into an online diary of sorts. Both of these methods will help you begin to connect with others that share common interests with you.

Traffic Geyser

This is another form of blogging with the added twist of using video marketing. Video blogging takes regular blogs and puts them on steroids. In an instant, the viewer can know exactly who you are by "seeing" you and building an almost personal connection with you via your video message. Mike Koenigs, the founder of Traffic Geyser, is a master at getting your message out there with video posts, and he provides a much-needed service of automating the distribution of your message to the ever-growing list of social media networking, bookmarking, and podcasting sites and directories.

Star Alerts

After you build a solid relationship and become a trusted cyberspace community member in "good standing," you can begin to venture out in new ways to build upon that relationship and even find ways to monetize your efforts. One such way is with a social networking service such as Star Alerts. This is an innovative service that capitalizes on the popularity of mobile phone devices and provides a means in which you can stay in touch with your fans by sending them "alerts" so they can follow your every move, activity, and upcoming event by feeding your fans interesting tidbits to keep them updated and informed on what you are up to. But this platform also provides a way to monetize this interaction with your followers:

>> **Social skinning:** Places your message on social networking sites such as YouTube, MySpace, Facebook, and Twitter

>> **Mobile landing pages:** Creates mobile-friendly landing pages that capture contact information and catch the attention of your fans.

>> **Media vault skinning:** Builds a one-stop collection of all your content and stores it in the vault for easy access

Expanding your reach worldwide

After you have mastered the art of social networking and gotten your legs under you, so to speak, now is the time to fine tune some of your skills to expand your market reach. The proper use of *keywords* (a method of indexing your content) is a way to ensure you will get noticed by the search engines and will be found by people who share similar interests and want to know what you're doing.

Think of your keywords as that which captures the essence of what your topic is all about — it can be in a form of one word or a phrase. How do you suppose a typical listener might come across your music? How will they find your songs — or you, for that matter? Most likely they will do an Internet search on topics that may have nothing to do with you specifically, but if your website contains content that may be of interest to something they are searching for, you may just land right at the top of their search results page.

Similarly, an important thing to think about when considering the worldwide exposure you can reach in today's digital world is the title (and subtitles) of your songs. Think of popular TV shows or movies, and if your song title has something similar to the latest hit TV series, you've just paved a golden path right to how many search hits your song receives just by the power of association with a topic, theme, or keyword.

OFF THE RECORD

At SXSW I heard a catch phrase several times that was buzzing around, "TV is the new radio." Essentially, if you want to be a known songwriter, you must infiltrate the competitive field of licensing your music to every media group possible: TV, advertising agencies, radio, video games, ringtones, sporting events, and so on. Music directors are music fans by nature. They want to break the next artist. They want to be the one who discovers the next Wilco or The Shins. This is a perfect avenue of visibility. And there is no easy way. You have to get on everyone's radar and be politely persistent. You have to gently say, "Here I am again and I am not going away."

— STEVE "SKILLET" KILLEN, SINGER-SONGWRITER, GUITARIST, SESSION PLAYER, AND FOUNDER OF HERON BLUE RECORDING WORKSHOPS

Now go ahead, and "boldly go where no man has gone before." Step into the spider web matrix of the Internet and explore it's smorgasbord of social marketing and networking opportunities. This is the place to build up and expand your community of family and friends. Although it may be scary and intimidating at first, when you get in and look around, you'll find yourself in familiar territory in no time at all. If not, you can always say, "Beam me up, Scotty" to come back and regain your courage.

IN THIS CHAPTER

» Writing songs for motion pictures and television

» Coming up with jingles for commercials

» Playing in the gaming market

» Creating songs for the theater

» Practicing the art of mixing music with visuals

Chapter **14**

Writing for the Stage, Screen, Television, and More

When a songwriter dreams, sometimes his flight of fantasy takes him to a gilded Broadway theater where his songs are being performed by the cast and orchestra of a long-running, live stage production. In his dream's next feature, he sneaks into the Cineplex for the 8:00 showing of the blockbuster movie where his music is underscoring the action and his song is featured as the "end title." Just before he awakens, he hears another of his songs being used as the theme music for the hard-hitting drama just picked up by one of the networks for its fourth consecutive season. Then just after the credits roll and the morning sun is peeking through his curtain, he hears yet another of his compositions, which has just been chosen as the slogan and rally cry of a new multi-million-dollar ad campaign. Ultimately, he wakes up — but the vision stays with him all that day and possibly his lifetime.

If you're anything like other songwriters, you've probably had some segment of this dream either in your slumbering or waking state. Dreaming is a big part of what songwriting is all about, and there's no question that writing for the stage, screen, and television is worthy dream fodder. Writing for these arenas can be inspiring and lucrative, as well as frustrating and asset depleting — depending on your luck, connections, perseverance, and talent. And yet, if any portion of this dream comes true, you'll leave a giant footprint on the road to success in the world of songwriting.

In this chapter, we show you some of the road signs, detours, entry ramps, curves, straightaways, and deceptive bends down the vast turnpike of stage, screen, and television — and we let you know how it relates to your songwriting.

Songwriting for Film

Whether it's creating the score for a motion picture or writing songs for specific scenes or areas in a film, this remains an incredible goal for every serious songwriter. The list of songs written for and inspired by motion pictures is long. Table 14-1 shows you just a few notable songs on that list.

TABLE 14-1   **Songs Featured in Movies**

Song	Movie	Songwriter(s)	Singer/Performer
"Footloose"	*Footloose*	Kenny Loggins, Dean Pitchford	Kenny Loggins
"I Don't Wanna Miss a Thing"	*Armageddon*	Diane Warren	Aerosmith
"Can You Feel the Love Tonight"	*The Lion King*	Tim Rice, Elton John	Elton John
"My Immortal" and "Bring Me to Life"	*Daredevil*	Amy Lee, David Hodges, Ben Moody	Evanescence
"Lose Yourself"	*8 Mile*	Eminem, L. Resto, J. Bass	Eminem
"Sweet Home Alabama"	*Multiple movies*	E. King, G. Rossington, R. Van Zant	Lynyrd Skynyrd
"My Heart Will Go On"	*Titanic*	James Horner, Will Jennings	Celine Dion
"Eye of the Tiger"	*Rocky III*	Jim Peterik, Frankie Sullivan	Survivor
"Accidentally in Love"	*Shrek 2*	Counting Crows	Counting Crows
"Live and Let Die"	*Live and Let Die*	Paul and Linda McCartney	Paul McCartney, Wings
"I've Had the Time of My Life"	*Dirty Dancer*	F. Previte, J. DeNicola, D. Markowitz	Bill Medley, Jennifer Warnes
"Iris"	*City of Angels*	John Rzeznik	Goo Goo Dolls

The various categories of music in movies include the following:

- » **Main title:** This is the song that opens the movie and is often heard throughout the picture in various styles and treatments. This song is vital because it pretty much sets the emotional tone for the entire movie.

- » **Songs for specific scenes:** These are the songs that are in the background, setting the mood for a specific location in the movie — sometimes the lyric can echo the action on the screen. The song can be featured prominently with a minimum of dialogue (love scenes come to mind), or the song can be barely audible, coming out of some cheap transistor radio on the beach. A somewhat recent trend has been to stick songs by hot groups into a scene, randomly and barely audible, basically so that they can be featured in the movie's lucrative soundtrack.

- » **End title:** This is the song that closes the movie and is another key position because it creates the impression that the movie leaves you with (and hopefully is the song that you'll be singing all the way home, like it or not). Generally speaking, the music supervisor likes to find a big artist for this "money" song positioning.

- » **Scoring music:** This is the music, usually instrumental in nature, that runs through the entire film. It exists to create moods behind the action that emphasize what we are supposed to be feeling. Great orchestrators are worth their weight in gold to a filmmaker because their work makes such a significant impact on a film — think *Titanic* or *Avatar!*

Understanding the role of the music supervisor

The *music supervisor* or *supe* is the right-hand person to the director and producer of a film when it comes to finding the right music to go with the action on the screen. Music supervision is a relatively new position in film making (it came into its own in the early '80s), alleviating much of the chaos and last-minute scrambling for music that used to take place in this business. The supe is the person who must understand the script backward and forward, the motivation of all the characters, the mood that must be set overall and in each scene, and, not least importantly, the budget available to work with.

He usually has a great deal of financial incentive to get the job done right. His per-picture fee can run as high as a quarter of a million bucks, and he often receives a substantial royalty on the soundtrack he puts together. That might more than make up for the nightmares of trying to make all the significant entities — film company, director, producer, songwriters, artists, actors, record companies, and music publishers — play nicely together!

Although the budget for a major motion picture is in the $35 to 65 million dollar range, the budget for the music might be a mere $1 to 3 million. It's often the last thing considered by directors, who are far more concerned with the actors, editing, and storyline than they are with the underscoring or specific songs. It's only in somewhat recent times that music has become much more than just an afterthought.

After the music supe meets with the director and producer to determine the film's needs, he then marks out the positions in the movie for specific songs (spots like main title, various key scenes, and the all-important end title as the credits roll). He'll also start making lists of artists and music producers to fill these slots, and contact songwriters, artists, managers, and publishers while combing the record charts to find hot artists to include (especially if there's going to be a soundtrack album). He'll also contact some of his favorite scoring composers to write music that enhances the underlying mood of each scene and start sending copies of the script (often rough drafts) to the artists, songwriters, and composers he is considering.

Never say no to a music supervisor's suggestion. Instead say, "I'll try it." You may be surprised just how well the idea works — and you might also keep your job that way, too!

Don't be too surprised if the song you labored over is practically lost in the context of the movie. Just like the ubiquitous *product placement* in films (that's when, say, Red Bull pays a film company megabucks for the lead character to down their signature drink while getting pumped for an extreme sport trick), often songs are placed inconspicuously beneath dialogue, just so the film company can put the song on the soundtrack album. If you have enough clout, and/or a great attorney, try to get the usage of your song specified in your agreement.

The supervisor must also choose the perfect person to *score* the movie. Scoring is the job of creating music that plays behind the action of a film. Sometimes it calls attention to itself, like the dramatic scores of Hans Zimmer in *Gladiator*, *Pirates of the Caribbean*, *The Dark Knight*, and many more, and John Williams in *Star Wars*, *E.T.*, three *Harry Potter* movies, *Jurassic Park*, and others. Other times, the background music is more subliminal, subtly emphasizing moods ranging from joyous to creepy. Try to think of the movie *Jaws* without hearing the ominous foreboding of sawing strings in the background as the shark is about to feast on human flesh.

Scoring is a different art than songwriting, although the two are related. Both crafts have to do with creating moods, but scoring does its job generally without words by laying textures of sound (from celestial to abrasive) on the musical palette with both subtle daubs and bold strokes. The score to a movie is often overlooked, but boy, would you ever miss it if it were gone.

Getting to the music supervisors

If you're getting the impression that music supervisors pretty much control the music to be considered in a film and that it might be important for you as a songwriter to establish good relations with them — you're right! But building a rapport with them, even if you are an established writer, is not always easy.

If you're signed with a major publisher, they'll undoubtedly have a wing of their staff that caters to the film industry. Many publishers will, in fact, put out monthly pitch sheets that list and describe films in the works that are in need of songs and even list the music supervisor in charge.

OFF THE RECORD

I used to be signed with a publishing giant who would routinely send out sheets to their writing staff listing movies that were looking for songs. Much of the time, it was on an all-skate basis, where you and a bunch of their writers would write a song on spec (in other words, you get no fees unless your song is chosen — I've learned another meaning for this abbreviation — "Don't spec to get paid!"). Many times I would bust my hump to get a song written and demo-ed only to hear the roaring silence as I waited for some response. I was never quite sure if the song got to the designated music supe, much less given a fair chance to be "tried to scene" in the actual film — when your song is actually put against the action to see how it works. If you get this far, consider yourself on the home stretch. I finally realized that I had to make personal acquaintances with the music supervisors themselves. When I did this, things started to pop. After one of the great Music & Tennis Festivals held in the '80s and early '90s (the brainchild of one of the authors of this book, "Coach" Dave Austin along with his good buddy, Phil Ehart, drummer for Kansas), I ran into noted music supervisor Budd Carr. He told me about a new John Candy movie he was advising called Delirious, and I ended up co-writing the end title, "Beyond Our Wildest Dreams" (beating out "Unforgettable" by Irving Gordon, if you can believe that!). No matter how good your publisher is, there's no substitute for personal contact.

— JIM PETERIK, PERFORMER, SONGWRITER, AND MULTI-INSTRUMENTALIST
FOR THE BANDS IDES OF MARCH AND SURVIVOR, PLUS WRITER OF HITS
FOR .38 SPECIAL, SAMMY HAGAR, AND OTHERS

The best way to get music to me is proximity at the right time. I was recently on a panel hosted by the Recording Academy, and a songwriter asked "How does one get songs to you?" I then asked if he had a demo CD with him — the answer was no, and I simply said, "Missed opportunity." Be ready for those special moments when opportunity meets preparation.

— BUDD CARR, MUSIC SUPERVISOR FOR TERMINATOR, JFK, WALL STREET: MONEY NEVER SLEEPS, EVAN ALMIGHTY, HOTEL RWANDA, ROCK STAR, AND PLATOON

There are specific magazines such as *Variety* and *The Hollywood Reporter* with websites that cater to the film industry and movie aficionados. Often they'll report on movies in the planning stage and films that are in progress. They'll usually list the film company, director, producer, and sometimes even the music supervisor. Start making inquiries and requests with your own professionally worded letter, or one from your music attorney, reflecting your interest in submitting songs for the project. If you have a publisher, have them make calls to music supervisors on your behalf, or obtain lists from them of the ones that you can approach yourself.

Understanding the creative side of songwriting for films

Writing for film can be a wonderful, though sometimes frustrating, experience. At its best, it gives a songwriter a wonderful storyline, already created, to expand upon. When you get good at it, you can read a script and songs will seem to leap off the pages of certain scenes. Capturing the essence of a scene without being too obvious is an art in and of itself. If you are a composer scoring a movie (as opposed to writing specific songs for certain scenes), most film companies will send you *rushes*, or film footage, of the *dailies* (the scene shot that day) from which to score. There is usually a very short turnaround time in which to complete deadlines.

Personally, I love a song that spotlights, fairly literally, the action on the screen. "Let's Hear It for the Boy" (written by Dean Pitchford and Thomas Snow; sung by Denise Williams) from the '80s smash feature Footloose is a great example of a song illuminating the storyline. But many directors (and thus many music supervisors) are squeamish about songs being too literal to the scene. It strikes them as corny or operatic (where the songs virtually are the storyline). I learned that the hard way with "Long Road Home," which I was commissioned to write for Backdraft. In the end, it was disqualified for

the line, "still we're keeping alive the flame" — flames being too literal to the fires that appeared in practically every scene.

—JIM PETERIK, WRITER OF 18 BILLBOARD TOP 10 HITS INCLUDING
THE PERENNIAL FAVORITE "EYE OF THE TIGER"
FEATURED IN ROCKY III

WORDS OF WISDOM

I look for music that makes the action in the scene comfortable or effective. When you are out to dinner at a romantic restaurant on a first date, Nine Inch Nails' music is probably not as appropriate as a jazz piano — although at times in order to heighten tension or amplify action, music can play against the grain of a scene. When looking for a song, sometimes the movie needs a big name or a familiar song for the scene to help the movie. So I'm not looking particularly for the best song for the scene; I'm looking for a combination of the best song for the scene from the right artist. At other times, it is purely the song that works best for the scene regardless if the song is from an unknown or known artist.

— BUDD CARR, MUSIC SUPERVISOR TO MULTIPLE OLIVER STONE FILMS

Songwriting for Television

Billions of viewers can't be wrong! And as long as there's TV, there's got to be music to go along with both its brilliance and inanity. The synergy between songs and television and the exposure you can receive for one of your songs being on a program is staggering. Many a song has languished on a shelf until some visionary director discovers it while station surfing in his Maserati and decides to feature it on the next episode of his series.

OFF THE RECORD

Sometimes all it takes for a great song to be recognized is one person in a position of power to hear it at just the right time. When Michael J. Fox's first show, *Family Ties*, featured an obscure song by Billy (Vera) and The Beaters, "At This Moment" (written by Bill McCord), the phones at the radio stations lit up with requests for a song that had been ignored for six years! Television can be one of the most powerful stimulants to record success.

Knowing what songs work well in television

Producers of television shows are constantly calling publishers to license preexisting songs for use in their episodes. But in addition to this, they also commission new songs, *incidental music* (the music that plays under specific scenes), and theme music to flesh out this season's "big push" series. Even though the budgets

CHAPTER 14 **Writing for the Stage, Screen, Television, and More** 257 are slimmer for TV shows and time limits are tighter, they're still a worthy goal for any songwriter, due to the exposure received and the monies generated by repeated performances of the same show. Can you imagine being the composer of the *I Love Lucy*, *Baywatch*, or *Cheers* theme? You could literally retire on those royalties!

The fees generated for writing the background music for a half-hour sitcom or drama might be around $10,000 (and you pick up the recording tab!). But for theme music, get ready to receive from $10,000 up to $100,000 for writing the main song for a "major push" series (and get the wheelbarrow ready to collect the performance dollars that ASCAP, BMI, or SESAC will be sending to your door!). See Chapter 17 for more details on performance dollars.

REMEMBER

When a song of yours is being licensed for a particular scene in a television show, your fee will be substantially lower than you might expect — usually between $1,000 and $10,000 — but don't forget the added bonus of performance fees generated by its use.

Recognizing the exposure value of television

Many songwriters and artists have been boosted to fame from exposure on television. Singer Vonda Sheppard found the public ear through her appearances on *Ally McBeal* (making major bucks for the songwriters featured in her inspired re-interpretations of soul and rock classics). In addition to Vonda-type stories, many songs have found an audience by being exposed on the small screen. You may find opportunities for title songs like "I'll Be There for You" (written by D. Crane, M. Kaufman, M. Skloff, P. Solem, D. Wilde, and A. Willis), the theme for the smash series *Friends* by pop-rock group The Rembrandts. Not only do they get their moniker on the *crawl* (the tiny and rapidly moving credits that roll as the theme music fades), but they get the added promotion of the weekly exposure on a network smash. This song was catapulted to #1 because of its extreme catchiness and the mass acceptance of this show. The Rembrandts just happened to capture the essence and demographic of this inventive ensemble comedy.

TIP

Keep in mind there's power in numbers, such as evidenced in the commercial phenomenon called *American Idol*. Writing a song specifically suited to one of those participants is not only an honor but a great opportunity for massive exposure. Even if it's just for your own personal practice in songwriting, make it a habit of creating songs that you feel would be perfect for one (or several) of the varied "Idol" contestants (that is if it's still going strong in the year 2030 — otherwise get out a recorded copy or find a re-run of the show). Besides, if you are never able to get one of your songs pitched to any of the top ten finalists, you may just come up with a "winner" for yourself!

Especially if you are a singer/songwriter, you can increase your chances of success by sending your songs to television production houses and *clearance services* (the agencies that specialize in licensing preexisting compositions for use in television shows). The song "Superman (It's Not Easy)" (written by John Ondrasik; performed by Five for Fighting) was brought to the public's attention by its inclusion in the WB channel's series, *Smallville* — the hook line, "It's not easy to be me," fit like a glove into the premise of Superman living among mortals in the small town of Smallville, U.S.A.

OFF THE RECORD

I was totally taken by surprise a few years back when Bo Bice sang my song "Vehicle" on American Idol. I'd been doing some co-writing in Nashville and wasn't checking e-mail, so I'm riding the elevator down to go to dinner when I get a call from our drummer. "Dude, get back up to your room! There's some guy that looks like Jesus covering the be-Jesus out of Vehicle." I ran back up upstairs and sure enough there was Bo doing a bang-up job covering my song. Turns out my publishing administrator had been trying to reach me to get my permission — then went with her common sense and granted the show the rights. I received a decent fee but the real icing on the cake was that he recorded the song (with Richie Sambora from Bon Jovi doing the lead work that I'd originally played) and it went on to sell more than 850,000 copies! Ah . . . but the power of television seems to have no equal.

— JIM PETERIK, WRITER OF 18 BILLBOARD TOP 10 HITS

TIP

As a budding songwriter, make a list of songs you think would be appropriate for some of your favorite shows, or better still, target certain shows to write for. Even if they don't hit their intended goal, they may serve as songs you can use or pitch for other applications.

WORDS OF WISDOM

I get asked all the time how a composer/songwriter gets their music into the right hands to be considered for television. My reply is simple: persistence in following your dreams. Keep your vision in front of you.

—JOHN D'ANDREA, COMPOSER AND ARRANGER ON PRODUCTIONS SUCH AS TV SERIES BAYWATCH AND FEATURE FILM DIRTY DANCING

Pre-fab groups like the Monkees and The Partridge Family (and okay, also The Brady Bunch) actually paved the way for songwriters for hire to submit songs to be considered by major sitcoms. As manufactured and artificial as these groups were, they inspired many catchy songs by the likes of songwriting teams like Carole King and Gerry Goffin, Neil Diamond, and John Stewart to do some of their best writing. Apparently TV is one of those media types that strike a responsive chord in people, whether you are merely watching or participating in its creation.

The hit show *CSI* uses The Who's classic, "Who Are You" to open every show. Aimee Mann's "That's Just What You Are" was regularly featured on *Melrose Place* and appears on the soundtrack for the show. It really doesn't matter the vintage or style of a particular song. In television, all that's in contention is the impact it has in context of the scene.

Getting to television music supervisors

Television, just like movies, uses music supervisors; they are your first choice in submitting songs to get yours placed on a show. In fact, because music budgets in television are almost always smaller than movies, a new songwriter usually has a better chance of getting their song on a TV show than in a movie. The music supervisor for television usually doesn't have the budget for an established or current hit, so when a great song comes across their desk that fits what they need, it's a win-win situation — they can usually get the song under contract within their budget and the songwriter/artist gets valuable exposure, not to mention a great credit and a reasonable amount of money to add to their bank account.

Many times *The Hollywood Reporter* or *Variety Magazine* will list production schedules and the music supervisors who are signed on. An annual publication called the *Music Supervisor Directory* lists over 600 music supervisors complete with their contact information. If you're really adventurous, you can also explore who the picture editor is for a show (the person who takes the film dailies and pieces them together into a rough cut for the producer/director to review the work in progress) and send that person your song as well. The picture editor usually likes to create their rough cuts to music for added impact, mood, and ambiance. When a producer/director is reviewing the rough cuts, they might just like the song so much they'll ask the music supervisor to include that song in the final cut.

Songwriting for Commercials

Okay, so you didn't become a songwriter to sell beer and tires, but neither did a great many famous songwriters of our time, who created a win-win for themselves by helping to sell products without selling their souls. The *jingle,* as it has been called inexplicably for the last three decades, is a source of inspiration and income for songwriters and composers that could well be considered manna from Heaven. Many composers and songwriters make a very good living writing specific songs for specific products. Some of these songs have actually crossed over to the hit parade. Songs like "No Matter What Shape (You're Stomach's In)" written by Stormie and Michael Omartian, performed by The T-Bones (from an antacid commercial); "I'd Like to Teach the World to Sing (In Perfect Harmony)" written by William Backer, Roger Cook, Roquel Davis, and Roger Greenway, performed by the Hilltop Singers and The New Seekers (which started life as a Coke jingle); and "Percolator Twist" written by Lou Bideu and Ernest Freeman, performed by Billy Joe and the Checkmates (the Maxwell House coffee song) have all percolated into Top 40 hits. Other songwriters have made millions by licensing their old hits to huge conglomerates for elephant bucks. Still others have actually found that leasing their latest release to a product line is a great alternative means to promote their record, especially when traditional airplay on radio can be so hard to come by.

Take a look now at the basic ways you can harness your songwriting talents to enter the world of commercials — and make big loot to boot!

Writing jingles from scratch

Writing a jingle from scratch requires the expertise of the songwriter to spotlight the product, service, or company in the desired light. Whatever the image of that company or product is — it's the goal of the jingle writer to cement that into the hearts and minds of the listening and viewing audience. Catchy melodies, rhythms, and catch phrases are the stock in trade of a good jingle. An effective jingle is like a hit song on speed — you only have 30 to 60 seconds (or less) to make your impression, get your message across, and set up the product you are helping to sell. Jingles are usually very simple, repetitive, and full of the kind of sound effects that catch the ear. To write a good jingle, it's important to get as much input from the client (the actual people writing the checks to the ad agency) as possible, and to get a clear-cut picture of the entire campaign they are planning. Oftentimes, a jingle house will do several treatments of the same slogan or catchphrase in an attempt to please the consensus at the company level. Many of the same principles we examine for writing a full-length song can be applied to writing a jingle. Rhyme, rhythm, and melody all come heavily into play. But remember, due to the time constraints of the average commercial, when it comes to the element of song structure, the jingle is often limited to chorus only.

Fees for coming up with a new jingle for a product can range as high as $50,000 and may include renewal fees for every period the lease is extended. In addition, the jingle writer will usually play on his own song, reaping heaps of additional income for radio, network, and cable television airplay from the musicians union. If he sings on the spot as well, he'll also receive payment from the Screen Actors Guild (SAG) and the American Federation of Television and Radio Artists (AFTRA). Now how does all that grab you?

For many years, my voice was heard in the context of commercials. I had what the jingle houses referred to as a beer and tires voice — kind of gruff and macho. I came to really respect the songwriters behind the jingles I sang. Can you remember, "Look out for The Bull, look out for the Schlitz Malt Liquor bull" or "The friendly skies of your land, United Airlines?" These were a couple of the memorable songs I got to sing. I also sang a treatment of "Good Vibrations" for Sunkist Orange Soda — the new hook was "I'm drinkin' up orange vibrations, Sunkist Orange Soda taste sensation." Finally when my own hits started coming and I hit the road, I pretty much had to give up the jingle scene. But I'll never forget those jingle producers telling me to "put more smile in it!" the time I had to sing "like a rice crispy," or the cat food commercial where my one enthusiastic line was, "The meat/fish group!"

— JIM PETERIK, WRITER OF 18 BILLBOARD TOP 10 HITS

Writing jingles from scratch makes up perhaps 50 percent of the work we do. The other 50 percent is adapting songs for new campaigns. Of the original songs I come up with, about 70 percent are instrumental tracks and 30 percent are sung. Fees vary greatly depending on the client's budget and the music house's reputation for success. Typical creative fees for a spot run anywhere from $5,000 to $50,000 (for a big campaign with a corporate behemoth like McDonald's). The jingle writer can also look forward to performance money when the jingle is played because both BMI and ASCAP monitor airplay activity on your commercial (but don't expect publishing income because it's pro-forma that the ad agency retains the publishing on songs it commissions). In addition, if you play and sing on your own spot, you'll be printin' money!

— MATT THORNTON, CREATIVE DIRECTOR OF TRACK ATTACK MUSIC HOUSE

If you're eager to break into the world of jingle writing, put together a reel of some of your best material. You may even want to "mock up" some jingles for products that may or may not exist to give examples of the kind of work you are capable of. Go around to the ad agencies in town and introduce yourself and your work. Another way to go would be to take your demo reel to existing music houses to try to get hired there. Sometimes learning the ropes and making contacts at an established company is the best primer for moving on later to your own company.

VISITING A MUSIC HOUSE

Often an ad agency will come up with a concept for a product that they've been hired to represent. They'll then contact a *music house* (a company whose job it is to create and record commercials) to turn the concept into the sound of music — and money. On staff at the music house are various musicians who specialize in providing the ad agency and ultimately the product honchos with what they need to sell their product. Sometimes they'll be asked merely to do a *treatment* (basically a different arrangement) of a preexisting jingle. Other times they'll be asked to do a *sound alike* of a famous hit that they'd like to use. Other times they'll request a commercial (or spot, in the jingle jargon) based on the original recording of a hit. But what really defines a great music house is its writer's ability to create new jingles *from scratch*.

Getting your songs placed in commercials

If you have a song or a number of preexisting songs that you think would be ideal for the commercial market, contact the various ad agencies and request permission to submit those songs to their musical supervisor. Whether you're an established songwriter or a beginner, this process is much the same. There are many well-known songwriters who compile samplers of all their hits to remind the various advertising agencies of their songs. All it takes is one "ear" at the agency to hear a song and say, "Hey, that would be perfect for our client's product!" Even as an unproven songwriter, if you put together a professional looking and sounding CD sampler of your songs (complete with lyric sheets and all contact information; see Chapter 15), one of them just might catch the imagination of an ad executive. Some of the big agencies you'd want to get your material to are Leo Burnett and ddb in Chicago, BBDO and Lintass in New York, and McCann Erickson in Troy, Michigan.

Songwriting for Video Games

Film and TV aren't the only markets to place your songs. Video game music has grown rapidly and is now a force to be reckoned with. The opportunity for exposure in this category is tremendous for some songwriters — and we're not just talking about the rock legends of Guitar Hero and Rock Band. Exposure via video games can sometimes propel indie artists/bands from relative obscurity to overnight sensation in very short order.

Think about the successful X-games sports-based video games that have provided massive reach for artists whose music is featured in these games — *Tony Hawk*, *Need for Speed: Underground*, or *Grand Theft Auto*. Also, take a look at the huge popularity of *Rock Band* or *Guitar Hero* — granted, the songs featured there are that of well-established bands and hit-makers, but you never know, anything could happen if you put your mind to it!

Just type "submitting music for video games" in your favorite search engine and see what pops up — a long list of possible outlets to submit your songs to in this ever-popular market. Always research both the credibility and professionalism of any service you choose to work with. Here are a few resources to check out (remember they're not limited to just video game submissions either — TV and film music licensing also fall under most of their areas of expertise):

>> Pump Audio

>> Rumblefish

>> Broadjam

>> Taxi

In addition to checking into what's available via online resources, you might also want to visit conventions such as GenCon and other big gamer conferences for inspiration as well as networking.

TIP

Now here's an outside-the-box thought — you're a hot (and very enterprising) new songwriter and decide to market your own music to the gaming world. You begin by posting your songs on the various online music distribution sites with the intent (and marketing angle) of people paying to download your creations and saving them to their own customized gaming soundtracks — a common feature on the latest game consoles by Xbox, Wii, and Playstation. Ha! You've now got your original music on the latest video game, were paid for it, and have the bragging rights to go with it!

Songwriting for Musicals

The excitement and lure of the Broadway stage has inspired writers to come up with some of the greatest songs of all time. Before there were motion pictures, there was the theater. Live dramatic presentations were the way playwrights and composers brought their stories to life. It remains, to this day, a vibrant messenger of emotion, song, and story. The excitement surrounding a top-notch musical can be electric — and to imagine your song being performed by a major star in the context of a powerful story is pretty good motivation to come up with a great one. Songwriting teams like Rodgers and Hart and songwriters like the Gershwin brothers made their considerable fortunes from the songs they wrote for Broadway musicals.

Submitting your songs for musicals

If you're a songwriter eager to break into theater, it may be best to start at the local level in community theater. You'll start to get a grasp of the breakdown of responsibilities of the various people who comprise a theater company and get to try out your music in front of a sympathetic audience. Try to make acquaintances with local directors and discuss their musical needs. Attend as many theater workshops and round tables as possible (for a comprehensive guide to U.S. theater companies and workshops, be sure to check out the book *Songwriter's Market*). And above all, attend as many top-notch musicals as you can afford to see where the bar has to be set to make it all the way to Broadway! Make contact with the musical director if you can — she'll be the one making decisions on what songwriters will be involved in a play's production. Your demos can be sent in care of that person to the musical's main production headquarters.

Understanding the creative side of songwriting for musicals

All the business stuff won't mean too much if you don't have some great songs to go along with the excitement and drama onstage. This is your chance as a songwriter to get large, wear your emotions on your sleeve and your heart in your throat. The scale of most productions is big enough to accept songs that are sweeping in their panorama of feeling.

WORDS OF WISDOM

I have learned to paint with broad strokes in the songs I write for the stage. I try to keep lyrics simple and not too busy because in an ambient theater, words are easily lost. All the great words in the world won't mean a thing if intelligibility suffers. Also, it is important to use musical devices that assure heightened drama — like key modulations at choruses and sometimes a second modulation upward at the final chorus. Extreme dynamics from loud to soft is another way to wake up your audience. Many of these writing cues were created for Broadway for specific dramatic effect. When I write rock 'n' roll, I have to hold myself back a bit from it from becoming too Broadway.

— JIMMY NICHOLS, MUSICIAN AND COMPOSER

Writing songs for musicals is much like writing songs for other purposes. Big titles and memorable melodic hooks become even more important in the theater. It's the goal of every songwriter who writes for musicals to send the people away singing the featured songs. Generally, the lyrics of these songs mirror the action and emotion of a particular scene. Keep in mind that the plot of a musical can be a constantly changing thing. With those changes, the songwriter has to be open to adapting his songs to the ever-changing shape and landscape of the play.

WORDS OF WISDOM

In writing music for musicals, flexibility is the key. Unlike writing a popular song, where the composer is in total control of the musical and lyrical content, in musical theater, oftentimes the composer must be cognizant of the ever-changing facets of the book. In Broadway terms, the book means the script of the stage play. If the director cuts a scene or wants quicker character development, the book is always changing; therefore, a song that was appropriate at one point of the play's development may no longer fit the new scene. Even when the play finally opens, there is inevitably fine-tuning of songs and scenes. Showboat was written 75 years ago and they're still fooling around with the book!

— DENNIS DEYOUNG, NOTED COMPOSER OF THE MUSICAL
ADAPTATION OF THE HUNCHBACK OF NOTRE DAME AND
FOUNDING MEMBER OF PLATINUM ROCK BAND STYX

Practice Makes Perfect

Throughout this book, we talk about preparation meeting opportunity. If you are serious about your songwriting, you can't do enough to prepare yourself for moments of opportunities. In this practice, we'd like you to pick three of your favorite shows. Record an episode of each on your DVR. Turn off the volume, and begin imagining what music you'd put under the scenes. Then also try your hand at writing a song that fits a particular scene — because these are your favorites, you probably know most of the lines anyway, so turning off the sound shouldn't hinder you much. As you do this, you may discover that you have a real knack and love for doing this kind of writing, so put your best work on a demo CD and then get your networking shoes on. Who knows when you'll be at the right place at the right time, and when the opportunity to get your CD to the "right people" will arise?

IN THIS CHAPTER

» Determining when your song is ready

» Getting the details in order

» Choosing the method to create your song

» Arranging the musical shape of your songs

» Recording the actual demo

» Assembling the package and sending it out

Chapter **15**

Getting Your Songs Heard: Making the Demo

The day will come when you've finally finished your song and it's time to put your heart and soul on the line to share your creation with the world. After all, your song won't do anyone any good sitting in your notebook! The first step in getting your song out there is to make a demonstration of the song — better known as a *demo*. A demo basically demonstrates your song's potential — in other words, it's a prototype or template from which the right industry people who may be interested in your songs can elaborate. It's like a sketch from which a fully realized masterpiece can then be painted.

In this chapter, we give you the inside scoop on how to prepare and produce a demo and get it in the hands of the right people.

Evaluating Your Options

There are many things to consider before you embark upon the considerable time and expense of cutting a demo of your song, but first things first. You need to run through a simple checklist of honest evaluation and critique to rate the readiness of taking your song to the next level. Here are a few questions to begin asking yourself in self-evaluating your song:

>> Is each line of lyric and melody the best you are capable of writing?

>> Is the song structure well thought out and effective?

>> Does the song have an interesting title and hook?

>> Does the bridge provide a new dimension?

>> Is the song capable of evoking true human emotion?

>> Will the listener find it interesting, easy to remember, and can they sing along with it?

Even though many songwriters now own the equipment to produce demos at home (see Chapter 11), when it comes to quality material and making a career out of songwriting, it may be wise to hire a pro rather than "cut off your nose to spite your face!" However, if you're simply making a hobby of songwriting and this isn't your livelihood, then by all means lock yourself away in the basement and get creative to your heart's content — who knows . . . one of your creations just might jump out and surprise us all.

Creating a "work tape" demo first

When you feel that your song is ready, a pre-demo version is a must in order to get some objective feedback from others. You'll need to create a rough recording of your song — a "work tape" version. With this in hand, you can go about getting song critiques in a variety of ways. You can get peer-to-peer critiques through songwriters' organizations such as The Songwriters Guild of American (SGA), the Nashville Songwriters Associations International (NSAI), and TAXI (refer to Chapter 13 for a detailed description of services provided by these organizations). You can also solicit feedback from your friends, family, and associates. You don't always have to agree with what you hear, but do try to be objective, and use what is being said for the benefit of getting your song in its best shape possible.

Defining the production components

While you are gathering as much feedback and constructive input as possible *before* you plunk down a considerable amount of time or dough producing a high-quality and professional demo, there are two very important things to consider from the onset: the type of production this song is going to require to do it justice, and how much moola you can afford to spend. True, cutting a demo of a ballad may not require much more than a polished piano or guitar and a top-notch vocal performance, but an up-tempo pop or urban tune may need the benefit of a whole lot more instrumentation and vibe. Get an overall picture in your mind as to what type of production you are seeking.

Deciding what purpose the demo serves

There are basically two types of demos; the song demo and the artist demo. You will need to determine in advance which of these two you are ultimately going after. Ask yourself whether you want to put yourself out there as a potential artist, or use this demo as a tool to get your song published and recorded by some other recording artist. If you are also looking to be considered as the artist, you'll need to set your standards high and have your vocals pitch perfect as opposed to when you are pitching your songs to someone else — either way is good, just be clear about your intentions from the beginning so you get the right finished product.

Knowing the competition

Even if you are recording your very first demo on your laptop computer program, it's wise to know the quality of work that's being produced by others. Quite often the quality of today's demos sound very much like the songs you hear on the radio. The professional standard of your competition is high and many of the demo singers legitimately should have their own record deals. It's a clear advantage to get the best musicians and players you can afford so your song has a fighting chance to stand out in the crowd.

TIP

If the thought of recording a demo makes your hands sweaty — and you're the type who would rather spend time creating lyrics and melodies — don't think you have to do it all on your own. There are options other than self-producing your own demo. Hiring a demo service (companies that specialize in doing the demo for you for a set fee) may be the way to go. Just make sure you let them know in advance what you want, and be very specific by providing samples of the sound you are looking for. Also be sure to get referrals, and shop around (and listen to their finished work to evaluate their quality) before deciding which demo service to hire.

Paying Attention to Details

First and foremost, a demo should be an effective representation of your song. It can be simple or complex, depending on the song itself. The demo doesn't have to be totally polished. However, as mentioned earlier in this chapter, the more professional it sounds, the better the chance of standing out in an already crowded and competitive market.

Picking your format

Other than the compact disc (CD), electronically submitted audio files (such as MP3s and other audio file formats) are pretty much the format of choice for demos nowadays. In the past, demos were always presented on cassette, but thankfully — because they sometimes run at wrong speeds, the quality is poor, occasional dropouts can be heard, and you can't just skip automatically to the song you want to hear — cassette tapes are basically a thing of the past. By using audio files or CDs, you can get away with having more songs in one demo presentation — a good idea in case the person you're sending it to doesn't like one song; in that case they can quickly jump forward to the next one.

Choosing the number and length of songs

Ideally, your demo should contain no more than three or four songs total. The producer, artist, or A&R person probably cannot absorb much more than that at one time — and because he's leaving for Aruba on Saturday, his time is kind of tight anyway.

Making sure the songs on your demo aren't too long, or too short, is also very important. However, don't compromise the song just for its length. Ultimately, the song dictates the length of the demo.

Ideally, a song that you're pitching should be under four minutes in length, but there are no hard and fast rules here. If the song is good at seven minutes, then let it be that long — just make sure you're not kidding yourself and that those seven minutes really work. (Please note that a seven-minute song is an extremely long one.) Also, keep intro lengths short and get to the first verse as quickly as possible. Many times the first verse is perhaps all the demo screener hears (due to the lack of time and patience) — yeah, that's not fair, but such is life!

TIP

Playing your song for friends is a good road test to see if you can hold their interest. Good friends will usually call a spade a spade and a clunker a clunker — and hopefully they'll still be your friends the next day! If they nod off while listening to your demo, consider editing the song (or finding some new friends!).

Your song and demo should keep moving and building; try to engage the listener's attention at all times.

Keeping it simple

Demos generally need to be very simple. Try to leave room for the potential singer to imagine what they can do to it to make it their own — just like they attempt to do via American Idol style.

A good demo song is an effective representation of:

REMEMBER

>> The lyric

>> The melody

>> The chords

>> The feel

>> The direction or genre

>> The heart and soul of the song

Overall, when creating your demo, always keep in mind that this is the way your song will be heard by the world. Make sure when all is said and done, whether the arrangement is simple or complex, or the production is rough or sophisticated, that it represents the song the way you think it should be heard. Take pride in the presentation at whatever level your budget dictates. If it gets across the essence of the song, it really doesn't matter how much (or how little) money you spend on it — the song will shine through.

Picking the Players

After you've finished your song, unless you're a one-man-band or a *DIY* (do-it-yourself) junkie, you'll need to create a team of musicians, programmers, and engineers to help see your vision through. (Refer to Chapter 12 for in-depth information on songwriting collaborations.)

Deciding whether to use musicians or machines

Many times, nothing beats the sound and chemistry of real musicians playing together. But often, due to financial restrictions or lack of contacts, you may be wise to consider programming your demo on a computer. A programmer can sequence the sounds of drums, keyboards, and bass. However, you may want to add a real guitar player after all the other pieces are on, in order to get a humanized sound to the track.

Using musicians

If you decide to go with real live musicians instead of using a computer to create your demo, you'll quickly see that there are no shortcuts to finding the perfect team of musicians to work with — it's all trial and error, and finding the right combination can take time. You'll need musicians who are intuitive to what's in your head and are a supportive presence to your talents. Creating a demo is like putting a puzzle together — you can only see the whole picture when all the pieces are in place. Look for reliable people who you believe "hear" what you're hearing in your head and can expand on that vision.

FINDING MUSICIANS

Finding musicians isn't as hard as you might think. Start by going to clubs where bands are playing. During a break, introduce yourself as a songwriter looking for musicians. Oftentimes, they'll be eager to do studio work (especially if there's pay involved) because it's a welcome change of pace from their "live dates." You can also check in the back pages of your local music publication for musicians for hire (request a sample of their work before booking them), place an ad yourself seeking top-notch studio musicians, or just type studio musicians in your online search engine and you'll be off and running with more resources than you'll ever need! In addition, by attending various writers' nights and showcases you'll inevitably find qualified people who are in attendance, or you may find qualified musicians quite simply by "word of mouth." You can also find talent by keeping your ears open at your local guitar center, as musicians are trying out new gear.

WORKING WITH MUSICIANS

In music, as in life, sometimes human interaction is the magic behind the music. Whether you're making a quickie demo or a big-budget master, the synergy created between musicians is often what brings a song to life.

WORDS OF WISDOM

Finding great players isn't enough. Try to use the people who don't feel they need to show off in order to earn their keep — find the ones that support the song and bring out the best in it and in you!

— JIM PETERIK, WRITER OF 18 BILLBOARD TOP 10 HITS
INCLUDING THE PERENNIAL FAVORITE "EYE OF THE TIGER"
FEATURED IN ROCKY III

Using machines

It used to be that all instruments had to be played by actual human beings. But with the advent of drum machines, samplers (a digital recorder that captures, or "samples," any sound source for playback onto your track), MIDIs (which stands for musical instrument digital interface whereby a musician can program his computer to communicate with a vast array of sound sources), and computers, everything has changed. Much of the music you hear on the radio today is created and perfected on computers. As a songwriter, this can be good news. By learning the craft of programming, you can literally be a one-person band — and courses (both online and offline) are offered at recording institutes and community colleges that can educate you in this amazing and ever-changing technology.

TIP

As a songwriter making a demo, learning programming, or finding a team player who's proficient at it, is important — especially if you're pitching your song to any of the areas that rely on programming so heavily, such as urban, hip-hop, rap, and dance-pop.

Programming your demo can have these advantages in certain situations:

>> Keeping your costs down by not having to hire as many musicians

>> Making your demo have a more current sound in certain genres

>> Adding flexibility to your demo by giving you the ability to build it up slowly and make modifications at the eleventh hour

OFF THE
RECORD

Recently, I came across the original demo I had made for "Hold on Loosely," which I co-wrote with Don Barnes and Jeff Carlisi for .38 Special. At the time, I thought it was pretty hot that I did it using a drum machine and playing all the parts myself. But in listening to it after some time had passed, I couldn't believe how stiff and mechanical it sounded after being used to the finished hit version, which included all the members of the band — giving it that human feel that only comes through human interaction. I found that whether it's the actual musicians playing together or the person who's programming the computer, it still comes down to the heart and soul of an actual human being.

— JIM PETERIK, WRITER OF 18 BILLBOARD TOP 10 HITS

Deciding who is going to sing

There are varying opinions and considerable debate on whether the songwriter should actually sing his own demo. On the one hand, the songwriter knows the song from the inside, and whatever he lacks in vocal ability is made up for in soul and feeling. However, the industry is accustomed to hearing polished vocals — so it may be best to give up a little feeling for the range, vocal texture, and overall technique of a great singer. The best of both worlds, of course (unless the songwriter happens to be a great singer), is finding a singer who really gets into the song and sells it for you with professionalism *and* the correct mood or feeling.

Making an Arrangement

The term *arrangement* refers to the musical shape that your song will take. Years ago, the arranger was arguably more influential than the producer in determining how a song would end up sounding. When Frank Sinatra changed from arranger Nelson Riddle to other arrangers, his whole style changed. In those days, the arranger wrote out the parts that virtually every instrument would play and the dynamics (louds and softs, playing and laying out) with which they would be played. Even the rhythm and feel were notated on paper.

At the demo stage, the arrangement is important because it serves as a template of how you envision the final version. The type of arrangement that you create will depend on the type of song you've written. The arrangement of a song indicates what marketplace you'll be targeting and how effective your presentation will be. For example, ballads often can be presented in a simple piano and vocal version with minimal percussion, if any. This approach showcases the melody and lyrics, which are the most important elements of a ballad. On the other hand, up-tempo songs — whether they are rock, R&B, country, gospel, or whatever — rely as much on the rhythm as anything else. You'll want to add powerful drums, pounding bass, cutting guitar, brass, and whatever else you feel is necessary to give the listener the full impact.

In any case, allow the person who's listening to your demo *feel* the song, not just hear it. And, when creating the arrangement for your song demo, keep in mind that a strong musical hook is often as important as the song itself. It won't make a bad song great, but it sure can elevate an average song and make it a slam-dunk. Often, it's those little intro riffs and figures that stick in your head well after the song has faded.

TIP

Ask your band members or studio musicians to add their own creative touches to bring musical spice to your song.

A lot of times, the artist, manager, or producer who's listening to these songs has had it up to his ears with fancy demos. Don't give them anything not to like. Many hit songs were originally presented as a demo with only piano and voice. Some have been cut on the strength of one voice singing into an answering machine. But there are other examples where the excellence of the arrangement and performance actually sold the song — some writers create what sounds like finished products to showcase their song. Ultimately, you have to go with your gut instinct and do what's right for you and your song.

WARNING

A good producer or publisher will see right through any gold paint and sparklers that you may have added to the demo thinking it would help compensate for what you feel your song may be lacking otherwise. If the song isn't solid at its core, you won't be able to disguise it with a fancy production. Let production be transparent, and let the song itself shine through. As they say in Nashville, you can't polish a cow chip!

Creating a chart

The songwriting team should come to a session with a *chart* of the song — a rough draft of the chord structure of the song. Chord charts can be presented in two different ways:

» **The chord root chart:** This is the traditional method, in which each chord is assigned a letter in accordance with its root note (the root or bottom note of a chord — if you played a C major chord — C, E, and G — the C would be the root). Jotting down any melodic figures (suggested bass lines, band stop times, or essential rhythmic figures) is also a good idea. Session musicians really appreciate some direction in terms of arrangement

» **The number chart:** Also known as the Nashville system, this is a method in which each chord is indicated by its number, and a "Maj" (for Major") or a minus sign after the letter to indicate major or minor (see Chapter 10 for more information). Here is a key with some helpful shorthand chart-writing techniques:

- **Major:** Upper-case Roman numeral (Nashville system)
- **Major:** Upper-case letter (*G* or *C*, for example)
- **Major:** Letter or number with "Maj" after it (*C Maj*, for example)
- **Minor:** Lower-case Roman numeral (*ii*, for example)
- **Minor:** Lower-case letter with "min" or minus sign after it (*g min*, for example)
- **Dominant 7:** Upper-case letter with "7" (*F7*)
- **Major 7:** Upper-case letter with "Maj7" (*C Maj7*)
- **Minor 7:** Lower-case letter with "min7" (*d min7*)
- **Diminished:** Lower-case letter with "dim" (*g dim*)
- **Augmented:** Upper-case letter with "Aug" (*C Aug*)

Notations should be made on the chord chart as to the sections of the song, clearly marking intros, verses, pre-choruses, choruses, bridges, repeats, instrumental sections, and whatever else. Often, musicians make their own notations on their chord charts to remind them of certain arrangement ideas.

Beyond that, it's up to the songwriter and his team of musicians to create a *head arrangement*. A head arrangement is where everyone makes mental notes (hence the word *head*) and suggests ideas as to style, feel, rhythm, genre, musical breaks, musical riffs, and hooks — all the nuances that take a basic chord chart and make it magic. Sometimes the spaces you leave in a song are as important as the notes you play. Arranging a song is all about the give and take between musicians — the sections of a song where one instrument will drop out, allowing another one to shine. These techniques will make your song demo more compelling to the listener.

TIP

If you come to your session without at least a chord chart, you'll waste precious studio time waiting for the musicians to write out their own charts as they listen to the song.

As the writer of the song, you'll probably have a pretty good idea of how you want your song to sound, but try to be open to the input of others you trust. Your arrangement choices will help to determine the following:

>> The musical direction your song will take

>> Which market is best suited to your song

>> How effective your presentation will be

>> What demographic target your song will find

TIP

Often there is a very fine line between the genres — and actually a lot of crossover among them. For instance, the borders are currently quite blurry between pop/rock and country. Sometimes it's just a slight change in the instrumentation of a song that skews the same song to two different marketplaces. Often, the addition of a pedal steel or fiddle can tip a pop song into the country market. Conversely, the addition of a distorted power guitar can beef up a country pop song enough to be pitched to rock artists. Sometimes, the vocal style has to be altered accordingly, but the drums, bass, and keyboards can often stay the same. Similarly, a pop/rock song can change into a dance/pop song by altering the feel of the arrangement and usually by substituting programming for live musicians.

Using an arranger

Having a team player called an *arranger* — the person who puts all the musical pieces in the right place and adds sonic musical color where it's needed — is well substantiated but not always required. If you've assembled a good team, the musicians and the engineer can all become the arranger. The songwriter can also act as the arranger, but in doing so, the songwriter must also put the arranger hat on and think like an arranger.

The days of hiring an arranger at the beginner's level are long gone. When you get your song cut and have a budget for, say, $10,000, then you can bring in an arranger and ask him, "Okay, here's the basic track, what do you hear?" He'll then say something like, "Oh wow, I hear an organ here, sleigh bells right there, and a 40-piece string section on the chorus."

REMEMBER

As the songwriter, the arrangement of your song will set the tone for how you want the record companies, the artist, and the managers to perceive it. Start with a mission statement of the marketplace (or marketplaces) you think your song can fit and make decisions accordingly.

Recording the Demo

Whether you decide that you're going to be using real musicians, programmed instruments, or a combination of both, you must also decide on how and where your song will be recorded.

Deciding where to record

Generally, your finances dictate where you'll record your demo. If you can afford it, use a professional studio. They can offer you a trained staff, top-notch equipment, and great coffee so you can concentrate on what you do best: creating music. If money is tight, perhaps you know someone with a decent home studio who wouldn't mind helping you out (plus making a few bucks on the side). Maybe you could even barter your musical talents in some way against free studio time. The most cost-effective way, of course, is to do it yourself on modest equipment you've installed in your basement or spare bedroom. If you have a fairly high aptitude for the technical, this may be your first choice. Just be sure not to let the technical details totally bog you down.

DIY — doing it yourself

These are great times to be living in if you're a songwriter on a shoestring budget. You can buy relatively inexpensive but superb digital home studio equipment (see Chapter 11 for more on home studios) and, for less than a few thousand bucks, create a recording studio in your spare bedroom. Becoming efficient at this will allow you to rival the production quality of what could only be done in the major studios just a short decade ago.

Of course, there are sonic differences between an inexpensive digital recorder and the professional setup at the downtown studio. But at the demo stage of a song, those differences won't determine whether your song will be well received or not. In fact, Alanis Morrisette's 13x platinum album *Jagged Little Pill* was recorded entirely on the Alesis ADAT system — a technology even at the time considered to be primarily a demo recording format. If the song is there and the soul is intact, that's all that really matters.

Lots of songwriters make their own demos and record all the instruments themselves — one overdub after another. They lay down the drum tracks or computer-based drum samples first, do a sequence, and then play all the instruments over that, adding vocals just before the mix-down phase.

To learn the technology of digital home recording, you can often find classes offered by local colleges. Check with The Recording Academy (NARAS) to see if they have any recording workshops on the horizon or if they can point you to one. Look in the back pages of home recording magazines like *EQ* to find schools that specialize in the recording arts. Music stores often have company-sponsored seminars on the recording gear they sell. Of course, as a last resort, you can always read the owner's manual and learn the old-fashioned way — trial and error until you get it right!

Using a professional studio

Even with the numerous improvements that have been made in home recording, many songwriters still choose to bite the bullet and spend bigger bucks in hiring professional recording studios. A commercial studio:

>> Supplies top quality engineers and staff

>> Provides a musically conducive environment away from your everyday home or office atmosphere

>> Provides you with more equipment options at a level of higher sophistication on every aspect, from a wide assortment of microphones to sound processing like de-essing (getting rid of those spitty s's) and pitch correction

>> Provides a place where your musicians can meet and not invade your private space

>> Allows you to concentrate on patching up your song instead of running patch cables

>> Furnishes you with generally some of the strongest darn coffee north of Brazil

Furthermore, professional studios make their reputation on service and reliability. If a machine goes down at home, the session is off until you can get it fixed. At a big studio, they'll generally have backups for just about every piece of gear — so the creativity and the momentum of your session rarely have to be broken up because of broken equipment.

REMEMBER

A home budget generally does not allow for the use of microphones that can cost upwards of $10,000 dollars. Also, you will not have access to a nice recording console. These can run over a hundred thousand dollars. The primary stages in your signal flow are essential to sweetening one's sound, so you want the best possible quality. Professional studios really do make a huge difference.

If you aren't inherently a technical person, it may be wise to use a professional studio. Many songwriters get so bogged down watching meters, reading manuals, and troubleshooting problems that the music gets lost in the shuffle.

Currently, you can rent a good demo studio equipped with an engineer for $50 or less per hour. Call around and find a good price, and avoid the expensive studios. Some studios specialize in cutting demos (as opposed to actual final album work) and make it easy by booking the room in three-hour session blocks, complete with recording engineer and often a selection of session musicians they'll supply for a package price. Studios like this (County Q in Nashville has made its reputation on this principal) pride themselves on total efficiency. If you come well prepared with songs and charts, you could cut as many as six or seven songs in a three hour session.

Finding demo services

In the back of many songwriting newsletters and music magazines (or by way of online search engines), you can find listings of demo services. The deal is, you send them a rough tape of your song (or the sheet music) and for a set fee they'll produce a finished demo for you. The quality of these services range from rip-off to amazing, so be sure to request samples of their work before you hand over your precious song. And always copyright your song before sending it anywhere (refer to Chapter 19 for more details).

Paying for the demo

How much you're able to spend on your demo will be determined to some extent by who's footing the bill. If you're signed to a publisher, there may be provisions in your contract that specify the conditions of making demos and the maximum cost allowable per song. Usually the expense is paid upfront by the publishing company and recouped from royalties due to the songwriter (often a good attorney can negotiate for only 50 percent of that cost, to be paid back from your earnings). There may also be language in the contract that states all demos must first be approved by the publisher — which means you'll have to do a great job of singing your song over the phone or do a decent boom box version for their approval. At any rate, it still behooves you to keep your cost down — you'll be paying it back someday!

Packaging the Demo

For a songwriter, the packaging that goes into selling your song doesn't need to be elaborate. In other words, your demo CD need not look like a CD in a record store with four-color printing or fancy artwork. The song — seldom the writer — is the star of the show. Few people really know what Diane Warren looks like, yet she is the writer behind scores of Top 10 hits. You'd walk right past Max Martin (who writes songs for Kelly Clarkson, Pink, Katy Perry, and others) and Mutt Lange (the writer behind hits for Shania Twain, The Corrs, Def Leppard, and the Jonas Brothers) without ever knowing it. Take note that it isn't necessary to have a photo of yourself on your demo package, unless you're presenting yourself as an artist as well.

REMEMBER

When packaging your demo, it's not about you — it's about the song. Presentation is important with a song demo, but it doesn't have to be fancy or elaborate to get attention.

Including contact information

Contact information is everything when pitching your songs. Next to the music itself, it is the single most important element.

WARNING

There have actually been cases where a song has been passed over by a producer who could not find a contact phone number on the label. Maybe the writer's information had been on the cover letter that accompanied the disc, but the letter had since been tossed out. Industry people get hundreds of songs a month — it doesn't take much to disqualify one for reasons like this.

The best and most economical way to package your song demo (other than to send it electronically via the Internet) is to house your CD in one of those clear, slim-line jewel cases. Then put all the pertinent information on the CD disk itself. That information would include:

>> The titles of the songs on the disc and their running lengths

>> The names of the songwriters

» The name of the songwriter(s)' publishing company (if any) and performing rights group (ASCAP, BMI, or SESAC)

» A contact phone number

» An e-mail address

» The copyright date (the date you recorded your demo)

WARNING

Be sure that your copyright date is within one year — no one wants to be pitched a song that's been around the block or is collecting dust and is dated.

Keep the information as simple as possible on the CD. For instance, if there is more than one writer, don't bother listing issues like who wrote the lyrics and who wrote the music. Similarly, there is no need to cram the label with every publishing company involved in a song. After your song is cut, there will be plenty of room on the final product to go into greater detail.

The audio CD is one of the best mediums for presenting your song in terms of quality and convenience for the listener. CD labels, jewel cases, and front insert cards (which are optional — see Figure 15-1 for an example) can be purchased at your local office supply or computer supply store. You can buy blank CDs in bulk on spindles quite economically, and you can easily learn how to *burn* them (copy them) by using an inexpensive CD-ROM burner, a piece of equipment that connects to, or is included in, your computer.

TIP

Sometimes, putting a simple graphic behind the information on your CD label can add a nice dimension to your presentation (check out the example in Figure 15-2), and provide a more compelling package.

TIP

There are many software programs that you can load into your computer to add graphics to your demo presentation. But if you don't have access to a computer or label maker, you can still use a sheet of sticky labels (available at your local office supplies outlet) for all the pertinent details and label the CD yourself.

Always have your contact number in two places: on the CD *jacket*, which is the card tucked inside the case, and on the CD label itself.

Other elements to go out with your song package include the following:

» **A cover letter:** A typewritten letter from the songwriter or publisher introducing you, the songs, and the songs' intended target. This page should include all your contact details.

» **A lyric sheet:** A typewritten listing of all the songs included on the demo, along with their lyrics. This sheet, too, should include all your contact details in case the other sheet gets lost.

FIGURE 15-1:
An example of a
CD jacket (or
insert) for your
demo CD.

Requesting permission to send a demo

If you send a demo without it being requested or *solicited,* you run a high probability of having it returned unopened. The record industry seems to be particularly vulnerable to lawsuits, so whenever someone listens to a song they have received unsolicited in the mail, they're leaving themselves open to possible copyright infringement litigation. If you can't hire a music attorney to solicit your song, send a letter (like the one shown in Figure 15-3) to the record company, artist, and others requesting permission to send a song to them for a specific purpose.

TIP

Also, when you call, ask if the recipient uses or requires a code word or an identifying mark on the outside of an approved submission package.

FIGURE 15-2:
An example of
the CD's label for
your demo CD.

As soon as you get an okay and you're ready to send your material, be sure to write on the envelope "REQUESTED MATERIAL," and any code or identifying mark if required. Make sure you have your name or company prominently displayed along with your return address on the package.

REMEMBER

A little protocol can go a long way. As a songwriter, you need every advantage you can get.

Making a lyric sheet

Including a typewritten lyric sheet with the song you submit is a good idea. Some A&R people, producers, and others will ignore the lyric sheet and rely on their ears alone, whereas others will follow along as they listen. Some will read the lyrics only after the song has initially grabbed them — so your words need to be intelligible on your demo. The lyric sheet then becomes icing on the cake. Take a look at Figure 15-4 for an example of a lyric sheet.

Sami Songsmith

1234 Melody Lane
Harmony, Tennessee 37654
(423) 324.5678 - songs@email.com

April 12, 2010

Mr. Sean Starmaker
A&R Department
Starmaker Music
4321 Chartmaker Terrace
Nashvegas, CA 95351

Dear Mr. Starmaker,

My name is Sami Songsmith. I am a 25-year-old songwriter from the tiny town of Harmony, Tennessee.

Although I do not yet have a hit to my credit, I have written over thirty copy-written songs and won my county's songwriting competition in 2008.

I would like your permission to send you a song for your artist Billy Bob Boyband. I feel I have one that would fit him to a tee. It is up-tempo pop with a bit of an alternative edge with what I feel is a very catchy chorus. Because I cannot yet afford to hire my own music attorney, I am asking your kind cooperation.

Looking forward to hearing from you by phone, fax, e-mail or mailing address.

Sincerely,

Sami Songsmith

Sami Songsmith

FIGURE 15-3:
Requesting permission to send a demo is a critical part of the submission process.

Sami Songsmith

1234 Melody Lane
Harmony, Tennessee 37654
(423) 324.5678 - songs@email.com
Lyric Sheet

"Dummy For A Song"

I stayed up all night long
Just trying to write this verse
But with every page of rewrites
My lyrics just get worse
We've all heard songs that bore us
Before getting to the chorus
So please don't fall asleep before I do

Chorus
I am just a Dummy For A Song
And I pray that other Dummies sing along
I'm a sucker for a hook
And a junkie for a book
That promises to help my pen along
And while I thumb these pages
I realize it's contagious
For I am but a Dummy For A Song

Bridge
It seems that I am running out of rhymes
So I'll cut right to the bridge to save some time
In Dummies I am told
It's okay to break the mold
I'm sure my big-time publisher won't mind

Verse 2
I worked the whole day long
To make my demo great
But every passing overdub
Only seals its fate
I'll try again tomorrow
Perhaps you'd let me borrow
A cup of adjectives, a sprig of rhyme

Chorus
For I am just a Dummy For A Song
And I pray that other Dummies sing along
I'm a sucker for a hook
And a junkie for a book
That promises to help my muse along
And while I thumb these pages
I realize it's contagious
Until I find a hook as good as "Thong"
I'll remain a Dummy For A Song

© Copyright 2002 Jim Peterik Music -- ASCAP

FIGURE 15-4:
Include a lyric
sheet in your
demo package.
Here's the song
example for Sami
Songsmith's
"Dummy For A
Song."

REMEMBER

The words to a song are as important as the music. Make sure they stand out in the mix and that they are well enunciated!

REMEMBER

If your demo presentation has a lot of unnecessary information, the listener will have a hard time finding the important stuff — like your phone number. Conversely, if a key element is left off the demo, it may end up in the circular file — otherwise know as the wastebasket.

Sending that Baby Out!

You've just written a song, finished the demo, and created a simple and attractive package for it. Now you'd like a certain artist to hear it — who is the best person to present your song to them? This is not the time to be a penny-pinching miser — go all out and try hitting as many people involved with your target artist as possible.

Getting your demo to the right people

It has been said that the definition of good luck is when "opportunity meets preparation." Now that your song is prepared, you need to know the people who can give your song that special opportunity! They include the following:

>> The A&R person at the record label

>> The president or CEO of the label

>> The artist's producer

>> The artist's manager

>> The artist's music attorney

>> The artist

>> The publisher

We cover each of these people in the following sections.

The A&R person

A&R is an abbreviation for *Artists and Repertoire* and indicates someone whose job it is to find talent and search out great songs for the record company's or publisher's artist roster. When you're a songwriter or an artist, this is a good person to get to know because he usually sits at the right-hand side of the CEO (who is usually too busy wining and dining to actually sit down and screen songs). You can find record company A&R executives by checking out the references listed on the online Cheat Sheet that applies to this book.

OFF THE RECORD

Sometimes the A&R person works hand in hand with a manager to get an artist together with a song. For example, the band Survivor had one song left over after recording their first album. It was a song called "Rockin' Into the Night," and their producer felt it didn't quite fit in with the rest of the album. The A&R person gave the song to .38 Special's manager, who then played it for the band — they loved it and the song became .38's first hit record.

The president or CEO of the label

In certain rare occasions, the head honcho at the label actually gets in the trenches and actively hunts for great songs for his artist. Sending two copies of your song to the label wouldn't be a bad idea — one to the A&R department and one to the president.

The artist's producer

Sending a song to an artist's producer really improves the odds of getting your song cut. The producer has a lot to say about what an artist will hear for a project, and if he has the confidence of the artist, he can influence what will and won't get recorded. Often, a producer will have a *listener* working for him — someone who screens for appropriate songs so the producer doesn't have to wade through thousands of songs himself.

WORDS OF WISDOM

Producers are usually looking for one particular type of song for a specific artist. Don't send a song to a producer unless you have one you think will fit. I once sent a producer friend of mine a song I knew deep down did not suit the artist. I mainly wanted to impress him with the song. Guess what? He wasn't impressed. If you go to the tool cabinet looking for a screwdriver, you may find a beautiful wrench but it won't do you much good. Don't wear out your credibility by sending inappropriate songs.

— JIM PETERIK, WRITER OF 18 BILLBOARD TOP 10 HITS

The artist's manager

The actual hands-on involvement of the artist's manager varies widely. Even if a manager doesn't listen personally to the songs submitted for his artist, he may pass them along to the producer or record company — especially if the songwriter has a proven track record.

The artist's music attorney

Because of the trust built up between an artist and his attorney, this is a really good office to get your song to. It isn't as conventional as some other places, and therefore falls into the "Gee, isn't he clever and enterprising" category. However, the top music attorneys in the business are very well connected, and it behooves you to get your songs in their far-reaching hands. The best-known champion in this category was the young songwriter who got important industry people interested in her songs simply by recording pieces of her best ones on their answering machines in the wee morning hours. Although we cannot go on record as recommending this practice, we do admire her fearless ingenuity.

The artist

If you could pitch your song to only one person, the artist would be the number one choice. No matter how strongly those around the artist believe in a song, it is still the performer who has to connect with it. The artist must believe the song is right for him in terms of direction, emotion, message, and feel. Collaborating with the artist can be so effective precisely for this reason: A co-writer can really get into an artist's head to see what makes him tick.

The publisher

Getting a song to the artist's publishing company may seem contrary to logic because they have their own songs to push. However, if they like your song enough, they just may pass it along to the artist or perhaps even suggest a collaboration between the two of you.

All of the above

Hitting as many bases as possible with a given artist is never a bad idea. If enough people in the artist's inner circle start talking about a song or a songwriter, they can create quite a buzz — and generally, the more bases you can cover, the better your chances of having a home run and getting your song cut.

TIP

Producers get songs pitched to them all the time. It's important that the song you send them is in keeping with the style of the artist that producer is working with. Even if the song is great in and of itself, it won't be considered unless it's artist-specific. Be disciplined and focus on the artist you're trying to reach — or you may not get a second chance.

OFF THE RECORD

Don't make apologies for the song or demo. A producer may lose interest in a song before he even hears it if all you can do is make excuses for the presentation. Never send a song out until you're confident you've captured the essence of the song — then of course, no apologies are needed.

Following up

After you've sent your solicited song or songs to a producer, artist, A&R person, manager, and others, you need to follow up with a phone call or e-mail to confirm it was received. After that's done, the next step is finding out whether it was listened to and how they liked it. You can do all of this with one phone call if you're lucky; but you may need to make several calls to get all the information you need. Persistence is a key element here, but you need to be sure not to come off as too much of a pest. Make sure your phone manners are pleasant and that you don't sound as desperate as you most likely are. Make sure you're not screaming at the kids, blasting the radio, or eating potato chips (bananas are okay) while you're talking to the head of A&R at J Records! It's also a good idea to have a pen and paper ready — with a list of things you want to cover in the phone call. If you've tried and failed repeatedly to get a response to a song, it may be that the interest is just not there.

5

Getting Down to Business

Just so all your best songwriting efforts don't languish on the shelf collecting dust instead of royalties, in this part, we get into the business side of music and songwriting. First we provide you with simple methods to make goals and deadlines work to your advantage. Then we look at the various ways your little ditty can make some serious dough. We also tell you about the business team you can assemble to make sure your songs get to the right homes and are protected and collected on properly.

Chapter 16

Creating Goals and Meeting Deadlines

The business of songwriting is, like so many other businesses, a matter of being at the right place at the right time with the right song. The true definition of "luck" is when *opportunity meets preparation*. This chapter is about making a habit of "getting lucky" by doing the work and being prepared — creating goals for yourself, achieving goals set for you by others, and ultimately meeting deadlines overall.

Creating Goals

When athletes use the word *goal*, they're referring to their trajectory reaching its intended target. Their score depends upon an achievement toward a goal in which effort is directed. In other words, if you know where you're going and put in the effort towards that purpose, you'll have a better chance of meeting your targeted goals. If you've not yet completed a song but have that burning desire to be a songwriter, think ahead and dream up or imagine what you'd like to accomplish — then set it as a goal.

Getting set to write for the first time

Put together an *action plan* — some kind of goal-oriented schedule that you hold yourself to. Your individual action plan will depend on your personal goals, but the process is an important step in getting started as a songwriter. A beginner's action plan might look something like Figure 16-1.

Put a timeline on your imagination. Don't be discouraged if you don't meet every goal on time. A schedule like the one shown in Figure 16-1 is meant to be a creative tool, not a pressure cooker.

OFF THE RECORD

Even as a beginning songwriter, I was very goal-driven. Although I hadn't yet learned the value of writing down goals in any kind of action plan, I'd always set my sights on a particular target. I told my seventh-grade class that I'd written a song before I had actually written it. Although I don't recommend this technique, it was perhaps my way of creating an unmovable goal for myself — if I didn't produce, I'd have been the laughingstock of Piper Elementary! Even though I didn't know the first thing about writing a song, I followed my instincts and used my rudimentary guitar skills to come up with "Hully Gully Bay" (sample lyric, "Where the sea is choppy and the shore is rocky and those hully gully sea gulls are wingin' our way"). The point is, I created a goal for myself and, through necessity, wrote a song.

— JIM PETERIK, PERFORMER, SONGWRITER, AND MULTI-INSTRUMENTALIST FOR BOTH IDES OF MARCH AND SURVIVOR, PLUS WRITER OF HITS FOR .38 SPECIAL, SAMMY HAGAR, AND OTHERS

Venturing out with your songs

If you're past the stage of figuring out the how-to's of songwriting, you've written or co-written several or more songs, and you'd like to get to the next step in your career, goals become even more important. Your next action plan might look something like Figure 16-2.

TIP

It's not enough to merely write out an action plan. Try to read it over weekly (or daily) to monitor your progress. Keep the plan in front of you at all times to keep track of the goals achieved and remind you of those that are still hanging out in the ethers.

- **Logging ideas:** I will gather up all the napkins, barf bags, grocery receipts, and other scraps of paper with scribbled notes of lyrical ideas, rhymes, and concepts, and organize them into one notebook. Or better yet, I will log them on my computer. I will log these ideas under specific headings like "Song Scraps," "Finished Verses," "Possible Titles," and "Song Concepts." And I will make sure to back them up regularly or keep them in a safe place.

- **Preparing the place to write:** I will designate an area of my living space as a writing room (probably that spare bedroom that my brother has finally vacated). I will start to research the marketplace for simple and economical equipment to document musical ideas and to eventually demo my own songs. I will also look into the cheapest way of soundproofing the room.

- **Getting myself ready to write:** I will bring my brother's old guitar over to Joey, the repair guy, to get it put into playable condition. I will then get my calluses back in shape by practicing along with every CD I own.

- **Learning the craft:** I will look for various songwriters' workshops and seminars in town to learn more about the craft and business of songwriting and hopefully find a co-writer to allow for feedback and to help put my ideas into a more tangible form.

- **Getting to know the masters:** I will enroll in a music appreciation class at the community college to get a better feel for the songs written by the masters in this field and buy at least one biography of a great songwriter or writing team.

- **Completing a song:** By midyear, I will complete an entire song and perform it for my friends.

- **Completing a demo:** By fall, I will complete a demo of my completed song.

- **Mailing out a demo:** I will research the process of soliciting songs and compile a list of everyone I wish to send my song to. I will learn the guidelines, submission requirements, and etiquette, and I will mail out and follow up with everyone on my Prospects and Contacts list.

- **Spending my royalties:** By this time next year, I will be in Cancun swimming with dolphins and spending my songwriting royalties.

FIGURE 16-1:
An action plan for the featherweight songwriter.

Sami Songsmith's Songwriting Goals
Middleweight Level

- **Setting up a studio:** I will get my home-demo studio up and running.

- **Compiling a CD demo:** I will decide on the four best songs I've written and demoed and compile a CD for solicitation.

- **Learning about copyrights:** I will learn all I can about copyright laws and register these songs with the U.S. Bureau of Copyrights.

- **Listing industry contacts:** I will compile a master list of publishers, producers, record companies, A&R people, artists, and entertainment attorneys based on my research of various industry source books and referrals from friends in the music industry.

- **Writing a contact letter:** I will draft a professional cover letter that will go out with every CD telling a little about myself and the songs included in the package.

- **Creating a CD label:** I will get a computer program and design a simple graphic for the CD.

- **Mailing out my demo:** I will send out my four-song CD package complete with all contact and publishing information, cover letter, and a typewritten lyric sheet adhering to proper submission requirements.

- **Following up with contacts:** I will follow up with each mailing by using either phone, fax, or e-mail.

- **Planning for spending royalties:** I will read up on Cancun and that whole swimming-with-dolphins vibe.

FIGURE 16-2:
An action plan for the middleweight songwriter.

OFF THE RECORD

For me, goals were always a big motivational tool — they were not always that cosmic. My first goal was to be popular with the opposite sex (music has a way of transcending social standing and physical appearance). My further goal was to make enough money with my passion of songwriting to afford a brand new Datsun 240Z. Of course, trying to enhance the world through creating great music can be the ultimate goal of any songwriter, but never underestimate the power of material goals in tandem.

— JIM PETERIK, WRITER OF 18 BILLBOARD TOP 10 HITS

Setting goals as a pro

If your songwriting career is finally up and running, you can most likely check off the items on the following list:

>> You've just signed a nice co-publishing deal.

>> Your home demo studio is up and running (you've even paid back your brother the money he lent you for the equipment and returned his guitar after buying a better one).

>> You have an entertainment attorney you're happy with to negotiate any deals that come along and answer your legal questions.

>> You even have a song on the debut album of a brand-new artist.

>> You have a *hold* (a hold is when a label is interested enough in your song to ask you to stop shopping your song until they've decided if they'll be recording it or not) with a time limit of one or two months imposed (sometimes the hold is even put in writing and can be from another label on a brand-new song of yours).

Because you're on your way to being a big-time songwriter, you may figure that setting goals is a thing of the past. Not so fast! Goals will now become more important than ever. Figure 16-3 shows what the action plan of an established songwriter might look like.

WORDS OF WISDOM

I have amassed a huge catalogue of songs through the years, and one goal that I've set before myself is creating a master computer file of all the songs I've written and all the vital info for each one. It'll be something I can refer to when I get a call from someone looking for a particular kind of song. My major goal is to continue writing the best songs I can, but my secondary goal is organizing my back catalogue so that it's more easily accessible — because songs don't do anyone any good sitting on a shelf!

— JIM PETERIK, WRITER OF 18 BILLBOARD TOP 10 HITS

REMEMBER

All the goals you set before yourself in the featherweight and middleweight phases of your songwriting journey have paved the way to even higher goals. Remind yourself every day of the reasons you got into songwriting in the first place and continually set new goals for achieving all the success you desire — and deserve.

WARNING

If you're the sensitive type who's prone to getting easily discouraged or disappointed in yourself, try not to set your goals unrealistically high. Still dream, but keep your visions in the realm of possibility to avoid unnecessary discouragement. However, there's something to be said about not putting limitations on your own success. Reach for the stars in strength, if you so desire, and try to let the disappointments just roll off your back.

Sami Songsmith's Songwriting Goals
Heavyweight Level

- **Finding artists to work with:** I will make a list of all the artists that are due to start a new record and scan my catalogue to see if I have any material that is suited for them, or see if my publisher or I can establish a co-writing situation with them.

- **Learning about artists' needs:** I will listen to the most recent release of these artists as well as their biggest hits to see where they are, where they've been, and where they need to go.

- **Getting a song cut:** I will set my sites on getting at least one of my songs cut by a major or up-and-coming artist.

- **Cataloguing my songs:** I will, once and for all, categorize my song catalogue as to song style, tempo, and lyrical theme (all positive love songs in one file, all up-tempo anthems in another, all death metal in yet another) complete with notes and the details of the song's creation, writers' splits, and so on.

- **Contacting the film industry:** I will make contact, either by myself or through my publisher with the various music supervisors for film companies, and target at least one of my songs to be included in a motion picture this year.

- **Promoting my song in advertising:** I will put together a composite CD of songs that I've written which may be appropriate for the advertising market and send them off to the various ad agencies. (Snag one big jingle campaign every five years and I can retire á la Bob "Like a Rock" Seger.)

- **Contacting other writers:** I will make a wish list of writers whom I'm dying to collaborate with and contact them personally, through either my publisher or theirs.

- **Choosing how many songs to write:** I will set a quota of songs that I'd like to write per month and attempt to meet that quota.

- **Choosing how many songs to sell:** I will set a quota of songs that I'd like to see recorded by other artists this year and I will motivate myself, my publisher or song plugger, or my manager to meet that quota.

- **Spending my royalties:** I will start pricing real estate in Cancun and find local builders who are well-versed in recording-studio construction. I'll also continue my research on swimming with dolphins.

FIGURE 16-3:
An action plan for the heavyweight songwriter.

Meeting Deadlines

Deadlines are a necessary part of the business of songwriting, so you may as well try to make them your friends. People are conditioned from preschool on with the reality of time limits — remember pop quizzes and ten-minute essays? It's no wonder that people seem to thrive on this kind of pressure later in life. People often take as much time as they're given, but the passion and urgency can be lost if they take *too* much time. You probably won't have to think hard before memories of being under the gun and sweating deadlines start surfacing in your mind. Making these inevitable situations work enables you to have more fun with deadlines and be creative in the process.

OFF THE
RECORD

I was a student who took a casual approach to school (usually doodling song ideas in notebook margins) until exam time came around, at which point I would cram like crazy. Give me a solid deadline, and my work will generally be sharper and more focused. If you have the reality of one of your songs about to be recorded, you're already imagining how embarrassing it would be if that song isn't great, so you're raising the bar and using the pressure to your advantage.

— JIM PETERIK, WRITER OF 18 BILLBOARD TOP 10 HITS

WARNING

Having all the time in the world can be a song's undoing. When you have too much time and opportunity to change, second-guess, and solicit too many opinions, you can ruin a perfectly good song.

There are many areas in the field of songwriting when time factors and deadlines may become an issue. Here's a list of but a few:

>> **Publisher's deadlines:** Often your publishing contract will specify a set number of songs that you must deliver each contract year. If you fail to meet that quota deadline, they may fail to pay you your final advance payment for the year or forget to renew your contract entirely.

>> **Movie deadlines:** If you're lucky enough to be commissioned to write a song for a motion picture, you may also be unlucky enough to develop an ulcer as you struggle against an unrealistic shooting schedule. Not only do you have to read the script, view the *rough cut* of the movie (that's the version that looks like it was edited by a machete), and write the song, but you generally have to demo the song (and demo it really well!) — all in about one week's time.

WORDS OF WISDOM

I'm certain that given enough time and opportunity I would have over thought and ruined some of my best songs. When Sylvester Stallone contacted Frankie Sullivan and me to write the main title for his upcoming Rocky III movie, I enjoyed the pressure of the deadlines we were presented with. When you keep the finish line right in your sites, it tends to sharpen your focus. The question is frequently asked as to how long it took to write "Eye of the Tiger." The correct answer is about a week. Perhaps the more insightful answer is that the song had been silently taking shape for a lifetime, and finally in 1982, opportunity met preparation and a song was born.

— JIM PETERIK, WRITER OF 18 BILLBOARD TOP 10 HITS

>> **Album deadlines:** When top-selling artists like Carrie Underwood and Faith Hill are looking for songs for their new albums, you can bet that every writer in Nashville is trying to come up with something fresh that will pique the artists', or their producers', interest. However, good as that song may be, if Faith and her team have already chosen the songs for her next album, unless your song is the next "Breathe," you're a dime short and a day late for that one. In contrast, there's also such a thing as being "early on a project" — where it's so early in the song-searching process that your song may be forgotten by the time the songs are being selected for the record — so it's best not to be too early or too late. Usually your publisher or *song plugger* (see Chapter 18 for more on a song plugger's role) will have the most current info on who's looking and when the deadlines for submissions are. Also there are various "pitch sheets" that you can subscribe to (such as Row Fax by *Music Row Magazine*) that give you a week-by-week snapshot of the artists currently looking for songs, specifying the kind of songs they need, whether co-writes are being considered, and what their timetable is for sending tunes.

OFF THE RECORD

I had an extremely embarrassing brush with deadlines early in my songwriting career. I'd just been signed as a writer with Warner Brothers Publishing, and I was overly eager to impress. My mentor at the company informed me that a prominent singer/guitarist was looking for material for his upcoming album. I had a song started called "San Pedro's Children" and was told that if I could finish it and demo it by the following week, I had a good shot of getting it cut. I finished it quickly, demoed it, and sent it in. Then I waited. The only thing that bothered me was that, because of the time constraints, I had to rely on my rudimentary grasp of the Spanish language (two years of study in high school) to create the section where the Mexican children could be heard singing God's praises just before the song hit the last chorus. On the demo, I started the section, "Viva Diablo con Noche . . ." and so on. I figured who's gonna know anyway, and it sure sounded Spanish-y. Well the artist loved the tune. So much in fact that he was soon in the recording studio singing those words, "Viva Diablo . . ." when one of the engineers of Mexican descent interrupted the session and asked John why he was singing, "The devil lives at night?" The singer then ripped my publisher limb from limb and he, in turn, tore into me. How does this story end? I took the time I should have taken earlier and got a proper Spanish interlude for my song with the help of the Spanish Council of Chicago. The song was completed the following week and the story had a happy ending. But every time I see a photo of this artist, I picture him with the veins popping out of his forehead over the audacity of that new kid signed to Warner Brothers.

— JIM PETERIK, WRITER OF 18 BILLBOARD TOP 10 HITS

WHAT TO SAY WHEN YOU MISS A DEADLINE

Rather than turn in poor work as a result of trying to meet a songwriting deadline (or is it rather a "dread" line?), look at this handy checklist of excuses the next time you are under the gun and out of bullets:

- "The dog ate my song notebook" (the old standby).

- "I'd written the lyric on an airsickness bag on the flight to meet with you, but the person next to me needed the bag."

- "The demo was all finished when the ProTools system went berserk and substituted my son's interactive Pokemon game. Do you have any kids?" (It's always wise to blame it on a computer glitch because many of us have the uneasy feeling that computers are out to get us anyway.)

- "The song would be finished except that I'm writing a new and better one right now and giving you a piece of the publishing for your patience!"

Seriously, unless you are writing songs strictly for personal use, to play for friends, and/or to creatively express yourself, you'll want to stay up with the flow of traffic on the music industry freeway. That means setting and meeting goals (at whatever level you are), meeting the deadlines that you've set for yourself (or that have been imposed upon by others), and finding ways to motivate yourself to do your finest work.

Practice Makes Perfect

Pinpoint what stage of the game you most likely fall into — whether it's just getting started or as an established songwriter. Then get organized and set your goals for the next 12 months and commit to achieving them one by one. Print those goals and post them somewhere you will see them on a daily basis — and read them often. Songwriting is a creative process, but you still have to treat it as a business if you plan to make a decent living out of it. The more you structure your time, stay focused, and remain disciplined, the better your chances will be for success — and you'll tend to have other songwriters out there saying, "Man, you sure get lucky!"

» **Predicting the future potential of your song**

» **Selecting your PRO**

» **Making money at retail**

» **Getting up to speed, digitally speaking**

» **Using your song to sell a product**

» **Taking your songwriting talents to the movies**

Chapter **17**

Ka-Ching: How Your Song Makes Money

I f you've written a song and either you or someone else wants to record it, you're now at the point in the songwriting process where you may just get paid for all your hard work and effort. In this chapter, we introduce you to ways of getting paid and some important organizations you need to know about — the ones that handle the royalties. We also discuss how your song can find opportunities in commercials and movies.

Forecasting Financials

Most of us write songs because we love to. Songwriting helps us express our deepest feelings and allows us to share them with the world. It's nice to know, however, that there can be a pot of gold at the rainbow's end, that we're not writing songs only for our mental health — we're earning a living at it!

Sources of income

The major sources of income for a songwriter are as follows:

>> **Performance royalties:** The performing rights organization that the song-writer and publisher are affiliated with, such as American Society of Composers, Authors and Publishers (ASCAP), Broadcast Music, Inc. (BMI), or Society of European Stage Authors & Composers (SESAC), calculates this sum every time his songs are played — whether through radio, television, movie theaters, or anywhere else in public, including digital distribution. (More on performing rights organizations later in this chapter.)

>> **Mechanical royalties:** Songwriters and publishers get paid on every CD, cassette, video, DVD, or other product sold that contains their songs.

>> **Commercial use:** Songwriters and their representatives negotiate fees to be paid when a company wants to use their song to sell a product.

>> **Motion pictures:** Motion picture companies that want to use one of your songs must first work out a deal with you and your publisher.

Splittin' up the pie

The amount of money you earn in the categories listed in the preceding section depends upon the following variables:

>> **How well you and your business team function as a unit.** For example, you'll have trouble receiving your performance royalties if you or your administrator fails to register your song with one of the performing rights societies. Also, when a film company inquires about the use of one of your songs, an inexperienced publisher, music attorney, or administrator may quote a fee that's either too low (thus underselling you) or higher than the market will bear (thus blowing the whole deal).

>> **How many people are sharing in the writer's credit.** Obviously, the more wedges cut, the narrower the slices will be — however, if there is nothing paid, 100 percent of nothing is still nothing, so be generous with those who help you succeed in generating revenues.

>> **How your publishing is split.** Some songwriters own their own publishing companies, and others have co-publishing deals. Writers who have signed away their publishing rights will make half as much money as those who own their own publishing companies — but once again, a percentage of *something* is always better than 100 percent of nothing. (See Chapter 12 for more on publishing companies.)

Joining a Performing Rights Organization

After you've recorded your music, it's important to join one of the performing rights organizations (or a PRO as they are often called) so that you can be paid royalties for the public performance of your music — whether that be for radio airplay, TV or movies, concerts, "elevator music," or even the music played while you are "on hold" waiting to speak to someone on the phone.

TIP

Technically you don't need to join until your songs get played on TV or radio, but a PRO can help your career before then by introducing you to collaborators, publishers, A&R, and other industry people. They also hold showcases from time to time that feature new talent, and they hold workshops and seminars designed to educate and connect their members.

The three major performing rights organizations — ASCAP, BMI, and SESAC — all are recognized by the United States Copyright Act of 1976. Their job is to monitor the music that is played in public and make sure that you get paid all royalties that you're due. Performing rights organizations collect license fees from the businesses that play music to the public, and then distribute them as royalties to the writers, composers, and publishers they represent.

If you act as your own publisher, the fee for joining a performing rights organization is different for each organization. These agencies bring in most of their money from the small percentage (around 4.5 percent) they take from money collected on your songs. If you are signed to a publishing company already, they'll usually take care of your performing rights paperwork (just requiring your signature) and pay the initiation fee for you.

OFF THE RECORD

There is always a debate among songwriters as to which performing rights group is the best. I once wrote a fair-sized hit with a writer who belonged to BMI. Because I was with ASCAP, we decided it would be interesting to see who made more money on the song per quarter, and determine once and for all which organization did a better job of collecting our royalties. The first quarter I won by a few thousand; the next quarter my co-writer won. By the end of the fourth quarter, the tally was just about equal. Even though the two societies have very different ways of calculating performance royalties, at the end of the day, they seem to do a comparable job.

— JIM PETERIK, PERFORMER, SONGWRITER, AND MULTI-INSTRUMENTALIST
FOR THE BANDS IDES OF MARCH AND SURVIVOR, PLUS WRITER OF HITS
FOR .38 SPECIAL, SAMMY HAGAR, AND OTHERS

THERE'S GOLD IN THEM THAR HILLS!

The #1 worldwide song of the year is likely to generate $1.6 million in revenue (for one year of sales and airplay). A single song could command $4,000 or more when used in a popular television show, and a standard popular song's lifetime earnings could total $11 million or more. In case you didn't know already, songwriting has the potential to generate a lot of revenue!

REMEMBER

Choosing a performing rights organization is an important decision, so be sure to find out as much as you can about these agencies and their collection methods before you make your final decision. But keep in mind that if the organization you join isn't working out for whatever reason, you can always change — you are not bound to them for life.

ASCAP

ASCAP, a nonprofit performing rights organization founded by a group of prominent, visionary music creators in 1914, has offices in New York, Atlanta, Los Angeles, Nashville, Miami, London, and Puerto Rico.

ASCAP states that its "primary purpose is to assure that music creators are fairly compensated for the public performance of their works, and that their rights are properly protected."

In 2008, ASCAP distributed a record-breaking $818.9 million in royalties to 370,000 composers, lyricists, and music publishers in all genres of music. There are no annual dues — only a one-time, nominal processing fee of $35 to apply.

Performance money is primarily collected through a blanket license. After operating expenses are deducted, ASCAP sends the balance to its member writers and publishers and to affiliated international societies.

A *blanket license* is the annual fee paid by music users (radio, restaurants, television, and so on — see the long list later in this chapter). The music user pays each of the performing rights organizations this modest fee for the legal right to play all copyrighted music as much as they want. In other words, one fee gets unlimited use for any music. The performing rights organizations require a quarterly report detailing what songs (and how often) the music user is playing to determine the fee that is charged.

Members who have belonged to ASCAP include classic songwriters from Duke Ellington to Dave Matthews, from George Gershwin to Stevie Wonder, from

Leonard Bernstein to Beyoncé, from Marc Anthony to Alan Jackson, from Henry Mancini to Howard Shore — as well as many thousands of writers in the earlier stages of their careers.

BMI

BMI, a nonprofit performing rights organization founded in 1939, has offices in Nashville, New York, Los Angeles, and London. BMI distributed more than $940 million in royalties (less general and administrative expenses) to approximately 400,000 songwriters, composers, and music publishers in all genres of music. There is no registration fee for songwriters — just remember that you'll be signing a two-year contract and can only sign with one PRO at a time.

As with ASCAP, BMI uses a blanket license to collect license fees. It then distributes the monies received to its writing and publishing members. Showcases, workshops, and podcasts that help members develop their skills and gain industry exposure are also offered, as well as health and life insurance programs, discounts on professional tools, subscriptions, and computer hardware and software.

Members who have belonged to BMI include classic artists such as John Lennon, Chuck Berry, Dave Brubeck, Willie Nelson, Carlos Santana, Elton John, The Beach Boys, Aretha Franklin, The Who, and Eric Clapton, as well as Janet Jackson, Faith Hill, Sting, Jennifer Lopez, Sheryl Crow, Jay-Z, 'N Sync, Britney Spears, Eminem, Mariah Carey, Kid Rock, Sarah McLachlan, Sting, Shakira, and Maroon 5.

SESAC

SESAC is a for-profit performing rights organization, with headquarters in Nashville and offices in New York, Los Angeles, Atlanta, Miami, and London.

OFF THE RECORD

SESAC was founded in 1930 as The Society of European Stage Authors and Composers. Since that time SESAC has significantly expanded the number of songwriters and publishers represented, and its repertory now includes all music genres.

SESAC's repertory, once limited to European and gospel music, has diversified to include today's most popular music. Members who belong to SESAC or have performed SESAC-affiliated songs include artists such as Bob Dylan, Neil Diamond, Rush, Garth Brooks, Jim Brickman, U2, Luciano Pavarotti, LeAnn Rimes, Mariah Carey, Alan Jackson, Cassandra Wilson, Jagged Edge, Gary Burr, Jimi Hendrix, Ricky Martin, Christina Aguilera, and UB40.

WHERE YOUR SONGS MAY BE PLAYED

By securing a license from these organizations, any song in the performing rights organization's repertory can be played legally. Without this license, music users are in danger of copyright infringement. The following list (not all-inclusive) gives you an idea of just how many places there are that might play or use your song and pay for that right. It's pretty awesome to think that your song could end up being played in so many different environments and that you would receive royalties from each:

- Airlines' background/foreground music service
- Buses
- Carnivals and circuses
- Colleges and universities
- Concerts and recitals
- Conventions, expositions, industrial shows
- Dance clubs and associations
- Dancing schools
- Festivals
- Funeral establishments
- Halls of fame, wax museums, and similar establishments
- Hotels and motels
- Ice-skating rinks
- Laser shows
- Meetings and trade shows
- Museums
- Online music sites
- Playgrounds
- Private clubs
- Professional speakers
- Radio stations
- Restaurants, taverns, nightclubs, and similar establishments

- Retail stores, shopping centers, and shopping malls
- Sporting events
- Symphony orchestras
- Television stations
- Theaters
- Theme and amusement parks
- Training and development sessions, educational or informational seminars
- Video services

SESAC is the smallest of the three U.S. performing rights organizations; however, they believe that their size is the largest advantage because they're able to develop individual relationships with both songwriters and publishers.

SESAC has a selective policy of affiliation — they audition songwriters and publishers before they become a member, and when accepted, there is no fee to join.

Knowing What Happens When Your Songs Hit the Streets

As a songwriter, not only do you make money every time your song is played on the radio, television, or in a variety of public places, you also get paid on the sales of every CD, cassette, video, or other product that contains one of your songs. The money from this source is called *mechanical royalties*.

Mechanical royalties

The word *mechanical* appeared in the 1909 Copyright Law referring to payments for devices "serving to mechanically reproduce sound." It's been a very long time since those original mechanical devices were used to reproduce sound, but the name lives on, and all the money paid to copyright owners for the manufacturing and distribution of records is still today called mechanical royalties — the rights to reproduce songs in recordings are called mechanical rights.

Through the end of 2012, the standard mechanical (also known as *statutory*) payment that the songwriter and publisher split is 9.1 cents per song. (That rate is reassessed every two years.) Doing the math, if you are the sole writer of a particular song, you will earn $91,000 on a million-unit seller. Often a record company will ask a writer for a reduced rate, such as 75 or 87.5 percent of statutory rate. Your willingness to accept a reduced rate will depend on just how badly you want a particular artist to record your song.

TIP

If you are a songwriter who handles her own publishing, you can obtain samples of mechanical licenses from your music attorney, administrator, or organizations such as the Songwriter's Guild of America. Or contact the largest of all mechanical royalty collection and licensing companies, the Harry Fox Agency, for information as to how to employ their services.

If an artist and his or her record company want to record and release one of your songs, or if a company of any kind (such as a cell phone company that licenses hit songs for users as ring-tone downloads) would like to use your song for a variety of other purposes, they must first obtain a mechanical license from you or your publisher. When a song is used on a CD, if it's the first time that song is being used, the artist or label must get the writer's written permission first.

The compulsory license

If a song has already been recorded and released for commercial sale, according to copyright law, anyone is free to record that song as long as the songwriter and publisher are paid and accounted to in accordance with what's known as a *compulsory license.* (The artist or label will usually attempt to obtain a traditional song license from you initially. If you, as the songwriter, fail to cooperate, they will just issue you a compulsory one.)

Synchronization royalties

Another potentially lucrative area of revenues for the songwriter is in *sync fees* (also known as synchronization royalties). This area of income for writers and publishers as well as independent artists and bands is derived from the licensing of songs for audio-visual uses, such as film and television (including commercials), video games, DVDs, karaoke, and video jukeboxes — basically anything that needs the music to be sync'd with a visual.

Because there is no statutory rate for these derivative works, they need to be negotiated in advance by a set up-front fee, back-end royalties, or a combination of both in order to be granted a *clearance,* or the right to use your music in this fashion. See more about putting your songs into film later in this chapter as well as in Chapter 14.

REMEMBER

Songwriters receive royalties from the first record sold and from the first time it's played on the radio or in public. On the other hand, artist's royalties are only paid out after the amount of money the record company has spent on production and promotion of the album has been recouped — and they're out of the red and into the black.

Using Digital Distribution to Your Advantage

There's good news in the music world, a debatable subject if you were one of the pioneers of the recording industry. A positive change we've seen since the digital age arrived is that there's more money for recording artists and labels (indie or otherwise) due to new copyright legislation. In the "old days" only songwriters and publishers got paid a performance royalty for any airplay collected by PROs, but artists, singers, and musicians were left out of the loop — until several digital legislative enactments in the '90s changed things up.

In addition to the income generated from traditional sources — think record sales, music used in films and TV, and music publishing — you'll most certainly agree that there is a constant stream of new and not so new income models becoming available to the songwriter. Having said that, much of what is cutting edge and new today will be obsolete in relatively short order, so keep an open mind as to the possibilities your future holds when it comes to making money with music.

TECHNICAL STUFF

SoundExchange is the nonprofit performance rights organization that collects statutory performance royalties, such as sound recording copyright royalties from satellite radio, Internet radio, cable TV music channels, non-interactive webcasts, and other digital services that stream sound recordings. Although ASCAP, BMI, and SESAC collect and pay royalties to the songwriters and publishers of songs, when the songs are recorded, it accrues an additional copyright for which that track's recording artists and copyright owner (like a record label) are paid statutory performance royalties by SoundExchange. The Copyright Royalty Board, created by Congress, has designated SoundExchange as the only entity in the United States to collect and distribute these digital performance royalties for featured recording artists and master rights owners. As to each performed recording, 50 percent of the royalties collected by SoundExchange are paid directly to the labels or copyright owners of the *masters, 45 percent of the royalties are paid directly to the featured artists, and 5 percent is paid to the AFM and AFTRA on behalf of the background musicians and singers. SoundExchange represents over 50,000 members, has processed over 170 billion spins, and paid out more than $360 million in royalties as of the end of 2009. Artists and copyright holders can register for free to be paid by SoundExchange for the performance of their recordings.*

— JAY L. COOPER, ESQ., ENTERTAINMENT ATTORNEY, VICE-CHAIR OF GREENBERG TRAURIG'S GLOBAL ENTERTAINMENT AND MEDIA PRACTICE, AND A SOUNDEXCHANGE BOARD MEMBER

WELCOME TO THE DIGITAL AGE

When digital technology and audio subscription services stepped into the mix and allowed us to pick and choose particular recordings on demand, the *statutory licenses* for digital audio transmissions for many media and entertainment companies (such as broadcasters, webcasters, and satellite and cable services that digitally transmit sound recordings) were impacted. Now there are specific types of performances that qualify for statutory licensing, whereas others are subject to *voluntary licensing* directly with the copyright owners (those that include on-demand transmissions that otherwise do not qualify for statutory licensing). Be aware that these voluntary performance royalties are not fixed and may be negotiated directly between the copyright owner and the sound recording copyright owners (SRCOs).

As confusing at this appears, what you need to know is that there are organizations out there that are watching your back for the most part. Rest assured you can be paid statutory performance license fees for digital cable, satellite television, and non-interactive radio services (such as DMX Music, Music Choice, XM, and SIRIUS radio), plus non-interactive webcasters like Yahoo!

To receive these statutory royalties, performers and labels must become an affiliate of one the new collectives (designated agents) such as SoundExchange or Royalty Logic — SoundExchange was created as a nonprofit organization to collect and distribute royalties to SRCOs, and Royalty Logic later formed as an independent performing rights organization for the negotiation, licensing, collection, and distribution of digital performance royalties. By default, if you do not choose one or the other, you will automatically become a distributee of SoundExchange. Do a thorough research on the services each of these collectives provides and make your choice, because in this case, not making a choice is in fact *making a choice* by default!

Music sharing sites and services

Music seems to be available just about any place you look nowadays. There are digital download services, streaming interactive subscription services, as well as non-interactive subscription services; video games, not to mention all the music you can access on your cell phone. Additionally, there a multitude of Internet destination sites that are music driven and visited by gazillions of people every day, such as *MySpace*. Here are a few examples of each:

Digital downloads

The biggie here is iTunes, but others include eMusic and Napster. Granted we are only talking pennies here for the artist (a net between $0.08 and $0.10 cents per $0.99 download), but those pennies do add up — especially when you're talking about billions of downloads sold just by iTunes alone.

Interactive subscription services

Service providers such as Rhapsody, Napster, and MusicNet allow you to create personalized radio stations and play lists. In addition to the same payments for digital downloads, these subscriptions also pay $0.01 to the record labels each time their recordings are streamed.

TIP

CD Baby not only provides songwriters and artists with a well-equipped platform to sell their songs and create their own personal websites, but it is also a very informative resource in the areas of interactive digital subscription services and royalty rates pertaining to the digital distribution of music.

Internet radio stations and non-interactive subscription services

Otherwise known as "terrestrial radio," satellite music subscription services such as MusicChoice, Sirius, and XM Satellite are still regular radio stations and as such there are no performance royalties paid outside of those paid to the songwriters and music publishers by way of ASCAP, BMI, and SESAC. Even so, things change at a rapid pace, so it might be a good idea to do an up-to-date search online to see what the latest and greatest is in this regards.

Video gaming

With wildly popular games such as *Grand Theft Auto* and *Madden Football* hitting the marketplace year after year, this is an area of great potential for not only massive exposure, but also significant revenues. See more on video games later in this chapter.

MobileTones and ringtones

A relatively new source of income for songwriters, publishers, PROs, and now record companies and their artists is the MobileTone (formerly known simply as ringtones). Cell phone carriers such as Verizon and AT&T provide their customers with access to music on their mobile devices for a fee, and in turn pay music publishers and/or songwriters approximately $0.10 or 10 percent of retail on that revenue stream (along with other performance royalties to ASCAP, BMI, or SESAC, and revenue splits to the record companies).

WARNING

May we mention once again that many of these revenue-sharing figures will most likely change rapidly as this market expands and redefines itself, so it's always best to grab your up-to-date numbers from a current online search.

Using Your Songs to Sell Products

One of the single most lucrative situations for you as a songwriter is when a product manufacturer decides that your song is to become the imagemaker for his company. It used to be that practically all songs used in commercials were created specifically for a product by ad agencies and *jingle houses* (companies that specialize in writing jingles for commercials).

But today, it seems that more and more major corporations are going with hit songs from the past and present, and they're creating their campaigns around these songs. "Revolution," performed by The Beatles (written by John Lennon and Paul McCartney), is now synonymous with the Nike brand. "Like a Rock," the platinum hit for Detroit's Bob Seger, will forevermore conjure up images of Chevy trucks climbing impossibly rugged terrain. The Ides Of March smash "Vehicle" (written by Jim Peterik) has become a rally cry for the entire GM line. Foreigner's smash "Double Vision" (written by Mick Jones and Lou Gramm) was certainly never originally intended to be the music behind Burger King's Double Whopper, but who would have guessed? As a songwriter, you'll never be able to plan these magical pairings. However, when you're writing a new song, it *is* fun to fantasize! (Refer to Chapter 14 for more about jingles.)

OFF THE RECORD

At the time "Eye of the Tiger" was released, I never dreamed I'd see Joe Izusu working out to that tune as part of a nationwide Izusu ad campaign. All a songwriter can do is to try to write a great song with staying power, and someday the right product might just find you!

— JIM PETERIK, WRITER OF 18 BILLBOARD TOP 10 HITS INCLUDING THE PERENNIAL FAVORITE "EYE OF THE TIGER" FEATURED IN ROCKY III

The money you can earn for the use of your song in a commercial can vary from one extreme to another and depends mainly on:

>> The size of the product's advertising budget

>> The popularity of the song

>> How much of the song is actually used in the commercial

>> The length of time that the song is contracted for

>> The area of the country (or world) that the ad covers

>> How good you or your publisher is at the art of negotiating

>> How desperate the advertisers are to get the song

>> Whether the song will be used for radio, television, Internet, or all three

A big hit song performed by a major artist for a major product can command upwards of $1 million for a year's usage. A more typical deal might bring $25,000 to $75,000 for an average-sized hit that's used in an ad campaign for a medium-sized company for a one-year period of time.

TIP

Even as an unproven songwriter, there may be opportunities for you to pitch your songs for commercial use. Contacting advertising agencies and jingle producers isn't as hard as you think. Use the same care with submitting material to them as you would with a record company or producer. And don't forget about local manufacturers, restaurants, dealers, and services that you could approach directly with your ideas for how your songs could be used to stimulate their business (and yours!). Check out Chapter 15 for more information on getting your songs into the right hands.

Making Money in the Movies

How many times have you walked away from the multiplex humming the title song of the movie you just saw? That's the power and synergy of combining the right song with the right scene. Motion pictures can be a great inspiration to a songwriter, as well as a tremendous source of income. Songs can be submitted to film companies, producers, and directors through your music attorney or your publisher — or you can do it yourself using the proper etiquette described in Chapter 15.

Due to my involvement in soundtracks in the '80s, I've had a fair amount of opportunities to try and repeat those successes. I had a good experience writing, such as "Beyond Our Wildest Dreams" for Delirious, *starring John Candy (co-written with Cliff Eidelman), but I've had some disappointing experiences as well. In 1990, I was commissioned to write the end title for the Robert DeNiro movie* Backdraft. *The movie supervisor sent me the script and a rough cut of the movie. I was blown away by the visual power of the film and the turbulent, yet loving, relationship between the two brothers in the film. I was also totally jazzed that the movie took place in my hometown of Chicago, and that my song would be playing underneath a majestic, smoke-tinged view of Chicago's skyline at dawn. I turned in what I thought was one of my best songs ever, entitled "Long Road Home." The music supervisor loved it, the stars loved it, but the director wasn't quite sure. The day before the film's deadline, he decided the lyric contained the word "fire" and was too literal to the story. He went with another song written and sung by Bruce Hornsby. I spent the next three days in my bathrobe! (By the way, that director was Ron Howard, and I haven't watched an episode of* Happy Days *since.)*

— JIM PETERIK, WRITER OF 18 BILLBOARD TOP 10 HITS

Getting your song into a film, or writing one specifically for a movie, is definitely something to shoot for. It would not be unusual for a song that was used in the beginning or end-title slot of a major motion picture to command anywhere from $25,000 to $100,000. Songs that are used in lesser scenes might bring in anywhere from $10,000 to $20,000. A complete score by a well-known composer could bring in $100,000 or more.

Of course, if your song is included in a hit soundtrack album, and your performance and mechanical royalties start kicking in, then order that Ferrari you've been drooling over — compliments of those royalties!

Every time a movie is shown on television, the songwriter gets money from the performance society he belongs to in accordance with established rates. Unfortunately, the songwriter gets no royalties when the movie plays in a theatre, so try to negotiate a decent flat fee upfront to compensate for this.

Having Video Games Pay to Play

It sure looks like the video game industry tore a page out of the "How Your Songs Make Moola in the Film Industry" manual. The game companies pretty much use the same model when it comes to licensing music for video games, mainly by offering a *buy-out* as opposed to paying a royalty per each game sold — as is the custom with CDs. These buy-outs are somewhere between $5,000 to $10,000 per master recording, and $5,000 to $10,000 for the musical composition embodied on the master recording for a short-term time period of about five to ten years of online use as well as any other *new media* format that may be developed in the future.

REMEMBER

There are many ways to turn your passion of songwriting into cash, but try to make sure money is not the main motivator. Let the cash be the fortunate result of your creative talent, hard work, and fair negotiations.

IN THIS CHAPTER

» **Assembling an awesome business team**

» **Choosing a music attorney before you need one**

» **Understanding the roles of a publisher**

» **Considering the use of a song plugger**

» **Looking at the roles of managers and agents**

» **Managing your money and business affairs**

Chapter **18**

Introducing the Business Players

Whether you've just finished your very first song or you already have a CD full of completed gems ready to go, your next step is choosing the right people to help your "babies" find a good home. Your success will depend not only on the quality of your song, but also on the specialized team that you assemble to market it. Your rock just won't roll unless your business team is rock-solid and your common goals are unified.

In this chapter, we look at the job descriptions of the various business players and give you some criteria for judging them. We discuss methods of locating the right people and suggest a few questions to ask that'll improve your chances of making all the right moves.

Putting Together Your Winning Team

A major step toward achieving success is choosing the right team to work together to get exposure for your songs and you as a songwriter. Granted there are some writers who thrive on the business side of this industry, but more typically, writers prefer spending their time creating new songs — not filling out forms, reading contracts, and making follow-up phone calls to record companies and managers. If you're a songwriter in this latter category, you'll need to find just the right people to help you so you can spend your time doing what you do best. Plan on getting one or more of the following experts on your side:

>> **Music attorney:** The expert in all the legal questions that you'll have, especially as you get further along in your songwriting. Music attorneys can also be instrumental in making the right connections for you.

>> **Song publisher:** The company — large or small, major or independent — responsible for one or more of a variety of duties on your behalf, including soliciting or shopping your song or songs to artists, record companies, producers, and artist managers; teaming you up with other writers and artists who write; and handling administrative duties, namely, filing copyright forms, filing notices with agencies to collect your mechanical royalties (see Chapter 17 for more on mechanical royalties), or collecting the money themselves.

>> **Song plugger or broker:** The person who will, for a monthly retainer or a percentage of the publishing rights upon his getting an artist to record your song, shop your song around to the music world. Releated to this is a *licenser*, or a song plugger of existing master recordings. A licenser acts as a liaison between the songwriter and all media avenues.

>> **Manager:** The person who has the ability to put you together with music attorneys, song publishers, and song pluggers. A highly qualified manager can oversee your songwriting career in its entirety and help you to make the best-informed decisions.

>> **Agent:** The person who will, if you are a performing songwriter, secure live engagements for you to give your songs and you as an artist the much-needed exposure.

>> **Accountant:** The person who keeps track of your songwriting income and the expenses you incur in getting your songwriting career off the ground; very useful for your financial planning and tax accounting.

When you're just starting out, you may have to function as a kind of one-man band until you can afford the luxury of hiring the services of others. You'll have to be very hands-on when it comes down to cutting demos, copyrighting, shopping (the process of soliciting your song to artists and artists' representatives), and registering your songs. If you can't afford to hire representatives in each category, review the job descriptions and see what duties you can undertake yourself.

First Things First: Getting an Attorney on Your Side

A music attorney should be one of the first business team members you add. Love 'em or hate 'em — in the music industry this person can be your best friend and ally, so hiring your attorney in the beginning will start your team off with the right offense (as well as a solid defense). Good attorneys don't come cheap, but a good one is worth his weight in gold because he can help you avoid the pitfalls so many of us fall into and guide you into fair contracts with reputable people. Because of the importance of this person's role, some say that if you choose to handle your own legal representation, you may end up with a fool for a client.

Seeing what a good music attorney can do for you

A good music attorney will have contacts with artists' managers, publishers, song pluggers, record company artist and repertoire (A&R) people, and the artists themselves. With a good attorney, you don't have to worry about not having 35 years of experience in the business. A desirable music attorney does all the following:

>> Makes sure that every piece of paper that you are asked to sign is fully negotiated in your best interest and makes sure that you fully understand what you are signing.

>> Puts you in touch with other potential team players such as publishers, managers, agents, accountants, and other songwriters.

>> Promotes you among their friends and associates and raises your visibility in the music world.

>> Adds credibility and prestige to you as a songwriter — if they in fact have the respect of their peers in the business.

>> Utilizes their network of A&R people, record labels, publishers, and artists to have them listen to your work.

>> Analyzes contracts previously signed for ways to permit them to renegotiate, expand upon, or even invalidate an unfair contract.

>> Upholds and defends your legal rights in the case of a dispute and deals with any *breaches of contract* (when someone fails to live up to their part of the bargain).

Hiring your music attorney

For starters, make a list of potential candidates' referrals you receive through other musicians. You can also call one of the performance rights organizations (PROs) such as the American Society of Composers, Authors and Publishers (ASCAP) or Broadcast Music Incorporated (BMI), because they can make helpful recommendations on a music attorney to handle your needs. There are also listings of music attorneys in publications such as the ones listed under "Putting Together Your Winning Team" earlier in this chapter. By the way, an attorney need not be in your home town to be effective. Although face-to-face contact is always preferred, with phones, fax, and e-mail, you can still get the job done no matter where you're located. Write letters of introduction to those on your list, and follow up with a friendly phone call and e-mail. If they fail to call you back after a few tries, they're either too busy for you or they lack in the courtesy you're looking for. Keep searching, and soon you'll find the one with the expertise you need who also happens to match your personal style.

WARNING

Although there are many top-flight, caring attorneys who reach out to bands, artists, and songwriters they've seen perform at various showcases to offer a helping hand (sometimes for free), they'll always ask the person if he already has legal representation. Beware of the ones who try to persuade you away from your current attorney — integrity goes a long way in any business.

After you make a solid connection with an attorney by phone, the next step, if at all possible, is to set up an interview at the attorney's office. You need to be in harmony with the person who's going to help you make tons of money with your music, so be armed with specific questions when you have your interview. Let the attorney's answers to each of the following questions help you decide whether or not you want this person on your business team:

>> **Is your practice limited to music?** A jack-of-all trade's attorney may not be the master of any. (Your dad's real estate attorney who "plays a little banjo" ain't gonna cut it.) Look for an attorney who specializes in music law. Next, find out what his specialty is within the music industry. For instance, if his forte is negotiating recording and publishing deals, make sure he also feels comfortable handling copyright issues and royalty questions, or has others on his staff that he can pass the baton to when the need arises.

>> **Whom do you represent?** See if, on his list of clients, you recognize the names of any big success stories that have inspired you. Also, check for any conflicts of interest. For instance, does he represent any publishing companies that may want to sign you to a future deal? That's something you may want to avoid.

>> **How much experience do you have?** This might tell you how much time he's going to have to spend with you. Find the one attorney who has enough experience in business to make you feel confident in his services, but also whose workload won't make you feel like you're at the bottom of his barrel.

>> **How much will your services cost?** You can expect a variety of options, and there are pros and cons for any of the following fee arrangements:

- **Retainer:** Simply put, this is when you pay your attorney a fixed advance, usually monthly, from which his fees and expenses are deducted. Remember to check those statements — how many copies did they really need to bill at a gazillion cents per page?

- **Hourly rate:** The attorney keeps track of the time spent on your behalf, and you're billed on a monthly basis. Expect the hourly rate to be $100 to $500 per hour, billed in 15-minute increments. In addition, all expenses for phone, postage, photocopies, and so on will be added to the bill, so brace yourself.

- **Fixed flat fee:** Usually, this is a fixed amount that's proposed by the attorney when a deal is being negotiated for your project — like when you're offered a huge amount of money and you don't know how much of your attorney's time you'll need, and you want to call him at all hours of the night! The fee could be $5,000 or even $100,000, depending on the deal (a good arrangement for those high-maintenance types).

- **Reasonable fee:** This arrangement is similar to the fixed flat fee; however, the amount is not arrived at until after the deal is completed — which could be sticky and lead to unpleasant surprises. If you're ever offered a reasonable-fee deal, be very cautious. Things may look good now, but just wait until the honeymoon period is over!

- **Percentage:** Now we're talking popular! Here's an arrangement most people would enjoy having. Typically, 5 to 10 percent goes to the attorney who negotiates the deal. This is based on whatever you receive, whether it's from an advance payment or from royalties down the road. With this type of arrangement, you get all the professional advice you need when you need it, and if there's no deal, there's no pay except for expenses — it's kind of like profit sharing with this type of arrangement. The attorney will be highly motivated to keep working with you when he sees big bucks added to his bank account.

>> **How strong are your contacts?** Let's face it. Networking and access are important aspects to consider as far as what this team player can offer you. An attorney's clients, contacts, and relationships are huge factors to take into consideration when making your choice.

After completing your interviews, asking your questions, and checking up on references, it's time to decide. Look at your notes and organize them into a pros-and-cons list for each attorney. Why would this attorney be good for you? What are his strengths and weaknesses? Take a look at your lists and see which attorney best fits your needs. Perhaps it may be wise at this point to whittle down your choices to just two or three attorneys, and then take some time to digest each of their answers and reflect on their personalities and contacts before making a final decision. When all else fails, ask your mother-in-law or the street-corner psychic to choose — or flip a coin!

Weighing Your Publishing Options

After finding the right music attorney, the single most important issue to consider is publishing. A publisher is the person or group of people responsible for managing the career of your songs. A good publisher, by being at the heart of the action of the music business, will be aware of all the various opportunities available for your song. Here is a list of the functions a music publisher may provide:

>> Soliciting your songs to artists, artist managers, agents, producers, A&R representatives at record labels, and to anyone else who has a connection to an artist looking for material.

>> Finding opportunities for you and your songs in film, television, and theater — the American Idols of the world, look out!

>> Putting you together with other songwriters in their publishing stable and even those outside their company.

>> Putting you together with other artists to collaborate on songs together.

>> Providing you with inside information as to which artists are looking for material so that you may have a specific focus and scan your back catalogue of songs for appropriate *pitches* (a pitch, in publisher's lingo, is the act of putting the right song into the right hands).

>> Critiquing your work and guiding the creative aspects of your growth as a songwriter.

>> Helping to negotiate contracts on your behalf with other writers, foreign publishers, sheet music publishers, film companies, and so forth.

>> Granting licenses to those who would like to use your song.

>> Handling administrative duties such as copyrighting your songs, filing notices with performance organizations (ASCAP, BMI, and SESAC) for songs that receive airplay, registering your songs with various agencies like Harry Fox that collect your mechanical royalties (the monies a writer and publisher receive on every record sold), collecting your mechanical royalties themselves, doing general accounting, and of course paying you your writer's royalties (generally on a quarterly basis).

>> Providing upfront money to a writer in the form of advances either in a lump sum, annually, monthly, or weekly — don't hold your breath here, but hey, it's happened before and could happen again!

>> Footing the demo bills on songs they've approved, and on occasion, even making the demos themselves. (Demos are the demonstration recordings of your song — see Chapter 15 for more details.)

>> Advising you on all aspects of your songwriting career and finding every opportunity possible for your song (everything from TV commercials and film, to uses by choirs and marching bands for that matter!).

If a publishing company likes your work enough to sign you as a writer, they may also be nice enough to give you some money, so you can actually stay afloat while indulging in your passion of songwriting. This money will come in the form of *advances* upon your future royalties (ha, did you think you wouldn't have to pay it back?), and it's doled out in either weekly or monthly portions, or it's given in one or two chunks during the year. Your music attorney may also specify in your contract with the publisher that the publisher will spring for your song demos, for lyric translations into other languages, and for the production of sheet music. If you happen to be an aspiring performer as well as a songwriter, they might even assist you in securing a record deal. The publisher will also administer your song — which means they'll take care of all the paperwork and registrations for your song, as well as collect all your royalties and disburse them to you, usually quarterly, along with a detailed accounting.

WARNING

If you are considering a publishing deal for your songs, *in most cases* there needs to be a monetary advance put on the table on your behalf — and don't give away the ship or even half of it for no money down!

If it sounds to you like a music publisher plays a vital role in the future of your song and songwriting career, you guessed right. However, finding the publisher to fit your specific goals is not always easy. You need to find a publisher that is not only passionate about your songs, but has the connections to find placement for those songs. The right publisher will know your songs almost as well as you do in order to make well-informed pitches. Also, you must be sure to get adequate attention from the publishing staff. Take a look at the types of publishing companies from which you have to choose (for lists of companies in each category, refer to the publications listed earlier in this chapter or consult the Music Publishers' Association):

>> **Major publishing companies:** There are a few behemoths out there that are certainly worth your consideration. When a large company is running on all cylinders, it's hard to beat. Many of them have the staff and track record to go the distance with your song. They have developed clout in the industry through the big name writers and artists they are associated with. The major publisher should also have the cash flow to offer you an advance and be generous in demo budgets. Companies like Warner/Chappell, BMG, Sony/ATV, EMI, and Universal Music Publishing Group all have great reputations for servicing their writers' needs. The fact that some publishers are affiliated with record companies seems only to be an advantage.

>> **Mid-sized publishing companies:** These companies still have the advantage of an adequate staff to handle your many songwriting needs — though the companies themselves are not as large. Often their stable of writers will be smaller, and they may have offices in one or two cities as opposed to worldwide. If you want the advantages of a major, but are afraid you'll get lost in the shuffle, a mid-sized company may be right for you.

>> **Independent publishing companies:** If you're not looking for big cash advances and want "a few good men (and women)" representing your songs, an independent publisher may fit your needs. These small independent companies will often make deals on a per-song basis — whereby you make a deal for one song at a time, usually with a two-year reversion clause, which means if they fail to place your song within that period, the publishing rights will go back to you. (The larger major companies will also make deals on a per-song basis, but focus more on acquiring song catalogues and signing songwriters as entities, as opposed to individual songs.)

WARNING

No matter which publishing option you choose, be sure to have the advice of a qualified music attorney on your side. Make sure every contract is fully negotiated on your behalf and that you understand what you are signing.

Whether you sign with a major, mid-sized, or small independent company, the range of compensation for representing your songs is the same. To understand better how a publisher is paid, think of a song you write as 100 percent. (If you wrote less than 100 percent of the song — for instance 50 percent, base your calculations on that figure being 100 percent of your share.) Of your 100 percent, 50 percent is the "writer's share" and 50 percent is the "publisher's share." Generally, when a publisher makes a deal with a new writer, unless that writer has a very powerful attorney or is an artist/writer about to break on his own, the publishing company will demand 100 percent of the publisher's share (in other words 50 percent of the income on the entire song). The length of your agreement is an important negotiation point, and whether you get the full rights to your songs back at the end of the agreement depends on you and your attorney's or manager's leverage in the business.

Co-publishing deals

Depending on your status as a songwriter and the power of your attorney, you can often enter into a co-publishing venture with an established publishing company whereby you get to split the publishing 50/50. (In other words, you, the writer, could retain 100 percent of the writer's share and in addition retain 50 percent of the publishing share — which equals 75 percent of the royalties.) Generally, the established company will want to retain administration rights, which will keep them in the driver's seat when it comes to many future decisions. (For instance, you as a co-publisher will not be allowed to sell your share of the publishing without the main publisher's consent.) Co-publishing deals are common for self-contained bands and artists with a built-in following that makes a publisher's job a lot easier. Co-publishing deals are also common for writer/producers with a built-in means for getting songs placed and connecting songwriters with extensive contacts with artists and their record labels.

OFF THE RECORD

If you research copyright law on the subject of "recapture," you will find that the Copyright Law of 1976 includes provisions that allow writers to terminate previous grants of rights and "recapture" their publishing as early as 35 years after the first date of publication — a method that assists writers from having to live with bad deals they may have signed early in their careers. More than 100 songs have reached their effective date of termination and have come back to the writers (or their heirs) who previously had never received any publishing money on those songs before.

Being your own publisher

As a writer, you might decide to *do-it-yourself* (DIY) and handle your own publishing duties. Here are some of the plusses of retaining your own publishing:

>> You get to keep all of the income your song ultimately generates, the writer's share and the publisher's share.

>> You have the freedom of making deals on a per-song basis with various independent publishers.

>> You avoid inter-company politics that have been known to exist within companies where one writer receives an advantage over another due to their track record or personal alliances with other staff members.

And, here are some of the minuses of being your own publisher:

>> You have to do much of the business duties and paperwork, and you have considerably less time to do what you do best — write songs!

>> You may lack the contacts to fully market your songs.

>> You miss out on collaborating with other writers on a publisher's roster.

If you have contacts of your own in the music business, have a flair for salesmanship, or you're an artist recording your own songs and therefore do not require song pitching, self-publishing may be an option for you. Here's a list of the steps to take when forming your own publishing company.

1. **Become a member:** Set up your company with one of the PROs — ASCAP, BMI, or SESAC (and for digital distribution, either SoundExchange or Royalty Logic). Generally they'll require that a recording of one or more of your songs is about to be released for sale, heard in a movie or on a television program, or has been broadcast on the radio.

2. **Choose your name:** Come up with three choices of names for your company in order of preference. The PRO will then do a computer search for names already taken and advise you accordingly. Unless your given name is extremely common, it's a good idea to name your company after yourself. Using your own name is another method of branding yourself. The other option is finding a highly creative name for your company that in all likelihood has not been used.

3. **File your name:** After you've locked in your name, go to your local county clerk's office and fill out the necessary forms to set up a DBA (doing business as) with the same name as your publishing company. (If your name is the name of the publisher, you can skip this step.) You should then open a separate business banking account under that name. You must also give notice through a local publication that gives the required notice that you are doing business under that name. (The county clerk's office can direct you in these matters.)

4. **File your copyrights:** Register the songs in your new company with the U.S. Copyright Office (Library of Congress). If they are already copyrighted, you'll want to register them again as published works.

5. **Register for royalties:** Be sure to notify your performing and mechanical rights organizations of all songs that'll be hitting the airwaves either on radio, television, or motion pictures (or sold to the public), so they can pay you and your company the performance royalties. (For an explanation of royalties refer to Chapter 17.)

Although it's relatively simple and cost effective to set up your own publishing company, you'll have to decide how important it is to you. If you can handle all the detail work necessary to be effective, and have the willingness to hit the phones to make contacts and follow up, more power to you. Your own publishing company could be an enjoyable and profitable venture. If not, you're better off to enlist the help of an already established company that has the experience to do it justice.

Working with administration deals

A good half-way point between signing away your publishing rights to a publishing company and doing it yourself is entering into an administration deal. In this arrangement, a writer would have his own publishing company, but would sign a deal with a publishing administrator to handle all the paperwork involved in running his company. For a commission of between 10 and 20 percent of the publishing royalties for the contracted period (typically one to three years), the administrator's job is to register copyrights, fill out ASCAP, BMI, or SESAC forms, grant licenses to those who want to record your song, and negotiate synchronization fees for those wanting to use your song in films or commercials. (A synch fee is paid to the writer for the right to *synchronize* their music with the a visual medium.) In addition, the administrator will collect your royalties and pay them out to you on a quarterly basis. Some administrators will use the services of an outside collection agency, such as the Harry Fox Agency, to do the royalty collection — others do it themselves.

Here are some plusses in making an administration deal:

>> The administrator takes a massive burden off the songwriter who runs his own publishing company, freeing him up for the creative side, including writing and *song casting* (getting the right song to the right artist).

>> You can retain your publishing rights because the administrator generally doesn't have ownership of the song, but instead is paid a percentage of the song's earnings for the contracted period.

>> You can harness the administration skill of a large experienced publisher without signing over a large portion of your publishing rights.

>> If you are a self-contained singer/songwriter or have a deal with an independent song plugger (see the following section on independent song pluggers), you may not require your songs to be shopped to other artists, and may only need someone to do your paperwork and disburse your money. So, why give up a major portion of your publishing share to a publisher.

And, here are some minuses of administration deals:

>> No monetary advances in the form of weekly salaries or yearly guarantees are made in administration deals. You must be solvent financially to handle all of the expenses incurred by you, the publisher.

>> Generally speaking, administrators do not do song solicitation, so the burden falls on you to hawk your songs and get them into the right hands.

>> There is generally no one at the administration level who gets involved in the creative nurturing and "songwriter's matchmaking" that many songwriters need to get their songs to the next level of excellence.

Dealing with foreign sub-publishing

Whether you decide to sign with a publishing company or act as your own publisher, collecting money from foreign countries will be a factor when you start having worldwide success. The local publisher in the various foreign countries is called a sub-publisher. The huge publishing conglomerates have branches in practically all territories which is certainly one of the advantages of going with a major. For the smaller companies and the songwriter with his own publishing, deals must be made on a territory by territory basis. A qualified music attorney can set up deals for you with the various sub-publishers worldwide. Generally a sub-publisher will collect all revenue on behalf of the main publisher on a given song and keep 15 to 25 percent for himself. If the sub-publisher actually gets someone to record another version of your song, he'll then retain 40 to 50 percent of the song's publishing revenue. Even though the world of foreign sub-publishing is a bit of an inexact science, it behooves the songwriter to make sure that his interests are being looked after worldwide — after all, it's potential for extra moola!

Considering an Independent Song Plugger

A song plugger is someone who actually solicits your songs to artists and their representatives on your behalf. Every publishing company employs a song plugger who listens to their writers' songs, decides who might be an effective pitch, and proceeds in getting your material to that person. A song plugger's main talents would include a great phone personality, as many personal contacts as possible, and the ability to "hear" a song and be able to not only assess its quality, but determine which artists might be the right match for those songs.

Sometimes a person with these talents will work on his or her own — independent of a publishing company. Here's an inside peek at the various aspects of an independent song plugger.

Putting a song plugger to work

Generally, an independent song plugger will work on a retainer basis (the big ones in Nashville command anywhere from $500 to $1,500 per month to pitch your songs). The reputable ones will only take you on if they feel you have material they can "get cut" (Nashville lingo for getting someone to record your song).

In addition to a monthly retainer, some successful song pluggers ask for and receive a bonus for getting a song recorded on an album, a further bonus if the song is released as a single (the cut that is pushed to radio), and an additional bonus if the song reaches the Top 30, Top 20, and Top 10 of the music charts.

Other independent song pluggers will make an agreement with a writer that he will receive anywhere from 10 to 50 percent of your publishing, if he gets you a cut. Generally, the song plugger will retain this share of your publishing for *life of copyright* (life of copyright on songs written after 1978 is the life of the last living author of a song plus 70 years — or sooner by "recapture" rule).

Agreements with song pluggers are generally one year in length so that at the year's end everyone can assess the success of the relationship. Some pluggers actually operate on a month-by-month basis, giving a writer the option of terminating his services at any time.

Considering the advantages of a song plugger

There are pros and cons to the various roads you can take as a songwriter. If you go with a song plugger, you can quite possibly retain ownership of your song and you can receive the extra degree of attention afforded by a song plugger's generally smaller roster of songwriters and songs to pitch. However, a publishing company can offer you advance money, pitch your songs, and administer your catalogue all in one fell swoop — but this service may be at the expense of giving up a significant portion of your songwriting income and freedom to do whatever you please with your songs. There is no right or wrong way — it all comes down to weighing the needs of your own personal situation.

To decide if a publisher or a song plugger best fits your needs, there are certain questions you'll want answers to regarding their services:

>> Are they specialized in the type of songs you are writing? Just like with publishers, some song pluggers' contacts run more toward one style and market of music than another. On the other hand, most publishing companies have individuals who specialize in all the various genres.

>> Does the company have a true passion for you and the songs you are writing? Do they see the bigger picture of your career as a whole or will they take any opportunity on your behalf just to make a quick buck?

>> Are you comfortable with their style of doing business? Do they get back to you on the phone and treat you with the respect you deserve? If not, they may not be getting back to potential producers or artists either — and the saying goes, "how you do anything is how you do everything!"

>> Can you negotiate a performance type of agreement where you give up no portion of your publishing unless the song plugger gets your song cut? If so, and he fails to find a home for your song, at the end of your agreement you're free to offer the song to another plugger or publisher.

Using a Manager or an Agent

As mentioned in the beginning of this chapter, a big step toward achieving success in the business of songwriting is choosing the right team to work together in getting exposure for your songs and for you as a songwriter. Managers and agents can play a big role in this mission, and here is a look at each of these roles.

Do I need a manager?

A *manager* does what the name says: They manage your business career. Choosing someone to guide you is a very personal decision and comes down to chemistry as much as it does ability, experience, and contacts. As a songwriter, a manager is not a necessity because your publisher is really the "manager" of your song catalogue, and your music attorney can handle many of your business affairs. A manager comes more into play if you are a performing songwriter. It's then all the more important to add this point person to your team.

Here's what a good manager can do for you:

>> Help you assemble your business team.

>> Assist you in getting signed with a publishing company.

>> Assist you in securing a recording contract as an artist.

>> Advise you on all aspects of your songwriting and performing career.

>> Make sure that your other team players are working for you to their full potential — applying pressure if necessary.

>> Network and make contacts on your behalf.

>> Make sure you get every dollar you have coming your way.

>> Inspire you to do your very best work.

Managers consult with you on every aspect of your musical career. They help you decide whether you should have a song plugger or a publisher, and then hook you up with one. Managers can also be a help in getting you connected with the right music attorney and accountant if you don't already have one.

A manager is the one who can do all these things for you, so if you're not really into the business side of songwriting, and you would just like to work on the creative side of things, hire a manager to be out there fighting for you on a daily basis. Your manager can be the one to assemble your entire team.

Some singer/songwriters like to be hands-on and become their own manager. Why would you want to do this? Because no one cares more about you than you do. You can have a manager out there working for you, but if he already has four or five other clients who are earning him a decent living, he may tend to point all his energy in that direction. A manager really has to believe in you to give you the time you deserve. Make a list of the pros and cons for using a manager to see if having one meets your particular needs.

WARNING

Steer clear of a manager who asks for a fee upfront against future commissions. This could be a red flag that he's either in dire financial straights, or that he doesn't really believe in you and is hedging his bets. Reputable managers don't charge for their services upfront. They make their money when you do, by taking a percentage. It's a good arrangement because the better you do, the better they do! That's pretty good motivation to try to make you a household name in the songwriting world.

Shop around. Be aware that there are different levels of managers, from the heavyweight who handles the superstars, to the well-respected middleweight, to the friend-who-loves-your-music featherweight who would fight for you to the finish. Compile a list of referrals from musician friends and check out online resources for names and phone numbers of managers. In this case, you may want to look for a manager in your geographical region — there is nothing like close proximity for good communication. However, if your manager is located in a music hub like Los Angeles, Nashville, or New York, he may do more good for you there. (Especially if you live way out in the boondocks!) Then set up interviews and prepare your list of questions, which may include the following:

>> **Whom do you represent?** Listen for any names you recognize and take note of any powerhouses.

>> **How much experience do you have?** You need to find a manager with far more experience than you have yourself. You don't need to be spending your time educating them — it should be the other way around!

>> **What genre of artist do you specialize in?** Look to see if this manager falls into your genres of choice.

>> **What is the cost for your services?** You can expect to hear a range of between 15 and 20 percent of your gross income. If a manager is really good, he'll more than make up for the money you're paying him.

>> **How many artists do you manage?** If his roster is large, does he have enough staff to cover all the detail work? Make sure you meet his entire team, from the front desk receptionist to any partners he may have — and make sure you're not relegated to one of his assistants without your full approval.

>> **How strong are your contacts?** Don't be afraid to ask just who his friends are in the music business. His reputation and connections directly impact how effective he'll be on your behalf.

What does an agent do for a songwriter?

In addition to a manager, a good agent may help you to reach your committed goals. If you're a performing songwriter, you'll need the right booking agent to find you steady work to promote your career whether you're at the club, county fair, or arena level.

As a songwriter, there are specialized agents that handle television, advertising, and film score placement for your songs. There are agents that find opportunities for writers in the video and interactive game market as well. Just as they are with managers, music attorneys, song pluggers, and publishers, an agent's reputation and connections are everything! Ask them where their strengths lie as an agent and make sure the answer coincides with your career goals. Whether they earn their 10 to 15 percent commission depends on the quality of the shows they schedule for you and how well they can interface with the other members of your team.

When there's good synergy between your manager and your agent, you have a better chance of succeeding in this very competitive business. Listings of booking agents can be found by searching the resource sites mentioned earlier, and you might also get referrals from your music attorney and your various musician acquaintances — but if you're not a performer too, you won't be needing a booking agent anyway, so spend your energy elsewhere.

You're in the Money: Hiring an Accountant or a Business Manager

Accountants are people who are skilled and trained in accounting — they are the number crunchers. Their role is to give advice and/or handle financial accounts, and depending on your particular circumstances, an accountant can be hired to do as little as your annual tax returns or a great deal more. If you just need an accountant to do your taxes, then you can probably get by without one who specializes in the music industry. But if you feel more comfortable with a music expert, then get an accountant who really knows the ins and outs of the music industry. The financial accounting business is complex when dealing with royalties and musical rights — very different kinds of animals that an everyday accountant might not fully understand.

Taking this one step further, if you have your accountant handle your entire financial situation, what they have basically become is your *business manager* — one who handles all of your business affairs. However, please note that due to ever-changing rules and availability of Schedule C deductions, that even for start-up songwriters it's absolutely important for anyone in the entertainment industry to obtain advice from a licensed tax practitioner, enrolled agent, or CPA with experience in entertainment industry reporting. These specialists usually don't cost any more than a regular tax professional but, depending upon where you live, it may be more difficult to find one.

Knowing what a good music accountant or business manager can do for you

You may want to hire an accountant who specializes in sources of revenue that apply specifically to a songwriter. You need to basically go through the same process you did when hiring your music attorney. Although you can consider an accountant who is a little more of a jack-of-all-trades, he still must have some understanding and experience in music accounting.

A desirable music accountant or business manager provides all the following services:

>> Helps you set aside (hopefully) large chunks of money to pay your taxes, which he'll calculate and submit on time.

>> Helps you understand such things as tax deductions and will get you saving all those little receipts for expenses that are business related.

>> Handles your money (makes deposits into and balances your bank accounts — pays the bills that you've had forwarded to his offices).

>> Provides you with a monthly financial statement of what your incoming and outgoing finances are, known to him as *accounts receivable* and *accounts payable*.

>> Gives you advice on investments, or refers you to professionals who can better advise you on what to do with your money.

>> Reviews your royalty statements and makes sure you're being paid accurately and on time.

Hiring a music accountant or business manager

Because the music accountant or business manager is probably the last person to add to your business team, you have plenty of time to find just the right one — unless, of course, you make it big overnight, in which case you'll have to put it into overdrive and find someone you can really trust right away.

Considering that by now you have an attorney and maybe a publisher, your search for referrals just got easier. Many times these music professionals work together, or at least have some experience or knowledge about others in the industry. In any case, round up a list of people to interview and book some appointments.

Every person on your business team is important, and the accountant or business manager is the one who handles what everyone seems to care about most — your money! You really need to feel good about this person, so be prepared with crystal-clear questions when you arrive for your interview. Let the answers to each of the following questions lend a hand in your decision to hire your music accountant or business manager and to complete your team of players:

» **Whom do you represent?** Take note of any recognizable names. (Although this in and of itself does not guarantee that your money is safe; many "big names" have been known to get ripped off!)

» **How much experience do you have?** He can have all the big-dollar clients in the world, but the music business is a unique animal. Listen to what knowledge he has about royalties, performance, and mechanical rights. Get a feel for his music knowledge and expertise.

» **How much will your services cost?** Accountants are similar to attorneys in this regard. Most of them charge by the hour, with a monthly retainer or percentage payment made upfront.

When choosing an accountant or business manager, be absolutely sure that he has the background and experience to do what it is that you're asking him to do (handle your professional career and earnings!). Make sure that he has some music-industry knowledge and know-how before signing him on. Then just keep those hit songs coming, so he can become a long-term team player!

Chapter 19

Looking at the Legal End: Dealing with Paperwork

B eing creative, working with melodies and lyrics, and producing songs can be very time-consuming. And on top of all this, having to deal with paperwork issues can be boring, overwhelming, and cumbersome — especially for artistic people. Nonetheless, ultimately this part of the songwriting process can make a huge difference in improving your chances of success. See Chapter 18 for more on song-related contracts.

Creative and linear thinking rarely go hand in hand, and most people tend to be stronger in one way of thinking than they are in the other. But in order to really be in control of your creative output, the more you understand about the business side, the more successful you'll be at meeting your goals. Even if you put together a business team to help you with the inevitable paperwork of songwriting (those hired to handle the publishing, legal, administration, and accounting), it's still your name that's scrawled on the bottom of the paper, so you can't just sit back and "watch the wheels go round and round." Taking the approach of, "Hey, I'm an artist; I don't need to know that stuff!" just ain't gonna cut it. Even surrounded by the best team possible, your basic understanding of the business is vital in helping your team function at 100 percent.

In this chapter, we discuss signing contracts, filling out forms, and keeping track of all the paperwork that's involved in songwriting.

Legal Deals: Creating Win-Win Contracts

"The best for all concerned" is certainly what you strive for when you're coming up with a contract. Although the music industry is full of stories about people getting taken to the cleaners, when structured right, it is possible for everyone to come out on top and win.

TIP

Getting things clear upfront, before you begin any business adventure, is always best. That way, you eliminate (or at least reduce) confusion about who gets what and how the credits and money are handled. In other words, get rid of any disagreements *before* signing any agreements.

OFF THE RECORD

My least favorite part of the music business is the "business of music." I'd rather spend all my time creating and performing songs. Unfortunately, without the business side of things, many of my songs would remain unheard or the income they generate will not be looked after properly. Over the years, I've come to value the various paperwork issues involved in my chosen field, whether it's protecting my song with a copyright, registering it with a performing rights organization (PRO), signing with a publisher, or filling out administration forms. The business side of songwriting isn't all as weird and mysterious as it first appears, and the better you understand what you're signing, the better you and your songs will be taken care of in the long run.

— JIM PETERIK, PERFORMER, SONGWRITER, AND MULTI-INSTRUMENTALIST
FOR THE BANDS IDES OF MARCH AND SURVIVOR, PLUS WRITER OF HITS
FOR .38 SPECIAL, SAMMY HAGAR, AND OTHERS

Understanding different kinds of contracts

Contrary to popular belief, contracts *can* be made simple. Yes, there are some deals that are still sealed with only a handshake (however, this is not a recommended practice!), and others can be as simple as a one-page agreement between you and a co-writer or musical-team player, outlining who gets what, when, and how. As your songs become hits, the contracts will definitely get longer and more complex — and your attorney will undoubtedly make sure that every *i* is dotted and every *t* crossed.

WARNING

Never let an unscrupulous publisher, manager, artist, or anyone else pressure you into signing a deal without fully understanding and agreeing to its terms. A popular ploy is to get you to sign on Sunday when lawyers' offices are closed. Another is to say that if you don't sign "right now," you'll blow the entire deal. You're better off letting the whole deal fall apart than having to live with an unfair contract. Beware of anyone who says they represent you *and* the other party in a contract. It's a common practice for the representative of one party (publisher, producer, co-writer, and so on) to approach a featherweight songwriter saying, "Hey, we have to do this deal *now* because. . . ." "Since I'm already working for [so and so] why don't I just go over the paperwork with you now, so we can get this show on the road?" Stay away from this type of situation at all costs. Songwriters need their own independent representation.

The day will undoubtedly come when you, as a songwriter, will have to sign on the dotted line to consummate a deal. In fact, you'll probably encounter several different kinds of contracts, and it is wise for you to be familiar with each of them ahead of time. In the following sections, we guide you through what to expect before you sign your name.

Publishing and co-publishing agreements

When a songwriter finishes the music, lyric, and/or music-with-lyric of a song, the songwriter is automatically the publisher of that song unless they've assigned the publishing rights to another company. (There is specific paperwork to setting up your own publishing company as discussed in Chapter 18.) However, because most songwriters lack the clout or industry connections to act as their own publisher and get their songs into circulation, it's usually necessary for songwriters to assign all or part of their publishing interest in their own songs to a third party. This third party can be a publishing company, record company, or manager acting as a publisher, song plugger, or song administrator.

A publishing or co-publishing agreement is the often-complex contract you're asked to sign when making a deal with a publisher (see Chapter 17 for more about what a publisher does). Whether the company you're considering is large or small, be sure to read and understand *every* word of the contract. If you're entrusting your precious songs and pledging half of the income (or a quarter of your earnings in a co-pub deal) from these songs, you'll want to do the following:

>> Make sure that the publishing company is treating you fairly regarding issues such as advances, demo costs, length of term, and *reversion of copyright* (if you don't get the rights to your song back at the end of your deal, they should treat you especially well financially speaking).

>> Make sure that your *submission quota* (the number of tunes you must create and turn into your publisher within a period of time) is reasonable. Often an unscrupulous publisher will specify an unrealistic number of songs to be completed each quarter, just so they can put you in breach of contract and stop paying you advances.

>> Make sure that the publishing company doesn't make you, the writer, responsible for obtaining a set number of *cuts* (the industry term for getting an artist to record and release one of your songs) — getting cuts is the publisher's job! Unless you are a really hot producer with a built-in avenue for your songs or a signed singer/songwriter — watch out for this one.

REMEMBER

Only so much can be spelled out for you in a contract. How hard the company will work on your behalf and how many of your songs they'll find homes for are factors you have to gauge by the company's track record, their reputation, and your own gut feeling about the people you'll be dealing with. That piece of paper is all you have to hold them to their promises, so make sure you understand it and that it's as comprehensive as possible.

Performing rights agreements

A performing rights agreement is the contract you'll sign with the American Society of Composers, Authors and Publishers (ASCAP), Broadcast Music, Inc. (BMI), or Society of European Stage Authors and Composers (SESAC), as well as SoundExchange or Royalty Logic for digital distributions — the agencies that monitor the airplay on your song and collect money on your behalf. The contracts are fairly simple and nonnegotiable. Your main concern should be that you understand the length of the agreement and how you can terminate the agreement if you're unsatisfied with their performance for any reason. More important than the actual contract is your understanding of how your performances are being calculated. (See Chapter 17 for more details regarding your songwriting income.)

OFF THE RECORD

It used to be that one of the determining factors for songwriters when they were choosing a performing rights organization was which one offered the largest advance of dollars against future royalties. Much to many songwriters' chagrin, both BMI and ASCAP stopped that practice back in the late '70s.

Performing rights forms

Performance royalties are the monies songwriters and publishers receive when your song is played (or in old terminology, performed) on the radio (satellite or online), network and local television, commercials, juke boxes, Muzak (the smooth versions you generally hear at the supermarket or mall), or in live performances, stores, night clubs, by marching bands, sung by choirs, at work-out clubs, for film, and anywhere else your song is helping to enhance people's moods and elevate the day. Performance royalties are paid by one of the performance rights groups such as ASCAP, BMI, and SESAC. After you have joined one of these groups, in order to get paid you'll need to fill out certain forms they supply (by mail or online — the latter being the obvious choice when wanting to contact one of the foreign performing rights agencies) when your song is about to be released.

The forms require you to supply accurate information regarding your name and publishing company, any co-writers and their publishing affiliates, address and Social Security numbers of all parties, all contact information, date of release of the product containing your song, and the writer's splits (the percent of each song that each writer has a share in). Take extra care in making sure all entries are correct because this is the only record they have to ensure you'll be paid correctly.

Mechanical rights agreement

Mechanical royalties are the monies that the songwriter and publisher receive from the sale of compact discs, tapes, videotapes, and DVDs. (The term *mechanical* stems from the old days when it referred to devices "serving to mechanically reproduce sound.") There are certain forms that you or your publisher need to fill out for your songs that get recorded, in order to assure you get paid on the units sold (if someone else wants to record one of your songs, they must also contact your designated mechanical rights agency). Whether you sign up with the Harry Fox Agency (many of the larger publishers actually hire Harry Fox to perform mechanical rights collection) or one of the smaller companies that specialize in royalty collection, you'll still get paid according to the statutory rate, set by Copyright Royalty Tribunal, of 9.1 cents per unit sold. (If you wrote 50 percent of the song, cut that figure in half.) If you are signed to a publisher, that company will handle this paperwork on your behalf. If you handle your own publishing, you'll want to team up with an administration agency to take care of your mechanical royalty collection and the issuing of song licenses. Record companies must account to them as to the sales of the units containing your song so you can be paid properly. The Harry Fox Agency is the largest administrator of songs (in fact, many publishers use Harry Fox themselves to do their administering as well), but there are other smaller administrators who do an excellent job, too. Most of these royalty collection services command anywhere from 5 to 10 percent for their services. Again, be sure to understand the scope of the agreement, the percentages withheld, and the terms of the contract.

TIP

If you choose a giant mechanical collection agency like the Harry Fox Agency, try to make a few personal acquaintances at the company so that you're more than an account number. There also needs to be one or two specific people you can count on to answer your questions as they arise. No matter how big the company is that you are dealing with, remember, it's ultimately *you* who are keeping *them* in business, so don't be afraid of asking questions and requesting explanations of their business practices.

Mechanical license payment rates are standardized, with all songwriters being paid equally according to a formula that changes occasionally over time. You can contact the Musician's Union or Harry Fox to give you the current rates.

Copyright forms

Copyright forms are important documents for you as a songwriter. Before you send your song out to the immediate world, you want to protect it from theft through copyright. Fill out these forms carefully and accurately. (You can find more information on copyrights later in this chapter.)

Synch rights agreements

Whenever someone wants to use your song in a movie, video, commercial, or any use where a song is synched up with the action on the screen, the company will issue you or your publisher a synch rights license for you to sign. The figures involved vary widely and are dependent on the popularity of your tune and how badly someone wants it. Thoroughly read the agreement and pay attention to the terms and the specific ways your song will be used.

Commercial music agreement

When a commercial manufacturer wants to use one of your songs to hawk his wares, he'll contact you or your publisher and offer you a contract to cover the song's use. These are actually quite simple and specify the following:

>> The product being advertised

>> The geographic area that the commercial will cover (anywhere from Southern Idaho, for example, to the entire world)

>> The media concentration (radio, TV, Internet, or all of the above)

>> The amount of the song being used

>> How long they want to use the song (if asked for an option of more time, make sure you or your negotiator up the ante for the next time around!)

REMEMBER

Having your song used in a commercial can be a great opportunity for you and your song. But after a song is used for a specific product, it may be eliminated from future use with other products — so make sure the deal you make is lucrative enough to make it worth your while.

Co-writer agreement

Whether it's scribbled on a napkin or specially worded by a high-priced attorney — this is the agreement between the songwriters as to how the songwriting credits will be divvied up. Standard forms can be obtained from the Songwriter's Guild or supplied by any good entertainment attorney.

WARNING

Contracts are only as good as the parties involved, and trust is still the number-one factor when signing a deal. When in doubt, rely on your gut and a reputable music attorney.

OFF THE RECORD

As soon as I've completed a song with a co-writer, I find that it's best to decide right then and there what the writing splits are going to be — when everyone can still remember the degree to which they've contributed. I've made the mistake in the past of waiting too long, only to have some confusion and fuzzy memories just before the song was about to be released.

— JIM PETERIK, WRITER OF 18 BILLBOARD TOP 10 HITS INCLUDING THE PERENNIAL FAVORITE "EYE OF THE TIGER" FEATURED IN ROCKY III

Knowing when to put the pen to the paper

When you are making a deal with someone regarding your career, property rights, potential earnings of your song, or whatever, get it in writing! If you think that you've found the right person with the right connections — whether it's an attorney, a publisher, or a song plugger — make sure that you spell out your mutual goals and set time limits to reach them. In other words, create a contract. It can be simple or complex, but the main thing is that you convert your mutual goals into a written level of understanding between those who'll be representing your songs, style, and ethics. Take a look at Figure 19-1 for a checklist of what a contract between a songwriter and a publisher should contain.

There's often a lot of hype prior to actually signing a deal. Try to use your instincts to know when it's the appropriate time to consummate an agreement. Again, here's where having an attorney on your team will help you decide when the time is right to sign on the dotted line.

TIP

Before you sign your name to any kind of contract, have a trusted music attorney look it over to make sure that it's both fair and properly written. In addition, ask yourself the following questions to see if you're ready to sign:

>> Do you understand everything you're agreeing to?

>> Do you trust the people you're signing the deal with?

>> Are you satisfied that you're getting the best deal possible?

>> Can you live with the term length of the contract and its possible restrictions?

>> Do you feel the agreement will help promote your career?

>> Will this contract motivate you to do your best work?

>> Is the Third Party Benefiting from my work more than I am?

Songwriter/Publisher Contract Checklist

☐ **Date of Agreement:** The birthday of your agreement.

☐ **By and Between:** Your name and the publisher's name.

☐ **The Composition:** List and define (title, words, and music) the song or songs that you assign and/or transfer to your publisher.

☐ **Time of Agreement:** Beginning on the date that you sign the contract for the length of time that you agree to work together (generally the time varies anywhere from 3 to 25 years) and also include some provisions to extend or terminate the contract.

☐ **Existing Agreements:** The contract should be subject to any existing agreements that either party is already affiliated (such as performing rights organizations).

☐ **Exclusive and Original Work:** Identify that you have the right to make the agreement for your composition(s) as exclusive and original work and that no other claim to the composition(s) has been made.

☐ **Rights and Responsibilities:** Clearly define who has the right to do what, and what each party is responsible for. Make sure you get credit where credit is due.

☐ **Publisher Agrees to Pay Writer:** An advance on royalties; upfront costs to produce a demo(s); percents of the: wholesale price, all net sums for foreign countries, piano copies, orchestrations, band arrangements, song books, licenses to reprint lyrics in books and magazines, and so on; fees for synchronization with sound motion pictures; and any other source not now known which may come after signing the agreement.

☐ **Method of Payment:** Include the when and how you will be paid by the publisher for each portion of the income. It should also be spelled out how the publisher will compute and credit your account, and your right to inspect the bookkeeping process.

☐ **Recording the Composition:** Set a date for the publisher to release a commercial recording of the composition and create a clause to terminate the agreement if they do not.

☐ **Defining the Writer:** If you are a co-writer and share the royalties, you need to clarify who the other writers are and how you divide up the writers' portions.

☐ **Time to Comply:** Define what and when items in the agreement should happen and identify all the "if this" or "if that" happens. Here's where you'll really need an attorney!

☐ **Termination:** If and when you or your publisher terminate the agreement, you need to include all the reasons and methods to do so. Also make sure that all of the compositions that you have assigned to the publisher are transferred back to you.

☐ **Arbitration:** In the case of an argument, you need to define just how you will settle the differences of opinion.

☐ **Cost for Legal Action:** Define who pays for what in the case of a legal battle.

☐ **State of Law:** The agreement will abide by the laws of (choose a state) for settling any legal action.

☐ **Signatures:** You, a witness, and the publisher all sign on the dotted lines: including names, addresses, and dates.

FIGURE 19-1:
A checklist for a songwriter/publisher contract.

Also, it's a good idea to watch out for any red flags in each agreement that you're asked to sign. Here is a list of ten of the most common offenders:

- **Publishing agreements that ask a writer to pay a fee to publish the song.** Reputable publishers take their agreed-upon percentage from the back end of monies earned. (In fact, publishers who take upfront fees to publish your tunes are generally not allowed to belong to the various performance rights groups!)

- **Publishing contracts that take a cut of your writer's royalties (as opposed to a piece of the publisher's share).** This practice is acceptable only in certain cases — be sure to consult your attorney before agreeing to this.

- **Publishing deals that make the writer responsible for getting a specific number of songs cut by artists.** This is the publishers' job — if you can help in the process, all the better, but the total responsibility shouldn't be on the shoulders of the songwriter.

- **Agreements between other individual songwriters that limit your percentage of the song to a set amount — no matter what portion of the song you've actually written.**

- **Publishing contracts that specify an unrealistic quota of songs that must be submitted in order to avoid suspension.**

- **Publishing contracts that don't count a song against your *submission requirement* (the amount of songs you agree to turn in quarterly) unless you are at least a 50 percent writer of that song.**

- **Contracts that have an unrealistically long term (usually anything over three years) and put all the reasons for termination on the publisher's side of the court.**

- **Publishing contracts that restrict you to writing only with other songwriters signed with that same publishing company.**

- **Publishing contracts that take 100 percent of your publishing without offering some kind of upfront or weekly monetary advance.**

OFF THE RECORD

Because the retail record business is not what it used to be, many record companies, when signing an artist or a band, will demand their publishing rights as another way to recoup on their investment. If you're an artist about to sign a record deal, have your attorney do his best at retaining at least half of your publishing.

- **Any contract that you are pressured to sign without the advice and counsel of a good attorney.**

TIP

Breaking a contract can be costly — so understanding exactly what you are agreeing to is vitally important. After getting all the advice from your professional, having discussions with friends and family, and even hashing it out with the guy next door, go on your gut feelings (using the information that you've gathered). More often than not, you'll instinctively know when and what to sign.

REMEMBER

When you have questions about the meaning of some wording or language in a contract, it's worth the money to have it looked over, explained, and perhaps modified by an attorney — never be too embarrassed to ask.

Finding resources in a hurry

Okay, so in an ideal world, you have already hired a top-notch music attorney and have the means to pay him — handsomely, we might add! However, sometimes the "real" world bites us in the butt and some do-it-yourself (DIY) songwriters need something in writing and need it fast (because something in writing is better than any verbal "he said she said" scenario). Here are a couple of alternative resources consider in a pinch.

MusicContracts.com

If you are looking for a nice collection of standard music contracts, this is a good resource for you — well-crafted documents specifically designed for use in music industry agreements. There's a fee to download these documents, but their prices are very reasonable in comparison to hiring a lawyer. These are formatted in Microsoft Word for easy editing, with descriptions in plain English to help you sift through all the legal jargon — such a deal!

MusicContracts101.com

This is another good resource that provides exactly what its title states — 101 music business contracts. Never fear when you have these contracts at your disposal because you can navigate the DIY legal waters with at least some basic tools at your side to guide you along — at least until you can afford the services of a real lawyer . . . and the sooner the better at that!

Protecting Your Songs with Copyrights

Before you solicit your song, protect yourself with a copyright. Your publisher or attorney can handle the filing of your copyrights, or you can do it yourself — just make sure that it gets done no matter what!

A *copyright* is basically a form of protection that is provided by the laws of the United States to the authors of "original works of authorship," which includes you, the songwriter. The small print and details may look a bit overwhelming at first, but in this section we make it simple for you.

The moment you've committed your song to tape, it's in what is known as *tangible form* and it's technically protected by copyright laws. However, if your copyright is ever challenged, you'll have a hard time proving the exact date of your song's creation if you don't actually file a copyright registration. This is why registering your song with the federal government is always a good idea — you'll be better protected in the event of a copyright infringement suit. You'll also be listed at the Library of Congress in Washington, D.C., if someone wants to look up the songs you've written.

Although no longer considered a legal substitute, a *poor man's copyright* was the old technique of recording your song on a cassette (or CD) and sending it to yourself. The theory was that if you don't open the envelope after you receive it back, the postmark would serve as a record of the date you originally created it. You can still do this method but only *in conjunction* with a government copyright and strictly as additional proof as to the date of a song's creation.

TIP

Copyright forms are available online — they're easy to fill out (these are not difficult to decipher since their revision in the early '90s), the electronic filing fee is relatively inexpensive (currently $35), and the copyright lasts for the lifetime of the composer (or the lifetime of the last surviving co-writer) plus 70 years.

Rounding up the right forms

The Copyright Office of the Library of Congress has all the forms you'll ever need for filing your copyright. They can provide you with the necessary paperwork and instructions for registering copyrights, changing your mailing address, changing the name of your song, updating a lyric, and myriad other options. You can either call them to request the forms, or you can download them online (using the PDF format). The Library of Congress's website is the best place to find all the most up-to-the-minute info regarding copyrights. It even includes links to some related sites such as performing rights societies (ASCAP, BMI, and SESAC) and to the Harry Fox Agency. The folks at the copyright bureau are usually quite willing to walk you through any questions you may have regarding forms or procedures.

In recent years the U.S. Copyright Office has simplified the forms needed for most works. Old forms such as PA and RA have pretty much been replaced with the single CO (or eCO for electronic filers). These forms are used for published or unpublished works of the performing arts, including

>> Musical works, including any accompanying words

>> Dramatic works, including any accompanying music

>> Pantomimes and choreographic works

>> Motion pictures and other audiovisual works

OFF THE RECORD

At first glance, $35 per form would seem to mean $35 per song. Not so! Here's the trick: The Copyright Office allows you to group songs together as a collection. A collection can be any group of songs you define — an album, a soundtrack, or just a bunch of songs you lump together and name. For example, each January I register all the songs I wrote the previous year. On the copyright form I group them as a collection, and name them something like "The Aaron Cheney 2010 Collection." Every song in the collection gets registered, and I only pay the fee once — pretty cool!

— AARON CHENEY, AUTHOR OF THE SONG GARAGE BLOG

REMEMBER

Copyright protection by law is legally granted to you as soon as your song is in fixed form. (That means recorded on any recording medium.) However, for additional protection we would always recommend filing an official Library of Congress copyright to back up your claims. When you solicit your songs, always affix the copyright symbol (©) and/or the written word "copyright," followed by the year of the song's creation and your name, to the CDs, tapes, sheet music, and any lyric sheets you send out or post online.

Filling out Form PA

Each songwriter's situation is a little different, so read the instructions before filling out your form. If you have a publisher or an administrator, they'll handle the filing of this form on your behalf. Figure 19-2 is an example of Form PA filled out for a songwriter who has completed a demo and is ready to send it off to artists, record labels, or other music-industry people. (You can use either this PA or a CO.) For this illustration, you'll note we've used Sami Songsmith's wife, Jennifer — because we know full well it's the women who truly control the money!

REMEMBER

The Copyright Office can take six to nine months, sometimes longer, to mail out Certificates of Registration — so don't panic. (The office routinely gets thousands of submissions per day.) After you've sent in your application, you can breathe a lot easier knowing that the song you worked so hard on has that extra degree of protection. If you file online, you'll receive a confirmation e-mail that your form has been received; otherwise, if you mailed an application, it's best to use a carrier such as FedEx or UPS that provides tracking and acknowledgment of receipt by the Copyright Office — doing so by U.S. mail may take several weeks or longer to confirm receipt (which only delays the "effective" date of the copyright registration because it's based on the day they *receive* it in their offices).

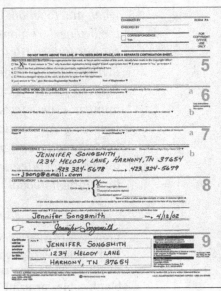

FIGURE 19-2: A completed sample Form PA.

Using the copyright notice

For published works, the law provides that a copyright notice (©) must be placed on all publicly distributed copies. Doing so is your responsibility! Here are the three things that, together, make up a copyright notice:

>> The symbol (©)

>> The year of creation

>> The name of the owner of the copyright

Here's an example of how the copyright notice will look: © 2010 Jennifer Songsmith.

Filling in the Blanks and Being Organized

As a songwriter, you have to be as good at the *organizational* elements of the business as you are at the *creative* aspects in order to give your songs the best chance for success. The bottom line is that you need to get organized.

WORDS OF WISDOM

Records are everything. When I send out a particular song, I keep a record of when and to whom it was sent. When I make follow-up calls on the song, I log the listener's responses. When I file my copyrights, I keep a duplicate for my records (which I destroy when the finals come back from Washington). When I write with someone new, I take down all their personal info — their name, address, phone number, date of birth, publishing company, and Social Security number. (These facts really come in handy when I'm filling out forms or supplying information to my administrator regarding the song we wrote.) It doesn't really matter if your method is high tech (sophisticated computer software that offers various organizational templates) or primitive (written down in a spiral notebook); the important thing is to have a system and to stick to it.

— JIM PETERIK, WRITER OF 18 BILLBOARD TOP 10 HITS

Endless organization methods are out there — you just need to find the one that works best for you. One method is to create a standard form with blank lines to fill in while you're on the phone or when you send out packages. Just make blank copies or print them right from your computer as needed. In the following sections, we provide a few sample forms that you can use to give you an idea. Naturally, you can come up with your own system by customizing the fields of information to include on the various forms (or tracking sheets) that you design.

TIP

If you're computer savvy, you may want to use an Excel spreadsheet for keeping track of your information. This is a great way to stay organized, and it has easy options to sort your data to suit your needs. Choose from an array of templates that are available online — then use it or lose it (data that is).

Using a prospects-and-contacts form

Figure 19-3 is an example of a form you can use to keep track of whom you know and whom you want to know — your contacts and prospects. This is your personal note-taking organization. Getting referrals from friends and associates is an excellent way to get in the door (and on the phone with) music-industry people. There are numerous industry sourcebooks in which you can find all the big names and their phone numbers; however, unless you're very lucky, you'll most likely have worked your way to the top in order to actually get through and talk with the "bigwig" personally.

THE IMPORTANCE OF GOOD ORGANIZATION

If you don't have a secretary (and even if you do), keep notes about what you've sent to whom and when it was mailed. You're developing rapport with new contacts, so write down the names of everyone from the receptionist to the assistant of the person you sent your package to.

Organization can make a big difference. If the head of A&R at Universal gives you a call, you'll want to be quick about responding to exactly what he has in his hot little hands. If you've sent dozens of packages out and can't remember what you sent to whom, well, you won't appear very professional now will you!

TIP

If you make contact with someone who says no to a specific request, ask if they can refer you to someone else who may instead say yes. Also, ask if they have any other suggestions for you to help achieve your goal (of finding a record label, attorney, or artist to sing your song).

Creating a song-history tracking sheet

When you start sending your songs out, you'll want to keep track of who has a copy of your song, and how it's faring on a submissions rating scale (such as for-get it, keep trying, possible interest, highly potential, and best of all, signed the deal on such-and-such date).

Figure 19-4, the song-history tracking sheet, is an example of the things to keep track of regarding your song.

Keeping track of your copyright registrations

As you go along writing tons of songs, you'll see how time flies. So the simple form shown in Figure 19-5 is used to help you remember whether or not you've already sent in the copyright registration form or not. Organization has a nice way of replacing confusion.

Songwriter Prospects & Contacts

(#) ≡

- ☐ Artist
- ☐ Manager
- ☐ Producer
- ☐ Publisher
- ☐ Record Company
- ☐ Song Plugger
- ☐ Other _____

Name

Title

Company

Address

City/State/Zip

Phone

Fax

E-Mail

Web Site

Referred By

Referred To

Notes

Follow-Up

FIGURE 19-3:
A prospects and
contacts form.

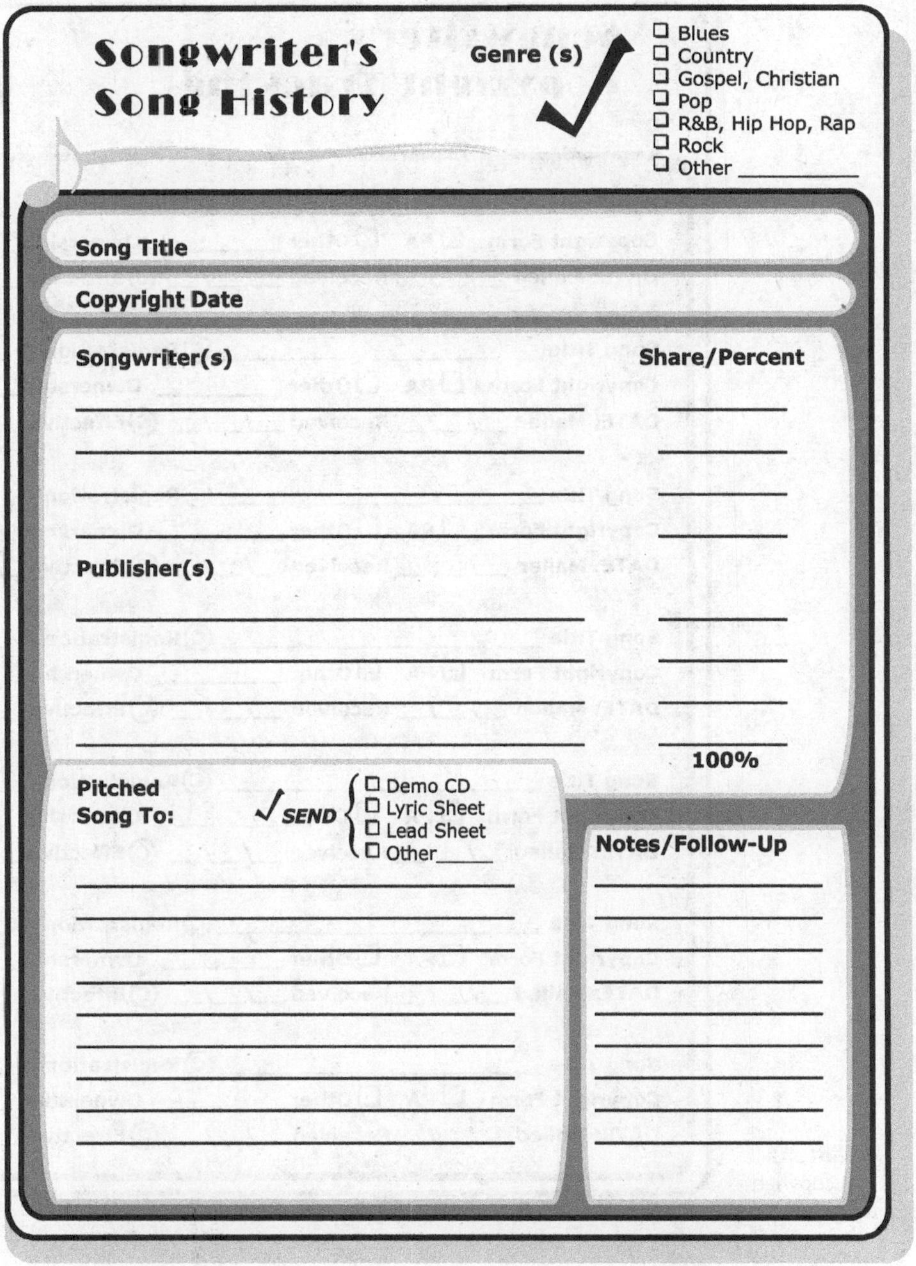

Songwriter's Song History

Genre (s) ✔

- ☐ Blues
- ☐ Country
- ☐ Gospel, Christian
- ☐ Pop
- ☐ R&B, Hip Hop, Rap
- ☐ Rock
- ☐ Other _____

Song Title

Copyright Date

Songwriter(s)	Share/Percent
_____	_____
_____	_____
_____	_____
Publisher(s)	
_____	_____
_____	_____
_____	_____
_____	**100%**

Pitched Song To: ✔ *SEND*

- ☐ Demo CD
- ☐ Lyric Sheet
- ☐ Lead Sheet
- ☐ Other_____

_____
_____
_____
_____
_____
_____
_____
_____

Notes/Follow-Up

_____
_____
_____
_____
_____
_____

FIGURE 19-4:
A song history tracking sheet.

Songwriter's Copyright Tracking

Song Title _____ ©Registration # _____
Copyright Form ☐ PA ☐ Other _____ Ownership _____%
DATE: Mailed __/__/__ Received __/__/__ ©Effective __/__/__

Song Title _____ ©Registration # _____
Copyright Form ☐ PA ☐ Other _____ Ownership _____%
DATE: Mailed __/__/__ Received __/__/__ ©Effective __/__/__

Song Title _____ ©Registration # _____
Copyright Form ☐ PA ☐ Other _____ Ownership _____%
DATE: Mailed __/__/__ Received __/__/__ ©Effective __/__/__

Song Title _____ ©Registration # _____
Copyright Form ☐ PA ☐ Other _____ Ownership _____%
DATE: Mailed __/__/__ Received __/__/__ ©Effective __/__/__

Song Title _____ ©Registration # _____
Copyright Form ☐ PA ☐ Other _____ Ownership _____%
DATE: Mailed __/__/__ Received __/__/__ ©Effective __/__/__

Song Title _____ ©Registration # _____
Copyright Form ☐ PA ☐ Other _____ Ownership _____%
DATE: Mailed __/__/__ Received __/__/__ ©Effective __/__/__

Song Title _____ ©Registration # _____
Copyright Form ☐ PA ☐ Other _____ Ownership _____%
DATE: Mailed __/__/__ Received __/__/__ ©Effective __/__/__

FIGURE 19-5:
A copyright
tracking form.

6

The Part of Tens

In this part, we go out on a limb and show you some noteworthy (ouch!) songs that have stood the test of time. Just so the limb doesn't break, instead of calling it "The Ten Best," we simply call it "Ten Songs You Should Know." These shining examples of the songwriting craft at its best are sure to inspire budding songwriters. Over time, you'll surely create your own list of the songs that really "float your boat," but this is as good a place as any to start your voyage. We also take a look at ten important song-related contracts that'll undoubtedly cross your path as you navigate the waters during your songwriting journey.

Chapter 20

Ten Songs You Should Know

There are endless lists of "Best Songs," and new lists are being formed every day. Some of these are based on the opinions of the authors; some are gauged by chart positions and sales figures. Whichever way you tally it, the greatest songs of any generation are the ones that matter the most to the listening public. Here's a list of our favorites and reasons why they've resonated throughout the years.

"Hey Jude"

This song not only had the longest run at the top of the charts for any Beatles single, it is also more than seven minutes in length — breaking one of the many rules of writing a radio-friendly hit! Although there are varied opinions as to whom this song was really written for (among those were Jane Asher, with whom Paul McCartney had a long-term relationship, and also John Lennon, who believed the song was written about him), it was Paul who confirmed what inspired him to pen this tune. Being particularly close to Lennon's first wife, Cynthia, and their son, Julian, "Hey Jules" (the original title to the song) was intended to comfort Julian during his parents' divorce. The original lyrics "Hey Jules, don't make it bad, take a sad song and make it better" take on a whole new perspective when thought of in terms of helping a kid dealing with his parents split. Later the "Jules" changed to "Jude" simply because it sounded better — apparently this mattered not to Julian, who years later bought the recording notes auctioned for 25,000 British pounds.

"Bohemian Rhapsody"

Another song that broke free of conventional songwriting structure was written by Freddie Mercury of the rock group Queen, who wrote this intended "mock opera" to be something outside the norm of the typical rock songs of the time. Although Freddie never personally revealed his inspiration other than to say it was a song about relationships, there was a Persian translation that claims the band said it is about a young man who has accidentally killed someone and then sold his soul to the devil. On the eve of his execution, he calls for the help of God and his angels to regain his soul once again. Other theories include a suicidal murderer hunted by demons just before his execution — at any rate, whether or not the lyrics are simply "random rhyming nonsense," the song is a compelling, haunting, and dynamic composition all at once.

"What's Going On"

"What's Going On," written by Marvin Gaye, Al Cleveland, and Renaldo Benson, is a landmark song in the history of Motown records and modern music in general. Marvin Gaye was "chomping at the bit" to express his inner emotions and social stance in the years prior to the record's release, and Berry Gordy's hit machine was not quite ready to break the mold of radio-ready hits such as Marvin's own "Heard It Through the Grapevine" (written by Norman Whitfield and Barrett Strong) and "Get Ready" (written by Smokey Robinson) by The Temptations. Always the rebel, Marvin convinced Berry to give him his head on this powerful track as a kind of test case — if it failed he'd go back to the formula, but if it was a hit, it was full speed ahead for Gaye's new sound. The song went right to radio and became a landmark hit in Motown's history. Suddenly many R&B artists were scrambling to be socially conscious and express the urban plight in America. Songs such as "Cloud 9" (written by Norman Whitfield and Barrett Strong) by the Temptations (exploring the lure of hard drugs in our society) and "Ball of Confusion" became massive hits and gave credibility to the genre of crossing dance grooves with Dylan-like slam poetry. Again, Marvin Gaye was a pioneer, visionary, and architect of a fresh new sound.

"Yesterday"

"Yesterday," written by John Lennon and Paul McCartney, has been played more than 7 million times in the twentieth century alone. No other song has been played more since it first hit the airways in the mid-60s. It also holds the *Guinness Book of Records* title as the most "covered" song in history — more than 3,000 versions. The story is told that McCartney woke up one morning with this tune running through his head — the song just came to him without a flaw. The Beatles and their producer George Martin recorded "Yesterday" with just a string quartet, acoustic guitar, and Paul's vocal. This song is well served by the simplicity of its production. "Yesterday" ranks third place in BMI's Top 100 Songs of the Century. According to BMI's calculation, 7 million performances are the equivalent of approximately 350,000 broadcast hours, or more than 45 years of continuous airplay!

"God Only Knows"

With haunting vocals by the late Carl Wilson, "God Only Knows" is considered by many to be the ultimate Brian Wilson song. Ironically, shunned by certain radio stations for its use of the word "God," this song climbed to the outer reaches of the Top 40 in 1966. This ode to a love that can't quite be verbalized properly features some of the most sensitive chord progressions of Wilson's career. With lyrics by one of his most inspired lyricists, Tony Asher, this song is one of the cornerstones of The Beach Boy's masterwork, *Pet Sounds*, along with "Wouldn't It Be Nice."

"Imagine"

"Imagine" was John Lennon's ultimate message to the world. John composed the song one morning on the white grand piano made famous in films and photos of him sitting at the keyboard. Lennon captured pretty much everything he believed in and stood for within this song — we are all one country, one world, one people, without boundaries or borders. "Imagine" is the most commercially successful of all Lennon's post-Beatles works. It peaked at #3 on its initial 1971 release, but ten years later was re-released and hit #1 — heralding the inner dynamics and longevity of the message.

"Satisfaction"

Not everyone was initially enamored with Mick Jagger and Keith Richards' collaboration, but lucky for the world, this song made it to the light of day. It's the signature three-note guitar riff that opens and drives this song (a Richards' middle-of-the-night inspiration, he woke up and recorded on cassette tape what he describes as 2 minutes of "Satisfaction" and 40 minutes of snoring!) plus the sexual overtones and anti-commercialism theme that initially kept it from being heard anywhere except on pirate radio stations. Considered by some to be one of the great rock songs of all time, this Rolling Stones #1 hit remains a favorite among many — the only one of three songs that was "not censored" during the 2006 Super Bowl XL halftime show — go figure!

"I Still Haven't Found What I'm Looking For"

This song by the rock band U2 began life as a demo created during one of their many jam sessions. Originally described as a "one-note groove" by bassist Adam Clayton and compared by The Edge to "Eye of the Tiger" being played by a reggae band, it was kept around for its drum beat — which later became the song's signature. Building from there, layer by layer, this song took life, and as Bono began singing a "classic soul" melody, The Edge slipped a piece of paper to him with the phrase he'd written in a notebook that morning for a possible song title — "I still haven't found what I'm looking for." Remember what we mentioned earlier about where ideas come from and the necessity of keeping great notes? Needless to say this song went on to become U2's second #1 single, following "With or Without You."

"Like a Rolling Stone"

"Like a Rolling Stone" is one of those songs that practically everyone that knows it remembers where they were when they first heard it — and got a buzz off its musical synergy. This song (like "Bohemian Rhapsody" mentioned earlier) just kept going far beyond the three-minute limit set by most radio stations to facilitate more commercials — and the lyrics were the usual brilliant stream of conscience Dylan. But what really hooked you in was the magical Hammond B3 organ (played by rock veteran Al Kooper) that's woven through the song like a silver thread. Funny thing is that Kooper was at the session to play guitar, but wasn't needed so he started idly doodling on the studio's Hammond B3. By the second take the song started to gel and Dylan told the engineer to turn up that organ (which up until then was buried deep in the mix). That's when the whole song came to life. Soon after the record hit #1, Al was inundated with session requests to add his "magic organ" to their songs — and this was an instrument he had only very recently started playing! A song is only as good as its arrangement and sonic textures, and this is the perfect example of a great song finding the simple signature from a casually played B3 organ.

"Somewhere Over the Rainbow"

Once in a while, a song comes along that's so great that it just never goes away. One such a song is "Over the Rainbow," composed by Harold Arlen in 1939 with words by E. Y. "Yip" Harburg — the pair who wrote the songs for the film *Wizard of Oz*. The melody suddenly came to Arlen while driving in his car. He had a tremendous feeling about the value of the melody and took it to Harburg, but Harburg didn't like it. To settle the matter, they drove over to Harburg's friend Ira Gershwin's house and asked him how he felt. Gershwin felt that Arlen had indeed come up with a great melody, and Harburg reluctantly wrote the words for "Over the Rainbow." Judy Garland sang the song in the movie, but the studio pulled it, saying it didn't fit the plot and that it was too slow. They only reluctantly put it back in the film after the associate producer, Arthur Fried, forced them to do so. The rest is history. "Over the Rainbow" was voted by the National Endowment for the Arts (NEA) and the Recording Industry Association of America (RIAA) as the #1 best song of the century, and it's been recorded by hundreds of artists ranging from Tori Amos to Zoot Sims — but arguably the most well-known recording of this song was done by late Hawai'ian artist IZ (Israel Kamakawiwo'ole), when he combined it with the song "What a Wonderful World."

Chapter **21**

Ten Common Song-Related Contracts You Should Know

While the right side of your brain is engaged in the creative pursuit of writing a song, challenge the left side and make sure it understands your legal rights and responsibilities. This will ensure that eventually the fruits of your labor will be served properly and you'll find some peace of mind.

In this chapter, we highlight some of the most common and vitally important contracts that are related to the business side of songwriting. Think of these contracts as your friends. They ensure that you and your hard work will be duly rewarded, your song protected, and the proceeds end up at the correct address — yours of course!

Single-Song Agreement

This agreement is used by music publishers to acquire songs from a songwriter on a song-by-song basis. A copyright assignment of the songs from the songwriter to the music publisher is always attached to this agreement or is included in the verbiage of the actual agreement. Publishers often use this agreement to develop a relationship with a writer before offering an exclusive agreement to that writer.

Exclusive Songwriting Agreement (ESA)

This agreement is used by music publishers to acquire all songs written by a songwriter over a period of time (for example, for a period of three years or for a period equal to the term of an exclusive artist agreement if the songwriter is also signed to an artist deal with a record label). Because you cannot assign an interest in property not yet created, a publisher will either issue individual assignments or songwriter agreements that parallel the terms of the ESA, after the songs are written and turned into the publisher. There may also be a Schedule A attached to the ESA whereby the publisher wants to acquire some or all of the songs of a songwriter that were written prior to the term of the ESA. Each of those songs would be listed on the Schedule A.

Copyright Assignment

This document is usually a one- or two-page document that contains the formal wording for an assignment of copyright in a composition from the songwriter to the music publisher. Most publishers require that these assignments be notarized by a notary public to confirm that the person executing the assignment is actually the songwriter named on the document.

Co-Publishing Agreement

This agreement is similar to a Single-Song Agreement (for an individual song) or an Exclusive Songwriting Agreement (for songs written over a period of time), except that the songwriter retains for himself a portion of the publisher's interest in the song (for example, 50 percent of the publisher's interest so that the songwriter retains 100 percent of the songwriter's portion of the songs and 50 percent of the music publisher's portion of the song).

Administration Agreement

This document is an agreement for a third party to administer the rights to a certain number of songs in a given country or territory. This agreement is usually executed by the music publisher or by a songwriter who has formed his or her own publishing company and needs someone to issue licenses (mechanical, sync, print, and so on) on their behalf and to collect the income generated by those licenses. This agreement usually covers administration only and does not include the active pitching of songs. Many music publishers use the Harry Fox Agency for the administration of their catalogs in the United States.

Sub-Publishing Agreement

This agreement is similar to an Administration Agreement except that this agreement is usually made between a publisher and another publisher outside of the United States (the sub-publisher). The sub-publisher is usually involved in the active pitching of the domestic publisher's songs and takes a greater share of the income from those songs if the sub-publisher secures a cover recording of that song in its home territory.

Performing Rights Society Affiliation Agreement

Before a songwriter or music publisher can collect performance royalties for the performance of a song (via airplay of the music by radio stations and performance of music in public venues), the songwriter and music publisher must execute an agreement with one of the performing rights societies (ASCAP, BMI, or SESAC) for that organization to administer the "performance" rights in those songs. Those societies issue licenses to all major radio stations and major clubs and venues, and collect substantial revenue from those licenses. The performing rights organizations (PROs) pay the songwriter and music publisher directly (usually on a 50/50 basis) for any performance income collected. This direct payment usually ensures that a music publisher cannot collect the songwriter's share of performance income to recoup any outstanding advances paid to the songwriter by the music publisher.

Mechanical License

This agreement is usually a short form document whereby a music publisher grants to a record label the right to record, manufacture, and distribute records embodying a specific song.

Synchronization License

This agreement is usually a short form document whereby a music publisher grants to a movie or television producer the right to sync music to visual images and to either broadcast that video or manufacture and distribute the video in videocassette or DVD format. Most producers of video content will attempt to secure rights for both broadcast and home video; however, most music publishers will want to retain home video rights so that they may negotiate a better fee if the television show or movie is commercially successful. This license does not cover the use of the sound recording because the producer of the video work must also negotiate and secure a license with the copyright holder of the master recording.

Digital Licenses

Most licenses for content to be distributed via a digital medium (such as the Internet) are a combination of the mechanical, synchronization, and print licenses, depending upon whether the material will be merely broadcast or a digital copy of the song will be actually delivered to an end user. This area of rights management is still basically in its infancy and continues to develop as new means of digital distribution and expression are introduced to the marketplace.

Index

Numerics

"24 Hours From Tulsa," 118

A

a capella, 62 (Found as "a cappella")
accented syllable, 158–161
accountant, 335, 336–337
action plan, 294–298
administration agreement, 329–330, 367
adult contemporary, 40–41
advances, 325, 329
advertising agencies, 263
advice songs, 129
agent, 320, 334
album deadlines, 300
"All Along the Watchtower," 57
"All Fall Down," 141
alliteration, 133
American Federation of Television and Radio Artists, 261
American Idol (television show), 258, 259
American Society of Composers, Authors and Publishers (ASCAP), 304, 306–307, 322, 342
anaphora, 101
Aquino, Mike (guitarist), 191–192, 195–196
Armageddon (movie), 99
arrangement, demo, 274–277
arranger, 276–277
artist, sending demo to, 288

Artists & Repertoire (A&R) person, 40, 286
assonance, 134
attorney, 320, 321–324
audio files, 270
Austin, Dave (mental performance coach), 170, 188, 225
Auto-Tune, 214
autotuning, 86

B

Bacharach, Burt (songwriter), 231–232
backbeat, 164, 166
bans, on records, 104
bar, beats in, 164
"Barbara Ann," 87
Barnes, Don (songwriter), 29, 191
beat
  backbeat, 164, 166
  definition of, 162
  downbeat, 167–169
  number in bar, 162
  off, 162
  on, 162
  syncopation, 164–169
The Beatles
  bridge use by, 123
  collaboration in, 223, 230
  extended standard form use by, 60
  formal structures of songs, 61
  hooks in songs, 87
Beethoven's Fifth Symphony, 77
"Black Horse and the Cherry Tree," 81–82
blogs, 22, 241, 249

bluegrass, 45–46
Blues For Dummies (Wiley Publishing, Inc.), 51
blues genre, 32, 51, 192
"Bohemian Rhapsody," 360
Boyle, Jeff (songwriter), 14
breach of contract, 321, 341
bridge
  description, 54–55
  instrumental, 186
  lyrics, 123–124
  melody of, 182, 186
  option aspect of, 186
  short form, 124–125
  in verse-chorus song form, 65–71
Broadcast Music Incorporated (BMI), 304, 307, 322, 342
Broadjam, 264
Broadway songwriting
  creative side of writing for musicals, 265
  submitting songs, 265
  word rhythm, 169
build, of song, 182
Building a Web Site For Dummies (Wiley Publishing, Inc.), 240
business manager, 335–336
business team
  accountant, 320, 335–337
  agent, 320, 334–335
  attorney, 320, 321–324
  business manager, 335–337
  choosing, 320
  manager, 320, 332–334
  publisher, 320, 324–330
  song plugger, 320, 330–332
buy-out, 317

American Society of Composers, Authors and Publishers, 304, 306, 322, 342

attorney recommendations from, 338

Broadcast Music Incorporated, 304, 307, 338, 342

joining, 305, 328

Royalty Logic, 312, 342

Society of European Stage Authors & Composers, 304, 307, 342

SoundExchange, 311–312, 342

personification, 101, 134

perspective, lyric, 127–129

Peterik, Jim (songwriter)

on beat, 164–165

on business of music, 340

on chords, 191, 195, 198

on Christian genre, 48–49

on collaboration, 222, 223, 227

on commercials, 261

on concepts for songs, 116

on country genre, 46

on co-writer agreements, 344–345

on dance-pop, 39–40

on deadlines, 299–301

on demo quality, 273

on films, 255, 256

on formal training, 9

on goals, 294, 297

on influences, 8–9

on jamming, 37–38

on melodic pre-chorus, 183–184

on melody, 173, 180

on musicians for demos, 272

on perfect rhymes, 147–148

on performing rights organizations, 305

on personal contacts, 255

on personal experience, 12

on recordkeeping, 352

on rhythm of words, 125, 161

on sending demos, 287

on song use to sell products, 315

on Songwriters Guild of America, 235

on soundtracks, 316

on television, 259

on Tori Amos, 33

on Web site use, 241

on writing to type, 131

Phillips, Mark *(Guitar For Dummies)*, 190

Piano For Dummies (Neely), 190

Piano Wizard (video game), 213

pickup notes, 161

pitch, 324, 330–331

pitch sheet, 300

places to write, 14

plagiarism, 94

Pod effects unit, 193–194

podcasting, 203

poetic devices, 131–134

poetry, 130–131

point of view, noticing a lyric's, 127–128

politics and protest as song concepts, 20

Pomeranz, David (songwriter), 160, 172

pop

adult contemporary (AC), 40–41

chords, 192–193

contemporary, 38–39

dance, 39–40

description, 38

electro, 38

genre, 32, 38–41

traditional, 38

pop country, 44, 46–47, 169

pop rock, 180, 192–193

power ballads, melodic chorus of, 184–185

pre-chorus

description, 54

lyrics, 121

melody of, 181–182, 184

in verse-chorus song form, 64–71

Pro Tools, 211

producer, sending demo to artist's, 287

product placement, 254

programming your demo, 272

pronunciations, changing to help rhyme, 149–150

Propellerhead, 211

prospects-and-contacts form, 352–353

publisher

being your own, 327–329

compensation, 326, 327

deadlines from, 299

finding, 325

functions provided by, 324–325

sending demo to, 288

sub-publisher, 320

publishing

administration deals, 329–330

companies, types of, 326

co-publishing deals, 327

do-it-yourself, 327–328

publishing agreement, 341–342

Pump Audio, 264

R

radio, Internet, 243

range of notes, 173

rap

genre, 41, 43–44

lyrics that make a statement, 104

melody, 181

rhythm of words in, 125–126

shifting accent of syllables, 169

V

Van Zant, Johnny (singer/
songwriter), 12, 149
Variety (magazine), 256, 260
"Vehicle," 64, 82, 126, 140, 259
verse
  chorus and, 185
  lyrics, 119–121
  melody for, 181, 182–183
  purpose of, 54
  repetition, 132
  rhyming across verses,
    149–150
  single-verse form, 55–57
  standard song form, 58–60
  two-verse form, 58
  verse-chorus form, 61–71
verse-chorus form
  description, 61–63
  lyric writing for, 122–123
  repetition of chorus, 133
  song examples, 63
  using a bridge, 65–66
  using a pre-chorus, 64–65
  using a pre-chorus and a
    bridge, 66–71
"Vida La Vida," 94
video games, 263–264, 313, 317
videos, as source of song
  ideas, 22
virtual recordings, 214–215
vocable, 118

W

waltz tempo, 164
"The Way," 77
Web sites
  creating your own site,
    240–241
  Internet radio, 244
  music distribution
    networks, 243
  online music stores, 242, 248
  resource, advice, and
    information sites, 244
  social networking, 241–242,
    246–247
  video and music sharing, 243
  virtual recording, 214
"What's Going On," 360
where songs are played, 309
"Wild-Eyed Southern Boys," 151
Wiley Publishing, Inc.
  Blues For Dummies, 51
  *Building a Web Site For
    Dummies*, 240
  *Creating Web Pages For
    Dummies*, 240
"Wipe Out," 84
"With Arms Wide Open," 110
words, rhythm of, 125–126,
  158–162
workshops, 236
writers' night, 233–234

Y

Yankovich, Weird Al, 106–107
"Yesterday,"60, 361
"Your Body is a
  Wonderland," 134
"Youth of a Nation," 104

About the Authors

Jim Peterik has enjoyed a 45-year love affair with music, and has written or co-written a memorable array of top-40 hits such as 38 Special's "Hold On Loosely," "Caught Up In You," and "Rocking Into The Night." As group co-founders, Jim and Frankie Sullivan also wrote the entire catalogue for Survivor, including smash hits such as "High on You," "I Can't Hold Back," "Is This Love," the #1 single "The Search Is Over," and the timeless ode to the fighting spirit — the triple-platinum, Grammy-winning, Oscar-nominated theme from *Rocky III*, "Eye of the Tiger." Today, when not spending time with family, Jim is busy discovering and producing new talent, in addition to focusing on projects like "Lifeforce" and his duet collaborations with Lisa McClowry. He also plays regularly with The Ides Of March and performs with his World Stage superstar lineup for special events.

Dave Austin has been in and out of the music industry his entire life. He can't help but be immersed in the energy of the music because it moves him in ways that are hard to define. Over the past 30 years, Dave, Cathy, and their good friend Phil Ehart (co-founder of Kansas) have produced and promoted a series of all-star concerts with some of the greats in the industry, including Carlos Santana, Melissa Etheridge, David Foster, Rush, Queen, Alan Parsons Project, and more. This dedicated trio has also gone so far as to create their own independent label and secure distribution through Universal when they found no takers for two of the bands they managed together, Geoff Byrd (a soulful singer-songwriter from Portland, Oregon) and The Orange Sky (a high-energy, reggae-rock band from Trinidad). Outside of music he is also a "mental performance" coach to professional athletes.

Cathy Lynn has always had a deep love of music, dating way back to her first real job at the young age of 15 when she became an usher and ticket taker at the Long Beach Sports Arena and L.A. Coliseum, logging in over 30 concerts in her first year alone. From being a huge fan to then rubbing elbows with the best during multiple years of producing charitable events such as the Music & Tennis Festivals, Cathy blended her ear for great music with her never-ending love for writing by composing "music inspired" screenplays for the big screen. Always a fan at heart, Cathy continues to instill her love of music to her own boys, enjoying their new favorites just as much as they do, and whether she's working one of her own book projects or ghostwriting for others, music is always a part of that creative process — either in the background for inspiration or in the forefront, woven into the stories.

Authors' Acknowledgments

The authors would like to give their heartfelt thanks to everyone who made this book possible. To Mary Ellen Bickford and Don Robertson, who gave their love and support and took the 1st Edition of this book to a higher note. As well as our friend Kenny Loggins for both his incredible music throughout the years and for his heartfelt words in the 1st Edition's foreword (cutting down the brilliant original four-page version to only two was like Chinese torture). A special thank you goes to our new friend Kara DioGuardi, who wrote the foreword to this 2nd Edition. Kara has a heart of gold, and her passion is evident in everything she does, from her songwriting to her judging on *American Idol* to her message in the foreword. Thank you, Kara, for your tenacity and for jumping in at the last minute to make this book even better.

Warm gratitude goes to our acquisitions editor, Tracy Boggier, and project editor, Natalie Harris, as well as copy editors Sue Hobbs and Krista Hansing and technical editor Steve Killen. Appreciation also goes out to all of the songwriters and industry people (including Sami Songsmith) who lent their words and wisdom to this project — we're especially glad to have you as a part of this team effort. Lastly, but certainly not least, we'd like to give a big thanks to Bill Gladstone and everyone at Waterside Productions for bringing life to this project and keeping it fresh and current with this 2nd Edition.

From Jim: Personal thanks goes to my wife, Karen, and son, Colin, for sticking with me through all of my songwriting endeavors — I couldn't have done it without you — and to my extended family and friends for their support and constant inspiration. Thanks also to my late mother and dad, Alice and Jim, who put the song in my heart and always seemed to put me and my music first, and to my dear sister Janice, who always brought me roses. Also to indie-artist Dave Cavalier, Marzette Griffith, and 20-year-old wunderkind Sijay— your music inspires me — as well as to Terry Becker, Yvette Arledge, Diana Dietrich, Jack Rossner, and Karen O'Connor. Extra special thanks to my brothers in The Ides Of March — you are the gift that keeps on giving — and to my buddy Scott May for his last-minute research, plus Steve Salzman and Mike Aquino for their 1st Edition input. Finally, I'd like to thank that higher power that inspires me and gives me the perspective and accepting love I need. You're truly my favorite collaborator.

From Dave: Personal thanks goes to my smart, talented, hard-working wife Cathy and our four amazing boys for putting up with me during self-inflicted hectic schedules, and to my entire extended family for allowing me the time and freedom to do what I do. Deep gratitude goes out to Jim (you crack me up) — without you the original book wouldn't have taken flight — and to all my fellow music compadres past and present: Phil Ehart, Kenny Loggins, Eliot Sloan, Cory Lerios, Dave Jenkins, David Pack, Kevin Cronin, Brian Anders, Kelly and Christy Moulik, Amy Isnor, Geoff Byrd, Steve "Skillet" Killen, Colby Hendricks, Matt "Bernie"

Burnett, Eric "Johnny Depp" Storm, Caleb Skinner, Nigel Rojas, Obasi Springer, Nicholas Rojas, Richard Hall, Jeff Glixman, Chris Horn, Donna Ross, Jimmie Haskell, Budd Carr, and Zach Horowitz. Mostly, a very special thank you goes directly to God from whom all my inspirations come — as long as I stay out of the way and let more of you in, good things will continue and more "inspired moments" will flow.

From Cathy: Personal thanks goes to my family, my faith, and my source of divine inspiration. Without any one piece of this puzzle, my life would be incomplete. Big thanks go to my co-writers Dave and Jim — you were much-appreciated saints during the occasions I became stressed over meeting our submission deadlines. Other special saints are my boys — all four of them! Having an age-appropriate son in each of the generational youth decades (preteen, teenager, 20-something, and 30-something!) during the writing of this edition was especially helpful in keeping my ears tuned to what is (or isn't) current and relevant, and I thank each one of you for your love, support, and patience (even when, at times, I showed no patience in return). I also offer a great appreciation for having awesome musicians at my fingertips when I needed relevant and technical advice on a dime — special thanks to Shane, Skillet, and Scott for always answering my emails so promptly when an urgent and burning question arose, even in the middle of the night. I'd also like to thank my new and old friends, Aaron and Chris, who contributed fresh ideas and perspectives to this book.

Publisher's Acknowledgments

Acquisitions, Editorial, and Media Development

Project Editor: Natalie F. Harris

Acquisitions Editor: Tracy Boggier

Copy Editors: Susan Hobbs, Krista Hansing

Assistant Editor: Erin Calligan Mooney

Composition Services

Project Coordinator: Katherine Crocker

Cover Photos: © photobyphotoboy/Getty Images

PERSONAL ENRICHMENT

Staying Sharp
9781119187790
USA $26.00
CAN $31.99
UK £19.99

Facebook
Carolyn Abram
9781119179030
USA $21.99
CAN $25.99
UK £16.99

Guitar
Mark Phillips
Jon Chappell
9781119293354
USA $24.99
CAN $29.99
UK £17.99

Investing
Eric Tyson, MBA
9781119293347
USA $22.99
CAN $27.99
UK £16.99

Beekeeping
Howland Blackiston
9781119310068
USA $22.99
CAN $27.99
UK £16.99

Digital Photography
Julie Adair King
9781119235606
USA $24.99
CAN $29.99
UK £17.99

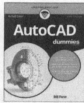
Meditation
Stephan Bodian
9781119251163
USA $24.99
CAN $29.99
UK £17.99

Pregnancy
9781119235491
USA $26.99
CAN $31.99
UK £19.99

Samsung Galaxy S7
Bill Hughes
9781119279952
USA $24.99
CAN $29.99
UK £17.99

iPhone
Edward C. Baig
Bob "Dr. Mac" LeVitus
9781119283133
USA $24.99
CAN $29.99
UK £17.99

Crocheting
Karen Manthey
Susan Brittain
9781119287117
USA $24.99
CAN $29.99
UK £16.99

Nutrition
Carol Ann Rinzler
9781119130246
USA $22.99
CAN $27.99
UK £16.99

PROFESSIONAL DEVELOPMENT

Windows 10
Andy Rathbone
9781119311041
USA $24.99
CAN $29.99
UK £17.99

AutoCAD
Bill Fane
9781119255796
USA $39.99
CAN $47.99
UK £27.99

Excel 2016
Greg Harvey, PhD
9781119293439
USA $26.99
CAN $31.99
UK £19.99

QuickBooks 2017
Stephen L. Nelson, MBA, CPA, MS in Taxation
9781119281467
USA $26.99
CAN $31.99
UK £19.99

macOS Sierra
Bob "Dr. Mac" LeVitus
9781119280651
USA $29.99
CAN $35.99
UK £21.99

LinkedIn
Joel Elad, MBA
9781119251132
USA $24.99
CAN $29.99
UK £17.99

Windows 10
Woody Leonhard
9781119310563
USA $34.00
CAN $41.99
UK £24.99

SharePoint 2016
Rosemarie Withee
Ken Withee
9781119181705
USA $29.99
CAN $35.99
UK £21.99

Fundamental Analysis
Matt Krantz
9781119263593
USA $26.99
CAN $31.99
UK £19.99

Networking
Doug Lowe
9781119257769
USA $29.99
CAN $35.99
UK £21.99

Office 2016
Wallace Wang
9781119293477
USA $26.99
CAN $31.99
UK £19.99

Office 365
Rosemarie Withee
Ken Withee
Jennifer Reed
9781119265313
USA $24.99
CAN $29.99
UK £17.99

Salesforce.com
Liz Kao
Jon Paz
9781119239314
USA $29.99
CAN $35.99
UK £21.99

Coding
Nikhil Abraham
9781119293323
USA $29.99
CAN $35.99
UK £21.99

dummies.com

dummies
A Wiley Brand